D1523667

Nabokov at the Movies

Nabokov
at the Movies

Film Perspectives in Fiction

Barbara Wyllie

McFarland & Company, Inc., Publishers
Jefferson, North Carolina, and London

LIBRARY OF CONGRESS CATALOGUING-IN-PUBLICATION DATA

Wyllie, Barbara.
     Nabokov at the movies : film perspectives in fiction / Barbara Wyllie.
          p.   cm.
     Includes bibliographical references and index.

     ISBN 978-0-7864-1638-7 (softcover : 50# alkaline paper) ∞

     1. Nabokov, Vladimir Vladimirovich, 1899–1977 — Knowledge — Motion pictures.   2. Motion pictures and literature.   3. Motion pictures in literature.   3. Motion pictures — United States.   I. Title.
PG3476.N3Z95   2003
813'.54 — dc21   2003014392

British Library cataloguing data are available

On the cover: A scene from *Sunset Boulevard* with William Holden and Gloria Swanson (BFI Collections)

Manufactured in the United States of America

McFarland & Company, Inc., Publishers
   Box 611, Jefferson, North Carolina 28640
   www.mcfarlandpub.com

In memory of
Gunter Wittenberg

Acknowledgments

Research for this project was funded initially by grants from the Ian Karten Charitable Trust (UK) and latterly by a postgraduate studentship from the Arts and Humanities Research Board, London. I am most grateful to the staff (both academic and administrative) of the School of Slavonic and East European Studies, University College London, and in particular, to Michael Branch, Carol Pearce, and Julian Graffy. I would like to thank my two supervisors, Arnold McMillin and Kasia Boddy (English Department, University College London), who not only kept me on track, but gave me invaluable support and advice, while always encouraging me to follow my instincts. I am also extremely grateful to my former director of studies at Cambridge, Jean Gooder, for her continued interest and assistance in my various (not simply academic) endeavors over the years, as well as Don Barton Johnson at the University of California, Santa Barbara, and Neil Cornwell at the University of Bristol.

As part of my research for this project, I spent a few days in the Nabokov archive at the New York Public Library, facilitated by grants from the Arts and Humanities Research Board, the School of Slavonic and East European Studies and University College London. I am most grateful to Stephen Crook and his colleagues at the Berg Collection for their help in making the best of my time there.

Finally, I would like to thank Ian and Mildred Karten for their great generosity and hospitality, and most especially Eva Wittenberg and her late husband, Gunter, to whom this book is dedicated, for enabling so many things in my life and for their tremendous kindness and understanding.

I am of course deeply indebted to all my friends, my parents and my brother James for their enduring faith in me, their patience and their love.

Table of Contents

Preface

This book was inspired by what I perceived as the lack of a satis-factory explanation for America's fascination with Nabokov. Critics have focused on his most controversial and overtly "American" novel, *Lolita*, and its remarkable evocation of postwar America but because of the par-odic aspect of the novel's overriding narrative voice have been reluctant to emphatically identify Nabokov's perspective as American. The phe-nomenon of *Lolita* and the fact that Nabokov set several of his other late works in the United States — or at least, recognizable versions of it — also fail to provide a convincing account for his enduring presence in con-temporary American culture. Finally, the rather flimsy argument that Nabokov took up U.S. citizenship and so qualifies as an American writer is, quite simply, inadequate.

Lolita is a highly cinematic work. Critics have commented on its allusions to the predominant movement of the period, film noir, but in the light of this, few have investigated further the potential for new inter-pretations of Nabokov's vision across the entirety of his oeuvre. As F. R. Karl commented, film functions as both a major "part of the American collective unconsciousness" and is its "primary shared experience."[1] Thus it could be argued that Nabokov's deployment of film in *Lolita* enabled him to communicate with the American psyche on a subliminal but extremely potent level, and is key to the novel's success. But was it a unique experiment? Looking back to Nabokov's pre–American work set against developments in cinema in both Europe and America during the 1920s and 1930s, it quickly becomes apparent that Nabokov utilized prevalent themes, styles, and techniques of film as a creative resource. *Lolita*'s cinematic quality, therefore, merely marked a stage in a deliber-ate process that extended back to Nabokov's earliest Russian fiction and would continue to be a feature of his later work, culminating in his penul-

1

timate novel, *Transparent Things*. Not only this, but his preoccupation with the medium parallels that of American writers from John Dos Passos and F. Scott Fitzgerald to Don DeLillo and Bret Easton Ellis.

Nabokov's passion for cinema serves, essentially, as a celebration of moving picture art. More importantly, however, it contributes to America's ongoing social and cultural exploration of the impact and significance of the cinematic experience. Nabokov's response to cinema, and to the literary medium that supported it, is perhaps best described by Canadian film director David Cronenberg:

> [Nabokov] absolutely adored movies, [he] went to see them all the time and talked about them. He understood the energy of movies, the narrative drive of movies and the collision of imagery. It's possible that he loved the movies whose literary equivalents he would have despised.[2]

Central to this study is the notion that Nabokov brought to his appreciation of film a different set of criteria than those by which he judged works of fiction. Thus, as Cronenberg contends, consideration of the cinematic elements of texts by authors Nabokov is known to have disliked—William Faulkner, for example—has a relevance in terms of the very particular dynamics generated by their incorporation of film, and is valuable for what they in turn reveal about Nabokov's deployment of the medium. In attempting to place Nabokov in America's literary and cinematic traditions, therefore, this study offers a comparative analysis of films and works of fiction immediately contemporary to him, regardless of declared familiarity or influence. The purpose of this analysis is not to identify explicit allusions but, rather, to elucidate affinities and demonstrate common perspectives, and ultimately to explore the ramifications of Nabokov's discourse with the American cinematic tradition into the last part of the twentieth century.

One

Nabokov and Film: Positive Versus Negative

[The movies are] a pastime for helots, a diversion for the uneducated, wretched, worn-out creatures who are consumed by their worries ... a spectacle which requires no concentration and presupposes no intelligence ... which kindles no light in the heart and awakens no hope other than the ridiculous one of someday becoming a "star" in Los Angeles.[1]

Nabokov's treatment of cinema and cinematics in his fiction is characterized by ambivalence. In certain respects it reflects the tradition of anti-film polemic epitomized by Georges Duhamel, but in many others, it communicates a genuine fascination for the medium and a profound consideration of its significance as a legitimate art form. Nabokov's deployment of the styles, themes and techniques of film encompasses every dimension of the cinematic experience, from the mechanical processes of exposure and projection to its potential as an alternative fictive narrative mode. Any analysis of his cinematic manipulations is, however, complicated by contradiction and ambiguity. Film exists in Nabokov's fiction as an overt and explicit parodic dynamic — evident particularly in specific characterizations — but also, and more fundamentally, discreetly and implicitly as a pivotal aspect of his creative aesthetic.

Critical Responses

Alfred Appel, Jr., in his seminal study, *Nabokov's Dark Cinema* (1974), described the presence of film in Nabokov's fiction as "the product of an anatomist's tour of the contemporary world, rather than a *cinéaste*'s total recall, a film buff's enthusiasm."[2] Concluding that his stance was essentially indifferent, arbitrary and negative, he proposed that Nabokov was merely an "average movie-goer" who had "seen more films than he [was] able or care[d] to remember."[3] A close examination of Nabokov's deployment of the medium in his work, however, demonstrates a far greater, more intimate and vital interest than Appel concedes, one which goes beyond the dimensions of mere reference or allusion, to establish it as critical in his exploration of themes of memory, mortality, and the imagination.

Nabokov's response to Appel's study was, nevertheless, essentially positive. He wrote to Appel shortly after the volume's publication calling it "a brilliant and delightful book."[4] Although he did not question the legitimacy of its central premise, he did express concern as to Appel's rather over-enthusiastic appropriation of references:

> Your basic idea, my constantly introducing cinema themes, and cinema lore, and cinema-metaphors into my literary compositions cannot be contested of course.... In due time I may add some remarks, but I already note that for the sake of an elegant generalization, you connect me, now and then, with films and actors whom I have never seen in my life. (I still do not quite know, for example, who this "James Bond" is). You and I and other Nabokovians will readily realize that stylistically you are slanting my works movieward in pursuit of your main thought; yet it would be rather unfair if less subtle people ... were to conclude I had simply lifted my characters ... from films which you know and I don't.[5]

Nabokov's objection to Appel's "elegant generalizations" suggests a far higher level of engagement than that of the "average movie-goer," in spite of his apparent ignorance of more recent cinematic icons.

Appel's analysis is primarily influenced by his perception of the parodic function of film in Nabokov's work, compounded by notions of *poshlust*—Nabokov's term for the "obviously trashy," false or vulgar[6]— which Appel identifies as a key dynamic. This perspective is supported by an image, cited in Brian Boyd's biography, of Nabokov choking with laughter before a particularly "inept American film,"[7] an impression which also could be interpreted, however, as indicative of a highly discerning critical sensibility responding, simply, to a very bad movie.

Although as Dabney Stuart argues, "the most frequent mode of artistic perception Nabokov employs by means of which to structure his 'novels' is the motion picture,"[8] his manipulation of the modes and themes of cinema has received very little critical attention since the publication of Appel's volume. Rather than examining the entirety of his work, commentaries have focused on isolated texts, particularly the overtly cinematic early novel *Laughter in the Dark* (1938) and Nabokov's first English story, "The Assistant Producer" (1943).[9] In many other texts, however, an implicit deployment of cinematic detail serves as an integral dimension of narrative structure, exposition of character, theme, and motif, even metaphysical discourse. At the same time, a definitive perspective on the significance of the medium is difficult to achieve, particularly as it is subjected to a method of deliberate obfuscation and is consistently presented as a provocative yet highly ambivalent mode. It is precisely these qualities, however, that characterize the nature of Nabokov's engagement with film and inspire his fascination, a response expressed by many of his protagonists, but perhaps most emphatically, by Darwin in the novel of 1932, *Glory*:

> "Funny thing," said Darwin one night, as he and Martin came out of a small Cambridge cinema, "it's unquestionably poor, vulgar, and rather implausible, and yet there is something exciting about all that flying foam, the *femme fatale* on the yacht, the ruined and ragged he-man swallowing his tears."[10]

The scene is both ludicrous and thrilling, but it is this juxtaposition of antagonistic forces that stimulates Nabokov's imagination and generates the dynamic of ambivalence pivotal both to the deployment of film in his fiction and to his protagonists' referential emulation of cinematic styles and icons.

Vladimir Nabokov, "Film-Buff"

Apart from incorporating modes and techniques of film into his fiction, Nabokov's engagement with the medium extended into a desire to participate in the industry itself. During his years in Berlin he worked as a film extra and auditioned as a movie actor,[11] wrote scenarios and screenplays and negotiated with film directors and producers over potential screen adaptations of his work. His cinematic ambitions were fueled by more than financial reward, however, being inspired by a genuine and avid regard for the medium. A fellow émigré writer, Ivan Lukash, recalled a particular episode with Nabokov in a Berlin cinema when, by chance, they found themselves watching one of the films in which Nabokov appeared as an extra. Although Nabokov was subsequently unable to remember the title of the film,[12] the experience evidently had a considerable impact:

> As his face gleamed and faded, he pointed himself out on the screen, but the sequence was over so quickly that Lukash simply scoffed, thinking Nabokov had invented this moment of stardom.[13]

Nabokov's excitement at this fleeting vision parallels the fervor with which many of his protagonists pursue their cinematic dreams. Former Moscow Art Theatre director Sergei Bertenson also recalled Nabokov's enthusiasm during negotiations with Hollywood director Lewis Milestone in the early 1930s. Apparently he "grew very excited" at Milestone's proposals, telling Bertenson that "he literally adore[d] the cinema and watch[ed] motion pictures with great keenness."[14]

Bertenson's depiction of Nabokov is far removed from the stern and dispassionate countenance exhibited in correspondence with Alfred Hitchcock or Stanley Kubrick thirty years later,[15] his dealings characterized by cool pragmatism. Nevertheless, Nabokov continued to reveal, if only occasionally, the enthusiasm of a film buff in less formal situations. In a letter to Edmund Wilson, for example, Nabokov describes his attempts to contact him during a recent visit to New York in fanciful emulation of a scene from a 1940s' film noir—"I rang up the Princeton Club—and slowly put down the receiver as they do in the movies"[16]—while Appel recalls Nabokov enacting, with mischievous relish, the opening scenes of Robert Siodmak's 1946 screen adaptation of Hemingway's story "The Killers":

> Nabokov and I entered the dimly lit bar of the Montreux Palace Hotel. Standing at the bar he ordered a scotch, and I asked for a well-known aperitif which was not in stock. "Good!" said Nabokov, "that's no drink for a man." Our rather tight-fitting overcoats still on, we began a three-way badinage with the barman.... "We're like Hemingway's killers," observed Nabokov, speaking out of the corner of his mouth in mock-gangster fashion. Pointing to his wide-brimmed grey fedora, placed in gentlemanly fashion on a bar stool, Nabokov said, "I should return it to my head, no?, and heighten the realism."[17]

In terms of his fiction, the cinematic elements of his first novel, *Mary* (1926), demonstrate Nabokov's intention to put his experiences to immediate artistic use. The "raw bit of 'real life'" presented by Ganin, the "tuxedoed extra,"[18] generates a sense of actuality and contemporaneity, but also epitomizes Nabokov's approach to the exploration of cinema throughout his work.

> Nothing was beneath his dignity; more than once he had even sold his shadow ... to work as a movie extra on a set ... where light seethes with a mystical hiss from the huge facets of lamps that were aimed, like cannon, at a crowd of extras, lit to a deathly brightness.[19]

Ganin's experience both expresses the impact of the medium on Nabokov's imagination and demonstrates the complexity of his response to it. While there is an explicit suggestion that there is something ominous and dangerous in the film-making process — "an undefinable but quite definite sense of mystery and dread,"[20] as Gavriel Moses describes it —

Gunmen Al (Charles McGraw, left) and Max (William Conrad) keep their eye on the door of the diner, waiting for Swede to enter. *The Killers* (Universal, 1946).

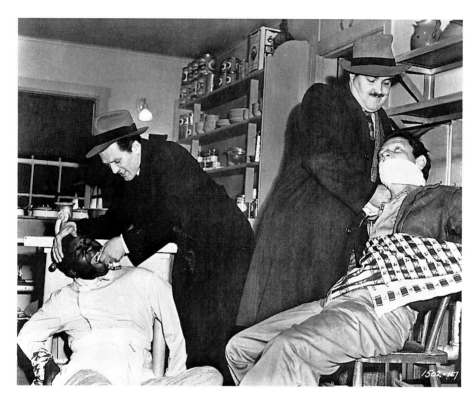

"I loved 'The Killers' and the film version, too: the first scene in the diner was superb, each detail so exact, the unappetizing kitchen in which the killers, working with frightening dispatch, truss together those innocent men"—Vladimir Nabokov to Alfred Appel, Jr. (Appel, p. 208). Here, gunmen Al (Charles McGraw, standing left) and Max (William Conrad, standing right) in the scene to which Nabokov refers.

there is also something intensely compelling in the idea of offering oneself up to annihilation by the overwhelming power of the studio lights, or being rendered utterly anonymous, engulfed in a vast crowd of strangers. The notion that "nothing was beneath his dignity" is, therefore, critical in the context of this sense of wonder, and there is also an implication of pride in this statement that counteracts its negative aspect. It is also significant that Ganin claims not to have sold *himself* but his "shadow," appropriately, to this phantom world. Conventional associations of life with light and death with darkness are subverted here, but the sense of conflict they generate remains unresolved. Ganin's stance, therefore, exemplifies both the inherent quality of Nabokov's treatment of film and the pivotal dynamic of ambivalence that permeates his fiction.

Nabokov's Camera Eye

Nabokov claimed to "think in images."[21] That his creative imagination was informed by the processes of film and photography was acknowledged also by his son, Dmitri, who stated that "his writing ... was all there, inside his mind, like film waiting to be developed."[22] Nevertheless, the elucidation of Nabokov's deployment of cinema and cinematics in his fiction is made problematic by a method of deliberate obfuscation whereby references function as implicit, elusive allusions, possessing only fragments of a discernible theme, concept or device. For example, in his autobiography, *Conclusive Evidence* (subsequently revised as *Speak, Memory*), Nabokov removed the key element of an explicit mnemonic association, rendering it indeterminate and oblique. The original passage, in which Nabokov describes a childhood memory of the family's house on Morskaia Street in St. Petersburg, appears in an incomplete, undated draft of a chapter titled "My English Education":

> In the gathering dusk the place acted upon my young senses in a curiously teleological way as if this accumulation of familiar things in the dark was doing its utmost to form the definite and permanent image which *a certain system of repeated exposure* did finally leave in my mind.[23]

In the published version, Nabokov omits the phrase "a certain system of," thereby revoking the initial, overtly filmic metaphor.[24] The relationship between memory and the processes of film and photography evident in Nabokov's fiction, however, irrevocably demonstrates the critical role of this association and the extent to which they are an abiding preoccupation, subject to perpetual reinterpretation and modification throughout his career.

Cinematic perspective is also integral to Nabokov's exposition of themes of memory and mortality. Processes of film and photography not only grant his protagonists a superhuman visual capability, but the calculated manipulation of the camera eye also offers them supremely privileged points of vantage which are crucial in their struggle to overcome the degenerative forces of time. The artificial quality of this mode of narrative presentation in turn magnifies preoccupying questions of objective and subjective cognition but also serves, paradoxically, as the only reliable means of apprehending "reality" in time and space. As Nabokov argues, the problem of perceiving any given situation as "real" can only be solved by means of "the apparatus to reproduce those events optically within the frame of one screen," namely, a "video" camera.[25] At the same time, the photographic image is perceived as an independent dimension and an alternative realm of existence, one which is both aspirational and terrifying. For Ganin, the submission of his shadow to this ghostly realm is profoundly disturbing and reductive, rendering him vulnerable, amorphous, transitory, and yet for others, particularly Humbert Humbert or Van Veen, film offers a form of refuge, the potential for transformation, the means by which to realize their creative ideals and, most critically, the promise of immortality.

Two

The Impact of German and Soviet Film on Nabokov's Early Russian Fiction

Nabokov's early work demonstrates the palpable influence of contemporary cinema, in particular the avant-garde experiments of German and Soviet filmmakers. Visually imaginative and challenging and technically innovative, the films of Lang, Wiene, Murnau, Eisenstein, Pudovkin and Vertov extended the possibilities of the medium beyond the limitations of conventional storytelling. Although the informing of Nabokov's imagination by German and Soviet silent film may have been only brief, lasting as long as the movements themselves, their impact should not be underestimated, nor the degree of their enduring presence in Nabokov's experience of cinema.

German Expressionist Film: Key Aspects

Early German cinema had strong ties with the theater and continued the tradition of experiment that had been prevalent since the turn of the century. Throughout the 1920s, the essence of Expressionism remained the primary inspiration for German filmmakers. Characterized by the Gothic, the fantastic and the grotesque, its principal themes were initiated by the Faustian legend of damnation through surrender to the temptations of decadence. The movement itself began to decline toward the end of the decade, but its long-term impact lay in the stylistic and technical innovations it inspired.

Expressionism focused upon the solipsistic experience of an individual in the face of the chaos and disorder of modern society, the solitariness of life in the new cities, alienation caused by mechanization and urbanization, and an intensely emotional response to these forces. Film offered the potential for greater freedom to explore these ideas than did theater, which was limited by its static sets, its confined spaces and the physical distance between actor and audience. These limitations were to some extent overcome by Max Reinhardt's development of Kammerspiel (chamber) theater, which reduced the size of stage and auditorium to promote an atmosphere of intimacy thus magnifying the audience's sense of engagement with the actors. Innovations in filmmaking paralleled developments in theater, and early cinema began as an essentially theatrical medium. Cameras were fixed and unmoving, and visual effects were created by elaborately constructed sets designed to generate deep shadows and surreal distortions, with only minimal additional lighting. Nevertheless, technicians and directors became highly versatile in adapting and utilizing the limited technical resources available, while the absence of sound placed the emphasis on visual communication, which in turn raised questions of the relationship of the audience to the form, and the nature of the reliability of visual perception.

The success of Wiene's *Das Kabinet des Dr. Caligari* (1919), for example, depended entirely upon the skill of set designers and lighting technicians to convey a nightmarish atmosphere of confusion and menace. The world it presents is that seen through the protagonist's eyes, "a distorted world, a world that looks like it is ready to collapse or explode and fly apart, without verticals or horizontals that would give a sense of weight or firm foundation. Structures seem to lean, twist, slouch, or rear back as if they were alive with the fear and violence of the story itself."[1]

For all its technical crudity, the film has a remarkable pace, scope and fluidity, created by the multi-dimensional construction of its sets combined with a sophisticated use of lighting to generate a sense of space and movement unobtainable in theater.

The pivotal dynamic of *Caligari*—the externalization of an individual's internal emotional and mental state — presented Expressionism's central conceptual premise in a skilful manipulation of cinematic visuals. Only three years later, filmmakers were already beginning to subvert and revise this premise, shifting the primary narrative focus away from

The Expressionist nightmare: distorted, twisting structures and extremes of light and shade. *Das Kabinet des Dr. Caligari* (UFA, 1919).

the visual expression of a subjective condition to a preoccupation with perspective and perceptual modes, emphasizing the importance of the camera as an independent narrative tool.

In *Dr. Mabuse der Spieler* (1922), Fritz Lang used the camera in a remarkable way, combining innovative editing techniques and visual effects with a combination of "close-ups," "reverse-angle" and "point-of-view" shots. Close-ups[2] were conventionally employed at a critical moment to amplify the protagonist's experience by focusing tight on the face, the most expressive vehicle of communication in silent film. In one of the film's most critical scenes, however, Lang extends the conventional impact of the close-up by deploying it in a sequence of reverse-angle shots[3] to dramatize the effect of Mabuse's hypnotic gaze on Wenk, the public prosecutor. As they confront each other across a card table, the camera alternately adopts the antagonistic subjective perspective of each man, the scene concluding in an extreme close-up on Mabuse's face:

> The struggle between the two wills is captured in this moment: the eerie face filling the whole screen is the visual abstraction of [Mabuse's] determination to conquer the police commissioner, while Wenk's resistance seems to be the force that keeps the face from bursting out of the screen. Mabuse's staring face ... seems to glow with a ghostly whiteness. Then Mabuse's head begins to move forward, growing larger and becoming disembodied, as everything else recedes into darkness. His head becomes an abstraction, filling the whole screen, his hair flying out wildly on all sides.[4]

This innovative sequence generates a visual ambiguity which is deeply disruptive, both in terms of the audience's response and the consequences for notions of representational reliability and authenticity. Lang's manipulation of point-of-view[5] shots dissolves the perceived autonomy of the camera perspective, such that, as its objectivity is compromised, so too is the audience's ability to distinguish what it sees. Thus the goal of Expressionism was extended to present more than one singular visual perspective, serving to undermine the audience's dependence upon the camera as a reliable mimetic tool.

By 1923 the use of visual effects had become complex and highly evocative, generated by adapted stage-lighting techniques borrowed from Reinhardt's Kammerspiel theater. In Robison's *Schatten*, the "hypnotic use of lighting, shadows, and mirror images that [dominate] the action of the film, whose world is one of deceptive likenesses, pervaded by reactions to appearances,"[6] obliterate concerns of either story or characterization. Apart from the evocation of atmosphere, Robison's film demonstrates a preoccupation with the synthetic nature and self-conscious aspect of the cinematic experience.

As John Barlow argues, the "illusion within the film ... mirrors the actual illusion of film viewing, suggesting that viewers can deal with the shadows haunting them as they discover themselves in the cinematic shadow play they are viewing."[7] This notion of participating in a self-declared and acknowledged piece of creative artifice has since been acknowledged as a key element of the overall cinematic aesthetic,[8] but it was also to become a recurrent theme of Nabokov's Russian and English fiction.

The Expressionist Nightmare in
Murnau's Der letzte Mann *and*
Nabokov's "Details of a Sunset"

The relationship of audience to screen was a fundamental aspect of the Expressionist experience. Reinhardt's Kammerspiel theater was an indication of a director's desire for total absorption by the audience in the action on stage, and film could offer an even greater proximity, an intimacy, a visual flexibility and control which was impossible to achieve in theater, no matter how small the stage and auditorium.[9] By 1924, film had adopted Reinhardt's Kammerspiel method and elaborated upon it, to an extent where the fantastic could be rendered as the everyday by granting dramatic significance to inanimate objects and thus extending the Expressionistic sense of the external manifestation of an intensely driven subjective consciousness. In Murnau's *Der letzte Mann* (1924), the central character's fate is governed by inanimate objects — a uniform, a trunk and a series of doors.[10]

The objects are used in the film as plot catalysts, but they also carry considerable symbolic weight. Nabokov's story of the same year, "Details of a Sunset," similarly employs a series of inanimate objects which as they recur, generate a subliminal, extra-textual meaning, at the same time acting within the narrative framework of the story upon both plot and character. The story relates the demise of Mark Standfuss, who is knocked down by a tram on the streets of Berlin. The significant objects — a workman's tent, some removal vans, a broken chair — are seen by Mark, and a sense of ominous foreboding registers, but the messages they convey remain undisclosed until the end of the story and then are revealed only to the reader. Mark's inability to perceive the significance of these objects is indicative of the blind naivety and trust he demonstrates in his human relationships. That he will experience tragedy, either in the form of a terrifying, fatal accident or in the discovery that his beloved fiancée has been deceiving him seems somehow inevitable, the presence of these signals of his fate serving, obtusely, as an attempt to prepare him, offering a glimpse of another realm into which he is soon to enter. These signals take the form of two visions, one grotesque and one divine. The first occurs at night:

> In the middle of a square stood a black wigwam: the tram tracks were being repaired.... On the other side of the fence, in a gap between the

> buildings, was a rectangular vacant lot. Several moving vans stood there
> like enormous coffins. They were bloated from their loads.[11]

With hindsight, the significance of the damaged tram lines becomes
starkly apparent to the reader, suggesting the wreckage caused by the
accident. The potency of the image of swollen coffins, however, has a
strong and immediate impact in the narrative, serving as a horrifying premonition of death, alerting both Mark and the reader to its inexplicable
proximity. The second vision presents a completely antithetical prospect,
however, seeming initially to be entirely unrelated and incompatible with
the first.

> The houses were as gray as ever; yet the roofs, the moldings above the
> upper floors, the gilt-edged lightning rods, the stone cupolas, the colon-
> nettes ... were now bathed in rich ochre, the sunset's airy warmth, and
> thus they seemed unexpected and magical, ... contrasting sharply, because
> of their tawny brilliance, with the drab façades beneath [p. 82].

If the first vision was a glimpse of hell, then this is a glimpse of
heaven, and yet Mark, in his state of perceptual blindness and at present
so replete with life, is, ironically, oblivious to their connotations. The
notion that Mark has no control over his destiny is underlined by the
suggestion that he has already begun, unwittingly, to be transformed
from a day person into a night person, and that two possible fates await
him, either one of utter physical and spiritual annihilation or one of transcendent beauty and peace, neither of which he has the power to choose.
These same visions return to him, slightly modified, after his collision
with the tram, as he lies unconscious, slipping, still oblivious, toward
death. Where before they existed independently of each other, one
belonging to night, the other to the day, suddenly they appear together,
confronting him in such a way that he cannot ignore them.

> The street was wide and gay. The colors of the sunset had invaded half
> of the sky. Upper stories and roofs were bathed in glorious light. Up there,
> Mark could discern translucent porticoes, friezes and frescoes, trellises
> covered with orange roses, winged statues that lifted skyward golden,
> unbearably blazing lyres.... Mark could not understand how he had never
> noticed before those galleries, those temples suspended on high.
>   He banged his knee painfully. The black fence again. He could not
> help laughing as he recognized the vans beyond. There they stood, like
> gigantic coffins. Whatever might they contain within? Treasures? The
> skeletons of giants? Or dusty mountains of sumptuous furniture? [p. 83].

In his dream state, Mark looks inside one of the vans only to discover that all it contains is a broken chair, minus one leg. Although Mark does not realize it, this incongruous image serves to cancel out one of his two possible destinies. This unremarkable, rather pathetic object then is, ironically, the ultimate symbol of his fate.

Mark's predicament echoes the Expressionist experience in which the protagonist's destiny pursues him in the guise of commonplace objects, their portent disguised by their very banality. Here, their message remains elusive; they defy perception and thus deprive him of any independent will, rendering him powerless and impotent. Death, however, grants perceptual revelation, proving to be a positive, liberating force, available even to the most unremarkable of heroes.

There is no such prospect for Murnau's hero, however. *Der letzte Mann* epitomizes Expressionistic art with its use of thematic and stylistic contrasts — extremes of light and dark, stillness and movement — and its central theme of a solitary individual helpless in the face of the forces of an urban metropolis which ultimately destroys him. The film also contains a strong social polemic. An underlying narrative irony tells of the futile existence of the working-class man in a decadent, capitalistic society that favors the wealthy and the beautiful, a narrative which grounds the film's reality in actuality. The narrative focus is, therefore, not truly Expressionistic, since the camera eye serves to expose the reality of the protagonist's situation, allowing the audience an objective insight into the forces dictating his demise. The shadows and darkness are not the product of his inner emotional and mental state but are external and independent, creating an atmosphere of hopelessness and alienation which pervades the modern urban world, lurking close to a fragile surface of glamour and sophistication.

Der letzte Mann is one of several Expressionist films which Nabokov particularly admired.[12] He also described Wiene's *Orlacs Hände* (1924) as "wonderfully macabre and bizarre":

> I remember perfectly certain scenes in Orlac: the nocturnal train crash in which the concert artist [Veidt] loses his hands — steam, smoke, infernal confusion — and the "executed" murderer's unexpected return, his broken neck bolstered by a terrible brace, his face masked, mechanical claws in place of the hands that have been grafted onto Orlac's limbs.[13]

As Appel cites, so impressed was Nabokov by Wiene's film that he transcribed the visual style of the scene of the train crash into his descrip-

tion of the railway which runs alongside Ganin's boardinghouse in
Mary:

> The black trains roared past, shaking the windows of the house; with a
> movement like ghostly shoulders shaking off the load, heaving moun-
> tains of smoke swept upward, blotting out the night sky. The roofs
> burned with a smooth metallic blaze in the moonlight; and a sonorous
> black shadow under the iron bridge awoke as a black train rumbled across
> it, sending a chain of light flickering down its length. The clattering roar
> and mass of smoke seemed to pass right through the house as it quiv-
> ered between the chasm where the rail tracks lay like lines drawn by a
> moonlit fingernail and the street where it was crossed by the flat bridge
> waiting for the next regular thunder of railway carriages [p. 90].

Nabokov's use of contrasts of light and dark in this passage and the
patterns of shadows and distorted reflections are overtly Expressionistic
in style, and the atmosphere of "infernal confusion" in Wiene's film which
made such an impact on him is powerfully amplified. The description
is, however, incidental to Ganin's situation; it is neither a reflection nor
an externalization of his inner emotional or mental state, possessing no
wider thematic implications for the novel. Although this may be a rather
crude exploitation of a powerful cinematic sequence, it is important in
that it confirms the close attention Nabokov was paying to film at this
time and his intention to use the medium as an aspect of his art. Nabokov
continued to demonstrate a close affinity with and fascination for cinematic visual styles and themes, not simply for the fictional effects they
could generate, but also for the implications for extending narrative perspective.

Mechanisms of Cinematic Visualization in The Eye

Nabokov's *The Eye* (1930) is distinctly Expressionistic, reflecting the
nightmarish quality of contemporary German film and its definitive preoccupations. Its central theme, as Nabokov described it, is "the pursuit
of an investigation which leads the protagonist through a hell of mirrors
and ends in the merging of twin images."[14]

The novel's narrator/protagonist, Smurov, is the first of many of
Nabokov's deluded heroes who indulges in solipsistic fantasy to the point
of insanity. Subsequent characters include Hermann Karlovich in *Despair*

(1936), Humbert Humbert in *Lolita* (1955) and Charles Kinbote in *Pale Fire* (1962). Smurov's referential use of the cinematic mode is distinctive because it is a new and unconventional phenomenon, employed together with the more familiar mediums of literature and theater. By 1930 the German Expressionist movement was in decline, due to the redundancy of silent film in light of the advent of sound and a combination of financial and political forces which were severely restricting the German avant-garde film industry. The style of *The Eye* is unequivocally inspired by this fading movement and would have been immediately recognizable to a contemporary reader as a parody of the cinematic style that had dominated the past decade of German cinema.

It is rare for Nabokov to spell out the intent of any of his works, but in his introduction to *The Eye* he alerts the reader's attention to the novel's principal emphasis—"not on the mystery but on the pattern" (p. 10)—essentially, the importance, above all, of the reader's ability to visualize the construction of his work. The key to unraveling the pattern lies in the network of images and motifs—the visual clues—incorporated in the text which, as they recur, develop in impact and meaning.

The rebellion of Expressionism took the form of distortion and, in particular, the distorted perspective of an individual which subverted, rejected and revised the conventions of visual apprehension. Smurov's self-inflicted predicament is a form of rebellion against the petty restraints and humiliations of everyday life. His paranoid delusion, that he has succeeded in committing suicide and has returned as another person who happens to be the complete antithesis of his former, pathetic self, is perfectly complemented by the cinematic perspective of his narrative.

The reincarnated Smurov sees the world as if through a camera lens. This allows him a distance and objectivity which would otherwise be unsustainable and also the possibility for self-regard which removes the pain of humiliation and rejection. The first key example of Smurov's cinematic reinterpretation of events is his presentation of the incident which anticipates his attempted suicide—the fight with his lover's husband, Kashmarin. Smurov depicts the scene in a series of stills, combined with slow motion and sudden rushes of action which transforms what was a brief skirmish into a lengthy battle. By thus amplifying the scene's dramatic impact, Smurov is able not only to disguise his humiliation, but also to render the anguish and torment he endures.[15] The episode borrows from silent screen melodrama, with Smurov's enemy playing the part of a Nosferatu,[16] a "jealous fiend ... with protruding eyes, dilated nostrils, and a lip replete with venom under the black equilateral triangle of his trimmed moustache" (p. 21). The actual effect of this, however, is more comical than horrifying, and the presence of Nabokov's ironic perspective is established. The scene can be read as a sequence of intercut long, medium, close-up, and point-of-view (POV) shots (as indicated in square brackets) which emulate the camera eye and generate dramatic pace and tension:

> [First-person POV close-up] He bared his teeth and got ready to hit me again. [CUT] The blow landed on my raised arm. [CUT to third-person long shot] Here I retreated and dodged into the parlor. [CUT] He came after me. ... [CUT to POV medium shot] When he caught up with me again, I tried to protect myself with a cushion I had grabbed on the run, but he knocked it out of my hand. ... I took refuge behind a table, and as before, everything froze for a moment into a tableau. [Freeze frame. CUT to POV close-up] There he was, teeth bared, cane upraised, and [CUT to POV long shot] behind him, on either side of the door, stood the boys [Freeze frame]: perhaps my memory is stylized at this point, but, so help me, I really believe that one was leaning with folded arms against the wall, while the other sat on the arm of a chair, both imperturbably watching the punishment being administered to me. [CUT to third-person medium shot] Presently all was in motion again, and all four of us passed into the next room [CUT to POV close-up], the level of his attack lowered viciously, my hands formed an abject fig leaf, and then, with a horrible blinding blow, he whacked me across the face [pp. 22–23].

Smurov recalls the fight as a combination of freeze frames and spurts of action which, while giving the impression of chaos, belies the control he asserts over the depiction of events. The sequence is structured in three distinctive sections characterized by (1) the POV close-up, (2) medium and long third-person shots and finally (3) the POV close-up again. The point-of-view shots are calculatedly deployed to reassert Smurov's subjective perspective and to dramatize the full horror of the violence he suffers. Nevertheless, it is not only Smurov who is seen to be participating in this filmic scenario. His description of the boys' behavior, for example, suggests that they are not only conspirators with Kashmarin but also conscious collaborators in Smurov's cinematic imaginings:

> The contemplative immobility of my two pupils, the different poses in which they froze like frescoes at the end of this room or that, the oblig-

ing way they turned on the lights the moment I backed into the dark dining room — all this must be a perceptional illusion — disjointed impressions to which I have imparted significance and permanence, and, for that matter, just as arbitrary as the raised knee of a politician stopped by a camera not in the act of dancing a jig but merely in that of crossing a puddle [pp. 23–24].

That Smurov recognizes his mnemonic distortions, however, serves as a key insight into the unreliability of his narrative and exposes the absurdity of his interpretations.

Smurov's assumed directorial control is constantly undermined by the reality he attempts to manipulate. His perception of personalities is corrupted by his desire to fulfill a fantasy, inspired by romantic heroes and heroines from popular novels or screen melodramas:

He was obviously a person who, behind his unpretentiousness and quietness, concealed a fiery spirit. He was doubtless capable, in a moment of wrath, of slashing a chap into bits, and, in a moment of passion, of carrying a frightened and perfumed girl beneath his cloak on a windy night to a waiting boat with muffled oarlocks, under a slice of honeydew moon [p. 43].

Smurov's emulation of such banal heroics could also be considered as a parody of the emotional extremes of Expressionist heroes, the intensity of their anguish and desire, and the ferocity of their actions. The adoption of different personae or "masks" (p. 59), as Smurov calls them, is also reminiscent of the mystic elements of Expressionist film as is the animation of inanimate objects which seem to conspire against him. For example, when stalking Roman Bogdanovich, Smurov finds himself standing alone in familiar streets that have become, in the darkness, forbidding and threatening:

Clouds rolled across the sky, assuming various grotesque attitudes like staggering and ballooning buffoons in a hideous carnival ... hunched up in the blow, [I held] onto my bowler which I felt would explode like a bomb if I let go of its brim.... The only witnesses to my vigil were a street light that seemed to blink because of the wind, and a sheet of wrapping paper that now scurried along the sidewalk.... I stood away from the street light; and the shadows afforded me a kind of hectic protection. Suddenly a yellow glow appeared in the glass of the front door [pp. 81–82].[17]

As in Wiene's *Caligari*, where contrasts of light and shade, blacks and whites and changing contours signal the presence of unearthly forces, here they also reflect opposing aspects of madness and sanity, the real and the surreal. There is no question that the scene depicted is that solely seen by Smurov and that the personification of objects — the clouds, the bowler hat, the street light, the wrapping paper, even the shadows — is the product of Smurov's distorting mind. His vision of his shadow, apart from being overtly Expressionistic in style, typifies the dilemma of the Expressionist hero, trapped in an internalized world, yet constantly bombarded and betrayed by everything around him:

> My shadow, as it plunged into the aura of the street lamp, stretched out and passed me, but then was lost in darkness [p. 84].

The notion of a conspiracy by inanimate objects, suggested in "Details of a Sunset," is here extended by Nabokov from a thematic element of Smurov's subjective narrative to a crucial plot device reminiscent of the trunk or the uniform in Murnau's *Der letzte Mann*. Here, Smurov's bowler hat functions as a motif which signals to the reader that he and the narrator are one and the same character. Nabokov betrays the hat's ownership three times, each time confirming that Smurov and the novel's narrator are one and the same and thus that Smurov is, in fact, alive. The hat first appears just before Smurov's attempted suicide. It is significant that on this occasion, as with the last, the hat is seen as a chance reflection in a mirror:

> A wretched, shivering, vulgar little man in a bowler hat stood in the center of the room, for some reason rubbing his hands. That is the glimpse I caught of myself in the mirror [p. 26].

Each time Smurov believes his reflection to be that of a third party, and for a brief instant he fails to recognize himself:

> As I pushed the door, I noticed the reflection from the side mirror: a young man in a bowler hat carrying a bouquet, hurried towards me. That reflection and I merged into one. I walked out into the street [p. 97].

The reader identifies this familiar cinematic visual effect as the "merging of twin images" mentioned in Nabokov's introduction, but there is no suggestion that Smurov acknowledges his own mirror image, and he is not aware of the significance of the bowler hat. It is the hat which gives him away to the reader in this instance, as it did to Roman Bogdanovich, on whom he spies:

> With a light thump, the bowler hat fell and rolled away on the sidewalk. I dashed in pursuit, trying to step on the thing and stop it — and almost collided on the run with Roman Bogdanovich, who picked up my hat with one hand, while holding with the other, a sealed envelope that looked white and enormous [p. 83].

The hat in this scene not only causes Smurov to be apprehended, but it reasserts his true identity both to the reader and to Bogdanovich, thus destroying the carefully constructed alter ego he parades and exposing the fragility of his delusions.

At the same time, however, as it deploys elements of Expressionism, *The Eye* also demonstrates an intriguing affinity with some of the key innovations in Soviet cinema during the 1920s and, in particular, with the work of Dziga Vertov. Indeed, there are aspects of Smurov's extraordinary perceptual dilemma, implied also in the literal meaning of the novel's Russian title, *Sogliadatai* (*The Spy*), which almost directly parallel the distinctive principles of Vertov's cinematic ideology of "kinopravda" (film-truth). Nabokov had seen films by both Eisenstein and Pudovkin in Berlin,[18] and it is likely that he was also familiar with Vertov's work, *The Man with the Movie Camera* having been released in 1929, a year before the publication of *The Eye*, to international critical acclaim.

Dziga Vertov and Smurov's Kino-Eye

Vertov began his career as a director of newsreels, producing over twenty films between 1922 and 1925. His first full-length film, *Kinoglaz* (*Kino-Eye*) (1924) established the method and philosophy of documentary realism as central to his art. Vertov believed human vision to be inherently flawed. Thus he replaced the human eye with the camera lens as the sole means of reliable visual perception. He considered the camera to be not only a perfect machine, a machine which would neither degenerate nor regress, but also a machine which had the potential for continual development and improvement. It also had a flexibility and versatility that far surpassed the capabilities of human vision:

The camera as superlative visual apparatus. *The Man with the Movie Camera* (VUFKU, 1929).

> The mechanical eye, the camera, rejecting the human eye as crib sheet, gropes its way through the chaos of visual effects, letting itself be drawn or repelled by movement, probing, as it goes, the path of its own movement. It experiments, distending time, dissecting movement, or, in contrary fashion, absorbing time within itself, swallowing years, thus schematizing processes of long duration inaccessible to the normal eye.
>
> Aiding the machine-eye is the kinok-pilot [cameraman], who not only controls the camera's movements, but entrusts himself to it during experiments in space. And at a later time the kinok-engineer, with remote control cameras. The result of this concerted action of the liberated and perfected camera and the strategic brain of man directing, observing and gauging the presentation of even the most ordinary things will take on an exceptionally fresh and interesting aspect.[19]

Through a highly defined creative process, Vertov transformed the ordinary into the extraordinary, presenting to the human eye, via means of superior technology, an enhanced vision of the world. The liberated camera, working within a documentary format had, Vertov believed, not only the potential for achieving realism on screen, but also the ability to perceive and project an extant hyper-reality invisible to the human eye.

> The main and essential thing is:
> The sensory exploration of the world through film. We therefore take as the point of departure the use of the camera as a kino-eye, more perfect than the human eye, for the exploration of the chaos of visual phenomena that fills space.[20]

Montage was a crucial element in the exposition of this hyper-realism, an editing technique pioneered by Sergei Eisenstein and widely used by Soviet and European avant-garde filmmakers during the silent era,[21] which also inspired the narrative style of American directors, particularly D. W. Griffith. Vertov deployed it as a means of extending the boundaries of perception, to challenge the imagination and the psyche of his audience, granting a more acute and vital perspective on the world. Unlike Eisenstein, however, Vertov was not concerned with transforming chaos into order. Eisenstein's purpose, in his treatment of montage, was to generate a specific effect on his audience, a method which he called a "montage of attractions"[22]:

> An attraction is in our understanding any demonstrable fact (an action, an object, a phenomenon, a conscious combination, and so on) that is known and proven to exercise a definite effect on the attention and emotions of the audience and that, combined with others, possesses the characteristic of concentrating the audience's emotions in any direction dictated by the production's purpose.[23]

Eisenstein's montage constructed a network of visual associations which supported the dramatic and thematic structure of his films. "The method of agitation through spectacle," he argued, "consists in the creation of a new chain of conditioned reflexes by associating selected phenomena with the unconditioned reflexes they produce."[24] Eisenstein's method was, therefore, quite distinct from Vertov's. Whereas Vertov employed "montage parallelism," a technique which engaged and challenged audiences on a primarily intellectual level, Eisenstein's concern was to provoke his audiences emotionally. His aim was to develop cinematic narrative through the "juxtaposition and accumulation [of] associations that produce, albeit tangentially, a similar (and often stronger) effect ... when taken as a whole."[25] Thus he endeavored to generate interest not in isolated shots, "but in the relationships between the shots,"[26] as part of an integrated and cohesive cinematic experience, a method which, incidentally, was to serve as a major influence on the construction of classic American film narrative.

Vertov was primarily concerned with the dynamism and disruptive impact of individual images. On the basis of his thesis of catching life "unawares," he developed a very specific cinematic method which involved filming documentary-style on streets, in fields, factories, homes, either from a hidden location, so as to remain unperceived by his subjects, or quite openly, yet discreetly, so as not to disturb everyday activity.[27] (His method did, however, often involve a substantial element of contrivance, and he would sometimes even set up a scene by creating a synthetic diversion.) Shots were calculated for maximum visual impact and filmed from different angles and distances, in motion, or from alternatingly high and low perspectives. Editing was crucial in the filmmaking process, being intellectually driven, with the intent always to produce abstract art. In this respect, Vertov's work was extremely influential in European avant-garde filmmaking and is particularly apparent in the German director Walther Ruttmann's film *Berlin: Symphony of a Great City* (1927). Vertov himself asserted this influence, describing Ruttmann's film as something to "be regarded as the result of years of kino-eye's pressure through work and statements, on those working in abstract film."[28]

Vertov's cinematic experiments culminated in one of the last Soviet films of the silent era. In its exploration and manipulation of the visual capabilities of an artificial eye, *The Man with the Movie Camera* deployed "every optical device and filming strategy ... available to film technology" at the time, in "an unprecedented complexity of cinematic design."[29]

Vertov believed utterly in the camera eye's constructive, expansive capabilities and its universal communicative force. In *The Eye*, however, Smurov cynically deploys the camera eye as a dehumanizing mechanism and as a means of indulging his solipsistic fantasies. Vertov endeavors to present the world in its truest, barest, most vital form, without emotional or psychological bias, arguing that "the 'psychological' prevents man from being as precise as a stopwatch; it interferes with his desire for kinship with the machine."[30] Ironically, Smurov's "kinship" with his own internal camera eye is deeply corrupted by his flawed psyche.

Nabokov's use of cinematics in *The Eye* is deliberate and not only relates to the novel's style, as it does in places in *Mary*, but is also crucial to its narrative and thematic structure. The central protagonist's preoccupation with visual distortion and corruption is informed by the style and artistic intent of contemporary film. Whereas Ganin's relationship with film is purely pragmatic, as he is content to remain anonymous and inconsequential, Smurov fancies that he is not only in a film but also has the starring role, and while Ganin has no control over the piece in which he has taken part, Smurov considers himself to be director, author, camera, and the product entirely of his own design:

> Whenever I wish, I can accelerate or retard to ridiculous slowness the motions of all these people, or distribute them in different groups, or arrange them in various patterns, lighting them now from below, now from the side.... For me their entire existence has been merely a shimmer on a screen [p. 91].

Compare this, however, with Vertov's very similar declaration:

> I am kino-eye, I am a mechanical eye. I, a machine, show you the world as only I can see it.
>
> Now and forever, I free myself from human immobility, I am in constant motion, I draw near, then away from objects, I crawl under, I climb onto them. I move apace with the muzzle of a galloping horse, I plunge full speed into a crowd, I outstrip running soldiers, I plunge and soar together with plunging and soaring bodies.[31]

Initially, the two statements appear to be declaring a shared spirit of intent. Both men assume a superior perspective, one of control and discipline. They are self-sufficient, de-humanized entities concerned only with capturing and rendering cinematic images. The distinctive difference, however, lies in each man's relationship with his subject. Vertov's depiction of himself is one of an independent, detached machine, possessing superhuman energy and dynamism. His human faculties are in complete submission to the camera, the camera enabling him both to extend the limits of his physical and imaginative capabilities and to grant him an equal status with his subject. His capitulation to the camera is part of a process of attaining a level of vital communion with the world. Smurov may have achieved a similar superhuman dynamic, but his transformation is profoundly cynical, resulting in a complete abnegation of his former self and a superior stance which leads only to utter and irrevocable alienation.

From the outset, the multi-dimensional quality of Smurov's vision is peculiarly cinematic. Smurov's tortuous self-consciousness is expressed in terms of an external eye scrutinizing his every move, through which only he can see:

> Yet I was always exposed, always wide-eyed; even in sleep I did not cease to watch over myself ... growing crazy at the thought of not being able to stop being aware of myself [p. 17].

Rather than trying to resist this extraordinary mode of out-of-body self-visualization or to construct complex alter egos (personae which he cannot sustain) to attract his gaze away from himself, Smurov eventually embraces his bizarre predicament. Although it is an act of self-relinquishment, it serves at the same time to liberate him from the constraints of physical being, which have, after all, meant only rejection and humiliation:

> The only happiness in the world is to observe, to spy, to watch, to scrutinize oneself and others, to be nothing but a big, slightly vitreous, somewhat bloodshot, unblinking eye [p. 103].

Inasmuch as a camera lens resembles the human eye, so this grotesque image is a physical incarnation of a mechanical visual instrument. At the same time, it is a remarkable echo of the image of an eye superimposed over a camera lens that concludes *The Man with the Movie Camera*.

The most intriguing element of Smurov's predicament is the gradual disintegration of vision as a reliable means of perception as his sense of control over what he sees increases. In a sense it is an ironic process of progressive reduction, which has its source in Smurov's deluded imagination and its end in complete solipsistic retreat:

> For I do not exist: there exist but the thousands of mirrors that reflect me. With every acquaintance I make, the population of phantoms resembling me increases [p. 102].

This also echoes Ganin's lament for his lost shadow and his sense of life seeming "like a piece of film-making where headless extras knew nothing of the picture in which they were taking part" (p. 31), yet whereas for Ganin the process is one of loss and dissolution, for Smurov, complete negation is a triumph.

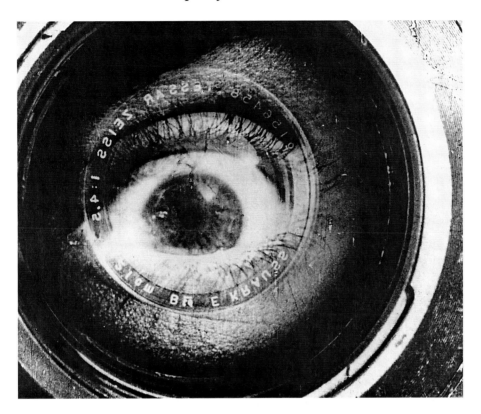

"To be nothing but one big, slightly vitreous, somewhat bloodshot, unblinking eye." The final frame of Vertov's *The Man with the Movie Camera* (VUFKU, 1929).

Manipulation of Cinematic Narrative in "The Leonardo"

Nabokov's deployment of cinematics extended beyond the era of silent, experimental film. His fiction of the 1930s demonstrates a sustained interest in cinema and an ability to draw equally upon the avant-garde and popular media, while assimilating film's most recent technical innovation, sound. "The Leonardo," a story published in 1933, demonstrates an intriguing manipulation of conventional narrative forms — the fairytale and the crime mystery — with a combination of theatrical and cinematic devices which, while initially familiar to the reader, are presented in such a way as to subvert all expectations.

The story's two strongest elements, cinema and the fairytale, are undercut by the theater and the detective story respectively, rendering a definitive reading impossible. Its narrative ambiguities remain unresolved; only a marginal sense of closure is afforded by the resolution of the story's central puzzle — the true identity of its enigmatic hero, Romantovski. In these terms, the story could be deemed an isolated experiment, were it not for the fact that it displays, in a concentrated form, the kind of elusive complexity which was to characterize Nabokov's future work.

In terms of cinema, the story contains three main devices. First, the narrative perspective is that of a film director, ordering scenes, interjecting in the middle of a piece of action, controlling the focus of the reader's attention. Second, scenes are visualized as if through a camera lens. The narrative demonstrates not only a visual scope beyond the capabilities of the human eye, but also a referential use of recognizable cinematic techniques, particularly montage. Finally, the narrative contains sudden shifts in pace, as if breaking into cinematic scenes, switching suddenly from third-person prose to unannounced dialogue, which drives the action in a series of abrupt and disorientating visual jolts.

Staging is a fundamental aspect of the story's presentation, and while it is overtly theatrical, it is also highly cinematic in its exposition. "The Leonardo" introduces a dynamic of ambivalence in relation to the roles of stage and film that recurs throughout Nabokov's fiction, essentially, in terms of its deployment as a narrative tool. Narrator/protagonists often explicitly emulate the theater, as they do painting or literature (for example, Hermann Karlovich, Humbert Humbert and Van Veen), but also, and at the same time, in combination with filmic images and devices. This serves to sustain rather than resolve questions of narrative intent, and, more fundamentally, to generate the principal of a fiction in which all modes of presentation co-exist on an equal plane.

As in Nabokov's later, overtly cinematic story, "The Assistant Producer," the narrator's role of director/producer is openly declared from the outset. The necessary objects are summoned to the scene, as props on a theater stage:

> The objects that are being summoned assemble, ... Hurry up, please.
>   Here comes the ovate little poplar, all punctuated with April greenery, and takes its stand where told, namely by the tall brick wall, imported in one piece from another city.... Other bits of scenery are distributed about the yard: a barrel, a second barrel, the delicate shade of leaves, an urn of sorts, and a stone cross propped at the foot of the wall. All this is only sketched and much has to be added and finished, and yet two live

people — Gustav and his brother Anton — already come out on their tiny balcony, while rolling before him a little pushcart with a suitcase and a heap of books, Romantovski, the new lodger, enters the yard.[32]

At the same time, however, the narrator announces the essential artifice of what he is about to present to his audience, as if to establish at the outset that this is not to be considered as a depiction of actual events. At this point the fairytale element of the story is established, which in turn implies that it contains some moral purpose, functioning, essentially, as a fable.

The narrator's perspective is granted superhuman capabilities. The manner in which scenes are presented demonstrates an ability to see beyond the range of the human eye, suggesting that the mode of perception is in fact a camera lens. This is established at the story's opening, as the narrator/director orders the scene:

> There remained, sunlit: the pushcart with the books, one barrel, another barrel, the nictating young poplar and an inscription in tar on the brick wall: VOTE FOR (illegible) [p. 358].

In this passage, the reader's attention is directed from one object to another, from a position overlooking the entire scene, and therefore at some distance. The sun functions as a spotlight, as on a film set, providing the key source of illumination. The reader's eye is guided from one relatively large object to another — the pushcart, the barrels, the tree — but then, suddenly, the focus is drawn to a detail on the wall, faint and mostly illegible. The pace of this shift in focus has a mechanical quality; it is the motion of a camera moving swiftly into close-up, with an accuracy which defies the capabilities of human sight. It serves to establish the narrator's all-seeing eye, and his ability to render the smallest and otherwise indiscernible of details confirms his superior visual capability and narrative authority.

The story also overtly deploys the techniques of contemporary cinema to generate visual dynamism and narrative pace. By including elements of Soviet silent film and German Expressionism, Nabokov is both acknowledging the role of cinema's innovations in extending modes of perception and demonstrating their value as narrative devices. In the following description of Anna, for example, Nabokov's use of an abstract image is distinctly reminiscent of early Soviet montage techniques:

> With head thrown back, she opened her mouth so generously that one
> could survey her entire palate and uvula, which resembled the tail end
> of a boiled chicken [p. 359].

The image is so striking and so bizarrely apt that in a brief flash, the reader
not only sees the pink, rubbery bird inside Anna's mouth, but for a
grotesque instant of surreal indulgence also believes it to be there. It
therefore functions exactly, and has the exact same impact, as montage,
while also contributing to the elements of the fantastic and the absurd
which underpin the story.

Later, during the scene in which the brothers and Anna visit Romantovski in his room, Nabokov utilizes a mode of visual and perceptual distortion which echoes Fritz Lang's *Dr. Mabuse*. As in the film, when Wenk
attempts to capture Mabuse by tricking him during a card game and
Mabuse's psychic powers begin to interfere with Wenk's mind, causing
him to see a contorting, expanding image of Mabuse's face before him,
so Romantovski, in a heightened state of anxiety, experiences a similar
perceptual distortion.

> Meanwhile the brothers began to swell, to grow, they filled up the whole
> room, the whole house and then grew out of it…. Gigantic, imperiously
> reeking of sweat and beer, the beefy voices and senseless speeches, with
> fecal matter replacing the human brain, they provoke a tremor of igno-
> ble fear [p. 361].

The effect of overwhelming intrusion, violation and disgust the brothers
provoke is depicted here as a nightmarish vision, and the fear Romantovski experiences is due to the realization of the potential for indiscriminate destruction generated by these two brothers, in the same way
that Wenk realizes his impotence in the face of the extent and force of
Mabuse's mysterious powers.

As the brothers have the capability to invoke such terror, so they
also have the ability simply to cancel someone out altogether, as if they
had all along been merely a figment of their imagination. On another
occasion, the brothers invite Romantovski to their room in order to get
him drunk, but, having extracted nothing of interest from him, they
become bored. Rather than have the narrative describing him leaving the
brothers in their drunken stupor and returning to his room, Nabokov
presents the reader with a tantalizing image of Romantovski simply dis-
integrating before their eyes:

> The boredom was suffocating and grim…. The brothers stooped, top-
> pled, yawned, still looking through sleepy tears at their guest. He, vibrat-
> ing and diffusing rays, stretched out, thinned and gradually vanished.
> This cannot go on. He poisons the life of honest folks [p. 363].

Nabokov is depicting the brothers' alcohol-induced hallucination, yet,
at the same time, the manner in which Romantovski disappears is strongly
reminiscent of a cinematic "dissolve,"[33] emphasized by the sudden shift
in narrative tone in the next paragraph, which signals the start of a new
scene. This serves both as a clever visual effect and a means of creating
a sense of conclusion while moving the action quickly forward.

Nabokov's tribute to film in this story even includes an actual visit
to the cinema. In one respect, this is an indulgence on Nabokov's part,
giving him an opportunity to gently ridicule the farcical efforts of inferior contemporary filmmakers:

> Specters conversed in trumpet tones on the newfangled speaking screen.
> The baron tasted his wine and carefully put his glass down — with the
> sound of a dropped cannon ball [p. 364].

It is significant that Nabokov is describing the most recent innovation in
film — sound — not simply because it confirms that he took an active
interest in the developments of the medium and was able to present very
accurately the primitive state of the technology in its first years, but also
because of its thematic relevance to the story. Sound is a crucial element
of the story's dénouement, and compared with its cumbersome use here,
Nabokov's utilization of sound in the subsequent murder scene is highly
sophisticated and has tremendous dramatic force. This does not so much
imply the superiority of fiction to film but perhaps indicates the potential of sound in cinema to create a similarly powerful dramatic moment.
This sequence, however, rather than reflecting the achievements of contemporary cinema, indicates the profusion of sub-standard imitations of
the work of innovators like Eisenstein and Lang, a general lack of technical and artistic understanding of their methods, endless referential and
wholly unoriginal reworkings of tired scenarios, and a glut of inept storytelling:

> And after a while the sleuths were pursuing the baron. Who would have
> recognized in him the master crook? He was hunted passionately, fren-
> ziedly. Automobiles sped with bursts of thunder. In a nightclub they

fought with bottles, chairs, tables. A mother was putting an enchanting child to bed [p. 364].

The fight scene in the nightclub, the speeding cars and the mother and child bear no relation to the dramatic focus of the film, the pursuit of the baron. These scenes exemplify a failed attempt at montage, while the principal idea of enhancing and developing meaning through abstract related images is completely missed, except for the notion that these images have in some way to *be* abstract. In this case, although the scenes are dramatic and emotive, they are so obtuse and chaotic that they are inherently meaningless and superfluous. Nevertheless, the film's central plot does have a direct bearing on Nabokov's scenario, one which is recognized by Romantovski. Once he is dead, it turns out that Romantovski was a master forger wanted by the police. Romantovski's reply to Anna's excited "Oh, that was wonderful!" (p. 364) not only refers to his own situation, but is also a subtle indication of Nabokov's attitude toward an audience's experience of cinema. That "in real life, it is all considerably duller" (p. 364) is an ironic comment on Romantovski's perception of his own drab and reclusive existence.

Yet Nabokov's attitude is more complex. While the comment develops the notion, hinted at earlier, that cinema is nothing more than a form of shallow, technical trickery, artistically vacuous and perhaps even culturally dangerous, its ephemeral, delicate, magical qualities also have an irresistible appeal. This is communicated by Nabokov's evocative description of the cinema's auditorium. The darkness inside the small cinema is a kind of "night" which is made to "flicker" by the "self-manufactured" light of the movie projector (p. 364). The implication that the interior of the cinema is somehow suffused with the exterior night suggests that there is something inexplicable connecting the two spaces, that the brick walls of the building fail to act as an effective barrier between the real darkness outside and the synthetic darkness inside allowing the two forms of "night" to merge. The scene is not depicted simply as the experience of sitting in a darkened room when the lights have been turned out, or of watching projected images on a flat screen, therefore. Rather, there is a surreal quality which is almost palpable. The "lunar" light of the projector has the power to disturb the stillness of the dark, to flicker like stars, and although this night and moon and these stars are all merely an illusion, the audience enters into the trickery, believing the transformation, and thus this artificial night is granted an enduring, transcendent mystique which cannot be diminished or denied.

As in film, the exploitation of physical appearance as an indication of character in this story delivers both visual immediacy and narrative economy. At the same time, such superficial interpretations can prove misleading. With respect to Anton and Gustav, for example, despite facial and physical differences — one thin, the other fat; one fair, the other dark — the fact that they both wear matching trousers of "identically checkered cloth enclosing tightly their prominent buttocks" (p. 359) confirms their fundamental similarity. That they are alike in such an unfavorable respect, oddly reminiscent of Tweedledum and Tweedledee,[34] is significant, since this lends them an aura of crass vulgarity and stupidity and at the same time a potential for irrational, unprovoked violence. The brothers fulfill this initial impression; yet Nabokov, careful to avoid simplistic determinations of character, confounds the impression of Romantovski's appearance. He is physically weak, cringing, and awkward, attributes which at first seem to complement his solitariness, his silence, his role as pathetic, helpless victim, and yet they turn out to be profoundly deceptive. In the conventional fairytale narrative, good and evil are unequivocally defined, dramatized by heroes and villains, but ultimately, no matter what occurs, good inevitably triumphs. In this story, Romantovski, although a victim, turns out to be far from innocent. He is revealed to be a greater criminal than either Anton or Gustav, a professional, no less, and an ex-convict, identified as the "leonardo"[35] of the story's title. While he may not be as dangerous as the twins, he is far more sophisticated, representing a form of cunning that parallels their thuggery. This subversion of an accepted and familiar fairytale scenario not only deprives the reader of a satisfactory moral resolution, but also transforms the story into a piece of crime fiction, thus requiring the reader not only to reinterpret it completely from this new perspective, but also to reconsider the narrator's intent, even to concede the possibility that none, in fact, may exist.

In light of this, the authority of the narrative is put into question, and yet a degree of control is asserted throughout as if to remind the reader of a guiding presence. These assertions take the form of authorial interjections, generating a sense of impatience and anxiety that either the story's impetus is being lost or the reader's attention is straying. The interjections also have the dramatic effect of shifting the visual focus of the narrative. At the beginning of the story, following a long description of the brothers' perception and opinion of Romantovski, the narrative suddenly switches to dialogue, which abruptly sets the action of the plot into motion:

> From the very moment he had appeared, rolling his pushcart into the yard, Romantovski had provoked a mixture of irritation and curiosity in the two brothers.... Additional eccentricities were noted: his light remained on practically until dawn; he was oddly unsociable.
>   We hear Anton's voice:
>   "That fine gentleman shows off. We should give him a closer look."
>   "I'll sell him the pipe," said Gustav [pp. 359–60].

That the narrator should need to interject at this point is questionable. His announcement suggests another motive at play, perhaps an undisclosed fear that the reader will not be able to follow the shift without such additional clarification. Yet, only a few lines later, the narrative switches again, this time more abruptly, to a scene in which the brothers confront Romantovski for the first time, under the pretext of selling him the pipe. The dramatic impact of this sudden switch is amplified by the absence of any introduction, compounded by the pedantic pace of the previous few lines of prose.

> The misty origins of the pipe. Anna had brought it over one day, but the brothers recognized only cigarillos. An expensive pipe, not yet blackened. It had a little steel tube inserted in its stem. With it came a suede case.
>   "Who's there? What do you want?" asked Romantovski through the door.
>   "Neighbors, neighbors," answered Gustav in a deep voice [p. 360].

The directorial interjections and the two long scenes of dialogue in which the descriptive passages concentrate on reported actions and responses resemble more a shooting script than a piece of narrative fiction. Critical scenes are related in a cinematic mode, therefore. At points where a series of events and a period of time need to be covered quickly, the narration reverts to a more prosaic mode.

The two key scenes which further the direction of the plot are presented in this cinematic style. The first occurs when the brothers invite themselves into Romantovski's room with their girlfriend, Anna, to interrogate and torment him, and the second when the brothers attack Romantovski in the street outside the cinema. Following the initial confrontation depicted, as before, predominantly in dialogue, Romantovski tries to get away from them, quietly and discreetly, but the brothers follow:

He turned and, holding his side, walked off along the dark rustling fences. The brothers followed, all but treading upon his heels. Gustav rumbled in the anguish of blood lust, and that rumble might turn any moment into a pounce [p. 365)].

This short passage is representative of the way the story combines a variety of narrative perspectives. Its opening takes the form of simple, reported, third-person narrative, but the concluding sentence demonstrates a subtle shift in emphasis. The narrative voice turns directly to the reader, and the sense of threat is transformed into a warning of imminent danger.

In the following passage the pace of the narrative slows, but the sense of threat does not diminish, and gradually the focus shifts to Romantovski's thoughts of means of escape. The dramatization of Romantovski's consciousness remains the focus of the action up to the point when he is stabbed by Gustav. At first it seems that the two interjections during this episode are, as before, made by the narrator. They do, after all, share the same characteristics, being abrupt, deliberate, didactic, yet somehow superfluous. In terms of Romantovski's present predicament, however, they have a dramatic relevance in emphasizing the invasion of his thoughts by these voices. As Romantovski registers them, so his sense of the proximity and threat of violation is amplified.

> Anna's voice: "Gustav, don't tangle with him. You know quite well you won't be able to stop. Remember what you did once to that bricklayer."
> "Hold your tongue, old bitch, don't teach him what must be done" (That's Anton's voice.) [pp. 365–66].

It is also significant that it is Romantovski's point of view that is asserted here, serving to concentrate the narrative perspective. The absence of a third party leaves nothing to undermine or dilute the dramatic force of the scene. This is also particularly cinematic, the abrupt declaration of each speaker (Anna and Anton) serving to transform the text, briefly, into the form of a screenplay, the intrusive immediacy of these directorial asides having a greater impact than the conventional first-person prosaic voice. Romantovski announces to the reader which voices he hears, directing the focus of attention as a film director does with the camera or a soundtrack.

The dramatic impact of the murder is generated by the sudden introduction of sounds other than voices, the brief skirmish and the stabbing being described solely in terms of sound. The violence and force of the fight are rendered in only two adjectives, "rasping" and "crunching," and the stabbing itself by a mere suggestion, the discernment of "a special sound — smooth and moist":

> He ran and seemed, as he ran, to be laughing exultingly. Gustav over-took him in a couple of leaps. Both fell, and amid the fierce rasping and crunching there occurred a special sound — smooth and moist, once, and a second time, up to the hilt — and then Anna instantly fled into the darkness, holding her hat in her hand [p. 366].

Cinematically, this makes an extremely powerful scene, since the audience never sees the stabbing but only *hears* it. From the point at which Gustav falls on Romantovski, the visual attention is focused on a pair of bodies tussling on the ground. The audience's vision is preoccupied, therefore, waiting for the next image to present the next stage of the action, its ears not utilized at all. Thus the shock of the stabbing is magnified by the quick and unexpected means in which it is dramatized but then is instantly deflated by the visual cut to Anna fleeing the scene.

The story's impact, its horror, bleakness, and deceptiveness are, however, irrevocably deflated by the declaration of directorial control in its final lines, which mirror its opening:

> It is all over now. Alas, the objects I had assembled wander away. The young poplar dims and takes off— to return where it had been fetched from. The brick wall dissolves. The house draws in its little balconies one by one, then turns, and floats away. Everything floats away. Harmony and meaning vanish. The world irks me again with its variegated void [p. 367].

Once again, the fairytale character of the narrative returns, but without a concluding moral, leaving only a sense of profound disturbance and frustration. Nabokov employs a similar act of narrative destruction in *Invitation to a Beheading* (1935–1936), but then for the purpose of estab-lishing the potential for liberation from repression. In "The Leonardo," Nabokov offers merely an unsettling and ambiguous cautionary tale.

Despair *and the Tyranny of Cinematic Perception*

In *Despair*, published in 1936, Nabokov further extends a preoccu-pation with film into the narrative itself. With the hero of *The Eye*,

Nabokov demonstrated the distortions of solipsistic paranoia and the potential for complete disassociation from reality, but in *Despair* he presents the reader with a text that is overwhelmed by the flawed psyche of Hermann Karlovich, obliterating every means by which to establish a context of actuality, obscuring entirely any evidence of an independent, controlling authorial presence in the crazed fabric of the narrative. Hermann Karlovich perceives himself not only as a literary genius *manqué*, but also as a great undiscovered film director. Considering that the structure of the novel takes the form of a diary it could be argued that the literary analogy would provide sufficient material for an examination of manic self-obsession. That Nabokov should choose to include the film in Hermann Karlovich's frame of artistic expression not only adds a visual and dramatic dimension to the narrative but also allows for an emphasis on vision to contextualize his mental distortions.

In an echo of Joseph Conrad's statement on the purpose of his artistic endeavors,[36] Hermann Karlovich declares that "an author's fondest dream is to turn the reader into a spectator," and yet unlike Conrad, he believes this "dream" to be impossible to achieve, a notion suggested by his concluding question — "is this ever attained?"[37] This statement could also be considered, however, as deliberately ironic, a calculated gesture of feigned self-deprecation, made by a man confident in the belief that he has, in fact, attained the unattainable. Hermann may succeed in turning his reader into a spectator, but his deployment of the cinematic mode has no specific artistic purpose but serves rather as a means of achieving an overriding authority over the narrative, the events it depicts and the persona he projects.

Hermann Karlovich openly declares the machinery of his exposition, whether it be cinematic or literary, to display the level of creative control he wields.

> In the meantime... (the inviting gesture of dots, dots, dots) alias Cinematograph, alias Moving Pictures. You saw the hero doing this or that, and in the meantime... Dots — and the action switched to the country [p. 46)].

Although he appropriates the mechanics and technology of control, they can only serve him if utilized with skill and integrity, qualities which he does not possess. This fundamental paradox is extended by his belief in his artistic and technical ability, although this delusion is persistently undermined by episodes of irrational, psychotic mania.

Nevertheless, his desire to assert his authority is demonstrated by his incorporation of film into notions of doubling in the narrative, which in itself raises the level of his determination to add significance to his life by creating not simply a means of self-reflection but also a means of gaining external control. The credibility of Felix as his double is enforced by Hermann's self-visualization as a movie actor, a persona with a defined role to play, possessing superhuman qualities such as being able to live "generally on air" and having indestructible "elastic hopes" (p. 77), qualities which are amplified by the belief in Felix as his antithetical reflection, his "star ghost" (p. 79). There is a dual irony at work here, in that the more involved Hermann becomes in the direction of this imaginary scenario in which he takes the starring role, the more synthetic and precarious it becomes, but these are the essential qualities of the art form which he manipulates. At the same time — in an ironic inversion of Vertov's philosophy — he attempts to transcend the inherent flaws of the form, insisting that the accuracy of his vision surpasses the camera eye:

> A film actor in a double part can hardly deceive anyone, for even if he does appear in both impersonations at once, the eye cannot help tracing a line down the middle where the heroes of the picture have been joined [p. 23].

Hermann persistently contradicts himself in his continual reference to film as a mode of interpretation in his apparent desire to emulate the art of cinematic illusion. The belief he has in his ability to perceive the cameraman's manipulations — "I started working from his feet upward, as one sees on the screen when the cameraman is trying to be tantalizing" (p. 68) — serves to enforce his superior position but is based on a denial of the cameraman's skill. The fact is that although to his mind, the cameraman is "trying to be tantalizing," the notion of contrivance produces a tantalizing image and is convincing because the cameraman understands the medium in which he is working and knows how to disguise his technique. Hermann's cynicism suggests, however, that there once was a time when he believes he was duped by sophisticated screen imagery, and the disdain he expresses for the medium here is nothing more than an arrogant posture adopted to conceal his true feelings of inferiority and impotence. He insinuates that the cameraman tries but does not succeed, his efforts being painfully apparent because of his inherent lack of skill. The dramatic irony of this assumption is that Hermann's demise is a direct result of his trying too hard, being too involved with the style of his scheme to account for trivial details. He is, therefore, just as much an amateur as his inept cameraman.

While literature and the theater provide Hermann with his principal narrative modes, film serves to reinforce his authorial/directorial role. In terms of his relationship with Felix, Hermann uses cinema as a ploy to attract him to his scheme. His role-playing, like Smurov's, is a combination of modes — literary, theatrical and cinematic:

> Although I have never been an actor in the strict sense of the word, I have nevertheless, in real life, always carried about with me a small folding theater and have appeared in more than one part, and my acting has always been superfine [p. 82].

Indeed, Hermann's chronicle is more reminiscent of a dramatic monologue, a piece played out before an audience, than a piece of fiction, being, after all, a work of autobiography, a celebration of self. Cinema is one of the many artistic resources from which he draws. At times, he displays an abandonment to the form, and particularly to screen melodrama, which echoes Margot's movie-inspired tantrums in *Laughter in the Dark*:

> I pushed her aside, almost knocking her off the divan, and started marching to and fro. I gulped, I sobbed. Specters of red melodrama reeled [p. 121].

The distinction here, however, is that Hermann is presenting an exaggerated version of events, whereas Margot's dramatization is for real. It is Nabokov who describes Margot's behavior, revealing her influences and aspirations to the reader, whereas Hermann, as narrator, has license to depict himself in whatever way he chooses, for maximum effect. Thus his manipulation of all artistic forms is both calculated and utterly false, serving, inevitably, to undermine the integrity of his narrative.

Hermann's solipsistic presentation of events is enabled by the specific technical capabilities of film. Gavriel Moses describes the bedroom scenes in which a dissociated Hermann finds himself watching himself making love to his wife as "a sequence of receding camera setups subject to the physical laws of perspective and distance,"[38] which establishes not only the theme of doubling in the narrative but also notions of voyeurism:

> I used to sit every night a few inches farther from the bed, and soon the back legs of my chair reached the threshold of the open door. Eventu-

ally I found myself sitting in the parlor — while making love in the bedroom. It was not enough. I longed to discover some means to remove
myself at least a hundred yards from the lighted stage where I performed;
I longed to contemplate that bedroom scene from some remote upper
gallery ... to watch a small but distinct and very active couple through
opera glasses, field glasses, a tremendous telescope, or optical instruments of yet unknown power that would grow larger in proportion to
my increasing rapture. Actually, I never got farther back than the con-
sole in the parlor, and even so found my view of the bed cut off by the
doorjamb unless I opened the wardrobe in the bedroom to have the bed
reflected in the oblique speculum or *spiegel* [p. 33].[39]

Although the analogy here is overtly theatrical, as Gavriel Moses points
out, "this omnipotent staging, carefully analyzed in terms of what would
be visible to an objective camera eye, is extended into a repetitive sequence
characterized by an ever-growing distance of viewer (voyeur) from the
scene,"[40] the overriding cinematic perspective being established ultimately
by the wardrobe mirror which serves as a screen enabling both a vision
of and a frame for the action.

Hermann's journey to the Koenigsdorf forest, where he murders
Felix, initiates the most starkly cinematic episode of the narrative. It has
the quality of a surreal passage through a timeless, lifeless zone from one
familiar, tangible realm to another, bleak and unknown, and is presented
as a series of black-and-white, mute images which appear as a sequence
of isolated stills:

> The colors of the day were reduced to a mere two: black (the pattern of
> the bare trees, the asphalt) and whitish (the sky, the patches of snow) [p.
> 134].

The impact of the two simple colors which signal his arrival is amplified
by their contrast with this pervasive grayness. In an echo of the solitary
red flag in Eisenstein's *Battleship Potemkin* (1925), the "red station-build-
ing" (p. 136) and the "yellow post" (p. 137) stand out violently bright
and bold, marking the end of the journey or transition, and the visual
change is compounded by the return of sound — "I got out of my car and
with a bang that was louder than any shot, slammed the door after me"
(p. 137). Not only does this anticipate the manner of Felix's demise but
it is also the first overt reference to Hermann's purpose since leaving
Berlin.

It is significant that Hermann chooses to describe this episode in terms of film, suggesting that it is the most appropriate medium in which to truly represent his sense of emotional and psychological dislocation and detachment. He also describes the shooting cinematically, in a manner reminiscent of Smurov's visual manipulations, allowing him a license with time and perspective which would not be available to him in reality. The act is over in an instant, but Hermann presents it in slow motion, dramatizing every detail from the pall of gunsmoke hanging in the air to Felix's changing expression and the gradations of his fall with macabre satisfaction, transforming the horror and violence of the scene into a kind of comic dance:

> He turned, and I shot him between the shoulders.
>
> I remember various things: that puff of smoke, hanging in mid-air, then displaying a transparent fold and vanishing slowly; the way Felix fell; for he did not fall at once.... I remember, too, the shuffling sound he made in the snow, when he began to stiffen and jerk, as if his new clothes were uncomfortable; soon he was still, and then the rotation of the earth made itself felt, and only his hat moved quietly, separating from his crown and falling back, mouth opened, as if it were saying "good-bye" for its owner.... Yes, I remember all that, but there is one thing memory misses: the report of my shot. True, there remained in my ears a persistent singing. It clung to me and crept over me, and trembled upon my lips. Through that veil of sound, I went up to the body and, with avidity, looked [p. 143].

The description is silent, and, as at the conclusion of the car journey, the silence is broken suddenly by a sound — the "singing" of the report in Hermann's ears. The sequence is rendered with deliberate precision, the visual focus cutting from one detail to the next, considering each frame as an isolated still, serving to deflate the horror of Felix's shooting. The pace of the narrative is slowed almost to a halt, and the effect is vertiginous. The gunshot is not registered, the only sound being the shuffle of Felix's feet in the snow, and this, combined with the negative-image quality of the scene which parallels Hermann's drive from Berlin, serves to dissipate utterly the emotive impact of the killing.

These two passages are the decisive moments of the story, and in their unadulterated cinematic quality they stand out against the strong literary character of the rest of the narrative. The use of a film scenario can function effectively in Hermann's narrative only if it has a supporting medium, however. In the final scene (which Nabokov added to his 1966 version), Hermann turns to film once again as a last artistic resort because his literary endeavor has been destroyed, but it proves to be a futile attempt to regain lost control and lost confidence and is ludicrous in its transparent artificiality:

> "Frenchmen! This is a rehearsal. Hold those policemen. A famous film actor will presently come running out of this house. He is an arch-criminal but he must escape. You are asked to prevent them from grabbing him. This is part of the plot.... Hold those policemen, knock them down, sit on them — we pay for them. This is a German company, so excuse my French. *Les preneurs de vues*, my technicians and armed advisers are already among you. *Attention!* I want a clean getaway. That's all. Thank you. I'm coming out now" [p. 176].

The deployment of film in *Despair* serves as more than simply a means of generating dramatic irony, however. Nabokov is touching on wider issues concerning the relationship between literature and film and the possibilities of combining the two modes to create new perspectives and narrative dimensions. *Despair* not only marks an important development in Nabokov's use of cinematics in the fabric of his fiction, but it also contains elements which both characterized contemporary American fiction and film and anticipated the visual style and narrative character of the seminal cinematic movement of the 1940s —film noir.

Three

A Medium Invaded: Cinema and Cinematics in *The Great Gatsby*; *King, Queen, Knave*; and *Laughter in the Dark*

> The world is no longer an extraneous object, full of other extraneous objects, but an image. In the last analysis, it is with this image of the world that we are vitally concerned.[1]

The impact of Nabokov's early cinematic experience is evident not only in his deployment of the styles and techniques of German Expressionist and Soviet film, but also in the ways in which film emerges in his fiction as a new perceptual and narrative mode. Nabokov's treatment of film in his Russian work is distinctive with respect to the close affinities it demonstrates with the cinematic preoccupations of contemporary American writers, particularly John Dos Passos and F. Scott Fitzgerald. The parallels that can be drawn between Dos Passos's integration of techniques of montage in his fiction or the manipulation of cinematic perspective in Fitzgerald's *Great Gatsby* suggest a shared response to film that was to determine Nabokov's place as a key figure on the postwar American literary scene.

Dos Passos and the Camera Eye

Inspired by the innovations of Vertov and Eisenstein, John Dos Passos developed a literary method which incorporated the most progres-

sive techniques and devices prevalent in the cinema of the 1920s and
1930s. According to Linda Wagner:

> Dos Passos' aim was, newsreellike, to present, to bombard, the viewer-
> reader with a spectrum of scenes and images, from which some sense of
> the real "history" being lived — whether personal or social — could accu-
> mulate.[2]

This process Dos Passos called "simultaneity."[3] He cited Eisenstein
and D. W. Griffith as principal influences and the technique of montage as central to the presentation of his fiction.[4] His first novel, *Manhattan Transfer* (1925), depicts contemporary urban life in a series of
juxtaposed scenarios. The novel is structured as a film, the action cut
into complete scenes which interchange and interweave, with a set of
characters whose stories either overlap or coincide or merely serve as
episodic *mise-en-scènes* providing a context of actuality in their shifts of
dramatic perspective. Each chapter is prefaced by a description of a scene
unrelated to the central narrative concern, presented as a piece of film
footage:

> Dusk gently smooths crispspangled streets. Dark presses tight the steam-
> ing asphalt city, crushes the fretwork of windows and lettered signs and
> chimneys and watertanks and ventilators and fire escapes and moldings
> and patterns and corrugations and eyes and hands and neckties into blue
> chunks, into black enormous blocks. Under the rolling heavier heavier
> pressure windows blurt light. Night crushes bright mild out of arclights,
> squeezes the sullen blocks until they drip red, yellow, green into streets
> resounding with feet. All the asphalt oozes light. Light spurts from let-
> tering on roofs, mills dizzily among wheels, stains rolling tons of sky.[5]

This visual depiction of New York city lights gradually overtaking
the night sky has the pace, movement and energy of Vertov's camera lens,
sweeping from the panorama of the skyline to focus upon a multitude of
details beyond the scope of the human eye. Vision takes on a mechanical aspect, and the inanimate object, by contrast, takes on life, becoming a breathing, writhing, oozing being. At the same time, the description
has a stream-of-consciousness quality generated by the absence of conjunctions, the profusion of verbs and adverbs and the repetition of adjectives.

In *USA* (1930–1936), Dos Passos adapted the literary mode of stream
of consciousness to the perspective of film in sections titled "The Cam-

era Eye," in which action is presented as newsreel footage, mimicking the moving-picture experience of reportage, montage, headline titles and sound. In doing so, Dos Passos created a kind of fictional documentary, an attempt to capture and render the essence of urban American life, which established cinema as a legitimate literary mode. Dos Passos openly declared his influence by Vertov, which Vertov in turn was to acknowledge:

> I am accused of corrupting Dos Passos by having influenced him with kino-eye. Otherwise he might have become a good writer, some say. Others object and say that if it were not for kino-eye, we wouldn't have heard of Dos Passos.
> Dos Passos' work involves a translation from film-vision into literary language. The terminology and construction are those of kino-eye.[6]

Dos Passos was not alone in adapting cinematic montage to his fiction. William Faulkner also used a process of what Bruce Kawin describes as "dynamic juxtaposition":

> One image, or shot, or signifier, is butted up against another, with no transitional apparatus, and it is left to the audience to divine the connection between the two elements.[7]

Faulkner's most overt use of fictional montage is demonstrated in the novels *The Sound and the Fury* (1929) and *As I Lay Dying* (1930), in which "characters and events repeat and collide with no regard for the conventions of chronology. All time is equal, all mental space accessible, right up to the edge of a cosmic, ineffable silence."[8]

For Dos Passos, however, the purpose of presenting his fiction in terms of film was also an extension of his notion of the artist as observer or "reporter." As such, the artist develops a sense of detachment and becomes, as it were, a voyeur, engaging only with the surface of things, never the substance. Carol Shloss cites *Manhattan Transfer*'s Jimmy Herf as representative of Dos Passos's experience:

> Jimmy Herf is not, in Dos Passos's novel, a privileged and uniquely suffering character. He is one of a group of young people who all experience variations of voyeuristic emptiness and who find that the "center," which they hope to approach through seeing images of it, does not exist.[9]

Shloss argues that this notion of visual estrangement anticipates Dos Passos's subsequent denunciation of America as an "image nation," a preoccupation epitomized by Ellen Thatcher's "glamorous emptiness."[10]

Ellen Thatcher embodies the experience of voyeurism central to Dos Passos's art and is depicted as highly self-conscious. She sees herself as a doll, a silent, gesturing marionette whose actions can be manipulated according to the demands of any given situation:

> Ellen stayed a long time looking in the mirror, dabbling a little superfluous powder off her face, trying to make up her mind. She kept winding up a hypothetical dollself and setting it in various positions. Tiny gestures ensued, acted out on various model stages [p. 334].

Ellen's self-negation is a direct result of her ruthless ambition, which has caused her to relinquish true love in favor of a promise of wealth and social status offered by George Baldwin. It is significant that, although she is a stage actress, she behaves as if she were a movie star. Here, the extent of her alienation is expressed by her vision of herself as a still photograph, a flat, two-dimensional, lifeless image, absent and empty:

> Through dinner she felt a gradual icy coldness stealing through her like novocaine. She had made up her mind. It seemed as if she had set the photograph of herself in her own place, forever frozen into a single gesture [p. 335].

Shloss argues that such references to the photographic image are indicative of Dos Passos's preoccupation with the inherent vacuity of modern life, whereby the process of turning oneself into a photograph becomes "the ultimate expression of alienation, the substitution of externally imposed norms for internally motivated action, the eclipse of innate character."[11] In Ellen's case, it is as this frozen, empty image that she remains, and the episode is concluded by the vision of her "drowning" in Baldwin's kiss, the ultimate gesture of total abnegation:

> Inexorably his lips closed on to hers. Beyond the shaking glass window of the taxi, like someone drowning, she saw out of a corner of an eye whirling faces, streetlights, zooming nickleglinting wheels [p. 336].

In visual terms this concluding scene is interesting when compared with the depiction of an earlier parallel episode between Ellen and Stan Emery. This scene also dissolves in a suggested kiss, but rather than presenting Ellen's acute consciousness of the kiss as something she detaches herself from by "drowning" in a vision of that which lies beyond the intimate space within the taxi, here Ellen and Stan seem to drown in each other.

> He put down the chair and came towards her brown and male and lean in the silly dressinggown. The phonograph came to the end of the tune and the record went on rasping round and round [p. 198].

The dramatic impact of both scenes relies on a sudden shift in visual focus. In this instance, the cinematic quality of this "cutaway"[12] is compounded by the phonograph, which provides a musical accompaniment to the scene, functioning as a soundtrack, and the scene concludes in an elegiac "fade."[13] The "rasping" record, the melody long finished, suggests not only the passage of time but more importantly, the shared oblivion of the embrace. That the visual focus is Ellen's is subtly implied as it shifts from the actual image of Stan approaching her to the perceived image of the phonograph, the level of emotional intimacy indicated by this sudden loss of vision, sight being replaced by sound. In the later scene, the narrative eye is unequivocally Ellen's, and that she saturates it, by contrast, with the rushing hypnotic dazzle of chrome and headlamps is expressive of her emotional death.

In *Manhattan Transfer* and *USA*, Dos Passos establishes a thematic link between techniques of film and characterization as a means of finding "a novelistic device for rendering the lives of people who remained exclusively concerned with form," who were concerned only with "the 'beauty' of their own images."[14] A preoccupation with image is also central to Fitzgerald's *Great Gatsby* and is indicative of a culture which, as Dos Passos describes, was "manipulated and subdued by photographs and by its own pictures of desire."[15]

Fitzgerald's Dream Cinema

Like Nabokov, Fitzgerald assimilated distinctive cinematic devices in his writing, except that his primary influence was American cinema, which, unlike contemporary European film, had strong links with traditional literary narrative. Although 1920s' American film did not share the German philosophic purpose and was not overtly influenced by experimental theater, the emphasis was still very much on exploiting the potential of visual effects, forced by the absence of sound. Silent movie directors depended on the flexibility of the camera for dramatic impact, and in the same way that Expressionist directors emphasized the importance of facial expression to communicate thoughts and feelings, so American directors pioneered the use of the close-up as a key filmic device. This, combined with an attention to gesture as a means of silent communication, made it an integral means of conveying meaning. The art of gesture, therefore, had a transcendent importance, but as Fitzgerald was to reveal, the primacy of image was one of the most fundamentally misleading and synthetic elements to influence contemporary American culture and society.

Fitzgerald, born in 1896, three years before Nabokov, had his first novel, *This Side of Paradise*, published in 1920. In 1923 he sold the film rights for $10,000. His second novel, *The Beautiful and the Damned* (1922), sold over 20,000 copies in its first year of publication, and the rights were bought for $2,250. In 1926, the year following the publication of *The Great Gatsby*, film rights were sold for $13,500, which amounted to just over $18,000 by 1933 from subsequent deals.[16] Fitzgerald maintained a close relationship with the American film industry throughout his career. Apart from the rights bought on his novels, he sold many short stories, offered film scenarios and synopses and was commissioned as a screenwriter on fifteen projects between 1924 and 1940, the year of his death.[17]

Fitzgerald's Hollywood career, however, was a failure. *This Side of Paradise* and *The Beautiful and the Damned* were never produced. Fitzgerald failed to sell the rights for *Tender Is the Night* (1934), *The Great Gatsby* being first released unsuccessfully in 1949. He received only one credit as a screenwriter — for an adaptation of Erich Maria Remarque's novel *Three Comrades*, directed by Frank Borzage in 1938. In 1937 he moved to California in a final attempt to get a foothold in Hollywood, but his unfinished novel, *The Last Tycoon*, and his last series of stories, centered around the dissipated hack writer Pat Hobby, only served to exemplify his frustrated career in films. Unlike his contemporaries Nathanael West, William Faulkner, Raymond Chandler and Ernest Hemingway, Fitzgerald was never able to adapt to the production methods of Hollywood screenwriting, even though he understood the system and the medium intimately.

In spite of Fitzgerald's failure as a screenwriter, his cinematically inspired novel of 1925, *The Great Gatsby*, both incorporates a specific filmic visualization and powerfully evokes the impact of the cinematic experience on the contemporary American psyche. Its cinematic quality extends to the execution of the action and to characterization, while themes of illusion and delusion and the notion of the inherent unreliability of vision central to the novel are developed by a sophisticated manipulation of filmic perspective. Human vision is deemed to be flawed, and yet it is also, paradoxically, the primary means of cognitive perception. At the same time, the world presented by the novel's narrator, Nick Carraway, is compromised by his subjectivity and his emotional attachment to the principal protagonists. Fitzgerald, therefore, demands that the reader both acknowledge the deceptive nature of the novel's primary visual perspective and collude in a conspiracy of self-delusion.

The novel's pivotal theme is the romance of image and the lie that it is, embodied in the novel's hero, Jay Gatsby. A self-made millionaire, he fabricates a persona, a history and an identity in order to attain his dream — Daisy Buchanan. There is an inherent paradox in the notion of attaining dreams, however. Although essentially intangible things, they are believed to be tangible by those who succumb to them. Gatsby's sole ambition, therefore, is to achieve the impossible, to replace the image of his dream with the dream itself.

> There must have been moments ... when Daisy tumbled short of his dreams — not through her own fault, but because of the colossal vitality of his illusion. It had gone beyond her, beyond everything. He had thrown himself into it with a creative passion, adding to it all the time, decking it out with every bright feather that drifted his way. No amount of fire or freshness can challenge what a man can store up in his ghostly heart.[18]

Nick Carraway's compromised perspective reflects and compounds Gatsby's deluded dream-vision, but unlike Gatsby, Nick possesses a degree of perceptual objectivity, afforded by his role in the novel as spectator and commentator. At the same time, his perspective is that of the camera lens, which grants him a depth and versatility of vision and enables him to witness events which would not normally be available to him. That his interpretation and experience of characters and events is almost entirely visual enhances the importance of vision and image as a means of communication, expression and interaction in the novel's world. It is also significant that Nick uses film as a frame of reference. The level of identification with cinema is fundamental to the characters' own sense of not who and what they are, but who and what they aspire to be—namely the perfect, enigmatic, black-and-white, two-dimensional images projected by a shaft of light through a strip of celluloid onto a blank screen. This is particularly true of the female characters in the novel, Daisy Buchanan, Myrtle Wilson and Jordan Baker.

Nick's cinematic referentiality is pervasive yet subtle. The sensation of film can be generated by a mere change in light or in pace, or by the deployment of specific, key words. The life of the novel becomes increasingly shadowy and ephemeral as these references recur and is compounded by the descriptions of characters in terms of cinematic visuals. Nick's perspective has an aura of detached objectivity; his voice is calm, his role passive. People and things revolve dizzyingly around him, indifferent to his presence, remote and inaccessible. His relationship to this world is exactly that of the movie-goer, sitting alone in the darkness, hypnotized by the show of light before him. The influence of film on Nick's vision is expressed in recurring motifs, as a "constant flicker" or "constantly changing light," serving often merely to qualify a description, or to identify a common experience:

> I began to like New York, the racy, adventurous feel of it at night and the satisfaction that the constant flicker of men and women and machines gives to the restless eye [p. 61].

The visual impression of the city is as exciting to Nick as the moving picture. He is a new arrival, and he finds himself equally fascinated and alienated by it.

> Over the great bridge, with the sunlight through the girders making a constant flicker upon the moving cars, with the city rising up across the river in white heaps and sugar lumps all built with a wish out of nonolfactory money [p. 73].

The pace of this description evokes the movement and flow of the cars crossing the Brooklyn Bridge, but the energy and vitality of the vision are tempered by a sense of its artificiality, from the sugarlump skyscrapers to the essence of the vision itself, depicted as a series of flickering celluloid frames on a movie screen. This serves to compound the notion that the Manhattan skyline is nothing more than a mirage, a "wish," built not on real wealth, on the grimy, well-thumbed, stale-smelling dollar bill, but on some kind of sanitized, bleached, ethereal currency. The description epitomizes Nick's attitude to wealth throughout the story, and in its reflection of the world of moving pictures it establishes an irrevocable link between these two realms of existence, both equally sophisticated in their power to delude.

At one of Gatsby's all-night parties, Nick's cinematic perspective is again deployed to render the particular visual quality of the scene:

> The groups close more swiftly, swell with new arrivals, dissolve and form in the same breath — already there are wanderers, confident girls who weave here and there among the stouter and more stable, become for a sharp, joyous moment the center of a group and then excited with triumph glide on through the sea-change of faces and voices and color under the constantly changing light [pp. 44–45].

Nick's viewpoint is that of the camera panning across a crowd, from time to time closing in on one individual, watching in close-up their interactions and movements and then pulling away again to offer the whole scene in panorama. The crowd moves together as if orchestrated in an elaborate routine conducted by an invisible director raised high above them on a boom. There is an unnatural smoothness to the flow of movement which is captivating, far removed from the ugly chaos of a semi-inebriated crowd of strangers, the present-tense narrative voice at the same time generating an intimacy and immediacy that is both involving and compelling.

Elsewhere, the effect of light serves to reveal a frailty and fragility underlying the apparent solidity of the world — reminiscent of the depiction of the Manhattan skyline and the spectacle of Gatsby's parties — which compounds the theme of flawed vision in the novel. The figure of Gatsby personifies the deliberate and conscious manipulation of image that pervades his world, and yet his highly calculated and carefully contrived persona is nothing more than an elaborate sham. His library, for example, may be genuine, but it exists merely as an impressive visual spectacle, which, ironically, is all that is ultimately required of it:

> "See!" he cried triumphantly. "It's a bona-fide piece of printed matter. It fooled me. This fella's a regular Belasco. It's a triumph. What thoroughness! What realism! Knew when to stop, too — didn't cut the pages" [p. 50].

Belasco was renowned on Broadway for his theatrical realism,[19] whereas Gatsby's world is built, essentially, on a fantasy, one that is closer to the Hollywood dream. Fitzgerald emphasizes the cinematic quality of Gatsby's elaborate and extravagant property with a specific deployment of lighting. On his return from the city one night, Nick sees Gatsby's house "lit from tower to cellar" as if on a film set. The lights are indeed so bright they make Nick's house next door look as if it is on fire:

> Two o'clock and the whole corner of the peninsula was blazing with light which fell unreal on the shrubbery and made thin elongating glints upon the roadside wires [p. 86].

In spite of the tangible brightness of the lights cutting into the night, the picture has a ghostly, ethereal aura which quickly dissolves its initial dazzling impact. At the same time, the slightest obstruction can obliterate it utterly — "only wind in the trees which blew the wires and made the lights go off and on again as if the house had winked into the darkness" (p. 86) — the touch of a mere shadow causing it to disintegrate before the spectators' eyes.

At the same time, image, to those who conduct their lives by it, has a power to communicate more volubly than any other form of expression. This notion, however, is undercut by an emphasis on the illusory and essentially ephemeral quality of visual perception and its associations with the transient, amorphous quality of photographic and cinematic images. This echoes Dos Passos's notion of the photograph as a "skin," or a "surface, a reference to something absent, a fragment, [expressing] something widespread and profound."[20] For Fitzgerald, however, that "something widespread and profound" is never defined. The guiding preoccupation of his protagonists is, solely, the desire "to be or to feel like a photograph" or "to be caught in, or have accepted, someone else's image of what one should be."[21] The irony is that Fitzgerald's protagonists do not consider this process as degenerative; the risk of an "eclipse of innate character" is not a matter for concern. Rather, the conscious manipulation of image, to a degree where existence becomes a continual pose for an invisible camera, is not only an expression of character, more faithful and more eloquent than words, but also a defining force, and one which is assertive of power and authority.

Gesture is, therefore, inextricably linked with this notion of the supremacy of image, its potency rendering language redundant. As Ronald Berman argues, the language of gesture echoes D. W. Griffith's emphasis on gesture as visual metaphor.[22] Gatsby and Daisy consciously manipulate gesture and image for calculated effect, and it is significant that neither of them displays a great facility with words, as if they have never considered them an adequate mode of expression. In spite of the context of silent film in which the novel was written, sound plays an important part. It is always the effect of Daisy's voice which is emphasized rather than what she is saying, and this is compounded by its haunting musical quality, "the kind of voice that the ear follows up and down as if each speech is an arrangement of notes that will never be played again" (p. 13).

Gatsby shares this same captivating quality, an enigmatic elegance which gives the illusion of intimacy but which in fact guarantees him an unencroachable distance. It is also by a conscious staging of their every move that Gatsby and Daisy generate this illusion without ever really giving anything of themselves. Whereas Daisy's finely tuned poise is the result of careful nurturing to befit her position in society, Gatsby, motivated by his need to be part of Daisy's world, has had to consciously cultivate it. Gatsby has to invoke tremendous effort to generate and sustain the charade that Daisy maintains so easily, a charade that would otherwise go undisclosed were it not for the occasional brief, although discreet, unguarded lapse. Here, for example, is one of the rare occasions when Gatsby unwittingly reveals his vulnerability:

> Fifty feet away a figure had emerged from the shadow of my neighbor's mansion and was standing with his hands in his pockets regarding the silver pepper of the stars.... [H]e stretched out his arms toward the dark water in a curious way, and as far as I was from him I could have sworn he was trembling [pp. 25–26].

To Nick's eyes, Gatsby has made an entrance perfectly suited to his reputation, but Gatsby does not know he is being watched, and what Nick does not realize and does not yet know is that he has caught him at his nightly vigil before the blinking light on Daisy's jetty on the other side of the bay. It is in this moment, when Gatsby believes himself to be alone, that he allows his emotions expression. It is appropriate that this should occur in the form of a rare, involuntary action — his trembling — and that this should function as a highly intimate and uniquely honest gesture. It is, perhaps, Gatsby's most eloquent gesture, and ironically, it is not for the benefit of an audience. Its power is conveyed by the fact that Nick is able to discern it from where he is standing some feet away and in the dark. Also, unlike elsewhere in the novel, Nick does not resort to the mechanics of a camera-eye close-up, which serves to amplify its evocative force and sincerity.

In public, however, both Gatsby and Daisy display a highly sophisticated ability to manipulate a setting to enhance their impact upon it. Nick's portrayal of Daisy is that of a screen diva, permanently conscious of her audience, ever seeking the perfect light, the most flattering angle, pacing every move to evoke an aura of ethereal fluidity and grace. Her first appearance is an enaction of exactly this:

> For a moment the last sunshine fell with romantic affection upon her glowing face…. [T]hen the glow faded, each light deserting her with lingering regret [p. 18].

Her skill is so great that her surroundings seem to be in collusion with her, complementing her, animated in an empathetic relationship of devotion. For Daisy, however, any display of genuine emotion is considered to be both distasteful and vulgar, but most of all it means loss of control. Love is a gift she chooses to bestow on certain privileged individuals, and she deems it to be neither exclusive nor something that she is obliged to reciprocate. Gatsby's passion is exciting only as long as she can keep him at a safe distance. Gatsby, therefore, profoundly misunderstands Daisy in expecting something of her she disdains. He does not realize that she can allow nothing to jeopardize the meticulous and delicate charade she is bound to sustain. A critical scene at one of Gatsby's parties, however, exposes Daisy's awareness of the fragility of her masquerade:

> Gatsby indicated a gorgeous, scarcely human orchid of a woman who sat in state under a white plum tree. Tom and Daisy stared, with that peculiarly unreal feeling that accompanies the recognition of a hitherto ghostly celebrity of the movies [p. 111].

The irony is that, coincidentally, Daisy has been confronted by the epitome of her aspirations. Here are two movie stars, standing before them in three dimensions, acting out a real-life scenario, and yet the scene remains highly cinematic. The scene is devoid of color — there is only black and white — the white plum tree and the white dress are set against the blackness of the night, and the moonlight is transformed into the beam of some remote spotlight. The couple are "scarcely human" but are no longer "ghostly" as they are on screen; they have become tangible bodies, although somehow they still retain their otherworldly quality. They are delicate, exotic flowers, not a crude mass of flesh and blood and bile. Nick and Daisy return to the scene later on to find it being played out to its resolution:

> They were still under the white plum tree and their faces were touching except for a pale thin ray of moonlight between. It occurred to me that he had been very slowly bending toward her all evening to attain this proximity, and even while I watched I saw him stoop one ultimate degree and kiss at her cheek [p. 113].

This is slow motion in live action, a beautifully choreographed scene of poise and elegance. The two have attained the perfection of gesture and movement of silent communication to which Daisy aspires. Although they are unaware that they are being watched, they still seem to behave as if they have an audience, although this does not prevent them from expressing the intensity of their desire. Daisy's reaction to this suggests that ultimately, for all their control and skill, screen stars are only pretenders to an art which Daisy has made her life's work, that once off screen, these people cannot sustain the charade of the moving picture, and thus are lesser mortals.

> "I like her," said Daisy. "I think she's lovely."
> But the rest offended her — and inarguably, because it wasn't a gesture but an emotion [p. 113].

The episode is also significant in that it exemplifies Fitzgerald's premise regarding the impact of particular scenes within a novel's structure:

> When you plot a scene in a book the importance of the scene cannot be taken as a measure of the space it should occupy.... I could tell you of plenty [of] books in which the main episode, around which swings the entire drama, is over and accomplished in four or five sentences.[23]

Although initially the scene seems to be inconsequential, it reveals critical aspects of Daisy's character and contributes to the novel's central thematic preoccupations, just as a short scene can be crucial to the exposition of filmic narrative.

The cinematically inspired dream-world of 1920s' America extends beyond the concerns of Daisy, Gatsby or Nick. Myrtle Wilson's affair with

Tom Buchanan is an attempt to escape the ash heaps of West Egg, the miserable grime of her husband's gas station and a marriage devoid of excitement or romance. It is an attempt to attain the unattainable, to take part in a dream that has no real place outside the movies. Unlike Daisy, Myrtle does not have the skill to sustain her role or the ice-cool ability to exploit and manipulate her world and is ultimately destroyed by emotions which she allows to overwhelm her.

Myrtle loses control twice in the novel—first at a party in Tom's Manhattan apartment and again when she mistakes Jordan Baker for Daisy. Both times, her reactions are depicted in terms of camera perspectives. In the first episode, the narrative eye pulls in close, excluding all others from the scene, reducing the focus from the crowded, noisy room to Myrtle, standing alone on an empty platform, drowning out the noise of the party with the noise of her hysteria:

> Her laughter, her gestures, her assertions became more violently affected moment by moment and as she expanded the room grew smaller around her until she seemed to be revolving on a noisy, creaking pivot through the smoky air [p. 35].

Myrtle's hysterics are reminiscent of the on-screen tantrums of movie heroines, but unlike these women, her rage is ineffectual, and she is exposed as ridiculous and undignified. Her humiliation is further magnified by the sound of her vulgarity, which is "noisy" and "creaking," and she is not even afforded a spotlight, like the light in which Daisy permanently basks, but is rather faded out by a haze of cigarette smoke.

The second episode employs similar devices to amplify Myrtle's responses. Like the zoom-in[24] focus used above, Nick's vision exploits the mechanical eye of the camera to sweep from Doctor T. J. Ecklenburg's enormous unblinking stare from a billboard poster to the more distant and considerably smaller glare of Myrtle's eyes from an upper-story window of Wilson's garage as Nick and Tom stop for gas. At this moment she has lost her self-conscious affectation. She is alone, without an audience, and unaware that anyone can see her, since only with a close-up shot could the details of her reaction be visible:

> So engrossed was she that she had no consciousness of being observed and one emotion after another crept into her face like objects into a slowly developing picture [p. 131].

The photographic analogy enhances the sense that it is a mechanical device which reveals Myrtle's private anguish. Berman comments that even here Myrtle is acting in accordance with the screen personae on whom she molds herself—"the lens sees Myrtle at the end of her illusions, her own little script about life over. Just like all of those other 'frantic' women on screen she dissolves into despair."[25] There is nothing staged about her death however. Myrtle's tragedy not only leads directly to Gatsby's demise but is also linked thematically to Gatsby's death. The elements which make Myrtle's death tragic, make Gatsby's tragic also. Each of them tries to enter into a world which is closed to them because of their humanity. As Wheeler Dixon points out, Myrtle's death is the result of an "ocular confusion."[26] In a world so dependent on vision, so informed and influenced by image, that a person could so critically mistake what they see is deeply ironic, and yet at the same time this simple fact belies the unreliability and inadequacy of vision in perceiving the truth, that ultimately all it can afford is a perspective, and often a corrupted one.

Nabokov's Russian Fiction and the American Film Perspective

The theme of "ocular confusion" is fundamental to the dénouement of "Perfection," a story written in 1932, but it is also significant in that it marks the emergence of a preoccupation with visual disruption, distortion and manipulation that was to dominate Nabokov's work for the next forty years. The story's hero, Ivanov, has "a passionate desire to experience everything"[27] but is unable to overcome an innate and inexplicable feeling of detachment and isolation:

> Ivanov daydreamed about the many things that he would never get to know closer, about professions that he would never practice, about a parachute, opening like a colossal corolla, or the fleeting, speckled world of automobile racers, about various images of happiness, about the pleasures of very rich people amid very picturesque natural surroundings. His thought fluttered and walked up and down the glass pane which for as long as he lived would prevent him from having direct contact with the world [pp. 339–40].

Ivanov's dreams are, however, only illusions of perfection that are, essentially, undefined and nebulous. In indulging in these hollow fantasies,
based on a vague ideal of freedom, romance and excitement, Ivanov not
only deepens his solitude but is also unconsciously reinforcing his sense
of being trapped behind the transparent and impregnable barrier which
prevents him from realizing his dreams. Ivanov's dilemma is powerfully
evoked by the image of a moth caught behind glass, its vision saturated
by the light all around it, compelled to move toward it, unable to find a
point of access but equally unable to stop seeking one, rendered blind to
its immediate dilemma by the prospect beyond.

Ivanov is the tutor to a young boy, David, whom he reluctantly
accompanies on a vacation at the beach. Ivanov has a weak heart and is
prone to fits of anxiety, particularly when he is called upon to do something that he is not comfortable with, in this instance, swimming and
sunbathing:

> When they came down to the beach after a fifteen-minute walk, Ivanov
> instantly became conscious of an acute discomfort in his chest, a sud-
> den tightness followed by a sudden void, and out on the smooth, smoke-
> blue sea a small boat looked black and appallingly alone. Its imprint
> began to appear on whatever he looked at, then dissolved in the air.
> Because now the dust of twilight dimmed everything around, it seemed
> to him that his eyesight was dulled, while his legs felt strangely weak-
> ened by the squeaky touch of the sand [p. 342].

It is significant that the primary effect of this brief attack should be
to impair Ivanov's vision, serving to intensify his isolation. When, at the
end of the story, Ivanov suffers another, and this time fatal, attack, the
accompanying "ocular confusion" is exacerbated by his panic at what he
believes to be the vision of David drowning.

> A wave surged, knocking off Ivanov's hat, blinding him; he wanted to
> take off his glasses, but his agitation, the cold, the numbing weakness,
> prevented him from doing so [p. 346].

Ivanov's distress is compounded by the literal impairment of his vision
by the "dark-yellow sunglasses" that David persuades him to wear, which
further amplify his sense of incapacity by "narrow[ing]" his vision. The
glasses also present him with an unsettlingly discolored aspect of the
world which seems to anticipate his fate — the "dying," "turquoise" sky

serves as a premonition of the water in which he is to drown, and the "sunset tinge" on the porch suggests not just the end of a day but the end of life itself:

> [T]he sun swooned amid a sky dying a turquoise death, and the morning light upon the porch steps acquired a sunset tinge.... His horizon was narrowed by the glasses, he was afraid of a sudden automobile [p. 345].

The "ocular confusions"— the subtle visual distortions brought about by his unpredictable heart— that have dogged the entirety of his short life, culminate, therefore, in this final scene, combining all at once to render him utterly blind. Ironically, however, at the point of death, Ivanov feels the sunglasses being removed from his face, and his vision is not only restored but granted a superhuman capability, and the ascent of his spirit is both enabled and dramatized by this visual release:

> The dull mist immediately broke, blossomed with marvelous colors.... [T]he Baltic Sea sparkled from end to end, and, in the thinned-out forest, across a green country road, there lay, still breathing, freshly cut aspens; and a youth, smeared with soot, gradually turned white as he washed under the kitchen tap, and black parakeets flew above the eternal snows of the New Zealand mountains; and a fisherman, squinting in the sun, was solemnly predicting that not until the ninth day would the waves surrender the corpse [p. 347].

The perspective from which Ivanov sees the world is that of a bird in flight, suddenly presented with a panorama of details and places, which in turn serves to reduce the size of the planet, allowing an immediate and total access to the world he sensed was always denied him in life. The irony of this marvel is that it is achieved only in death, and yet the sense of liberation and wonder is overwhelming. At the same time, this newfound visual capacity is reminiscent of Vertov's camera, zooming and swooping, capturing every tiny detail of a scene, or of the sweeping shots of vast spaces and huge crowds in the films of Eisenstein, Griffith or DeMille. A similar rapid visual retreat is used in the depiction of Albinus's car accident in *Laughter in the Dark*, which transforms this sense of glorious ascent into something at once terrifying and banal. That Ivanov's death is dramatized in literal terms— his soul departing from his body— but also, and more significantly, in visual terms, establishes the centrality of modes of perception to Nabokov's artistic philosophy.

In many ways, "Perfection" is the direct precursor to Nabokov's penultimate novel, *Transparent Things* (1972), in its explicit proposition of the notion of perspective as fundamental to the apprehension of immortality.

Nabokov's *King, Queen, Knave* (1928), published only three years after *The Great Gatsby*, displays a similar treatment of aspects of film. *King, Queen, Knave* is visually extremely vivid, pervaded by themes of cinema and cinematic techniques which extend from plot to characterization. In 1967 Nabokov showed his newly translated manuscript to the actor James Mason, who played Humbert Humbert in Stanley Kubrick's 1962 adaptation of *Lolita*. Mason responded with great enthusiasm:

> It reads aloud very well and would, I am sure, dramatize even more effectively, being constructed with much flash. It is true that inner thoughts play an important role but even more dazzling is the unfailing sequence of one splendidly *visual* scene after another.[28]

Mason was eager for the novel to be adapted for screen. Columbia Pictures had already expressed an interest, which Mason offered to pursue on Nabokov's behalf.[29] Whether Nabokov had elaborated the novel's existing cinematic imagery deliberately with the possibility of a film adaptation in mind is impossible to know, however. Since Kubrick's *Lolita*, Hollywood's interest in Nabokov's work had become almost overwhelming. In the summer of 1968, British director Tony Richardson began filming *Laughter in the Dark*, and then in October, a whole year before its publication, "a succession of movie moguls" from Paramount, CBS, Twentieth Century–Fox and Columbia made bids for the rights to *Ada*.[30]

The changes Nabokov made to the original Russian novel, *Korol', Dama, Valet*, have been detailed by Jane Grayson in her volume *Nabokov Translated*.[31] Apart from certain key additions — the cinema across the street from Franz's apartment, the posters for Goldemar's movie, *King, Queen, Knave*, the references to a famous German star, Hess, and his film, *The Hindu Student*—the cinematic content of the English version almost exactly matches that of the original. Indeed, Grayson's comparison of the two texts reveals the extent to which Nabokov merely elaborated and emphasized aspects of plot, theme and characterization. "The motivations of the main characters become clearer, their expression becomes more colorful," she contends. "At the same time, authorial humour and irony continually intervene to expose their weaknesses and deflate their dreams."[32]

The most conclusive indication of the primacy of the cinematic theme in *Korol', Dama, Valet*, however, is "the ever present image of the cinema — that modern master of the art of illusion."[33] Although in the following commentary, all references are made to Nabokov's translation of 1968, all references have been checked against the original Russian text, and, in order to maintain a sense of chronology and context, only those details which correspond with this first version have been considered.

Like Myrtle Wilson and Daisy Buchanan, Martha, the sole female character in *King, Queen, Knave*, is infatuated with the movies. An avid movie-goer, she models herself on the screen heroines she idolizes and conducts her life in a perpetual enactment of cinematic scenes. The extent of Martha's immersion in the world of film is conveyed in the manner in which Nabokov first introduces her. Seen through Franz's eyes, the description is entirely visual, for she does not speak, the emphasis being solely on her appearance and what this reveals about her. Although appearances can be misleading and are often proven so in Nabokov's fiction, here, as in film, they provide important clues to Martha's personality, and the closer the attention paid to the image, the more telling its details become:

> The lady wore a black suit and a diminutive black hat with a little diamond swallow. Her face was serious, her eyes cold, a little dark down, the sign of passion, glistened above her upper lip, and a gleam of sun brought out the creamy texture of her neck at the throat with its two delicate transverse lines as if traced with a fingernail across it.[34]

The "dark down" is starkly incongruous set against the deathly pale of Martha's skin, which is accentuated by her black suit and hat. It is the strongest and only form of life emanating from this almost-corpse, the faint strangulation-like marks on her neck being indicative of some violent demise. What Franz finds attractive about her is initially difficult to comprehend, yet the perverse and subversive connotations of vampiric erotica associated with her neck and her pallor suggest a form of attraction which smacks of masochistic fascination and fatal submission. Franz is easy prey, being both socially and sexually naive. As it is, Martha seduces Franz primarily for fun but subsequently finds in him the perfect accomplice in her plot to murder Dreyer. Her attitude toward Franz is apparent from the outset:

"Dazzled and embarrassed, and so very young," she reflected with a mix-
ture of contempt and tenderness, "warm, healthy young wax that one
can manipulate and mold till its shape suits your pleasure" [p. 31].

The demonic associations are developed further here. Martha is no
longer a vampire but a witch, yet it is interesting that Martha interprets
her power in visual terms. She speaks of shaping and molding until she
has the perfect image. She does not have the capability to manipulate
Franz psychologically or emotionally, but she sees him as a kind of doll,
like the mannequins in Dreyer's shop window — someone she can transform outwardly to suit her every need. Her ability to use her looks to
get what she wants is her power. She is not interested in dealing with
personalities, and her victim is equally incapable of functioning on that
level. It is ironic also that Franz at this point has broken his glasses and
cannot see, which renders him completely impotent and utterly vulnerable to Martha's manipulations, further confirming that vision is his primary means of relating to the world.

Martha Dreyer's identity is based solely on wealth and sexuality.
The Dreyers exemplify a *nouveau riche* class of self-made entrepreneurs
who have literally bought their social status. They are extravagant, decadent and spoiled, strongly reminiscent of Fitzgerald's mercantile mil-
lionaires. Like Myrtle Wilson, money offers Martha a route to glamour
and sophistication, an entry into an otherwise closed world which she
perceives to be epitomized by the movies. For Martha, sex and money
are the tools by which she can achieve her dreams; they are her means of
self-expression and the elements she believes will provide her with a sense
of personal fulfillment. She is, therefore, spiritually and morally vacuous
and, among others of equal degeneracy, extremely dangerous.

Franz is just as taken in by the appeal of glamour, but it is its underlying decadence which he finds so irresistible. In a description reminiscent of Dos Passos's nighttime Manhattan, Franz is out on Berlin's streets
dazzled by the lights and the glitter which are reflected everywhere in store
windows and glistening asphalt. Nevertheless, as in his first encounter
with Martha, there is also something luridly seductive about the streets'
surface gloss:

> The luster of the black asphalt was filmed by a blend of dim hues, through
> which here and there vivid rends and oval holes made by rain puddles
> revealed the authentic colors of deep reflections — a vermilion diagonal
> band, a cobalt wedge, a green spiral — scattered glimpses into a humid

upside-down world, into a dizzy geometry of gems. The kaleidoscopic effect suggested someone's jiggling every now and then the pavement so as to change the combination of numberless colored fragments [p. 74].

The vision is deeply erotic, the lights oozing, spurting and squeezing into the darkness, while the juxtaposition of red and black echoes the vision of Martha's neck and lips in the train compartment. This is not a cold, hard, brittle, white world of translucent, delicate, remote beauty, but a very physical, tactile world, intimate and provocative.

> Meanwhile shafts and ripples of life passed by, marking the course of every car. Shop windows, bursting with tense radiance, oozed, squirted, and splashed out into the rich blackness [p. 74].

The potency of Franz's response parallels that of the cinema audience, intoxicated by the sensational impact of a calculated combination of color, movement and light which has the power to transform what is merely a two-dimensional spectacle into a palpable, sensual experience.

Martha's preoccupation with cinema, therefore, is highly appropriate in her superficial world. She craves the attention which Daisy Buchanan so expertly manages — "She longed to remain in this oval lake of light" (p. 124) — but somehow it seems to constantly elude her. Nabokov exposes Martha's pretensions as Fitzgerald does Myrtle Wilson's, and the weakly fabricated façade with which she attempts to conceal her ignorance and vulgarity, while the phony construction of her world echoes the synthetic charade which epitomizes Gatsby's:

> "Grandpa," Martha would say, indicating the genuine article with a wave of her hand that indolently included in the arc it described the anonymous nobleman to whose portrait the deceived guests' gaze shifted [p. 36].

She, like Gatsby, has taken pains to construct a lie, and although she does not have the style or elegance of Gatsby, she does, nevertheless, get away with her fraud. The distinction between Fitzgerald's characters and Martha, however, is the almost psychotic nature of her obsession with film, whereby everything is interpreted and expressed in cinematic terms, to an extent where even her inner feelings of frustration are visualized as filmic images — "Dreyer was spreading out monstrously before her, like a conflagration in a cinema picture. [He] filled the whole bedroom, the whole house, the whole world" (p. 199).[35]

Everyone in the novel knows and uses the power of image, whether it be Franz in his meager way — "The sharp autumn air, the surration of tires — this was the life! Add a new suit and a flaming tie — and his happiness would be complete" (p. 51) — or Dreyer, and it enables them to create for themselves a false identity which they can project to the world at large.

Dreyer, like Gatsby, is conscious of the power of image. The depiction of him "sitting in his office (a huge quiet place with huge unquiet windows, with a huge desk, and huge leather armchairs)" (p. 88), echoes Gatsby's carefully contrived and staged existence. Dreyer creates for himself a vast, grandiose setting in the midst of which he sits silent and enigmatic, yet all powerful, fully aware of and confident in the effect of this visual statement. This is compounded by the description of Dreyer's office, which emulates a camera panning across a set. From the resting point of detail — Dreyer at his desk — the narrative perspective pulls away to reveal first the interior of the room and then, defying physical barriers such as doors and walls — "[traversing] an olive-green corridor past glass expanses full of the hurricane-like clatter of typewriters" (p. 88) — pans at speed and at height over an area which seems to continue into infinity.

Dreyer's omniscient, all-pervasive, yet discreet presence is also deeply threatening and displays a highly skilled manipulation of visual effect which is also overtly cinematic. Even when sitting in the back of a taxi cab he is able to capitalize on the dramatic impact of the slightest gesture — "Dreyer remained mysteriously silent. He might have been asleep, had not his cigar glowed rhythmically" (p. 67). This is both reminiscent, in its Gothic connotations, of German Expressionist film and anticipatory of American noir imagery. Once again the associations of red and black are restated, here implicating Dreyer and emphasizing the extent of his control while serving to magnify Franz's passivity and ineptitude.

The extent to which cinema invades the world of the novel generates powerful dramatic irony. Nabokov amplifies this in his 1968 translation by adding the construction of a movie theater in its midst. The building has a direct bearing on the outcome of the story and stands as a symbol of the merging of the actual and cinematic worlds which would normally exist apart from each other. The strongest suggestion of the folly of allowing the boundaries between the actual and the fantastic to become confused lies in the three car crashes which occur at intervals in both versions. To Martha, who knows no personal fear, the first of these is more irritating than alarming. The second, however, touches Martha more profoundly because it touches her dreams. A German movie star is killed (Kurt Winter becomes Hess in translation),[36] an actor whom she fancies Franz resembles — more to suit the fulfillment of a fantasy than anything else. In the English version, the fact of his death is to her an outrage, but it is not the suddenness or the violence or the tragedy of this man's demise which shocks her, but the impossibility of it. Film stars are immortal in her eyes, and she is trying to attain immortality by emulating them. Suddenly, inexplicably, her belief is proven to be misguided, and also, more importantly, is her aspiration to immortality. Death to Martha is something which can be staged, organized, planned, calculated; it is neither arbitrary nor unpredictable. Death is also something that happens only to other people; she does not believe that it could either invade or interfere with her life:

> "People generally make all kinds of plans, very good plans, but completely fail to consider one possibility: death. As if no one could ever die. Oh, don't look at me as if I were saying something indecent" [p. 136].

In Nabokov's translation, the irony of Martha's demise is compounded by her blindness to and the reader's likely misinterpretation of the warning signals contained in the poster for the opening film at the new cinema. Its title, "King, Queen, Knave," signals to the reader that it has a direct bearing on the novel, and the images it presents serve to prefigure the climactic episode at the beach, where Martha attempts to drown Dreyer. Finally, the costumes worn by the actors pictured — "the King wore a maroon dressing gown, the Knave a red turtleneck sweater, and the Queen a black bathing suit" (p. 216) — also indicate how the protagonists will assume their respective roles.

The predominant colors, red and black, are restated here to emphasize the connection between the images and the three central figures of the story. The film poster, however, is misleading, for when the costumes appear in the narrative, as expected, they are displaced, Martha taking the red turtleneck and Franz the robe. As in Myrtle Wilson's case, Martha's emphasis on visual control is shown to be fundamentally flawed and unsustainable, but Nabokov is also suggesting the folly on the reader's part of relying too much on such arbitrary symbols. Apart from exposing Martha's misguided arrogance, this strong visual image also, therefore, serves to undermine the reader's ability to accurately recognize and

interpret Nabokov's visual signals, the implication being that the obvious symbols, such as the film poster, are not to be trusted. The more eloquent motifs are those which are the least obvious, for example, the
connotations generated by the name of the model of Dreyer's car—
Icarus—which is involved in two accidents. Martha's blind ambition parallels that of Icarus himself, and the analogy is reinforced by the link
between Dreyer and Icarus's father, Daedalus, who, like Dreyer, was an
inventor of robotic mannequins.

The complexity of Nabokov's use of cinematic motifs in his early
work is most overtly apparent, however, in *Kamera Obskura* (1933) or
Laughter in the Dark (1938). Over thirty years later Nabokov made the
following comment, in rare and explicit terms, on the novel's specific
intent:

> I wanted to write the entire book as if it were a film.... [T]he scenes and
> dialogue ... follow a cinematic pattern.... On the whole it was a gen-
> eral idea. I wasn't thinking of the form of a screenplay; it's a verbal imi-
> tation of what was then termed a "photoplay."[37]

Nabokov made few changes to his English version, essentially only
to render it more attractive to film producers.[38] As Appel points out,
"Nabokov's stated intentions provide neat critical guidelines,"[39] and critics have assessed the novel as a deliberate piece of film parody, the theme
of cinema pervading plot and characterization, but also the style and
structure of the novel. The latter, however, is an aspect of Nabokov's cre-
ativity which has been largely overlooked. In Dabney Stuart's chapter
"*Laughter in the Dark*: The Novel as Film," his analysis of the novel's
structural parallels with film is relegated to a footnote in which he cites
five main features:

1. Short scene-length chapters
2. Stage or set directions
3. "Subliminal frames" or flash frames
4. Flashbacks
5. Camera perspectives[40]

The very fact that such devices are incorporated into the narrative
demonstrates Nabokov's attempts to fuse the two genres—literary and
cinematic—not only to complement the thematic structure of the novel,
but also to lend it new technical and perceptual dimensions. On the one
hand the technical elements—short scenes, set directions—provide a

structural frame in which the action takes place, generating an immediacy and pace specific to film. On the other, the technical devices combine with the perceptual dimensions of the novel — the "flashbacks" and "flash frames" — giving the characters a highly sophisticated mnemonic visual capability, but at the same time amplifying the irony expressed in the novel's central theme of physical and moral blindness.

The cinematic techniques Nabokov employs also declare his guiding presence in the narrative, generating a sense of cool authorial detachment and heightening the parodic effect. Particularly remarkable are scenes in which Nabokov employs camera vision enabling the focus of attention to shift from detail to panorama and back again with the effect of undermining the main drama taking place. There are two examples of this — a scene between Axel Rex and Margot at a hockey match, and Albinus's car crash. In the crash, which Nabokov "saw vividly as film,"[41] he emulates a "tilt shot,"[42] pulling up and away from Albinus inside the car to reveal a privileged aspect on the scene.

> The bends became more and more frequent. On one side soared the steep cliff; on the other was the ravine. The sun stabbed his eyes. The pointer of the speedometer trembled and rose.[43]

Nabokov focuses close in on the speedometer needle before pulling back rapidly — "A sharp bend was approaching and Albinus proposed to take it with special dexterity." He suddenly changes not only the focal point of his description, but also the pace of movement. As Albinus drives faster and in worsening conditions, the narrative correspondingly slows down almost to a halt, and then as the danger increases, so the visual focus is retracted, serving to distance the reader from Albinus's predicament:

> High above the road an old woman who was gathering herbs saw to the right of the cliff this little blue car speed toward the bend, behind the corner of which, dashing from the opposite side, toward an unknown meeting, two cyclists crouched over their handlebars [p. 236].

At the most critical point of the sequence the narrative perspective shifts from Albinus to that of the anonymous old lady standing high above the road, who, although incidental to the scene's outcome, is crucial in terms of its visual disclosure. In this way Nabokov avoids the melodrama of a detailed description of the accident from Albinus's point of view without undermining the suspense generated by this skillful deployment of cinematic perspective.

At an ice-hockey game, a similar sudden shift of perspective is deployed at a crucial moment to deflate its dramatic import and to create a comic effect. This time Nabokov interrupts the dialogue between Axel and Margot, and when he returns to them, he does not pick up the conversation where he left it but rejoins it in mid-exchange, thus indicating his indifference to their dilemma and its insignificance to the world at large.

> "No Margot, he'll not marry you."
> "And I tell you he will."
> Their lips continued to move, but the clamor around drowned their swift quarrel [p. 151].

Nabokov turns the narrative attention to the game, gradually focusing in on the detail of the goalkeeper's leg pads from the prospect up in the stand, in the same way that Nick Carraway moves his focal attention from T. J. Ecklenburg's eyes to Myrtle Wilson's. Again the pace of the sequence correspondingly slows from a rapid sweep to a freeze frame:

> The crowd was roaring with excitement as nimble sticks pursued the puck on the ice, and knocked it, and hooked it, and passed it on, and missed it, and clashed together in rapid collision. Shifting smoothly this way and that at his post, the goal-keeper pressed his legs together so that his two pads combined to form one single shield [p. 151].

The graceful conclusion of this sequence is, however, interrupted by Margot's interjection — "It's dreadful that you've come back" (p. 151) — which serves to reassert her narrative priority. In focusing on the hockey game and on particular players, Nabokov causes Axel and Margot, albeit briefly, to pale into insignificance, and their quarrel is reduced to an inconsequential squabble, but this visual diversion proves to be unsustainable as the dialogue resumes.

Stuart also emphasizes the parodic aspect of the novel, arguing that Nabokov is employing the cinematic mode to expose the moral vacuity of both the characters and the medium itself and to imply the folly of attempting to displace the actual world with movie-inspired fantasy. There is, however, another dynamic fundamental to the experience of the novel which Stuart fails to consider — humor. *Laughter in the Dark* is essentially a black comedy, driven by Nabokov's sense of *poshlust*. If cinema is considered as both an element of *poshlust* and a medium which also generates it, then the effect of its presence in the central theme of *Laughter in the Dark* is to eradicate any sense of real tragedy in the novel. As Julian Connolly comments:

> In its manipulation of cinematic motifs, *Laughter in the Dark* affirms a basic truth in Nabokov's fiction: those who live their lives through the derivative patterns of conventional art display both a poverty of the imagination and a sterility of the soul.[44]

Considered in film terms, the novel would classify, plot-wise, as melodrama, but this would leave it devoid of humor, which is an element constantly employed to deflate the portent of the protagonists' experience. As Brian Boyd points out, "most of all [Nabokov] enjoyed the grotesqueness of the cinematic cliché,"[45] and Margot is the epitome of this.

> Margot had only a very vague idea of what she was really aiming at, though there was always the vision of herself as a screen beauty in gorgeous furs being helped out of a gorgeous car by a gorgeous hotel porter under a giant umbrella [p. 30].

The comic quality of her vision is contained in the over-application of the adjective "gorgeous" and thus Nabokov gently bursts Margot's delightful cinematically inspired dream bubble, sardonically revealing its clichéd absurdity.

Margot is in essence the literary sister of Myrtle Wilson in that she shares an equal desperation to construct another world into which she can some day escape. The distinction between the two women lies in the epitome of the dream that Daisy Buchanan presents, which is further distilled by the real movie star at Gatsby's party, thus relegating Myrtle to a level from which she could never rise. Margot's disastrous venture into film acting serves merely as an extension of her movie-saturated existence, but her delusion is so profound and her conceitedness so great that she is incapable of recognizing the impossibility of her dream.

There is also a highly comic element to Margot's behavior, particularly when in a state of anger or frustration she adopts the movie-star persona, emulating, say, Greta Garbo's most recent passionate role,[46] although she is often seen to be playing to an absent audience.

> "Good Heavens, how shall I do without him?" said Margot aloud. She
> leaped to the window, flung it open and was about to throw herself out
> [p. 38].

Her specialty is the dramatic exit, but the grandiose gestures that
are so eloquent on screen become cumbersome and ridiculous in a real-
life scenario. Again irony is generated by the obvious lack of an audience
and the bathos of the gesture, having a solely self-satisfying function.
On another occasion, Margot has an implicit ulterior motive in making
a dramatic exit — "In her distress she went to the dance hall as abandoned
damsels do in films" (p. 38) — adopting the role of a "damsel in distress"
in the hope that she might be rescued by a rich man. Despite her efforts,
however, she remains unnoticed, even by her own family:

> She sold her fur coat and the money kept her until the spring. Two days
> before this transaction she felt an ardent longing to display herself to her
> parents in her splendor, so she drove past the house in a taxicab [p. 39].

The timing of the comic release in this passage is crucial. Nabokov
skillfully deflates Margot's pretensions by concentrating the comedy on
one image — that of her buried in the back of a taxi. For all her opulence
and glamour, Margot ought to realize that no one will notice her unless
she rides in something that will attract some attention. A taxi is hardly
going to achieve this, and why does she not stop to visit her parents,
instead of parading hopefully past their house? The only person, it seems,
who does notice her, regardless of the circumstances, is Albinus.

While Margot embodies a cinematic ideal, Albinus provides the
means for the mode of cinema to pervade the novel's narrative. From the
very outset, Nabokov establishes both the invasion by film of Albinus's
psyche and the extent to which his actions are governed by his consciousness of its influence on him.

> Before Albinus' eyes there appeared a fine dark rain like the flickering of
> some very old film (1910, a brisk jerky funeral procession with legs mov-
> ing too fast) [p. 18].

Not only is there a sense of the hypnotic power of the moving picture image, akin to the flicker of images in *The Great Gatsby*, but Albinus's preoccupation with film enables him to identify the footage evoked,
indicating an intimate knowledge of even the most unremarkable aspects

Felicitas (Greta Garbo) has Leo von Harden (John Gilbert) utterly in her thrall. *Flesh and the Devil* (MGM, 1926).

of cinema. It is interesting that Albinus's frame of reference here should be so completely anathema to Margot's — grainy, patchy, silent, speeded-up, documentary-style footage of an anonymous and morbid event versus the grace and elegance of a fanciful Hollywood production.

Albinus is often presented in a state of reverie induced by the vision of Margot, yet Nabokov subtly undermines the quality of Albinus's rapture. In one instance he is seen "[gazing] lovingly at her childishly upturned face which looked very white in the blaze of the street lamp" (p. 56). The beauty of the vision is undermined by the banality of the source of light — not the moon, as would be expected, but a "street lamp." Margot is also often seen, through Albinus's eyes, cast in a soft, white light, as Daisy Buchanan is. Yet, whereas Daisy engineers her pose to catch the available light in order to maintain the level of control she has of the way others perceive her and the way she wishes to be perceived, the instances in *Laughter in the Dark* are a result of Albinus's contrivances to fulfill and subscribe to his cinematically informed imagination.

Margot's skill in emulating screen goddesses does not, therefore, increase; rather, it is Albinus's deluded vision which escalates to a point where it overrides every other faculty of perception, long before the event of his physical blinding.

> Margot sat up and smiled plaintively. Tears only added to her beauty. Her face was aflame, the iris of her eyes was dazzling, and a large tear trembled on the side of her nose: he had never before seen tears of that size and brilliance [p. 119].

At this point the aspirations of these two characters merge. Margot, who so desires to be a screen icon, becomes one in Albinus's eyes. The image, incidentally, also distinctly echoes the on-screen close-up of an anonymous actress in Nabokov's story, "A Letter That Never Reached Russia" (1925): "[T]he huge face of a girl with gray, shimmering eyes and black lips ... approaches from the screen, keeps growing as it gazes into the dark hall, and a wonderful, long, shining tear runs down one cheek."[47] Albinus at last finds a tangible embodiment of perfection attainable only in films, something he is seen to be searching for even before he meets Margot, but something he believes she possesses because of where he first meets her — in the cinema.

When he first sees Margot she is described as a "creature gliding about in the dark" (p. 23), but initially it is more the sensation of her in the "velvety darkness" (p. 20) of the cinema which attracts him, and ironically his first good look at her is colored by his initial sense of physical attraction compounded by the context in which she appears — "He stared at her face almost in dread. It was a pale, sulky, painfully beautiful face" (p. 21).

Albinus so wants to see beauty in Margot's face because of the realm from which she seems to emerge that he ignores its pallor and the predominant aspect of her personality — sulkiness — which it expresses, although at the same time it presents the archetypal image of the screen diva. Once they are together, Margot's play-acting is extremely effective on this man so preoccupied with film imagery. No matter how vulgar and contrived her behavior is to the reader, to Albinus, Margot's passionate role-playing is genuine and overwhelming.

> There were stormy scenes at home, sobs, moans, hysteria. She flung herself on the sofa, the bed, the floor. Her eyes sparkled brilliantly and

wrathfully; one of her stockings had slipped down. The world was swamped in tears [p. 192].

After days rehearsing in front of a mirror, Margot perfects her act and gradually begins to work on Albinus to become the sole image he sees, so that he relinquishes all power over her and becomes her slave.

> She returned home and when Albinus put down his paper and rose to meet her, she tottered and pretended to faint. It was an indifferent performance but it worked [p. 99].

While Margot's dismal failure as a movie actress proves irrevocably that she is no screen goddess, it fails to deflate the vaunted image of her which Albinus so cherishes. Albinus is cruelly and brutally victimized as a result of his slavish devotion to the visual incarnation of a romantic ideal, and, it could be argued that, in destroying him so utterly, Nabokov is condemning the potency of the cinematic image and the filmic perspective as an alternative mode of perception. At the same time, however, Margot, who calculatedly generates and manipulates a cinematic persona, apparently thrives, indicating that the fundamental issue is not the validity or otherwise of film as an alternative fictive dimension, but the deployment and incorporation of cinematic elements as a means of establishing and maintaining autonomy and asserting control, both in terms of characterization and narrative.

The extent of Nabokov's deliberate emulation of the techniques and devices of film in *Laughter in the Dark* and its extension of themes and ideas already explored in previous works indicates that the medium had a greater artistic significance than either Julian Connolly or Dabney Stuart proposes. The patterning of themes and motifs, the shifting narrative perspectives, the use of specific and sophisticated cinematic modes of presentation — panning and tilt shots, close-ups, long shots, even "flash-forwards"[48] — combined with scenes structured as film sequences establish the importance of the mode in Nabokov's creative designs and extend beyond the purposes of mere parody.

Also far from parodic, Nabokov's treatment of cinematics in the story "Spring in Fialta," written in 1936, is controlled and subtle. Film is discreetly integrated into the story's narrative structure and is pivotal in the realization and dramatization of the processes of memory.

Cinematic Motif in "Spring in Fialta"

The story is told in the form of a series of flashbacks, an immediately recognizable cinematic device. Within these flashbacks a network of motifs emerges which seems to indicate a conspiracy of inanimate objects reminiscent of Murnau's *Der letzte Mann* and Nabokov's early story, "Details of a Sunset." As Gavriel Moses points out, in *Laughter in the Dark* Albinus is "surrounded by ... actively engaged objects," including mirrors, doors, odd pieces of furniture, which offer alternative commentaries on particular scenes or even "foreshadow narrative events."[49] In "Spring in Fialta," specific inanimate objects have a visual power, their appearances triggering a set of associations and an underlying pattern that indicate a guiding force behind events where they initially seemed to be arbitrary and irrelevant. The realization of the significance and role of these inanimate objects is gradual, and this allows the reader to undergo the same process of gradual enlightenment that Victor, the story's narrator, experiences on returning to Fialta and his past. Each time the objects recur, the reader is forced to reassess their meaning and their bearing on the story's principal cathartic event. Victor's lover, Nina, dies in a crash on a mountain road when her car collides with a circus van. The event is prefigured by the circus posters, indicating its presence in town early in the story, and the pageant that occurs toward the end, the recurring visions of an inkstand in the shape of the mountain on which Nina dies, and the *Z*-shape image of Nina's reclining body that reflects the pattern of Victor's encounters with her and the winding mountain road where the crash takes place. These images combine with Victor's sense of premonition, which is described, significantly, in terms of film (note also the reappearance of the Icarus):

> A yellow long-bodied Icarus that looked like a giant scarab ... in the lacquer of its elytra a gouache of sky and branches was engulfed; in the metal of one of the bomb-shaped lamps we ourselves were momentarily reflected, lean film-land pedestrians passing along the convex surface.[50]

The memory itself is like a film which is being constantly rerun. Its visual potency does not diminish, but the picture has an ephemeral, deathly quality, being essentially a reflection, a distortion and a reduction of living things to a fragile transparency. This in turn is compounded by the implications of destruction contained in the image of the "bomb-shaped lamps," and this premonition of death is further developed by the silent quality of the description, the memory being mute like the dead.

> The three of them wearing motoring helmets, getting in, smiling and waving to me, transparent to me like ghosts, with the color of the world shining through them, and then they were moving, receding, diminishing (Nina's last ten-fingered farewell) [p. 426].

It is not just the memory which has become film, but the people also. Even in life they behave as two-dimensional celluloid images dependent on light to make them visible, in the same way that Daisy Buchanan and Gatsby require light to come alive. Nina's appearances throughout Victor's life have been sudden and unexpected; like staged entrances, they are contrived for maximum impact. As with Fitzgerald's characters, speech is essentially redundant, and although gesture is not Nina's primary means of communication it enables her to maintain her enigmatic distance. It is appropriate therefore that Victor's last vision of Nina should be that of her waving, reminiscent of Jay Gatsby's elegiac gestures, powerful enough to be seen as the car recedes into the distance, more eloquent and lasting than any speech.

Cinema is essentially a medium of artifice, driven by the innate paradox that realism can be achieved only through a highly conscious manipulation of visual tricks and is dependent for its success on an audience's willing suspension of disbelief. Fitzgerald saw the effects of this on the American psyche and the potential force of its influence, but he also saw the potential, as did Nabokov, for literature in its wake. By incorporating this new art form, its techniques, its styles, and its vocabulary into their work, Dos Passos, Fitzgerald and Nabokov were creating new fictive dimensions, at the same time addressing the questions relating to realism and artifice emerging from this new medium. To interpret Nabokov's purpose merely on the basis of Julian Connolly's comment would be misguided, therefore. Even in *Laughter in the Dark*, Nabokov demonstrates a far more complex relationship with cinema than the exploitative, satirical stance that Connolly identifies.

For Fitzgerald and Dos Passos, 1920s' America was concerned only with the fulfillment of a fantastic, elaborate and impossible dream of glamour, perfection and self-sufficiency projected by Hollywood. Yet American writers continued to incorporate cinema and cinematics in their work, as it in turn adapted and developed during the 1930s, so that by the 1940s, film was securely established at the vanguard of American culture, transformed from something potentially degenerative and alienating into a challenging force for technical and artistic innovation.

Four

A Common Vision? Traces of Noir in Nabokov's Russian Fiction and American Writing of the 1930s

During the 1940s and 1950s a distinctive canon of films was produced which distilled and extended the issues raised by the growing preoccupation with image in American culture and society. In terms of the Hollywood industry, the films themselves presented a new and disturbing vision of America which conformed neither to the dictates of formulaic production codes nor to established cinematic visual conventions. They were concerned primarily with an alternative depiction of contemporary America, not as a place of glamour and romance, but one of crime, corruption, decadence and moral oblivion. Film noir, as this series was to be called,[1] distilled the visual style of European cinema between the wars and combined it with the tough, "hardboiled" character of American popular fiction, which was growing in dominance during the 1930s.

American Film Noir: Definitions and Interpretations

Although essentially an element of Hollywood's "B" picture output, the significance of film noir in America's cinematic tradition should not be underestimated, particularly in terms of its fusion of American and European film-making expertise. A balanced perspective on the nature

of these films has been difficult to achieve, however. Critics have emphasized the contribution of émigré filmmakers to an extent where the American aspect of these films is virtually eclipsed and the origins and character
of film noir take on an entirely European dimension.[2] Nevertheless it is
true to say that

> the influx of foreign directors and other craftsmen before and during
> World War II — most notably the German "refugees": Fritz Lang, Robert
> Siodmak, Max Ophuls, William Dieterle, Billy Wilder, Otto Preminger
> had previously helped to refine film noir's distinctive visual style. This
> was not merely low-key photography, but the full heritage of German
> Expressionism: moving camera; oddly angled shots; a chiaroscuro frame
> inscribed with wedges of light or shadowy mazes, truncated by fore-
> ground objects, or punctuated with glinting headlights bounced off mir-
> rors, wet surfaces, or the polished steel of a gun barrel.[3]

The key term in this commentary is "refined," confirming the notion that
film noir was and remains an inherently American medium, for the origins of noir can also be traced in American film and fiction, particularly
the "hardboiled" detective story and the gangster movies of the 1930s.

The first acknowledged film noir was a wholly American product.
The Maltese Falcon (1941) was a remake of a previous Warner Brothers
release directed by Del Ruth in 1931. It had an American director, John
Huston, and was adapted for the screen by American crime writer Dashiell
Hammett from his novel of 1930. The noir cycle, however, can be located
even further back in the American tradition, to the late 1920s, with Josef
von Sternberg's *Underworld* (1927) and Lewis Milestone's *The Racket*
(1928). Both these directors were European-born American nationals,
and in a sense they embody the fusion of perspectives which informed
the films of the 1940s.

Hollywood's film industry had always been very aware of European
cinema, adopting and adapting film ideas and techniques for its own
purposes, while maintaining a closely guarded autonomy. Although many
European directors were invited to work in America in the 1920s and
1930s, they found they had little artistic freedom and were expected to
submit to the direction of the studios. Émigré directors Lubitsch, Dieterle
and Curtiz had "succeeded by dint of submerging their foreignness in a
typically American style of film-making or [by] inventing their own fantasy of foreignness specifically for the American market."[4] These three
were responsible for some of the most commercially successful films to

be made in Hollywood between the wars, films concerned predominantly with extravagant adventure and romance. It was the work of Fritz Lang, however, which enabled subsequent émigré filmmakers to retain to some degree the style and character of their European origins.

Lang's first American release, *Fury* (1936), was a huge hit, significantly because of the sense of the alien and the unfamiliar it brought to American cinema. As John Russell Taylor argues:

> Lang was different. In acclimatizing to the American cinema he had the advantage over most of the other earlier German imports in that his films in Europe, for all their frequent elaborations of costume and set, their powerful atmospheres, had been firmly based on narrative. American cinema was, and has remained, primarily a place for telling stories — the significance of the film is articulated through the plot and the pacing of the story. And *Fury*, whatever else it may be, is a relentless piece of story-telling.[5]

Lang became one of the most prolific of the noir directors, producing nine films in the canon after *Fury*. His particular hallmark was "a deep strain of paranoia." He was "[obsessed] with the mechanics of plot" and rather than constructing "sequences of action to illuminate characters, he [built] traps, horrible boxes from which his characters [could] not escape ... like a designer of very abstruse and pessimistic games."[6] Lang's films typified the noir scenario and set the standard for others to follow. At the same time, they expressed a very contemporary American preoccupation:

> The moral ambivalence, the criminality, the complex contradictions in motives and events, all conspire to make the viewer co-experience the anguish and insecurity which are the true emotions of contemporary *film noir*. All the films in this cycle create a similar emotional effect: *that state of tension instilled in the spectator when the psychological reference points are removed.* The aim of *film noir* was to create a *specific alienation.*[7]

Alienation was also a fundamental dynamic in American filmmaking. Karen Hollinger describes film noir as a "deviant genre within the classical Hollywood tradition," reflective of "the ideological contradictions, disequilibrium, and disturbing imbalance characteristic of the World War II and postwar periods."[8] Yet, Hollinger argues, the films neither function as "safety-valves for wartime angst, alienation, and discontent"[9] nor

offer any form of closure or resolution, but rather serve merely to dramatize the social, cultural, and psychological conflicts symptomatic of
1940s' America.

Paul Schrader categorizes the noir cycle in three phases. The first
falls between the years 1941 and 1946, the wartime period, which he
identifies as the phase "of the private eye and the lone wolf."[10] Films were
inspired by the crime fiction of Chandler and Hammett and directed by
American and émigré directors alike, including John Huston, Orson
Welles, Alfred Hitchcock, Fritz Lang, Robert Siodmak, Michael Curtiz,
Howard Hawks, Lewis Milestone, Edward Dmytryk and Otto Preminger.
The second, precursed by Billy Wilder's *Double Indemnity* (1944),
Schrader defines as the "postwar realistic" period of 1945 to 1949, characterized by films which "tended more toward the problems of crime in
the streets, political corruption and police routine."[11] These films shied
away from the romanticism of the first phase and often possessed an
underlying political or moral agenda, quite distinct from the amoral anar-
chy of the earlier noirs.

Welles's *Lady from Shanghai* (1948), however, is exceptional in this
context not only in its adherence to the original themes of film noir, but
also in its overtly exotic and Expressionistic style, generating chaos and
confusion by the use of deep shadows and acute camera angles. Characters are cast in extremes of light and dark, often in silhouette and sometimes only in shadow, evoking in them an amorphous, elusive quality
which undercuts the realism of the film's setting and the very contemporary concerns of the story. A recurring shark motif is deployed throughout the film as a metaphor for the destructive triangle of Bannister, Grisby
and Elsa, into which O'Hara is almost fatally drawn. It is introduced by
O'Hara's fishing story, its allusions to Elsa confirmed in a scene in an
aquarium in which a furtive conversation between O'Hara and Elsa is
backgrounded by grotesquely enlarged and distorted sea creatures. The
film's climax — the shoot-out sequence in the hall of mirrors of a Cali-
gari-like "Crazy House" — skillfully incorporates the nightmarish, fantastic quality of German Expressionist film with the hardboiled American
scenario of betrayal, deception and violence.

Schrader cites 1953 as the end of the cycle, although Welles's *Touch
of Evil* (1958) is also recognized as one of the last of its kind. This third
phase (1949–1953) Schrader describes as a period of "psychotic action and
suicidal impulse. The noir hero, seemingly under the weight of ten years
of despair, started to go bananas. The psychotic killer, who in the first

period had been a subject worthy of study ... now became the active protagonist."[12] These films took the original primary elements of noir — social alienation, amorality, decadence, sexual degeneracy and violence — to their extremes. At this point, their production was dominated by émigré filmmakers, in particular Otto Preminger, Max Ophuls, Billy Wilder, Robert Siodmak, Edward Dmytryk and Jacques Tourneur, although there were significant contributions from American directors including Nicholas Ray, George Marshall, Henry Hathaway and Gordon Douglas.

The notion, however, that the sole ambition of émigré filmmakers was to make this type of film is misguided. Directors often came to projects through a combination of coincidence and coercion. The studio system did not allow for the kind of power, influence and control which came with the brief emergence of *auteurism* in the late 1960s and early 1970s. The only mobility within the studio system was among technicians and cinematographers, and each studio retained an independence and self-sufficiency which prohibited the sharing of ideas or processes with any other studio, thus promoting jealous competition. Yet, as Silver and Ward describe,

> the years of production immediately after the war, with film more able to incorporate exterior locales, more mobile cameras, and more filmmakers, both foreign and domestic, ready to test the limits of technical innovations, became the most visually homogeneous of the entire noir cycle. In a random selection of productions, such as *The Big Clock* (Paramount) [Farrow/Seitz], *Cry of the City* (Fox) [Siodmak/Ahern], *Strangers on a Train* (Warners), [Hitchcock/Burks], *The People Against O'Hara* (MGM) [Sturges/Alton], *Out of the Past* (RKO) [Tourneur/Musuraca], *Criss Cross* (Universal) [Siodmak/Planer], and *Dead Reckoning* (Columbia) [Cromwell/Tover], seven different directors and cinematographers, of great and small technical reputations, working at seven different studios, completed seven ostensibly unrelated motion pictures with one cohesive visual style.[13]

The "cohesive visual style" of film noir was achieved by the manipulation of technical devices inherent in both European and American filmmaking. Particularly evocative was a highly calculated and specific use of lighting, which combined conventional devices with technical innovation, defined by Place and Peterson thus:

> *key light*: [a] primary source of light directed on the actor from above and to one side of the camera ... producing sharply defined shadows. Used in isolation [it has] the effect of cutting through deceptive facades.

fill light: ...a soft, diffused or indirect light that "fills" in the shadows
    created by the "key."
back light: [which] shines directly on the actor from behind, creating
    highlights and form, differentiating him from the background.
low-key lighting: noir lighting. The ratio of "key" to "fill" light is great,
    creating areas of high contrast and rich, black shadows.... *[N]oir* hero-
    ines were shot in tough, unromantic close-ups of direct, undiffused
    light, which create a hard, statuesque surface beauty that seems more
    seductive but less attainable, at once alluring and impenetrable. Also
    [it creates] a sense of sinister foreboding.
kick light: produced by moving the key light behind and to one side of
    the actor, below or high above to create unnatural shadows and strange
    facial expressions. Used in conjunction with restricted depth-of-field
    to pull in focus on the face.[14]

Extremes of light could also alter focus, increasing depth of field, whereby
focus could be extended into the background of close and medium shots,
bringing everything in the frame into sharp relief. This was used in conjunction with high- and wide-angle shots and extreme close-ups, which
would focus on the area of the face between the chin and the brow, known
as "chokers."[15] Another legacy of German Expressionist film, "the use of
oblique and vertical lines," was also adapted for the American scenario:

Obliquity adheres to the choreography of the city, and is in direct oppo-
sition to the horizontal American tradition of Griffith and Ford [i.e., the
grand-scale panoramic landscapes of the American West]. Oblique lines
tend to splinter a screen, making it restless and unstable. Light enters
the dingy rooms of film noir in such odd shapes — jagged trapezoids,
obtuse triangles, vertical slits — that one suspects the windows were cut
out with a pen knife. No character can speak authoritatively from a space
which is being continually cut to ribbons of light.[16]

This use of oblique lines is particularly evident in Wilder's *Double
Indemnity*, establishing Walter Neff, the film's protagonist/narrator, as a
condemned man. From his first meeting with Phyllis Dietrichson, the
shadows of Venetian blinds and window frames repeatedly cut across him
to suggest not only his unconscious entrapment by her but also the fatal
consequences of his submission to her. These and other visual devices,
particularly reflected images in mirrors and windows, and unbalanced and
restricted frames, combined to generate film noir's characteristic claus-
trophobic atmosphere of threat and paranoia.

High contrast noir lighting. Harry Morgan (Humphrey Bogart) and "Slim" (Lauren Bacall) are interrogated by Captain Reynard (Dan Seymour, foreground), and Lieutenant Coyo (Sheldon Leonard, right). The harsh white light above Reynard's desk starkly illuminates Morgan's and Slim's faces, intensifying their vulnerability and amplifying the sense of threat generated by Reynard, while Reynard's bodyguard (Aldo Nadi, left) looks silently and menacingly on. *To Have and Have Not* (Warner Bros., 1944).

That the predominant visual style of film noir was inspired by European film and, in particular, German Expressionism is not in question. Yet the ready assimilation of the noir sensibility and the continuing presence of noir as a formative influence in American cinema indicates the extent not merely of its impact on the American psyche but, more significantly, suggests that the noir vision was also inherently American, a perspective apparent in both the film and fiction of the inter-war years.

The dazzling impact of reflective surfaces. Dana Andrews as a bewildered Detective Lieutenant Mark McPherson in *Laura* (20th Century–Fox, 1944).

The Maltese Falcon *and* Sanctuary: Seminal Noir Texts

While Fitzgerald's *Great Gatsby* is a text infused with the themes and techniques of film, Dashiell Hammett's *Maltese Falcon* resembles a screenplay rather than a piece of narrative fiction. It has the character and structure of film, its twenty short chapters functioning as independent scenes, the action progressing through them principally in the form of dialogue.

Hammett began his writing career by contributing stories to serial publications — *Black Mask* being one of the best known and most popular — serials which produced a very particular kind of crime fiction and encouraged a very specific approach to the craft. As Raymond Chandler was later to comment, "the technical basis of the *Black Mask* type of story was that the scene outranked the plot in the sense that a good plot was one which made good scenes."[17]

This emphasis on plot driven by sequences of scenes echoes Fitzgerald's comment, "action is character,"[18] and his emphasis on the importance of a solitary, key scene in directing narrative. Chandler, however, took this notion a step further by arguing, unequivocally and in full acknowledgement of the role of this parallel medium, that "we who tried to write it had the same point of view as the film makers."[19]

This notion of "point of view" is centered in narrative stance. Dennis Dooley has emphasized the significance of the nature of Hammett's third-person narrative voice in simultaneously involving and distancing the reader:

> The voice of Hammett's narrator is strictly neutral, no speaker at all, but an objective, totally impartial voice that betrays not the slightest hint of affection or adulation concerning the detective hero. It is a voice that does not care whether Spade lives or dies, whether good triumphs in the end, or even whether the reader is impressed or exasperated by the main character's actions. And as such it is a logical extension of Hammett's earlier break with the popular conventions of the day.[20]

The detached, objective neutrality of the narration, Dooley argues, marks a break with the tradition of narrative didacticism in crime fiction — a moralizing, stabilizing voice which guarantees the prospect of good ultimately surmounting evil — and maintains a precise distinction between these antagonistic forces. Hammett's narrative stance, however, obfuscates these concerns, confuses the distinctions, causing the hero's role as the arbiter of justice and truth to vacillate.

> Spade does not ... narrate his own story. Instead he is only another character, albeit a central one, in it. In fact the reader goes nowhere Spade does not go and sees nothing that Spade does not see, though he does not go everywhere Spade goes or necessarily sees everything he sees. And he is never once allowed to know what Spade is thinking or feeling. Which leaves the reader just as much in the dark as everybody else with regard to his motives.[21]

Such narrative distancing parallels the alienating effect of film noir, the camera's objectivity enabling subtle contradictions, complexities and ambiguities to register rather than be reported. How far it can be argued that Hammett was influenced directly in this by contemporary film can be inferred from the state of cinema in the late 1920s. In 1930, the year of *The Maltese Falcon*'s publication, sound was introduced into film, although screen dialogue was, in those initial years, extremely primitive and unsophisticated, stilted, ponderous, affected, remaining very much tied to the melodramatic, gesturing style of the silent era. Hammett's dialogue in *The Maltese Falcon* anticipates the natural quality and flow of screen dialogue that developed during the 1930s. Its almost literal transposition into John Huston's screenplay for the 1941 Warner Brothers' release was to determine the tone and character of the noir scenario.

At the same time, Hammett's novel exhibits the visual emphasis of silent film. As Dooley comments, "the most remarkable thing about this suspenseful and complex tale is how much of it is played out in silence — or, to be more precise, the silences between the hard-bitten dialogue."[22] Action and dialogue, therefore, drive the narrative; the characters' movements are depicted in precise detail in order for the reader to have an exact visual picture of their placing in the scene and the specific significance of any single movement within it. The attention to detail which realizes these highly choreographed scenes is also a cinematic feature, employing a visual focus and direction which is more mechanical than human, its speed and accuracy generating a sense of immediacy and pace. The close-up frame of a face, the tracking of the subtlest change in expression, and the smallest shift in posture generate an intense stillness and tension. Conversely in fight scenes — for example, the struggle between Spade and Cairo, which takes place in chapter five — the action is depicted in a series of slow-motion images in close focus, rendering the precise choreography of the action and magnifying the force of the violence:

> Spade's elbow dropped as Spade spun to the right. Cairo's face jerked back not far enough: Spade's right heel on the patent-leathered toes anchored the smaller man in the elbow's path. The elbow struck him beneath the cheek-bone, staggering him so that he must have fallen had he not been held by Spade's foot on his foot. Spade's elbow went on past the astonished dark face and straightened when Spade's hand struck down at the pistol. Cairo let the pistol go the instant that Spade's fingers touched it. The pistol was small in Spade's hand.[23]

Hammett's scenes are visualized as if through the viewfinder of a camera; they are not depicted in terms of 20-20 human vision, but are boxed, their perimeters restricted, serving to limit the focal field. The geography of a scene, therefore, takes on a particular importance, having a specific narrative purpose. In chapter eight, for example, the characters are gathered in Spade's sitting room, and Brigid O'Shaughnessy is sitting in an armchair beside a table looking across the room toward the door:

> The girl put her feet down on the floor and looked warily from Dundy, holding Cairo's wrist, to Tom Polhaus, standing a little behind them, to Spade, leaning against the door-frame. Spade's face was placid. When his gaze met hers his yellow-gray eyes glinted for an instant with malicious humor and then became expressionless again [p. 74].

Hammett shows the reader what Brigid sees but gives her the vision of a camera. The placement of the four men in the room gives the scene a three-dimensional effect, a clever optical trick which overcomes the two-dimensional plane of the screen image, serving to enhance their positioning and to suggest some significance. Here the implication is of potential entrapment; Brigid is surrounded by these four men, and their stance serves to isolate her. This is immediately undercut by the irony of the conversation between Dundy and Brigid and Spade's implication in it, indicated by the shift of narrative attention to him, and from this the reader is given an insight into Spade's attitude to Brigid, without resorting to the conventional process of reporting what he is thinking or feeling.

> She looked at Spade again. He did not in any way respond to the appeal in her eyes. He leaned against the door-frame and observed the occupants of the room with the polite detached air of a disinterested spectator [p. 74].

A great deal of emphasis is placed on eyes as vehicles of communication. Characters use their eyes overtly as a means of silent communication, establishing an intimacy and a frankness often lost in speech.

> Brigid O'Shaughnessy sat up straight and looked at Spade with surprised blue eyes. He patted her shoulder inattentively. His eyes were steady on Guttman's. Guttman's twinkled merrily between sheltering fat-puffs. ... Cairo, hands on thighs, leaned forward in his chair, breathing between parted soft lips. His dark eyes had the surface-shine of lacquer. They shifted their focus warily from Spade's face to Guttman's, from Guttman's to Spade's [p. 174].

Such optical conversations also serve as dramatic pauses, generating tension and suspense by delaying the progress of the action.

This emphasis on optical communication is also apparent in William Faulkner's *Sanctuary* (1931), the notion of sanctuary in the novel being essentially one of silence and darkness. Language is an impotent form of communication, and thus the ability to speak, to tell, proves in the novel to be redundant. Horace, the lawyer whose livelihood and *raison d'être* is founded upon the power of language to protect and preserve justice and freedom is ultimately frustrated by the power of colluded silence, demonstrated by Goodwin, Temple and Popeye. In the absence of dialogue, the narrative emphasis is transferred to vision. In a world that is deaf and mute, sight becomes the primary means of perception and communication.

Alan Spiegel describes William Faulkner's *Sanctuary* as his "*Hollywood* novel."[24] Indeed, it was filmed in 1933 as *The Story of Temple Drake*, but by this time Faulkner had already become well established in Hollywood, having been noticed as early as 1926 by the director Howard Hawks. Hawks first directed a Faulkner screenplay in 1932, an adaptation of his short story "Turn About," and they continued to work together until 1954, their long and successful collaboration culminating in 1944 with *To Have and Have Not* and *The Big Sleep*. During this period Faulkner also worked with Ernest Hemingway, Charles Brackett, Jean Renoir, Irving Thalberg, Darryl F. Zanuck, Nunnally Johnson and Jules Furthman and continued to work in television until the late 1950s.[25]

The cinematic quality of *Sanctuary* is, however, very particular. As Spiegel comments, "the entire narrative surface of this novel seems to have been composed not just with any camera eye but with a specifically American camera eye."[26] Faulkner, he argues, generates an effect of "depthlessness" in his fiction which serves to both estrange and mystify. As a visual device it parallels the experience of film, the "depthlessness of the retinal image [being] equaled by the depthlessness of the photographic image," causing the details of a scene to be brought to a continuous plane of two-dimensional visualization, creating an "equality of insistence on the consciousness of the viewer."[27] In turn this forces the visual focus of a scene to be emphasized, and as it is achieved in film by mechanical means, by the close-up shot or slow-motion frame, thus it is in fiction, by controlled and calculated shifts in narrative attention and pace.

The central preoccupation of *Sanctuary* is watching; the novel's protagonists move in and out of the narrative's visual plane, focusing and refocusing attention, defining and redefining character and action. Almost every character in the novel is afforded a cinematic visual capacity. In some instances it functions merely as an incidental device, in setting a scene or providing a moment of dramatic pause or shift in focus, whereas in more crucial scenes, it is the only means of achieving some degree of insight into the nature of a character or a relationship. The only character who is denied this facility is Popeye. At no point in the novel does Faulkner offer a perspective from his point of view; rather, his depiction remains constant and fixed. Popeye, therefore, epitomizes Spiegel's notion of "depthlessness." Depicted as "sinister and exteriorized,"[28] Popeye is "virtually immune to inquiry," and Faulkner's deployment of "an extremity of depthless portraiture"[29] has a dehumanizing effect. It is significant that Popeye's first appearance is as a vision — "He saw ... the shattered reflection of Popeye's straw hat, though he heard no sound"[30] — establishing from the outset his elusive, evasive presence which is both insubstantial yet palpable, its resonance compounded by its silence.

Popeye appears throughout the novel as he is first seen, always with the same look and the same gestures and the consistent absence of dialogue, serving to reinforce his opacity and the corresponding visual impact of his presence.

> A man of undersize, his hands in his coat pockets, a cigarette slanted from his chin. His suit was black, with a tight, high-waisted coat. His trousers were rolled once and caked with mud above mud-caked shoes. His face had a queer, bloodless color, as though seen by electric light; against the sunny silence, in his slanted straw hat and his slightly akimbo arms, he had the vicious depthless quality of stamped tin [p. 5].

The implications of depthlessness in Temple are harder to define. She is strongly reminiscent of Fitzgerald's Daisy Buchanan, first appearing in the novel as hard, brittle, superficial; her looks masklike, shallow, and her actions mere gesture, insubstantial, frivolous, hollow:

> Her face was quite pale, dusted over with recent powder, her hair in spent red curls. Her eyes, all pupil now, rested upon them for a blank moment. Then she lifted her hand in a wan gesture, whether at them or not, none could have said [p. 23].

Temple's personality is defined by her appearance, by a movement, a gesture, subtle aspects almost indiscernible to the human eye or which would at least lie beyond its normal visual perimeters. This is the vision of a camera eye, focusing in close from a remote spot on a moving figure in dim light, and it is appropriate that Temple should be witnessed by a mechanical source, serving to compound her depthlessness. It is also significant that her introduction in the novel is reminiscent of Popeye's, the emphasis being on her silent movement, establishing an incongruous connection between them which is further reinforced by the associations of "stamped tin" with the metallic "glitter" which characterizes this scene.

> The town boys ... watched her enter the gymnasium upon black collegiate arms and vanish in a swirling glitter upon a glittering swirl of music, with her high delicate head and her bold painted mouth and soft chin, her eyes blankly right and left looking, cool, predatory and discreet.... Later, the music wailing beyond the glass, they would watch her through the windows as she passed in swift rotation from one pair of black sleeves to the next [p. 22].

These qualities are sustained throughout the first half of the novel, enabling Temple to maintain a precarious distance, although they soon prove to be ineffectual in the face of real physical threat which brutally exposes the naivety of her childish affectations and her oblivious disregard for any notion of consequence.

Temple experiences palpable threat for the first time in the figure of Popeye. From her first encounter with him at Goodwin's house, the "old Frenchman place" (p. 8), she is acutely aware of the emblems of Popeye's presence — the cigarette, the straw hat — and as she flits from room to room, trying to find a place of refuge, the visual perspective is given to her, so that her experience becomes the reader's.

> On the square of sunlight framed by the door lay a shadow of a man's head and she half spun, poised with running. But the shadow wore no hat, so she turned and on tiptoe she went to the door and peered round it. ... With the tail of her eyes she thought she had seen a thread of smoke drift out of the door in the detached room where the porch made an L, but it was gone. [She] saw Popeye watching her from the corner of the house, his hands in his pockets and a slanted cigarette curling across his face. Still without stopping she scrambled on to the porch and sprang into the kitchen, where a woman sat at a table, a burning cigarette in her hand, watching the door [p. 32].

The sense of perpetual darkness which pervades the Old Frenchman place, even by day, is amplified by the contrast between the brightness of the sunlight outside. With the onset of dusk, as the last remnants of light diminish, the potential of total darkness becomes tangible and with it the absence of any means of refuge or sanctuary. Ironically, the conventional notion of darkness providing protection and concealment is overturned, and Gothic associations of evil unleashed by night are initiated. Even the old blind man sitting out on the porch senses the lengthening shadows and moves his chair into the remains of the sunlight for warmth and security. As the light wanes, Temple also seems to undergo a transformation, or rather, incongruously, her essential ephemerality becomes more apparent, underlining the notion of her being defined by light, of her gaining her substance and her strength from it, so that without it she becomes as incorporeal as the shadows. Thus her fragility and vulnerability are amplified, serving a dramatic purpose of intensifying the sense of threat which seems to increase with the fading light.

> Temple leaned around the door, past his dim shape, her face wan as a small ghost in the refracted light from the dining room.... Between blinks Tommy saw Temple in the path, her body slender and motionless for a moment as though waiting for some laggard part to catch up. Then she was gone like a shadow around the corner of the house.... [H]e turned his head and looked down the hall just in time to see her flit across the darkness towards the kitchen [p. 47].

At the same time, the depiction of her here functions as an ironic echo of the vision of her at the beginning of the novel, also at night, having, as it were, undergone a similar transformation, as a "speeding silhouette," her "long legs blonde with running ... vanishing into the shadow beside the library wall" or simply as "a final squatting swirl of knickers or whatnot as she sprang into the car waiting there with engine running" (p. 22), a vision now punctuated by fear.

Manipulation of narrative visual perspective is also used to depersonalize. This serves to amplify the degree of Temple's physical, emotional and mental trauma following her rape and subsequent continued abuse by Popeye. This is powerfully dramatized by the depiction of Miss Reba as strangely disembodied, the emphasis placed on her physical presence, most particularly her voice, with the visual attention, which is Temple's, fixed permanently away from her face. That Miss Reba should be preceded by her two dogs on her first entrance immediately establishes her disembodiment in Temple's eyes. Once inside the room the visual focus remains on them and on the tankard in Miss Reba's hands as she

sits and talks to Temple, generating an aura of the grotesque and communicating Temple's alienation and revulsion.

> [The dogs came] climbing and sprawling on to the bed and into Miss
> Reba's lap with wheezy, flatulent sounds, billowing into the rich pneu-
> masis of her breast and tonguing along the metal tankard which she
> waved with one ringed hand as she talked [p. 100].

As Miss Reba begins to speak, the visual focus does not, as would be
expected, move to her face but stays with the tankard, closely following
the movements of her hands upon it.

> She drank beer, breathing thickly into the tankard, the other hand, ringed
> with yellow diamonds as large as gravel, lost among the lush billows of
> her breast [p. 100].

Temple's ability to dissociate herself from physical trauma is demonstrated in other previous instances and is dramatized cinematically. For
example, she sits "rigidly" and "quietly," as Gowan drives his car into a
tree, then as she is thrown from the car her perspective becomes more
acutely objective so that she only *feels* herself "flying through the air,"
her consciousness dominated by "a picture of two men peering from the
fringe of cane at the roadside" (p. 29). The notion of voyeurism is applied
even here, in a bizarre scenario of the victim watching the witnesses
watching the victim. Having confronted Popeye for the first time during a lift into town, she finds herself "moving towards the door with
Gowan's hand in the small of her back, her head reverted, her heels clat-
tering" (p. 37), and she adopts a similar visual perspective later as she
struggles to get away from Popeye in his car:

> When they passed beneath lights she could see him watching her as she
> struggled, tugging at his hand, whipping her head this way and that. ...
> One finger, ringed with a thick ring, held her lips apart, his fingertips
> digging into her cheek. With the other hand he whipped the car in and
> out of traffic, bearing down upon other cars until they slewed aside with
> brakes squealing, shooting recklessly across intersections [p. 163].

As in the scene with Miss Reba, the focus is again drawn to fingers,
this time Popeye's fingers clawing at her face. Cinematically this functions as a choker close-up as before, but now in slow motion, the frame,
as it were, completely filled as her face is filled with his fingers. Suddenly,

the perspective shifts to his other hand, and as it does so the narrative focus draws quickly back to reveal the context of the scene. The narrative pace correspondingly quickens, underpinned by the alliterative force of "whipped," "slewed," "shooting," "squealing," which dramatize the movement of the car. Once again the relationship between the two is voyeuristic — Temple watching Popeye watching her as they fight — although for different purposes: Popeye to increase the enjoyment of inflicting pain, Temple to divorce herself from Popeye's touch.

The novel's central theme of watching is distilled in the character of Tommy. Tommy's mental handicap grants him a simplicity, an innocence, a purity of vision. He is able to concentrate his attention on the smallest detail with mesmeric force and undistracted focus. It is significant that the pivotal scene of the novel — Temple's rape — is depicted through his eyes, Tommy voyeuristically watching from outside the window, like the boys watching Temple at the dance, fascinated, uncomprehending, yet here not in awe but in fear. Every move inside the room is described in deliberate detail as if some kind of precise choreography is being witnessed. Tommy's vision takes on a superhuman quality, demonstrating a capability afforded only to the camera in its ability to draw its focus to extreme proximity, to enlarge the smallest detail, to convey the subtle yet critical effects of light and shade. The climactic point of the scene is, however, denied the reader, since Tommy moves away from the window and, with him, the narrative focus. The narrative perspective as Tommy enters the bedroom with Popeye after the rape switches to Ruby, and the horror of the rape is communicated by Ruby's vision of Tommy's eyes. This not only dramatizes the gradual realization by Tommy that something despicable has occurred and communicates the level of trauma pervading the room, but also confirms to the reader that which has only been implied up until this point.

> Tommy's pale eyes began to glow faintly, like those of a cat. The woman could see them in the darkness when he crept into the room after Popeye, and while Popeye stood over the bed where Temple lay. They glowed suddenly out of the darkness at her, then they went away and she could hear him breathing beside her; again they glowed up at her with a quality furious and questioning and sad and went away again and he crept behind Popeye from the room [p. 56].

Again Tommy's eyes have an inhuman quality, their glow is both animal and mechanical, as if lit by some artificial or mystical energy. The mechanical quality of Tommy's vision is also transferred to Ruby, enabling her to focus on the glow of his eyes, which is made larger and more penetrating by the absence of any other light in the room. Ruby is, therefore, also implicated in the act of voyeurism which is initiated by the boys outside the dance hall and by Tommy at the bedroom window, marking a sinister prelude to Popeye's activities as disclosed later in the novel, the consequences of such voyeurism being to distance the witness from the subject, serving to absolve responsibility, to dissociate, to deny.

The preoccupation with watching and the treatment of perspective in the work of Hammett and Faulkner distinctly parallels Nabokov's manipulation of modes of perception in his Russian fiction, but notions of voyeurism and depthlessness were also to be central in the exposition of Humbert Humbert's experience in his major American novel, *Lolita*.

Fate, the "Double Bind" and the Femme Fatale: Formative Noir by Nabokov and Cain

While much of Nabokov's Russian work reflects the visual style of Soviet and German Expressionist film, it also displays a close affinity with American film noir. This is not merely by dint of a shared proximity to film noir's most overt and widely acknowledged cinematic influence but is also evident in terms of a similarity in tone and style, of theme and perspective. Silver and Ward's definition of film noir is based upon two primary elements; a distinctive visual style and a consistency of characterization.[31] They argue that the psychological dilemma of the noir protagonist is generated by a weakened moral awareness which gradually loses the battle against a strong urge to succumb to something he knows is likely to destroy him. While these characters are seen to embody "America's stylized vision of itself, a true cultural reflection of the mental dysfunction of a nation in uncertain transition,"[32] it is evident that "dysfunction" is also a prevalent quality of Nabokov's protagonists.

Nabokov's early work features characters who are, either in male terms, anti-heroes — alienated, estranged, solitary, even psychotic — or in female terms, *femmes fatales*— seductive, cold, manipulative and mercenary. They are individuals caught up in destructive, three-sided relationships which often involve a central criminal act and who become overwhelmed by an ensuing struggle for power and, ultimately, survival, driven by a compulsive obsession with an object — real or imaginary —

of desire. The protagonists of *The Eye* and *Despair*, for example, demon-strate precisely this compulsion for self-destruction, instigating situa-tions which lead not necessarily to total annihilation, but to a state of disintegration and marginalization.

As Alain Silver and Elizabeth Ward argue, alienation and obsession are primary motivators of the noir protagonist:

> Many, if not most, noir figures ... may seem more acutely despondent or alienated because they have been idealistic or romantic.... [I]t also seems that events must conspire to crush these positive indications.... This resignation to being annihilated by a relentless, deterministic abstraction is the only, bitter solace that the noir vision permits.[33]

Obsession replaces idealism and becomes a means of obliterating the reality of alienation, and it "erodes the sense of free will as it undermines the character's ability to make rational decisions."[34] Fatalism, therefore, is inextricably bound up in this psychological scenario and is dramatized in the "double bind," a situation in which protagonists are compelled to choose between two "equally bleak alternatives,"[35] a stalemate which serves only to deepen their impotence and frustration.

This dilemma is not confined to Nabokov's psychotic heroes, how-ever. A classic noir double bind also ensnares the feckless Franz in *King, Queen, Knave*. His weakness is tempered by greed, and in this he com-plements Martha perfectly, but he is not unique in his vulgarity and lack of moral integrity, for none of the novel's three protagonists displays any qualities which might command sympathy or respect. That the novel is devoid of either heroes or victims is significant in terms of noir, gener-ating the characteristic effect of alienation and aversion in the audience, and is reminiscent of the moral oblivion which pervades the work of James M. Cain and William Faulkner. The sardonic tone of the narra-tive voice, however, disguises the depravity of Nabokov's characters, and only brief insights are afforded which expose their true natures. The more dubious aspects of Franz's character, for example, are eclipsed both by his overriding ineffectual incompetence and by Martha's seductive power, yet he cannot be considered entirely as a victim.

> He might have passed, indeed, for a perfectly respectable, perfectly ordi-nary salesman, were it not for a blend of details that only a detective of genius might have discerned — a predatory angularity of nostril and cheekbone, a strange weakness about the mouth ... and those eyes, those

eyes, poorly disguised by glasses, restless eyes, tragic eyes, ruthless and helpless, of an impure greenish shade with inflamed blood vessels around the iris [p. 79].

That his eyes reveal the more telling yet otherwise undisclosed aspects of his character — restlessness, ruthlessness — parallels the emphasis which Hammett, Cain, Faulkner and Chandler place upon eyes as the only remaining means of honest communication in a corrupt world. Franz's glasses provide an expedient means of concealing what prove, ultimately, to be key personality traits, but it is also ironic that his eyes otherwise communicate nothing of significance, which is further compounded by the fact that no one makes any attempt to discern anything in them anyway.

That Franz's façade of innocence is essentially fraudulent is also confirmed by his readiness to be seduced by Martha and his response to the prospect of being a "kept" man. Franz is aware of the consequences if he and Martha fail in their murderous schemes, but while he is afraid of Dreyer, like the typical noir protagonist he cannot resist either his own or Martha's will, a helplessness which is openly acknowledged — "Franz no longer had a will of his own; the best he could do was to refract her will in his own way" (p. 161). By the time they are well under way with their plans, this feeble self-abandonment has transformed into a delight in the possibilities of danger:

> In those days ... young Franz was oblivious to the corrosive probity of his pleasant daydreams about Dreyer's dropping dead. He had plunged into a region of delirium, blithely and lightheartedly.... [T]here now lurked ... something strange — a little eerie and shameful at first, but already enthralling, already all-powerful. Whatever Martha said, however charmingly she smiled, Franz sensed an irresistible insinuation in her every word and glance [pp. 138–39].

Despite Franz's attempts to resist Martha's will, his concession to her and to fate is consistent with his personality, and his impotence is thus made more plausible. At the very beginning of the novel, before Franz encounters Martha on the train to Berlin, he finds himself sitting opposite a disfigured man, his repulsion compounded by the fear of some inevitable horror lurking within him.

> The shudder that had passed between Franz's shoulder blades now tapered to a strange sensation in his mouth. His tongue felt repulsively alive; his

palate nastily moist. His memory opened its gallery of waxworks, and he knew, he knew that there, at its far end somewhere a chamber of horrors awaited him [p. 3].

Franz's fear is irrational and inexplicable, yet it indicates a conscious awareness of the forces of fate which threaten to destroy him. Incongruously, the fact that these forces are contained within him allows him a degree of control which he does not have when confronted by an external force of destruction in Martha, a force truly to be reckoned with. That Franz is so concerned with the horrors within him that he is blind to their presence in the outside world accounts for his extreme gullibility. His subjugation by Martha is, however, distinct from Albinus's by Margot in that although both men are foolish and naive and delude themselves into believing that the prospect of realizing their romantic dreams lies in the form of a deceitful, self-seeking, amoral woman, Franz becomes complicit in Martha's murderous schemes, whereas Albinus is the sorry object of Margot's malicious plans.

Albinus's perception of and response to Margot is primarily visual, and it seems that her mirrors, which dominate their house, magnify his consciousness of her image and its unattainability.

> Now, the vision of the promised kiss filled him with such ecstasy that it seemed hardly possible it could be still further intensified. And yet beyond it, down a vista of mirrors, there was still to be reached the dim white form of her body [pp. 58–59].

This notion of endless reflection which serves at once to distance and ensnare is a key theme in film noir. Here it emphasizes the futile delusion that Albinus lives, whereas in *The Eye*, mirrors are employed to amplify and assist Smurov's paranoid fantasies to a degree where he revels in the notion of losing his identity in infinite reflections: Smurov's reference to mirrors is a metaphor for the myriad personalities he has and will continue to assume, whereas the profusion of mirrors in *King, Queen, Knave* do no more than offer a faithful image of the subject in reverse, providing a two-dimensional, flat, depthless reflection. This serves primarily as confirmation of the subject's physical presence, but it is inherently superficial, insubstantial. At the same time the mirrors seem to participate in the maintenance of a veneer of normality which conceals the prevalent activity of covert deception in the novel by granting the characters a means of ensuring flawless presentation.

The parallels between the typical noir scenario and the destructive triangles of manipulation and deceit in Nabokov's *King, Queen, Knave* and *Laughter in the Dark* are marked, and the notion of fate which dominates the fiction of Cain and in turn 1940s' film noir is also fundamental to the predicaments of the protagonists of *The Eye* and *King, Queen, Knave*. Smurov's submission to the workings of fate establishes his weakness — "my whole defenseless being invited calamity. One evening the invitation was accepted" (p. 18). His destiny is defined by an unexpected yet predetermined external event, the parallels with film scenarios being underlined by the manner in which he perceives this process — "It was then that a whole wall of my life crumbled, quite noiselessly, as on the silent screen" (pp. 20–21).

It is significant that Franz interprets his dilemma in terms of film, for it reflects the abiding preoccupation with cinema exhibited by his American counterparts. Like Myrtle Wilson or Margot, the only frame of reference by which Franz determines how he should act is provided by the movies. Film's highly stylized representation of phony myths offers him an alternative perspective, giving Martha's scheme a ludicrously fantastic aspect, and thus lessens the implications of his collaboration. Franz envisages Dreyer's murder as a scene from a gangster movie or a Western, and he is particularly careful to play out a faithful rendition down to the smallest irrelevant detail in a futile attempt to ensure his own protection.

In his translation, Nabokov emphasizes the cinematic aspect of Franz's imagined scenario by inserting the qualifying phrase "as they do in American movies":

> From its threshold he would fire half a dozen times in quick succession, as they do in American movies. For appearance's sake, before vanishing, he would take the dead shopkeeper's wallet [p. 179].

Fatalism is also key to the novel's scenario, but unlike Smurov's experience, it infects Martha's consciousness in such a way that she believes it to be working in her favor. Martha is a dissatisfied wife. She is married to a philandering husband who has openly enjoyed many affairs. By the time Franz appears on the scene, she is ready to take a lover and immediately recognizes Franz's potential. Although she knows that she will have to engineer their affair, she is confident that destiny is on her side:

"I'm an idiot," she said. "What's the matter? What's wrong with me? Why worry? It must happen sooner or later. It is inevitable" [p. 56].

As in the typical noir scenario, fate intervenes at critical moments, transforming coincidence into destiny. Martha interprets Dreyer's escape from a car crash not only as a sign from the fates, inspiring her plan to dispose of him, but also as a response to a premonition, as she idly blacks out Dreyer's name in her address book. Again, Nabokov emphasizes Martha's fatalism in his English translation by adding the notion of her interpreting this gesture as a "spell" which doesn't work (p. 128), a spell which she quickly converts into a "miracle" (p. 133). Martha's superstitions are confirmed, finally, by a further miracle, which occurs when they closely escape being surprised by Dreyer returning home early from a skiing holiday, an event that serves to finally sanction her mission as her rightful destiny.[36]

In terms of noir, Martha is an archetypal *femme fatale*, sister to Hammett's Brigid O'Shaughnessy and Cain's Phyllis Dietrichson (*Double Indemnity*), while prefiguring the arch screen temptresses Kathie Moffett (*Out of the Past*, 1947), Elsa Bannister (*The Lady from Shanghai*) and Norma Desmond (*Sunset Boulevard*, 1950). Her beauty and glamour have a coldness reminiscent of the "hard, statuesque surface beauty" of the noir heroine which Place and Peterson describe — the same seductive yet unattainable, alluring yet impenetrable qualities, evoking the noir scenario's characteristic atmosphere of "sinister foreboding." She has a chilling capacity for cruelty, displaying no remorse at the deaths of her chauffeur or her favorite film actor, and exhibits scornful delight in other people's suffering:

> The day before it had started to thaw, then the freeze had set in again. That morning a cripple walking in front of her had slipped on the bare ice. It was frightfully funny to see his wooden stump erect while he sprawled on his stupid back. Without opening her mouth, Martha broke into convulsive laughter. Franz thought she had uttered a sob and went to her side in confusion [p. 126].[37]

Martha is, in a sense, a nascent yet flawed *femme fatale*. She fails in her mission, and her death only proves the irony of her misguided fatalism and the folly of her greed. Margot, on the other hand, displays a greater self-sufficiency, a refined cunning and ambition more akin to the noir heroine. She is ruthlessly determined to achieve her destiny by any

Elsa Bannister (Rita Hayworth), the archetypal *femme fatale*: cold, ruth-less, ambitious. Here she looks down disdainfully at her butler, Sidney Broome (Ted de Corsia), who has just been shot by her husband's law part-ner, George Grisby, and is bleeding to death all over her kitchen floor. *The Lady from Shanghai* (Columbia, 1948).

available means. Margot is skilled at exploiting scenes of confrontation with Albinus, yet her malice takes on a new sadistic dimension after she meets Axel Rex. In one episode, she "[suggests] burning a hole in [Albinus's] palm with her cigarette" and, when she starts, Albinus does nothing to stop her — "though perspiring freely, he kept smiling like the little hero he was" (p. 133). Although this prefigures the humiliation to which Margot and Rex subject Albinus later on in the novel, this little scene establishes the lengths to which Albinus is prepared to go to pacify Margot and thus implicates him in his own eventual destruction.

Although a contemporary of Hammett, James M. Cain was not a crime writer in the tradition of *Black Mask*. Rather, his work has been described in terms of the "tough guy novel,"[38] fiction which centers around a criminal act from the perspective of the criminal. David Madden, in his book on Cain, describes the relationship between film and the tough guy novel thus:

> Essential to tough movies and novels is speed of impact. The short tough novel, like a movie, may be experienced in one sitting; like the movies, tough novels are particularly expressive products of our fast-moving culture. As Edmund Wilson has pointed out, many serious novelists who do not write for the movies have been influenced by their pace, themes, characters, tone and attitudes.[39]

The Postman Always Rings Twice (1934) is perhaps Cain's most cinematic novel in its deployment of the techniques of film and its manipulation of themes of illusion and delusion. As in Nabokov's *The Eye* and *Despair*, the narrative of Cain's central protagonist, Frank Chambers, has the quality of a confessional monologue, informal and conversational, generating a strong sense of character and instantly establishing a relationship of familiarity and intimacy with the reader. This device was to be transcribed directly to the screen, Cain's first-person narratives defining the character of the film noir "voice-over," which in turn became a predominant feature of noir, exemplified by Preminger's *Laura* (1944), Vidor's *Gilda* (1946), Welles's *Lady from Shanghai* and Wilder's *Sunset Boulevard*. Narration is sparse, serving only to introduce or locate a scene, the plot being driven predominantly by dialogue. Action is described precisely and succinctly, while allowing for the resonance of occasional specific, significant details which create a subtext of visual motifs that underpin the action and complement the novel's thematic ideas. As David Madden argues, "*The Postman* ... satisfies 'movie values,' partly because it was written like a movie 'continuity.' Its sixteen chapters are comprised of scenes. Within these scenes, short units — sometimes only eight or ten lines — approximate camera shots."[40]

The reader's attention is guided, focused, shifted, manipulated; the action is shown, as it were, to a passive audience, and the emphasis is placed heavily on visual communication, so that the reader develops an awareness of the narrative ramifications in the detail and geography of every scene.

The central criminal act of the story is Papadakis's murder, and yet the novel is preoccupied primarily with the relationship between Frank Chambers and Cora, Papadakis's wife, Cora being the principal subject of visual attention. Alienation is generated here not by narrative neutrality, but rather by the emotive force of Frank's subjective perspective. Unrestrained sexual energy overwhelms the narrative, driven by Frank's response to Cora's appearance, which defines his conception of her character. At the same time, this focus on the surface of things, the dependence upon appearance to communicate an inner, otherwise undisclosed essence is key to film. Frank presents his story in purely cinematic terms, exploiting the two principal dramatic elements of film — vision and dialogue — to offer an essentially autocratic, two-dimensional, ultimately limited portrayal of events. It could be argued that Cain is merely attempting to generate a sense of authenticity by having Frank present the story in his own terms rather than granting him a more literary narrative capability. Madden, however, argues that Frank's simplicity of presentation conceals a far more complex personality:

> An aura of deceit and fear hangs over most Cain novels. His characters are afraid, partly because they cannot separate reality from illusion. One trap is their sense ... of being the creator and controller of a little world of their own which thus appears real and knowable. But a hovering atmosphere of fear, deception and treachery produces a cynicism in Cain's characters [pp. 97–98].

Frank's subjective, solipsistic perspective fuels his suspicion and distrust of the world and particularly, paradoxically, of Cora, the woman he supposedly loves. It is ironic, but also appropriate, that within this world of treachery and deceit he chooses an illusory and insubstantial medium to depict it. Frank's choice is fundamentally flawed, however. Driven by an acute yet suppressed awareness of his inadequacy, Frank attempts to gain control where he has none, and this culminates in his relationship with Cora. The response Cora provokes in him is both corrupting and destructive, and yet its believed reliability proves ultimately to be a delusion. Cynicism affords no protection; rather it promotes Frank's passivity, which in turn encourages him to pursue the illusion, no matter what the consequences.

Cora's first entrance in the novel establishes Frank's solipsistic perspective. He is talking with Papadakis when she enters the room, silently, unobtrusively, yet Frank interrupts his conversation with Papadakis to report, "Then I saw her,"[41] causing an abrupt shift in narrative focus which is further emphasized by the contrast of this curt statement with the more fluid, relaxed dialogue preceding it. As he sees her, the reader sees her, an effect reminiscent of a "jump" cut[42] which focuses full visual attention on Cora, instantly communicating her impact on Frank such that Papadakis and their conversation are instantly forgotten.

This is a significant moment in terms of Frank's narrative authority and his need to maintain control, for Cora's effect upon him is to cause him to revoke it utterly. This then establishes the nature of their relationship at the outset and predestines its outcome, for it is a relationship essentially founded on conflict. It is interesting that Frank's attempts to gain control are manifested in attempts to control or dominate Cora, and in such scenes he demonstrates an ability to manipulate circumstances to his advantage, as a film director manipulates the action on a set and the audience's vision of it. Frank displays a cool composure and a sense of purpose when he speaks to Cora for the first time — "I shot it right close to her ear, almost in a whisper" (p. 7). It is as if he knows exactly the effect of this action upon her and calculatedly exploits his self-assurance in a way which betrays an ability to perform, the movement being played out like a screen direction. The visual effect of this provocative gesture is reminiscent of a choker close-up, the focus pulled tight on his lips and her ear, establishing an immediate sense of illicit physical intimacy and collusion between them. Soon after this, Frank approaches Cora again. He seems to set the scene, and everything in it serves to aid and reflect his purpose.

> Soon as he was gone I locked the front door. I picked up a plate that a guy had left, and went on back in the kitchen with it. She was there.
> "Here's a plate that was out there."
> "Oh, thanks."
> I set it down. The fork was rattling like a tambourine [pp. 9–10].

Frank's tension and anticipation are communicated through the sound of the rattling fork, which also serves to determine the significance of the plate, which has held the visual focus since the scene's opening. Frank's anxiety is further communicated in the next phase of the scene, by a combined aural and visual echo of the rattling fork in a rattling door.

> Somebody was out front, rattling the door. "Sounds like somebody try-ing to get in."
> "Is the door locked, Frank?"
> "I must have locked it."
> She looked at me, and got pale. She went to the swinging door, and peeped through. Then she went into the lunchroom, but in a minute she was back [p. 10].

The irony of Frank's deception is underlined by the repetition of the notion of the locked door in their dialogue, which also generates a sense of entrapment, enclosure and concealment. Although it seems that Frank is not in control of the situation, the premeditated act of locking the café door suggests incontestably that he is, which exposes his apparent nervousness as a fraud.

The central theme of irrevocable destiny in Cain's novel is played out to its ultimate conclusion in the car accident, in which Cora is killed. The impact of the scene is delayed, presented from Frank's subjective point of view, having the effect of dramatizing the full horror of the crash.

> When I came out of it I was wedged down beside the wheel, with my back to the front of the car, but I began to moan from the awfulness of what I heard. It was like rain on a tin roof, but that wasn't it. It was her blood, pouring down on the bonnet, where she went through the wind-shield. Horns were blowing, and people were jumping out of cars and running to her [p. 82].

The image of Frank wedged down inside the car is depicted very specifically, giving the reader a clear vision of the geography of the scene. At the same time, the picture excludes everything and everyone else, magnifying Frank's visual and physical incapacity. The sensory focus is transferred to sound, denying the audience any visual aspect on the scene, so that its full horror is conveyed aurally. At the same time this is com-pounded by the irony of Frank's confusing blood with water, which is amplified by the implications of meaning associated with these two antithetical substances. The reader shares Frank's suspicion that it is not rain pounding on the car's bonnet because of the emphasis on the unnaturalness of the sound, its "awfulness." Once Frank realizes what is happening, the focus does not return to him but remains on the vision of Cora's blood pouring over the car; the shift from sound to vision is triggered by the sound of car horns, which takes Frank's attention away from the inside of the car to the scene outside, and momentarily, the visual perspective becomes detached from his subjective experience and sweeps out and away from the car like a camera on a crane, panning over the full panorama of the scene. The effect of this very cinematic device is not only to grant the reader a privileged perspective on the scene, but also to dramatize the emotional impact upon Frank of the suddenness and violence of Cora's death, the shock creating this instant of objective detachment in the narrative, this momentary disembodiment.

In *Laughter in the Dark* Nabokov manipulates perspective in a similar way to generate suspense. The novel's closing scene is also distinctly noir in character and is depicted explicitly as a cinematic sequence:

> Stage-directions for last silent scene: door — wide open. Table — thrust away from it. Carpet — bulging up at table foot in a frozen wave. Chair — lying close by dead body of man in a purplish brown suit and felt slippers. Automatic pistol not visible. It is under him. Cabinet where the miniatures had been — empty. On the other (small) table ... lies a woman's glove, black outside, white inside. By the striped sofa stands a smart little trunk, with a colored label still adhering to it: "Rouginard, Hôtel Britannia."
>
> The door leading from the hall to the landing is wide open, too [p. 292].

Although apparently visualized as a stage set, the implicit cinematic quality of the scene's presentation overrides its stated theatricality. The narrative perspective has the abrupt and merciless quality of the camera eye as it focuses on each aspect of the scene, dispassionately cataloguing, in intimate yet depthless close-up, a sequence of equally significant and inconsequential details in a cyclical motion from a fixed point in the room, beginning and ending at the open door. Not only does this generate suspense, but it also undermines the impact of the vision of the dead man, who, significantly, remains unidentified (although the reader knows it to be Albinus), indicating that he is not the primary focal object, but that there is some other, more important activity occurring else-

The aftermath of violence. Joe Gillis's body is dragged from Norma Desmond's pool. *Sunset Boulevard* (Paramount, 1950).

where, beyond the visual dimensions of the scene, suggested by the concluding image of the door opened onto the landing. The scene also anticipates the visual dynamics of film noir in its depiction of the aftermath of violence — reminiscent of such seminal sequences as the slow tracking shot across Walter Neff's desk that opens *Double Indemnity*, or the vision of Joe Gillis floating face down in Norma Desmond's swimming pool.

Definitive Noir Motifs in the Work of Hammett, Faulkner and Cain

A legacy of the silent era, the visual motif offered an economical means of communicating information more succinctly and directly than any dialogue. In Nabokov's early work they function both as pivotal narrative devices and as an eloquent means of defining, identifying and developing character. Noir filmmakers combined visual motifs with their deployment of acute camera angles, choker close-ups, obliquity, and extremes of light and shade to generate the aura of irrevocable destiny fundamental to the noir scenario. In film noir, a mundane object could take on considerable and significant meaning according to its presentation in the visual narrative, perhaps the most famous example of this being the glass ball containing a snowstorm which appears at key moments in Welles's *Citizen Kane* (1941).[43] Another frequently deployed motif is the cigarette, used to draw attention to or away from a particular character or cathartic moment, to create a dramatic pause or to magnify tension before the conclusion of a murder or a seduction. Visual motifs can also be contained in a small physical detail, for example, a scar, or in the case of Hammett's Sam Spade, the figure "v," which characterizes his face.

In Hammett's *Maltese Falcon*, appearances are presented as both a reliable and deceptive means of communicating character. Spade's complexity, the paradoxes innate in his character, are expressed in the physiognomy of his face. His looks are described in detail in the very opening paragraph of the novel, a description emphatic in its implications, although his "satanic" quality is balanced out by, as the reader discovers, an essential goodness, a sense of unimpeachable honor and a determination to be true, maybe not to others, but at least always to himself.

> Samuel Spade's jaw was long and bony, his chin a jutting v under the more flexible v of his mouth. His nostrils curved back to make another, smaller, v. His yellow-gray eyes were horizontal. The v *motif* was picked up again by thickish brows rising outward from twin creases above a hooked nose, and his pale brown hair grew down — from high flat temples — in a point on his forehead. He looked rather pleasantly like a blond satan [p. 3].

The "v" motif is picked up and repeated throughout the text, and there are at least eight other instances where it appears[44] as a reminder of the less appealing side of his nature, compounding the shifting status of the central narrative stance while emphasizing the notion of Spade's enduring solitariness. Hammett employs this declared motif as an economic and evocative visual device which serves both to reinforce the cinematic quality of the narrative and to extend the notion of vision as an unreliable mode of perception. In turn, Spade is almost taken in by Brigid's innocent looks, while the notion of visual deception is transferred to the falcon statuette, which turns out to be a convincing fake. The ramifications of this are intriguing, suggesting that the central cinematic perspective of the narrative is, after all, inherently flawed and that such an emphasis on visual perception can offer only ambiguity and equivocation. In a sense, therefore, *The Maltese Falcon* reproduces not only the themes and techniques of film, but also the dynamic of illusion inherent in the cinematic experience.

As in *The Maltese Falcon*, Cain deploys visual motifs to signify a particular character, and here, like the "v" of Sam Spade's face, it is Cora's mouth which becomes a focal point. On a superficial level, this motif can be interpreted as the symbol of Frank's perception of her, the mouth being a highly erotic, sensual part of the body, and at the same time acutely sensitive, expressive and vulnerable.

The focus on Cora's mouth as an image primarily of promiscuity and sexual power is an example of Frank's subjective appropriation of a perception of her which is essentially inaccurate, confirmed by the way in which this perception changes, as the narrative progresses, in direct relation to his changing attitude toward her. From the novel's outset, Frank's depiction of Cora's mouth is indicative of his perception of her as an object of blame. His response to her from the outset has been only negative and destructive. Her mere presence causes him to abandon his autonomy, his judgment, his independence and, worst of all, to provoke him to acts of extreme violence:

> Except for the shape, she really wasn't any raving beauty, but she had a sulky look to her, and her lips stuck out in a way that made me want to mash them in for her [p. 6].

Her lips become an emblem of their passion, of physical possession and intimacy; bitten, swollen, sore, tender, they epitomize the violence and antagonism that characterize their relationship:

> I bit her. I sunk my teeth into her lips so deep I could feel the blood spurt into my mouth.... Her mouth was all swelled up where I had bit it.... I went over and looked at [it]. The swelling was all gone, but you could still see the toothmarks, little blue creases on both lips. I touched them with my fingers. They were soft and damp. I kissed them, but not hard. They were little soft kisses. I had never thought about them before [pp. 10–11].

At the same time, Cora's mouth becomes expressive of the impact of events upon her. By the time they get to court, her sulky pout has changed to a nervous twitch, and while this communicates her inner state, it also suggests that Frank's perception of her has changed. There is no mention of her lips, the focus of her eroticism, but only of her mouth, and there is a concern expressed in Frank's attention and an empathy for her suffering:

> I kept trying to see Cora's face. But all I could get of it was the corner of her mouth. It kept twitching, like somebody was jabbing a needle into it about once every second [p. 52].

This vision of Cora's mouth is seen from a considerable distance, yet is presented in extreme close-up, offering a revelation of detail beyond the scope of normal vision. As if to emphasize the minuteness of the image, Frank uses a still more intimate one, that of the needle jabbing the corner of Cora's mouth, an appropriately silent and discreet torture. This combination of almost imperceptible details, however, serves to magnify them adversely, both in terms of meaning and visual impact. From Frank's perspective, the initial implication of this image is to establish Cora's sudden isolation, now standing accused of murder, but more significantly, the rift in their relationship, which is confirmed in the following scene. Once again, the detail most revealing of Cora's true feelings is her mouth, and here it confirms her anger.

> "Flim-flammed! I'll say I was. You and that lawyer. You fixed it up all right. You fixed it up so I tried to kill you too." ...
> I tried to talk to her, but it wasn't any use. When she got so that even her lips were white, under the lipstick, the door opened and Katz came in [p. 53].

After cross and double cross, this breach between them continues to widen, to a point at the end of the novel when even though they are finally acquitted and reunited, it is evident that their relationship is irrevocably damaged. Cora has developed a toughness which surpasses even Frank's, demonstrated in the scene with the blackmailer, Kennedy, again expressed by the vision of her mouth:

> She came back there with us, with the gun.
> "If I give you the sign, he gets it."
> She leaned back and an awful smile flickered around the corner of her mouth. I think that smile scared Kennedy worse than anything I had done [p. 74].

In Faulkner's *Sanctuary*, the two most eloquent motifs are cigarettes and matches, two essentially inconsequential objects which, with every new appearance, develop associations of power, control, subjugation, and terror.

Popeye is never seen without a cigarette; he is always about to light one, is lighting or idly smoking one. The simple gesture of striking a match and lighting a cigarette becomes emblematic of his character and is an eloquent, dramatic visual device which communicates Popeye's cold indifference, his sly, ominous presence.

> Popeye stood in the door. His hat was slanted across his face. He took a cigarette from his pocket, without producing the pack, and pinched and fretted it and put it in his mouth and snapped a match on his thumbnail.... In the door Popeye watched her, the cigarette curling across his face [pp. 8–9].

Popeye's cigarettes also punctuate the key dramatic scenes of the novel. At moments of intense suspense, horror or despair, the cigarettes appear, providing an obtusely elegiac accompaniment to the scene, creating a dramatic pause, a moment of poise and stillness in acute contrast to the violence which has already occurred or is about to take place. The dramatic function of Popeye's smoking also suggests a ritualistic significance which is played out in the novel's final scenes, when Popeye is in jail, awaiting execution for a crime he did not commit. He smokes ceaselessly, methodically placing the spent cigarette butts in neat rows on the floor of his cell, the intensity of his absorption in this inane activity indicating his utter indifference to his fate.

Matches possess equal dramatic potential. The quick movement of striking a match is deployed as a means of shifting narrative attention, and the lingering focus on a dying flame creates a momentary pause, generating dramatic tension. Faulkner uses a match as a means of introducing Tommy's visual perspective:

> Popeye came out the door. He lit a cigarette. Tommy watched his face flare out between his hands, his cheeks sucking; he followed with his eyes the small comet of the match into the weeds [p. 49].

At the same time, the pause in the action which this ordinarily inconsequential gesture creates serves to discreetly assert, or rather, reassert Popeye's inexplicable authority and to establish Tommy's equally inexplicable submission to it. As in film noir, these visual motifs never become reduced to static symbols, however. Each time they appear they possess new connotations, and the dimensions of their significance grow. Temple's final vision of Popeye is one which both reasserts the by now familiar image of him but also offers a new perspective. It is, also, highly cinematic:

On the run. Harry Fabian (Richard Widmark) anxiously lights a cigarette. *Night and the City* (20th Century–Fox, 1950).

> Where the drive joined the lane that led to the highroad a long touring car was parked. When they passed it Temple saw, leaning to a cupped match, Popeye's delicate hooked profile beneath the slanted hat as he lit the cigarette. The match flipped outward like a dying star in miniature, sucked with the profile into the darkness by the rush of their passing [p. 170].

In a novel devoid of closure this is the sole vision which offers any potential for resolution. In the repetition of the cigarette motif it echoes Temple's initial encounters with Popeye at Goodwin's house. It also echoes the vision, as seen through Ruby's eyes, of Temple and Popeye in his car leaving for Memphis, and of Popeye's vigils, watching Miss Reba's brothel from his car parked in the street outside. The discarded match also echoes what Tommy witnesses on the evening of the rape, and Popeye is seen drawing on his cigarette with the same sucking in of his cheeks. Initially therefore, the image seems to offer nothing new, yet these same actions for the first time take on some meaning, for the discarded match is somehow indicative of Temple's liberation, of Popeye's capitulation, while at the same time suggesting that in spite of this, Temple, like the match, is spent, used up. There is also a quality of beauty in this vision which seems inappropriate considering the extent of Popeye's depravity and perverse cruelty. The untypical adjective in the passage, "delicate," associated more with Temple, is here attributed to Popeye for the first time to imply, incongruously, a kind of bizarre union or at least an element of sympathy. Conversely, this could denote the extent of Temple's assumption by Popeye that he now possesses the most precious and fragile elements of her being, which she can never regain. This is suggested by the image of the discarded match, "a dying star in miniature," which is emblematic of her soul, destroyed finally and utterly along with the image of Popeye's "delicate" profile in a kind of conspiratorial act of violence by the rush of the passing car in which she is a passenger.

Dark Illumination: The Origins of Noir Lighting in The Big Sleep and the Work of Cain, Faulkner and Nabokov

In terms of its implications for plot and characterization, Raymond Chandler's use of light, or rather, lighting in *The Big Sleep* (1939) was unique for its time, but it also provided the visual style that came to epitomize 1940s' American film noir. Chandler's manipulation of light in this novel is employed nowhere else in his fiction to such a consistent degree, to a point where it is key in evoking not only the novel's mood, as it is in film, but also its thematics.

The central theme of *The Big Sleep* is obscurity — actual, physical, psychological, emotional — and thus an emphasis is placed on light as the sole means of overcoming it. Considerable attention is paid to light in all its forms, artificial and natural, and its placing and effect, yet paradoxically, this focus upon light only serves correspondingly to sustain and sometimes even increase the depth of the novel's darkness.

Light plays an important role in Marlowe's detective work, much of which takes place at night, and the practical necessity for illumination takes on thematic implications, suggesting that in this mode of almost constant obscurity, light is paramount in the processes of visual and cognitive apprehension. The turning on and off of lamps and light switches becomes a dramatic device generating impact and contrast, the often uneven quality of artificial light serving to magnify the spectacle of a scene and the depth of the surrounding darkness, while at the same time enhancing mood, tension and suspense.

Light or lighting is overtly presented as a carefully conceived and orchestrated element of the narrative and is more cinematic than theatrical in its fluidity and variety and the speed and force of its dramatic and

physical intimacy, serving to obliterate utterly all sense of a world other than that inside the darkened cab.

> The darkness inside the taxi slid and swayed as quarters and halves and whole squares of ashen light passed from window to window across it. Margot was sitting so near that [Albinus] felt the blissful warmth of her body [p. 57].

The movement of light inside the taxi suggests that its forward motion has been somehow arrested, that it is standing still in a void of time, which both amplifies the erotic quality of Albinus's experience but also evokes a sense of serenity. This particular effect is echoed in *Sanctuary* in the scene of the fight in Popeye's car but is utilized for a very different purpose. The reader is afforded glimpses of the action as the moving car is lit intermittently by streetlamps. The sense of visual deprivation is dramatized by the focus on Popeye's fingers in Temple's face, yet the horrifying vision of Popeye's eyes upon her is amplified by their sudden and brief illumination. This contrast of light and dark, of extremes of visual sensation, from utter deprivation to almost excessive saturation is used throughout Faulkner's narrative but is particularly associated with Temple and Popeye, employed to depict Temple's quick, ephemeral delicacy and the oblique, opaque, depthless, enigmatic threat of Popeye, at the same time rendering them irrevocably bound.

Extremes of light are also used for dramatic effect by Cain in *The Postman Always Rings Twice*, particularly, for example, in a scene in which Frank finds himself alone in the kitchen in the middle of the night, standing in total darkness, listening to Papadakis and Cora arguing. Light is crucial to the scene's impact. The sudden transition from total visual deprivation to complete visual saturation is compounded by the inverted effect of sound, which is amplified in darkness and reduced in the light.

> I slipped into the kitchen, and stood there listening. But I couldn't hear anything.... [A]ll I could get was the sound of my own heart, going bump-bump, bump-bump, bump-bump.... I thought that was a funny way for my heart to sound, and then all of a sudden I knew there was two hearts in that kitchen....
> I snapped on the light.
> She was standing there, in a red kimono, as pale as milk, staring at me, with a long thin knife in her hand.... When she spoke it was in a whisper that sounded like a snake licking its tongue in and out [p. 28].

Light is also deployed by Nabokov's protagonists to assert control. Franz sees Martha's will in terms of a powerful light — "Under the long ray of her gaze he gave way as usual" (p. 124) — persistent, blinding, penetrating, paralyzing, like an enormous, relentless studio spotlight which exposes his every flinch. Dreyer too seems to be conscious of the power afforded by the manipulation of light. Franz's first visit to Dreyer's department store takes place at night, and the scene is lit by a flashlight and a solitary light bulb, which serve to deepen the surrounding darkness, to distort the scale and layout of the store's interior, evoking an ominous, surreal atmosphere. Dreyer's flashlight picks out disparate items, and they take on a curious, grotesque significance, their visual impact disproportionately exaggerated by its beam:

> Dreyer led Franz over a waste of dark carpeting into the shadowy depths of the hall. He flung off in passing the canvas of a small table and trained his light on cuff links sparkling like eyes on their blue velvet cushion. A little further with playful nonchalance he tipped off its stand a huge beach ball which rolled soundlessly away into the dark [p. 73].

The lighting of the scene also enhances its dramatic significance. Dreyer exploits this opportunity to show off to his nephew, to demonstrate his omniscient power, his supremacy within this little empire, and his control and authority are asserted in the manner in which he manipulates light and darkness.

Again, such a calculated manipulation of light is demonstrated by Goodwin in *Sanctuary*. Using one of the novel's principal motifs, a match, Goodwin deploys this otherwise unremarkable source of light to maximum dramatic effect, to communicate, silently yet unequivocally, his dominant position.

In order to dramatically enhance the visual experience of darkness in this episode, Faulkner is very specific about which parts of the house are lit. There is light only in the kitchen, the dining room and the back bedroom where Temple is to sleep, and then it is only dim lamplight. When Goodwin finds Temple in the kitchen she is crouching in pitch blackness, consequently serving to magnify the impact of the light of the match that he strikes to see her with. The match provides instant but temporary light, lasting only until the flame "reached his fingers" (p. 38) but is sufficient both for him to see her and to ensure that she knows that she has been seen, while establishing that he, Goodwin, has control of the facilities of sight and that at any time he can deny them to her, thus asserting his power and confirming her subjugation.

The visual effect of contrasts of light and dark also serve, as they do in film noir, to generate a sense of mystery, of portent. In "Details of a Sunset," the street takes on a "mirrorlike murk," but light also carries the hint of other worlds, and the eerie beauty of the night illuminated by indeterminate light is suggestive of this:

> The last streetcar was disappearing in the mirrorlike murk of the street and, along the wire above it, a spark of Bengal light, crackling and quivering, sped into the distance like a blue star.... The spark went out. The roofs glistened in the moonlight, silvery angles broken by oblique black cracks [p. 79].

This notion of light's ability to transform is central to the metaphysical dimensions of Nabokov's work. Its distinctly cinematic effect and quality grant it a dramatic immediacy, but at the same time, as a medium containing its own physical and metaphysical aspects, it complements and extends themes and concepts already extant in the fiction. Even in the most incidental of scenes, Nabokov's deployment of a cinematic perspective and cinematic lighting has a noticeable effect.

The affinities with the work of Americans displayed in Nabokov's Russian fiction is evident not merely through his adoption of prevalent cinematic modes, but also in a darkness of vision, tempered by a sardonic yet equally black humor. That this stance was more than mere experiment is confirmed by Nabokov's first "American" novel, *Lolita*, which conspicuously assimilates and deploys the details, concerns and character of immediate postwar American culture and society and most particularly film. In *Lolita*, Nabokov extends his treatment of cinematics to combine elements of not only American noir (as generally acknowledged by critics)[47] but also another contemporary film genre, "screwball" comedy, as reflective of the novel's dominant preoccupation: the consequences — dramatic, thematic, perceptual — of juxtaposing two antithetical, conflicting entities, namely Europe and America, in the guise of Humbert Humbert and Lolita respectively.

Nevertheless, *Lolita* was not the first of Nabokov's new English fiction to display a deliberate and cohesive treatment of cinematics. Of the first works published after his arrival in the United States in 1940, "The Assistant Producer" (1943), *Bend Sinister* (1947), and his autobiography, *Conclusive Evidence* (1951), written in serial form between 1947 and 1950 and revised in 1967 as *Speak, Memory*, demonstrate various aspects of Nabokov's cinematically inspired imagination but, more significantly, suggest that Nabokov was developing his own thesis of cinematics, establishing film as the means by which he explored and evolved notions of time, memory and perception, concepts which were to feature together for the first time in *Lolita*.

Five

Images of Terror and Desire: *Lolita* and the American Cinematic Experience, 1939–1952

Nabokov arrived in America in May 1940. Over the next ten years he published his first two English novels, *The Real Life of Sebastian Knight* (1941) and *Bend Sinister* (1947); a volume of short stories (*Nine Stories*, 1947), which included "The Assistant Producer" and "Time and Ebb," a volume on Gogol (1944); and verse translations of Pushkin, Lermontov and Tiutchev. By the end of the decade he had completed his serialized autobiography, *Conclusive Evidence*, and begun work on *Lolita*. During his first years in the States Nabokov also pursued the other career he had planned for himself before leaving Europe — that of a university lecturer. In 1941 he began teaching at Wellesley College, combining this with lepidopteral studies at Harvard's Museum of Comparative Zoology, where in 1942 he became a research fellow. On vacations he toured America as a visiting lecturer, using these trips as an opportunity to hunt for new species of butterfly. In 1947 he took up a position at Cornell, where he stayed until 1959.[1]

Nabokov once described himself as being "as American as April in Arizona."[2] America, Nabokov claimed, was the "only country where [he felt] mentally and emotionally at home."[3] One of the key figures responsible for developing this feeling was, undoubtedly, Edmund Wilson, with whom Nabokov enjoyed a protracted, albeit "unbalanced"[4] friendship for over twenty years. They met within months of Nabokov's arrival in the States, and, as Simon Karlinsky notes, Wilson "became something of an unpaid literary agent and adviser for Nabokov [and] was behind every important literary outlet that Nabokov was to find in his early years in America."[5] Wilson played a central role in facilitating Nabokov's engagement with the American literary scene, at the same time introducing him to the work of various key figures, including Henry James, William Faulkner and Delmore Schwartz, whose story, "In Dreams Begin Responsibilities" (1938) Nabokov was to cite as one of his favorites.[6]

That Nabokov gives a specific reason for so liking Schwartz's story is significant for what it reveals about his own artistic priorities. In a piece written in 1972 for the *Saturday Review*, Nabokov describes the story as a "[miraculous blend of] an old cinema film with a personal past."[7] The extent of Nabokov's own fascination with the creative possibilities of combining two such apparently disparate elements — memory and film — is implied by the notion of the process as "miraculous," and yet Nabokov's own treatment of these elements in his fiction establishes this process as integral to his art and thus more a matter of design than of either accident or mere experiment.

Memory as Film: "In Dreams Begin Responsibilities"

Schwartz's story serves both as a reflection of the impact of cinema on prewar American consciousness, in the tradition of Fitzgerald or Dos Passos, and a premonition of the changing aspect of the cinematic experience, signaled, more emphatically, by Nathanael West's apocalyptic Hollywood novel, *The Day of the Locust* (1939). Both works signify an increasing intensity in the level of engagement with film, and as Hollywood's fantasy world became ever more potent and appealing, so the desire for it to dispel mundane reality acquired a greater urgency, a desire which, according to West's perspective, could only generate frustration, anger, and, ultimately, violence and destruction. While Schwartz's story takes a more individualistic approach and is less overtly cataclysmic, it nevertheless communicates the power of cinema to overwhelm the imagination and provoke extreme perceptual crises.

> I am anonymous, and I have forgotten myself. It is always so when one goes to the movies, it is, as they say, a drug.[8]

In a dream Schwartz's protagonist goes to the movies to escape, to "forget himself" like thousands of other movie-going Americans. The story is dramatized cinematically to generate a sense of transient detachment which renders both the protagonist's dream state and the experience of movie-going:

> I feel as if I were in a motion-picture theater, the long arm of light crossing the darkness and spinning, my eyes fixed on the screen [p. 1].

He finds, however, that the film being shown is the story of his parents' life before he was born, and rather than being able to lose himself in the images on the flickering screen, he is confronted by a sequence of scenes which force him not only to witness events that he wishes had never taken place because he knows too well the future pain they have caused, but at the same time to endure the humiliation of having his very private, "personal" past reduced to nothing more than an entertaining diversion for the general public. As the film progresses, Schwartz's protagonist becomes increasingly panicked. He shouts at the screen in a desperate and futile attempt to command the events of the past which he knows full well are beyond his control, events that have already been captured for eternity and fixed in a precious and closed medium.

> I in my seat am shocked more than can ever be said, for I feel as if I were walking a tight-rope a hundred feet over a circus-audience and suddenly the rope is showing signs of breaking, and I get up from my seat and begin to shout once more the first words I can think of to communicate my terrible fear ... "What are they doing? Don't they know what they are doing?" [p. 8].

His frustration is mirrored by only one of the characters in the film, a photographer who is seen framing stills of his parents as a recently engaged couple:

> The photographer charms me. I approve of him with all my heart, for I know just how he feels, ... as he criticizes each revised pose according to some unknown idea of rightness [p. 7].

Being forced to revoke an "idea of rightness," whatever that may be, lies at the crux of the story. The dream is part of a process of letting go, and the empathy Schwartz's protagonist feels with the photographer has a self-effacing quality, as if he already realizes the folly of trying to assert a level of control in life that can be achieved only in art. This notion of futility is also extended into the screening of the film itself, in its jumps and flutters, and to the act of watching, as Schwartz's protagonist has to leave the auditorium twice in fits of panic. The photographer too seems to be thwarted in his attempt to control the scene:

> Sighing unhappily, [he] goes back under his black covering, holds out his hand, says: "One, two, three, Now!," and the picture is taken, with my father's smile turned to a grimace and my mother's bright and false [p. 7].

The dream is essentially an act of voyeurism. The scenes lie beyond the perimeters of the protagonist's personal memory, having occurred before he was born, and yet these privileged visions serve not to enlighten or reassure him, but to cause him greater pain and anguish.[9]

Yet its protagonist is, as it were, caught out by his conceit, for, ironically, the realization that what he witnesses is not exclusively his, that his "personal past" is being relinquished to the handful of strangers he sits among, reinforces his sense of alienation from not only the film itself, but also the people that it features, those who are responsible for his very existence.

Schwartz's story is significant not only as a reflection of cinema's role in defining and informing the consciousness of late–1930s' America, but also in its strong parallels with Nabokov's own use of cinematics in his fiction. The conflict within Schwartz's story between the autonomous authority of film and the scope it offers for imaginative expression is particularly significant when considered in terms of Humbert Humbert's struggle to maintain artistic control in *Lolita*.

Lolita: *Nabokov's Hollywood Novel*

Nabokov began work on *Lolita* in 1948, finally completing the novel in December 1953. It is set within a specific time frame, and the American part takes place between 1946 and 1952. In creating his child heroine, it was necessary for Nabokov to acquaint himself with every defining aspect of her world, a world which, in contemporary postwar America, was dominated by Hollywood. Film infuses Humbert Humbert's narrative. It indicates the level of his self-consciousness and is the medium by which his present and past realities are perceived and his fantasies realized. In spite of this, however, the precise extent of Nabokov's knowledge of contemporary American cinema is almost impossible to ascertain. In an interview with Alfred Appel in 1970, Nabokov cites scenes from films by the Marx Brothers and Laurel and Hardy, mentioning also Charlie Chaplin, Buster Keaton and Harold Lloyd as among his favorite slapstick comedians.[10] There are also specific films cited in Appel's volume, *Nabokov's Dark Cinema*, including Siodmak's *Killers*, and Ernst Lubitsch's 1939 comedy, *Ninotchka*. Evidently, Nabokov continued to be a regular movie-goer after he arrived in America. His son, Dmitri, recalls how his father "loved the cinema" and used to take him to Saturday-morning shows, matinées and "shorts" in Boston and Cambridge, featuring Abbott and Costello, the Three Stooges, the Marx Brothers, Buster Keaton, and comic-book heroes the Falcon and Superman.[11] The fact that Nabokov did not see Welles's seminal *Citizen Kane* until 1972, when it was shown on Swiss television,[12] indicates also that his movie-going was probably more ad hoc than deliberate and perhaps most influenced by what might have entertained his son. Nevertheless, the presence of film in Nabokov's fiction from 1940 on indicates the extent of his assimilation of this mode of popular culture as a fundamental element of his work and, perhaps more significantly, demonstrates a close affinity with the concerns and preoccupations of contemporary America.

In *Nabokov's Dark Cinema*, Alfred Appel describes *Lolita* as a "vision of love distorted and coarsened in the crooked glass of Hollywood,"[13] a statement which is more an assertion of his own subjective and essentially negative position regarding film in the novel than a reflection of Nabokov's more positive stance. The comment is, in fact, a deliberate echo of a statement made by Nabokov in an interview for the *Paris Review* in 1967, in which he proposes that "a tinge of *poshlust* is often given by the cinema to the novel it distorts and coarsens in its crooked glass."[14] The important distinction between this original assertion and Appel's, however, is that Nabokov is describing a very specific process, the transformation of fiction into film, and not the effect upon fiction of a calculated deployment of cinema and cinematics. Appel's premise is, therefore, based upon a misinterpretation and an incorrect assumption that Nabokov shared Appel's negative opinion of cinema. The presence and deployment of film in *Lolita* does not designate it entirely as an element of *poshlust*. Indeed, far from being something which "coarsens" and "distorts," it serves to clarify and refine and is an eloquent and evocative means of communicating the subtlest ideas and emotions. Nevertheless,

Appel's volume stands as the single major study of cinematics in Nabokov's fiction, and his commentary on *Lolita* is persuasive, detailing the echoes of many films and aspects of American popular culture contemporary to the novel.

Film in *Lolita* is generally considered to serve as a means of establishing the aesthetic conflict between Humbert Humbert and Clare Quilty. Alfred Appel argues that Humbert Humbert's antipathy toward Quilty is rooted in the apparent antagonism between high and low art, with Quilty's active engagement in the Hollywood machine as a filmmaker, screenwriter and semi-celebrity designating his lowly status, the elements of popular culture he represents necessarily abhorred by Humbert Humbert as a figure whose heritage of European poetry and philosophy is an overt and defining influence. Humbert Humbert's reference to and deployment of cinema in the narrative is deemed, therefore, to be a cynical manipulation of an inferior medium, designed, primarily, to denigrate Quilty. He is quick to emphasize Quilty's involvement in second-rate cinema and pornography as grounds for condemnation, and yet the cinematic details of the early part of the novel indicate that he is, in fact, not so far removed in inclination from his arch rival. This not only undermines the perceived degree of distance between the two men but also has intriguing ramifications in the subsequent revenge scenario. Once the proximity of these two protagonists is recognized, Humbert Humbert's superior stance is instantly deflated, and the nature of his relationships with Charlotte Haze, Lolita, and indeed America itself assumes a far more complex and ambiguous guise.

Humbert Humbert Goes to the Movies

During their first year of travels Lolita and Humbert Humbert "[take] in, voluptuously and indiscriminately, ... one hundred and fifty or two hundred programs."[15] This not only confirms the level of Humbert Humbert's exposure to contemporary American cinema, viewing, on average, a film every other day, but also suggests the degree to which the experience has saturated his consciousness. Particularly significant are the words he chooses to describe their movie-going — "voluptuous" and "indiscriminate" — which convey the notion of him allowing Lolita this indulgence in order merely to satisfy his own sexual cravings, giving him an opportunity to fondle her, anonymously, in darkened movie theaters.

In the light of his assimilation of almost every aspect of contemporary cinema, however, his words also convey a sense of sheer, irresponsible joy in this film-going ritual which is expressed in his presentation of the movie theaters themselves as magical, alluring visions, "dripping with jewel fires" (p. 116).[16] Whatever his motives, it is evident that, far from regarding filmmaking as an inferior artistic endeavor, Humbert Humbert actively celebrates it, emulates and exploits it, recognizing its influence, acknowledging its codes, its definitions, its styles. It is misconceived to position Humbert Humbert in antipathy toward Charlotte, Lolita or Quilty because of their constant reference to and identification with film, for he demonstrates precisely the same level of deference to it. He is not alone even in his cynicism and thus is brought ever closer to Quilty.

Appel's contextual analysis also ignores the significance of the role of film in the first part of the novel, the section set outside America, and the extent to which Humbert Humbert's obsession with film is established in this opening section, details which have profound consequences in any examination of the role of cinematics in the novel. How far Humbert Humbert's perspective is informed solely by his subsequent experience of American cinema is hard to discern, especially since it becomes inextricably linked with his passion for Lolita. Early in the narrative, however, he describes himself "discussing Soviet films with expatriates" in Paris (pp. 15–16), which suggests that his passion for film originated in the days of silent movies, long before he came to America. While the overt cultural context of Humbert Humbert's consciousness is European, his assimilation and deployment of film parallels that of all the principal characters in the novel, and rather than being regarded as a cynical manipulation of an inferior medium as a means of enabling him to control situations and the people in them, it can be interpreted as an attempt at self-initiation, the adoption of this foreign American art form being a demonstration of a sincere desire to understand, to conform and to belong.

Cinema and Humbert Humbert's Sexual Consciousness

Film and photography are fundamental to an understanding of Humbert Humbert's sexuality. They play a central role in the earliest "sexual events" (p. 11) of his life, before he encounters his first love,

Annabel Leigh. Recalling his time spent in the south of France as a child, he describes "a solemn, decorous and purely theoretical talk about pubertal surprises in the rose garden of [his] school with an American kid, the son of a then celebrated motion-picture actress whom he seldom saw in the three-dimensional world" (p. 11). Instantly, the link with American cinema is established and the validity of the two-dimensional screen image confirmed. Not only does this boy introduce Humbert Humbert to his sexuality, but his maternal connection with Hollywood instills the event with a quality of glamour and mystery, creating a set of associations that will remain at the basis of his perception and experience of desire for the rest of his life. This event occurs in conjunction with "some interesting reactions on the part of [his] organism to certain photographs, pearl and umbra, with infinitely soft partings, in Pichon's sumptuous *La Beauté Humaine* that [he] had filched from under a mountain of marble-bound *Graphics* in the hotel library" (p. 11). This experience serves to consolidate the particular relationship, in Humbert Humbert's imagination, between sexual stimulation and image, in other words, voyeurism.

Much of Humbert Humbert's early sexual activity involves voyeuristic episodes in which he is depicted as solitary and anonymous, seeking furtive gratification from chance glimpses of young girls in public places:

> How marvelous were my fancied adventures as I sat on a hard park bench pretending to be immersed in a trembling book. Around the quiet scholar, nymphets played freely, as if he were a familiar statue or part of an old tree's shadow and sheen. Once a perfect little beauty in a tartan frock, with a clatter put her heavily armed foot near me upon the bench to dip her slim bare arms into me and tighten the strap of her roller skate, and I dissolved in the sun, with my book for a fig leaf, as her auburn ringlets fell over her skinned knee, and the shadow of leaves I shared pulsated and melted on her radiant limb next to my chameleonic cheek [p. 20].

The distinctive character of these episodes is generated by the necessity for distance. For example, the vision of "a nymphet in the act of undressing before a co-operative mirror" becomes exciting to him only because it is "isolated" and "removed" (p. 20). At the same time, however, his pleasure is tempered by a fear that his perversity is somehow corrupting these objects of desire.

> I had possessed her — and she never knew it. ... But would it not tell sometime later? Had I not somehow tampered with her fate by involv-

ing her image in my voluptas? Oh, it was, and remains, a source of great
and terrible wonder [p. 21].

Humbert Humbert's admission of depravity serves also, most
significantly, to undermine his superior position to a level below even that
of Quilty's. Quilty may deal in the business of pornography and even
indulge from time to time in the corruption of innocents, but the power
of Humbert Humbert's imagination is such that by merely engaging in
these voyeuristic activities, innocents are corrupted without his ever need-
ing to lay a finger on them.

Film, Photography and the Mechanisms of Memory

Cinema may be fundamental to Humbert Humbert's sexual consciousness, but it is also central in defining the unique quality of his
memory. The process of remembering is a process of visualization, acti-
vated and realized either as film or a photograph. As Humbert Humbert
explains:

> There are two kinds of visual memory; one when you skillfully recreate
> an image in the laboratory of your mind, with your eyes open ... the
> other when you instantly evoke, with shut eyes on the dark innerside of
> your eyelids, the objective, absolutely optical replica of a beloved face,
> a little host in natural colors (and this is how I see Lolita) [p. 11].

The two forms of "visual memory" are subjective and objective
respectively, the latter being, essentially, a direct emulation of the cinematic experience, the "dark innerside" of the eyelid serving as the screen
upon which mnemonic images are "instantly" projected. Humbert Humbert's narrative is both an act of the imagination — the creation of a world
in the "laboratory of [his] mind" — and one of deliberate and conscious
recollection, and thus the process of reliving the past becomes the process
of the narrative as a whole. Humbert Humbert confirms to his
reader/audience that his memory is faithful by claiming it to be "photographic" (p. 40), that is, devoid of either decay or corruption by time or
subjective distortions. His photographic memory is an exceptional gift,
for it enables him to present accurately, for example, every word of the
diary he kept five years before, when he first came to live at the Haze

house in Ramsdale. The contention is, therefore, that his narrative is both reliable and trustworthy, and compared to the diary of his closest predecessor, Hermann Karlovich, his version of events is, due to its accuracy of detail and emotional candor, compelling, compounded by the fact that it is also, apparently, both a confession and a plea for absolution. The quality of his mnemonic powers do indeed seem to defy the ravages of time and the defects of the mind, and the cinematic analogy effectively designates them as more mechanical than human and thus invulnerable to deterioration or corruption, at the same time enhancing the manner in which these memories are realized. Like the images which travel along the projector's beam in Schwartz's story, "visions of Lo [vibrate] all along [his] optic nerve" (p. 160) or else appear as snapshots in real or imaginary photo albums. Indeed, the entire narrative is a process of him "leafing again through ... miserable memories" (p. 13), images he returns to again and again:

> In a secluded nook under a naked light, I was turning the enormous and fragile pages of a coffin-black volume almost as big as Lolita [p. 262].

Humbert Humbert invites his audience to look with him, to share the revelations of the past, yet his commentary upon these images denies the spectator an independent experience of them. Here, for example, Humbert Humbert's description is tainted by the definition of the color of the album as "coffin-black," which instantly suggests that this is the album of a person who is already dead, even though at this stage in the narrative Lolita is still very much alive. The reader is left to conjecture as to what exactly he is referring, for Humbert cannot know that Lolita is to die after him in childbirth. Either this is an emotive expression of remorse at the suffering he has caused her or a deliberate ploy to alert the reader to the possibility that she will meet some untimely and violent death, perhaps even by Humbert Humbert's own hands, a notion introduced by the concluding images of his "Carmen" song—"And the gun I killed you with, O my Carmen/The gun I am holding now (Drew his .32 automatic, I guess, and put a bullet through his moll's eye.)" (p. 62).[17] This is part of a sinister game he plays, never allowing the reader to be absolutely certain of his motives or his intentions, while claiming that his narrative is a faithful depiction of events, reinforced by a medium recognized for its reliability—the persistent, fixed form of the photographic image.

The ambiguous nature of Humbert Humbert's narrative is also reflected in the contradictory roles he assumes as, alternately, poet and cinematographer. It abounds with allusions to poets and men of letters ancient and modern, generating the illusion that he considers himself to be a contributor to this great literary tradition, and yet he claims to be "no poet" but "only a very conscientious recorder" (p. 72). His deployment of film and photography bears this out, suggesting that his narrative is more a demonstration of an exact science than a work of art. The notion of whether he is a poet or a technician is also linked with the question of his being a murderer, and he is seen to adopt either role depending on its expediency in serving in his defense.

> Nowadays you have to be a scientist if you want to be a killer. No, no, I was neither.... Emphatically, no killers are we. Poets never kill [pp. 87–88].

Although Humbert Humbert adopts various guises — poet, author, actor, photographer, filmmaker — the centrality of the camera image to his perception of the world is a constant. It informs his imagination, his memory, his sexuality. Ultimately, it is Lolita in the form of a "cinematographic still" (p. 44) which is most precious to him, for in this "immobilized" and immortalized state he can possess her entirely. She will never leave him, she will never die, and she will remain forever just out of reach, perfect and invulnerable, in the domain which allows him to adopt his ideal role, one that affords him the most potent satisfaction — that of the voyeur.

Humbert Humbert's system of memory is a process of visualization dependent upon the deployment of the mechanisms of film. Recollections are presented cinematically utilizing perspective, light, and shade to generate visual impact. He perceives his life as "divided tidily into ample light and narrow shade: the light pertaining to the solace of research in palatial libraries, the shade to my excruciating desires and insomnias" (p. 32). As the narrative progresses and his desires begin to overwhelm him, so the shadows lengthen until everything is depicted in a series of varying shades of gray, from the night shades and the obscurity of shuttered motel rooms to Quilty's cars — even flowers become gray like "smoke" (p. 236). Thus Humbert Humbert's world is gradually transformed into the black-and-white prints in Pichon's magazine or the images on a movie screen. The grayness of the narrative also reflects the color of Lolita's

eyes, and the significance of the connotations attached to gray — of ill-
ness and death[18] — is evident and is extended to her very surname, Haze,
which serves to suggest not only her brief life but also the nature of her
presence in Humbert Humbert's consciousness as an elusive, transitory,
amorphous image. The all-pervasive grayness of the narrative is punctuated only by the occasional bright red, pink, blue or green, the impact
of these colors seeming to suggest some special significance, and yet, ultimately, they fail to function as consistent motifs. Rather, they establish
temporary connections. For example, Lolita's "Aztec Red" swimsuit (p.
237), which mirrors Quilty's car — "the red fiend" (p. 247) — serves to alert
the reader/audience to their complicity. At the same time, the narrative's
overwhelming grayness is also a reflection of Humbert Humbert's emotional state as a doomed, grief-stricken man, and while it is appropriate
in terms of the narrative's cinematic quality, it also communicates the
confusion and despair of his present and past predicaments.

The Corruption of Objectivity: Humbert Humbert's Camera Eye

Film also offers Humbert Humbert a means of establishing an
autonomous authority over the narrative. It enables him to maintain a
distance between his interior and exterior worlds, and, like Hermann
Karlovich, he constantly steps back from or out of the picture. He is
director and star of his own movie, asserting exclusive control over and
offering a unique insight into the scenario and the characters playing
within it, including himself, that is, until he meets Lolita, who alone has
the power to disrupt his autonomy. The camera eye also seems to be at
once both his own and an independent mechanism, the images it records
allowing him a rare objective vision of himself:

> As I lay on my narrow studio bed after a session of adoration and despair
> in Lolita's cold bedroom, I used to review the concluded day by check-
> ing my own image as it prowled rather than passed before the mind's red
> eye [p. 188].

The notion of "review" is also distinctive as a cinematic process, and
Humbert Humbert is here emulating the role of the film director in viewing the "rushes"[19] at the conclusion of each day's shooting. By adopting

the camera eye as his own, he establishes a subjective tyranny over the narrative, to an extent where it is impossible to know how much of what is being presented is actual or a distortion. The camera eye, therefore, functioning in direct antithesis to its conventional role, is used to confuse and obfuscate, to depict constantly vacillating perspectives from scene to scene. At the same time, Humbert Humbert maintains that the camera eye is an independent witness to events, an unprejudiced, detached recorder, yet still, rather than being a means of condemning him by the evidence of his crimes that it collects, it serves merely as "an innocent camera catching [him] on [his] dark way to Lolita's bed — what a magnet for Mnemosyne!" (p. 262), essentially an ally and an agent of memory.

Not only is Humbert Humbert's consciousness saturated by film, but he also deliberately adopts its styles and techniques to realize his creative impulse. Particular scenes and sequences of events are presented cinematically. The beginning of part two, for example, reads as a series of "compilation cuts,"[20] giving a rapid, condensed overview of his travels with Lolita in a dizzying succession of varied locations, a sequence signaled by the repetition of the phrase "*nous connûmes*" and concluded with the obliterating roar of a night train:

> We came to know — *nous connûmes*, to use a Flaubertian intonation — the stone cottages under enormous Chateaubriandesque trees, the brick unit, the adobe unit, the stucco court.... *Nous connûmes* (this is royal fun) the would-be enticements of their repetitious names — all those Sunset Motels, U-Beam Cottages, Hillcrest Courts, Pine View Courts, Mountain View Courts.... *Nous connûmes* the various types of motor court operators, the reformed criminal, the retired teacher and the business flop, among the males; and the motherly, pseudo-ladylike and madamic variants among the females. And sometimes trains would cry in the monstrously hot and humid night with heartrending and ominous plangency, mingling power and hysteria in one desperate scream [pp. 145–46].

Humbert Humbert's presentation of certain key scenes is also particularly reminiscent of a visual device typical of Raymond Chandler's fiction, a technique which Spiegel describes as "anatomization," akin to the choreography of movement and precise attention to the geography of a scene or location also evident in Dashiell Hammett's work. In film, Spiegel argues:

the camera ... conveys more detailed information about how animated
things and beings look when they move through time and space than
perhaps any other artistic or mechanical invention.... The camera places
a new and concentrated attentiveness upon the infinite number of phases
that constitute the shape of any single action and thus brings to human
consciousness a new accretion of process images and an increased awareness of process itself.[21]

This precise delineation of detail within a confined field of vision is apparent in Chandler's early story, "The Curtain" (1936), which was used as a
basis for *The Big Sleep*. The first instance of this comes at the beginning
of chapter two, the cinematic mode having already been established in
the story's opening, which consists almost entirely of unembellished dialogue. Particularly striking are the fast switches in visual focus and the
changes in pace they accompany.

This episode features the shooting of Larry Batzel and his discovery by Chandler's detective hero, Carmady. The shooting itself is never
shown, and the process of discovery is presented in a sequence of scenes —
structured in the narrative as separate paragraphs — commencing in Carmady's apartment, from where he hears the gunshots, and depicting his
gradual progress into the hallway, down the back stairs, into the alley-
way and finally the yard, where Batzel lies. The episode's visual pace generates a sense of urgency which is at the same time frustrated by delayed
visual revelation, akin to Spiegel's anatomization. This, however, grants
the ultimate vision of Batzel's body considerable dramatic impact.

> Larry Batzel lay on his face, with his hat a yard away from his head, and
> one hand flung out to within a foot of a big black automatic. His ankles
> were crossed as if he had spun as he fell. Blood was thick on the side of
> his face, on his blond hair, especially on his neck. It was also thick on
> the cement yard.[22]

The manner in which the body is described became a recurrent device
in Chandler's fiction. Rather than describe the scene as a total visual spectacle, the visual focus moves in detail in *reverse* sequence over the body.[23]
First the face, then the hat are shown, but neither of these images confirms
the reader's supposition that this is a dead man. Confirmation, as in many
other instances, comes only with the final detail, in the final frame, as it
were. From the hat and the gun, the attention switches to Batzel's ankles,
a part of his anatomy the reader would have the least concern with. It is

as if Chandler is taunting his readers by purposefully denying them the one crucial detail they require, and it is almost at a point where the suspense is beginning to wane that Chandler grants them the conclusive image. From the ankles the focus "cuts" to the blood on Batzel's face, on his hair and neck and on the ground beside him. That Chandler is intentionally delaying the resolution of the scene is confirmed by this final vision, which draws the attention back to the opening image of the paragraph, that of Batzel's face then seemingly free of blood. Although the function and effect of this episode are overtly cinematic, they would be impossible to achieve in film without resorting to visual trickery, and yet the level of actuality and immediacy generated by the combination of close-ups, medium shots and flash-frame stills forces the reader to suspend disbelief and is a skilful exploitation of a necessary element of the audience's role in the cinematic experience.

As in the scene with Larry Batzel, Humbert Humbert presents the revelation of Charlotte's accident in a series of close-up cuts, and he has a specific reason for this.

> I have to put the impact of an instantaneous vision into a sequence of words; their physical accumulation in the page impairs the actual flash, the sharp unity of impression [p. 97].

Humbert Humbert's "sequence of words" functions, however, as a sequence of cinematic frames, converting the still image into a piece of anatomized film. As Chandler does, Humbert Humbert starts from the edge of the scene, working around its perimeters and then moving gradually inward, postponing the vision of Charlotte's body until the very end, painstakingly registering every other detail but the one the reader/audience is anticipating. Even when the camera eye finally falls on Charlotte she is concealed by a "laprobe" (p. 98). Humbert Humbert is not, however, attempting to spare the reader/audience the anguish or horror of the spectacle of Charlotte's "mangled remains" (p. 98), for he immediately goes on to describe every stage of the accident, a sequence which, note, he did not witness himself but is imagining on the basis of what he has been told.

The entrances of Charlotte and Lolita in the narrative also utilize this technique of anatomization. Humbert Humbert's attitude of apathetic curiosity concerning his new landlady is generated by the pace of her entrance and a visual perspective that is fixed and confined. Visual

attention is focused initially on an inconsequential inanimate object sitting in Charlotte's hallway, an "old gray tennis ball" (p. 37) (note its
color), leaving Charlotte's appearance at the top of the stairs to be registered aurally. She is eventually acknowledged by the subsequent switch
of visual focus to another incidental (gray) object — her cigarette ash —
as it falls into Humbert Humbert's field of vision:

> There came from the upper landing the contralto voice of Mrs. Haze,
> who leaning over the banisters inquired melodiously, "Is that Monsieur
> Humbert?" A bit of cigarette ash dropped from there in addition [p. 37].

As Charlotte descends, the perspective remains fixed on the middle of
the staircase, revealing her gradually from the feet up in a visual process
available only to the restrictive perimeters of the camera lens. It is
significant that the concluding shot is not of Charlotte's face but of her
cigarette, implying that it is this which designates her character, the ash
having provided the prelude to her entrance, and thus the scene is
afforded visual closure:[24]

> Presently, the lady herself— sandals, maroon slacks, yellow silk blouse,
> squarish face, in that order — came down the steps, her index finger still
> tapping upon her cigarette [p. 37].

The focus upon the cigarette invokes Humbert Humbert's cool
indifference to and disinterest in Charlotte, a lack of emotional engagement which characterizes his relations with her. The fixed visual perspective and the pace of the action within it emphasize the key aspects
of her appearance — her clothes and her cigarettes — which epitomize the
elements of her limited allure. Lolita's entrance into the narrative is, in
contrast, sudden, overwhelming and highly emotive. The "blue sea-wave"
which "[swells] under [Humbert Humbert's] heart" (p. 39) at first sight
of her is dramatized by a rapid "crash" zoom,[25] which focuses abruptly
in on the subject from a medium shot of Lolita turning on her sun mat
to a choker close-up of her gaze, and it is his turn to be regarded with
cool indifference by this "starlet" (p. 65) who basks in the sun as if in
the glare of a huge spotlight.

> I was still walking behind Mrs. Haze through the dining room when,
> beyond it, there came a sudden burst of greenery ... and then, without
> the least warning ... from a mat in a pool of sun, half-naked, kneeling,

turning about on her knees, there was my Riviera love peering at me over dark glasses [p. 39].

At the same time, there is a consciousness of the inadequacy of words to express the visual impact of a scene, and no matter how faithful and precise his memory, it cannot match the quality of film. Twice Humbert Humbert bemoans the absence of a real-life camera with which to capture particular superlative moments. Film would have eloquently rendered the grace and harmony he senses in "the curious pattern, the monogrammic linkage of [his and Lolita's] simultaneous or overlapping moves" (p. 58), as Lolita wriggles and squirms in his lap on Charlotte's davenport, and would likewise have captured the marvel of Lolita on the tennis court:

> I could have filmed her! I would have had her now with me, before my eyes, in the projection room of my pain and despair! [p. 231].

Humbert Humbert seems, however, to be incongruously unaware of the ability of his memory to store these visions as film, for the spectacle of Lolita's tennis game is presented as a highly anatomized, slow-motion sequence which serves both to amplify and enhance the vision to a degree available only in film, serving to immortalize Lolita's every movement:

> The ball when it entered her aura of control became somehow whiter, its resilience somehow richer, and the instrument of precision she used upon it seemed inordinately prehensile and deliberate at the moment of clinging contact [p. 231].

Humbert Humbert's frustration is, essentially, at the impossibility of "screening" this mnemonic vision. He can relive the moment in his mind's eye, but he cannot present it to anyone else, he cannot make someone else see what he sees, he cannot bring Lolita to life in another's eyes.[26] This declared inadequacy, however, could be interpreted as a cynical ploy to generate sympathy by imbuing critical scenes with a beauty and mystery they never had, exploiting the language and techniques of cinema to transform either the most mundane or sordid episodes into moments of transcendent romance. The most overt example of this is his cinematic staging of the episode at The Enchanted Hunters, signaled by the arclights which illuminate the exterior of the hotel as they would a set in a film studio. Nowhere else in the narrative does he refer to this particular form of lighting, used exclusively in film and photography for the intense, white light it produces.[27]

The presence and effect of lighting in this episode are given special emphasis and are established from the outset as Humbert Humbert and Lolita drive up to the hotel in the darkness—"Under the arclights enlarged replicas of chestnut leaves plunged and played on white pillars" (p. 117). This vision instantly evokes the setting's cinematic associations. In an image anticipating the later allusion to *Gone with the Wind* (p. 156), the illumination of the hotel accentuates its old Southern Confederate style and lends it a magical, ephemeral quality. It is significant, also, that the atmosphere of "enchantment," which is so fastidiously evoked— "I had gradually eliminated all the superfluous blur, and by stacking level upon level of translucent vision, had evolved a final picture" (p. 125)— is directly linked with the cinematic experience, for it attests not only to Humbert Humbert's calculated deployment of film in the narrative, but also to the delight he takes in setting the scenes in which he is to star.

The machinery of film provides the perfect setting, but it seems also to be complicit in Humbert Humbert's sinister scheme, since these same arclights are to facilitate his way to Lolita's bed.

> The door of the lighted bathroom stood ajar; in addition to that, a skeleton glow came through the Venetian blinds from the outside arclights; these intercrossed rays penetrated the darkness of the bedroom and revealed the following situation.
> Clothed in one of her old nightgowns, my Lolita lay on her side with her back to me, in the middle of the bed. Her lightly veiled body and bare limbs formed a Z. She had put both pillows under her dark tousled head; a band of pale light crossed her top vertebrae [p. 128].

Alfred Appel has remarked on the noir effect of the lighting in this scene,[28] but also notable is the way in which light is deployed in a process of gradual revelation, the rays of light extending from the window drawing the visual attention from across the room to Lolita lying asleep on the bed. The combination of extremes of light and shadow and the delayed revelation of the central subject of the scene generates a sense of tentative anticipation while the quality of the light creates an aura of delicacy and tenderness. In a skillful manipulation of cinematic technique, the camera eye moves across the room and comes to rest on the sleeping figure. The visual focus is drawn in close on the "pale light" which falls on the back of Lolita's neck, concluding the sequence with an intensely romantic and beautiful image. That Humbert Humbert is exploiting the machinery of film for his own purposes, here enabling him to transform what is simply an attempt to force himself on a twelve-year-old girl whom he has taken the trouble to drug in order that she be rendered utterly helpless, into an idyllic scene of innocent love is confirmed by the nature of the superhuman speed in which he "[slips] into his pyjamas" (p. 128). The sordid business of Humbert Humbert preparing himself for rape is obliterated, conveniently, by yet another cinematic process — this time, editing — enabling him to complete this maneuver with the "kind of fantastic instantaneousness which is implied when in a cinematographic scene the process of changing is cut" (p. 128).

The question remains, however, as to Humbert Humbert's purpose in depicting this elaborate and exact process of transformation. In the light of the imagined jury who sit in judgment of him, is this very subjective dramatization of events not an attempt to influence them, to generate sympathy, to encourage them even to reinterpret their understanding of events? Or is it possibly a defense presented by a man wholly innocent of any conscious or deliberate malice but simply overwhelmed by uncontrollable desires? In only one scene in the entire narrative does the latter case apply, as he begs a pregnant Dolly Schiller to run away with him.

At the point where Humbert Humbert breaks down completely, the visual attention is deflected and objectified, as if in an attempt to evade the ultimate humiliation of being *seen* at his most pathetic. Yet the effect of this is to generate, in one of only two or three instances in the narrative,[29] sincere sympathy for this man who is desperately trying to salvage just the smallest trace of dignity. By shifting the narrative focus to Lolita, his state can be inferred only from the way she responds to it. An occasional, very brief and embarrassed remark from her indicates to the reader what is happening, and in this very understated way the emotional force of the scene is tellingly communicated.

> "I think," she went on — "oops" — the envelope skidded to the floor — she picked it up — "I think it's oh utterly *grand* of you to give us all that dough. It settles everything, we can start next week. Stop crying, please. You should understand. Let me get you some more beer. Oh, don't cry, I'm so sorry I cheated so much, but that's the way things are" [p. 279].

Humbert Humbert's visual focus is engaged only when Lolita drops the envelope, signaling to the reader that he is not in fact looking at her, but deliberately away from her, at the floor, fixedly and unseeing, as he listens to her. This is the only instance where the cinematic aspect of the narrative collapses, along with Humbert Humbert, as it were, and the reader is left to imagine the vision of him weeping before Lolita. The scene is pivotal in that, for the first and only time, he concedes narrative authority to Lolita and in doing so relinquishes his tyranny over her, a tyranny, however, that although revoked in reality, can be quickly restored in the realms of his imagination through his manipulation of the codes and formulas of film.

Film as Refuge and Inspiration

Humbert Humbert expresses his desire for tyranny by referring to the actions of characters in films, extending this to his pre–American past. In Berlin, when confronted by his cuckolder, the émigré taxi driver Maximovich, he immediately transforms the relationship between him and his wife Valeria into a scenario from a gangster movie. Maximovich is "le gredin," the villain, and Valeria "his moll" (p. 29). Film offers refuge in that it provides a ready catalogue of tried and tested scenes from which to draw, enabling him, in this instance, to restore, if somewhat flimsily, his sense of pride.

> The vibration of the door I had slammed after them still rang in my every nerve, a poor substitute for the backhand slap with which I ought to have hit her across the cheekbone according to the rules of the movies [pp. 29–30].

Charlotte and Lolita are both evaluated in terms of screen icons, a criterion which Humbert Humbert extends even to himself. He describes Charlotte as a "weak solution of Marlene Dietrich" (p. 37), designating her instantly as a rather pathetic figure, enslaved, like so many other suburban American women, by Hollywood, living out a fantasy of glamour, beauty and romance which they will never attain.

His first response to the "starlet" (p. 65) Lolita, however, is to adopt the pose of her leading man, and the vision of him "[passing] by her in [his] adult disguise (a great big handsome hunk of movieland manhood)"

(p. 39) establishes his very willing concession to film lore for the purpose of attracting her. He is more than happy to acknowledge his resemblance to "some crooner or actor chap on whom Lo has a crush" (p. 43), oblivious, it seems, to the irony that the "actor chap" is in fact Quilty, who is pictured on the Drome advertisement above Lolita's bed.

Nevertheless, Humbert Humbert skillfully capitalizes on cinema's role as a universal mode of reference, to an extent where even total strangers, or mere schoolgirls, are able to identify the resonances, as one of them comments: "'First time I've seen a man in a smoking jacket, sir — except in the movies of course'" (p. 189). The initial vision of him in his "adult disguise" is particularly revealing, however, for it implies that he still believes himself to be a child, a notion which betrays his sense of being locked in the past, trapped in time from the day he loses Annabel Leigh, and thus confirms that he considers Lolita to be her reincarnation. At the same time, this "movieland" pose demonstrates the extent of his appropriation of film iconography and his belief in it as a potent force not only for seduction but also for self-aggrandizement. Ironically, it is from this assumed position that he fantasizes about the same movie-inspired romantic scenarios in which Lolita is steeped, musing over the possibility that this "modern child, an avid reader of movie magazines, an expert in dream-slow close-ups, might not think it too strange ... if a handsome, intensely virile grown-up friend" (p. 49) should make sexual advances toward her. The scene is borrowed from her dreams, and complying with them he imagines her seduction as a screen seduction, with Lolita melting and compliant in his embrace — "I knew she would let me do so, and even close her eyes as Hollywood teaches" (p. 48). In Humbert Humbert's eyes, therefore, he and Lolita are perfectly matched, each in their cinematic heaven, the filmic mode essentially giving sanction to his designs upon her.

Humbert Humbert's active emulation of screen heroes begins with Valeria, continues with Charlotte and Lolita and culminates in his contest with Quilty. When in flight with Lolita he assumes the persona of the gangster, the outlaw on the run with his moll, and following Quilty's trail he becomes the hero of the Western or film noir, the innocent wronged, forced into violence by the evil of his enemies. Even his prison-cell confession belongs in the tradition of film noir's condemned narratives, spoken by the soon-to-be or already dead heroes Walter Neff (*Double Indemnity*), Jeff Bailey (*Out of the Past*), Frank Bigelow (*D.O.A.*, 1949) and Joe Gillis (*Sunset Boulevard*).

The assumption of screen personae is not exclusive to Humbert Humbert, however. Indeed, Lolita's guises, or rather, those that are assigned to her, are significant in terms not only of his immersion in movie lore, but also, paradoxically, of the level of his detachment from her. The variety and number of roles she plays and the fact that she is consistently portrayed as everything but her real self are indications of Humbert Humbert's inability and failure to achieve any meaningful intimacy in their relationship and confirm that she is never more than an object of desire, fed by his imagination. It is not until the nymphet Lolita is killed stone dead by the vision of a pregnant Dolly Schiller that he claims to see the real person and to love her. Yet how far can this sentiment be trusted, when the entirety of the narrative has been an elaborate creation of a movie-inspired fantasy? Surely it is at this point that Humbert Humbert realizes he has lost Lolita forever, indeed that he never really had her, and like the "lovely and fast" photograph of Charlotte as a girl (p. 100), she belongs to him only in memory, in the sole dimension in which he is capable of love.

Lolita, Archetypal Hollywood Heroine

Lolita assumes four identifiable screen guises — the Hollywood starlet, the *femme fatale*, the fugitive moll and the screwball heroine. At the Haze house during the first months after Humbert Humbert's arrival, she plays the role of Hollywood starlet — bold, mischievous, flirtatious, tantalizing, untouchable — innocently oblivious to the evil which lurks about her. Despite Humbert Humbert's increasing frustration and desire, he does not attempt to seduce her outright but merely feeds from her image, indulging in voyeuristic flights of fancy, as he did in his European parks. This he achieves to a point of sublimation on Charlotte's davenport, for not only does he successfully conceal his arousal from Lolita, but he even manages to dispel the element of risk which endangers them both.

> Nothing prevented me from repeating the performance that affected her as little as if she were a photographic image rippling upon a screen and I a humble hunchback abusing myself in the dark [p. 62].

Humbert Humbert legitimizes this episode by equating it with pornography, negating Lolita's presence by consigning her to a two-dimensional image on a screen and reducing his role to that of an anonymous voyeur. This is significant not only in terms of his opinion of Quilty the pornographer, but also because it epitomizes the position he assumes in defense of his actions. Nevertheless, Lolita is able to keep Humbert Humbert guessing. When she leaves for Camp Q she is still the starlet, but when he goes to fetch her he discovers a new persona — the *femme fatale*.

This is the first scene in which they are alone together, and it is presented cinematically, consisting almost entirely of sharp, punchy, fast-paced dialogue which is compounded by the absence of identifying markers, so that the speech has the fluency and economy of an on-screen exchange. Lolita is tough, cynical and provocative, apparently in command:

> "Talk Lo — don't grunt. Tell me something."
> "What thing, Dad?" (she let the word expand with ironic deliberation).
> "Any old thing."
> "Okay, if I call you that?" (eyes slit at the road).
> "Quite."
> "It's a sketch, you know" [p. 112].

Apart from the stated irony, her use of the term "Dad" assumes greater implications of meaning when considered in its slang form as a term referring to a woman's lover. Combined with the notion that she is participating in a "sketch," this emphasizes Lolita's consciousness of the scene's artificiality and her role in it, as well as being a sardonic comment on the unnaturalness of the situation, an attempt to signal to Humbert Humbert her unease. Nevertheless, she seems afraid to expose her vulnerability and instead conceals it with a veneer of brash vulgarity which serves both to embarrass and consequently alienate him. She accuses him of no longer caring for her and, when he asks why, replies, "Well, you haven't kissed me yet, have you?" (p. 112), playing out in grotesque faithfulness her newly assigned role. Nevertheless she maintains her authority by attempting to undermine Humbert Humbert's command of the scene by overtly criticizing his driving, peppering her speech with expletives to further antagonize him:

> "The fruithead!" remarked Lo. "He should have nabbed *you*."
> "Why for heaven's sake?"
> "Well, the speed in this bum state is fifty, and — No, don't slow down, you dull bulb. He's gone now" [p. 113].

The scene shows Lolita vacillating between the guises of *femme fatale* and screwball heroine, at once dangerous and comical. She mocks Humbert Humbert in a way that communicates her awareness of his intentions, "comfortably" calling herself a "Bad, bad girl," a "Juvenile delinckwent, but frank and fetching" (p. 113), adopting a childish lisp in order to exaggerate the perversity of the scene. Yet there is also a futility in her words, for no matter how plain she makes her feelings on the situation, there is a sense that she knows ultimately there is nothing she can do to escape his clutches.

This episode, however, is paralleled by a later scene during their second tour of America, this time pursued by a still anonymous Quilty. They stop at a gas station, and while Humbert Humbert is away from the car, Lolita and Quilty have a brief consultation as to the next stage of the journey. On returning, Humbert Humbert catches a glimpse of the stranger and asks Lolita why they were talking:

> "Now I want to know exactly what he said to you and what you told him."
> She laughed.
> "If he's really a cop," she said shrilly but not illogically, "the worst thing we could do, would be to show him we are scared. Ignore him, *Dad.*"
> "Did he ask you where we were going?"
> "Oh, he knows *that*" (mocking me) [pp. 218–19].

The fear and uncertainty have gone from her voice. Her authority is no longer a pretence but is tangible and is expressed by the repeated use of the term "Dad," which generates the same connotations as before, and yet this time she makes a point of emphasizing it, as if to ensure that Humbert Humbert does not miss the irony. She even dares to insinuate that she is in some way conspiring with this stranger, confident that she has in Quilty a protector of her own choice, and when Humbert Humbert seems to be getting close to discovering the stranger's identity, she skillfully deflects his curiosity.

> "I thought," I said kidding her, "Quilty was an ancient flame of yours, in the days when you loved me, in sweet old Ramsdale."
> "What?" countered Lo, her features working. "That fat dentist? You must be confusing me with some other fast little article" [pp. 221–22].

It is Lolita in this guise of a worldly, predatory female — a "fast lit-tle article" — who seduces an innocent Humbert Humbert, the familiar elements of noir—sex and fate — which combine to overwhelm him and set them both on a perilous, fugitive course. In this scenario betrayal is inevitable, and in a true depiction of the archetypal noir heroine, Lolita shows neither mercy nor fear when facing Humbert Humbert's accusa-tions in Beardsley. "Mocking [him] with her heartless vaporous eyes" (p. 203), she sits defiant "right in the focus of [his] incandescent anger" (p. 204), returning his gaze with authority and candor, and the reader knows ultimately, long before the event, that Humbert Humbert's remonstra-tions will be futile and that he is doomed.

Once Lolita has escaped from him she assumes the guise, in Hum-bert Humbert's camera eye, of the fugitive heroine, in the tradition of Bonnie and Clyde, on the run with her partner in crime, Clare Quilty. Although here Lolita's partner is Quilty, there is a sense that Humbert Humbert is gaining some kind of vicarious pleasure from imagining them together, as if he were somehow in Quilty's shoes. Lolita's escape with Quilty is a direct mirroring of her travels with Humbert Humbert, the principal difference here being that Lolita is Quilty's willing passenger.

This role is significant in that it extends the notion of female empow-erment represented by the noir heroine. Here it spills over into the myths of the Wild West, of infamous criminal gangs like the James brothers of the 1870s and 1880s, and Bonnie and Clyde's Barrow gang of the early 1930s, gangs which "[captured] the public imagination because they [took] chances, and because often, they [enjoyed] dramatizing their lives."[30] This scenario is anticipated in the narrative by the films Hum-bert Humbert cites as Lolita's favorites — "underworlders" and "western-ers" (p. 170) — and by his description of them together as "meek fishy [Humbert] and dangerous Dolores Haze" (p. 172). It could be argued that the image of Lolita as a gun-toting outlaw is a direct allusion to Bon-nie Parker, who began her life of crime at the age of fifteen and was barely twenty when she met Clyde Barrow. In the four years they were together, they earned their reputations as "public enemies" by killing twelve peo-ple in holdups across America's southwestern states. Humbert Humbert's use of Lolita's proper name elevates her, as it were, to the status of a Bon-nie Parker, but it also signifies his estrangement from her and his sense that she no longer belongs to him. That she is still a mere child is utterly forgotten, as he is carried away by the romance and excitement of this vision of Lolita as a gunslinging bandit. He even further dramatizes the fantasy with a poem, again in an echo of the poems Bonnie Parker published in local newspapers in a deliberate effort to glamorize herself and Clyde. Humbert Humbert's poem betrays not only a knowledge of American folklore and the kind of crude popular verse Bonnie Parker produced, but also the facile, ludicrously improbable image of the American West promoted by Hollywood:

> Officer, officer, there they go —
> In the rain, where that lighted store is!
> And her socks are white, and I love her so,
> And her name is Haze, Dolores.
>
> Officer, officer, there they go —
> Dolores Haze and her lover!
> Whip out your gun and follow that car.
> Now tumble out, and take cover.
>
> Wanted, wanted: Dolores Haze.
> Her dream-gray gaze never flinches.
> Ninety pounds is all she weighs
> With a height of sixty inches [pp. 256–57].

Humbert Humbert's scenario also echoes the 1950 film release *Gun Crazy*, inspired by the legend of Bonnie and Clyde, which focuses on the romantic partnership of two "rebellious characters who actively choose to be criminals."[31] *Lolita*, like *Gun Crazy*, combines elements of both film noir and the Western, while *Gun Crazy* distinctly parallels some of *Lolita*'s principal preoccupations.

Bart Tare, the hero of *Gun Crazy*, is, like Humbert Humbert, depicted as an innocent, corrupted by a psychotic obsession. His weakness is guns, rather than nymphets, and this perversion causes him to become marginalized until he encounters Laurie Starr, her entrance into his life — like an "apparition, a dream come true"[32] — having a similar impact as Lolita's on Humbert Humbert's. There is, however, no central revenge motif in *Gun Crazy*; the couple are fugitive criminals eventually run down by the police, yet there are other narrative aspects which echo Nabokov's novel. For example, in *Gun Crazy*, "the high-speed getaways, together with ... scenes of the couple in transit, shape [it] as a road movie, the constant movement and furious action a graphic expression of their nomadic life together and its illicit pursuit of happiness."[33] This is essentially Humbert Humbert's perspective on his travels with Lolita, except for one crucial distinction — Lolita is not his willing partner in crime, but rather his "cross-country slave" (p. 150), essentially, his hostage. Neither are they hunted down, but they know only that they must inevitably settle to escape the suspicion of the authorities. Like *Lolita*, *Gun Crazy* "[plays] off and [parodies] the Western, [building] inevitably towards the final showdown, the most venerable of the Western's rituals, which Bart ironically revises and redirects by killing his soul mate."[34] Humbert Humbert also "revises and redirects" the "final showdown" by maintaining a level of ambiguity as to who the target of his revenge will be — Lolita or Quilty.

The "moll" is perhaps the figure Humbert Humbert relates to most closely. Lolita is defined as such early in the narrative during the episode on Charlotte's davenport, when Humbert Humbert attempts to distract her with his "Carmen" song. It is not coincidental that the role is continued after Lolita's escape by Rita, whom he picks up in a bar "somewhere between Montreal and New York" (p. 258) and abandons just as casually two years later. Rita is the epitome of a "fallen woman," and yet her suitability for the role in no way undermines the depiction of Lolita as moll. By contrast, Rita is a lonely, pathetic creature, a drunk who has been ostracized by her family and married, disastrously, three times. Her relationship with Humbert Humbert typifies the gangster/moll dynamic. He tolerates her, she worships him. For almost a year he consigns her to a motel in order to save himself the social embarrassment of being seen with her. Also typical of the moll, Rita has a self-destructive streak which often gets the better of her — she plays Russian roulette with Humbert Humbert's revolver, for example — and attracts her to dangerous and worthless men. Apart from Humbert Humbert, she manages to get mixed up with a "crook" (p. 259), almost gets picked up again by another stranger in another bar, and through a lack of supervision on Humbert Humbert's part, somehow has her appendix removed and winds up in jail for stealing some furs. Rita represents the predicament of the real-life moll, not the glamorized Hollywood version, and not even the fantastical movie-inspired character that Lolita becomes in Humbert Humbert's imagination. She is a sordid object of neglect and abuse, pitied but never respected, existing in a twilight world of drunken oblivion, seedy nightclubs and degenerate losers.

Lolita's final assumed cinematic role is that of the screwball heroine, a role closely linked to those she has already played, yet distinct from them in one fundamental way — comedy. Jim Kitses argues that there is a "direct line of descent from screwball heroine to noir's spider women.... If we strip Capra's professional women of their jobs and Sturges's gold-diggers of their conscience, we discover noir's dark ladies."[35] Invert this observation and Lolita's progress is explained.

The screwball comedy emerged as a Hollywood film genre in the late 1930s and is epitomized by William Wellman's *Nothing Sacred* (1937), Leo McCarey's *The Awful Truth* (1937), and Howard Hawks's *Bringing Up Baby* (1938). The genre continued into the 1940s and belonged to the tradition of farce, comedy arising from relationship conflicts, misunderstandings and romantic power struggles, with plots being driven by a "comic battle of the sexes, with the male generally losing."[36] The screwball comedy is located in contemporary middle- to upper-class American society, where money is never an issue, and everyday life is generally chaotic but essentially secure. In this scenario the male protagonist is depicted as ineffectual, naive and unsophisticated, characteristics which are amplified by the presence of the screwball heroine, who, by contrast, is manipulative, scheming and ambitious, that is, with regard to the object of her desires.

In many ways, Humbert Humbert presents himself as an absurd figure, utterly at Lolita's mercy. This is an effective means of disguising the true nature of their relationship, Lolita in reality being terrorized by threats of reform schools and orphanages, constantly reminded that her mother is dead and that she is a child alone with no family to protect her. Nevertheless, Humbert Humbert emphasizes the notion of his being a foreigner in a strange land, granting Lolita the illusion of command. Like the screwball hero, he enjoys "abundant leisure time,"[37] in which he pursues a spurious and obtuse academic career, "a profession seemingly nebulous to many Americans."[38] His unease in American suburbia parallels the screwball hero's "anti-rural and anti-small town values,"[39] yet as Wes Gehring argues:

> Although screwball comedy characters occasionally attack the country hayseed, they seldom attack the country setting itself, no doubt because

Opposite, top: The screwball heroine maintains the upper hand. Katharine Hepburn and Cary Grant in *Bringing Up Baby*, RKO, 1938. *Bottom:* Professor Potts (Gary Cooper) visits his new research subject, nightclub singer and gangster's moll Sugarpuss O'Shea (Barbara Stanwyck). Mobsters Asthma Anderson and Duke Pastrami are played by Ralph Peters, foreground, and Dan Duryea in closet). *Ball of Fire* (RKO, 1941).

Western culture has long considered the pastoral backdrop a classic location for the awakening of romance, even screwball style.[40]

The proximity of this aspect of screwball comedy to the Western is
marked. As Philip French comments, the "contrast between open land
and the town, between the illusion of freedom and the necessity of compromise, between a relaxed association with nature and a tense accom-
modation to society, lies at the roots of the genre,"[41] and this is also
exactly Humbert Humbert's predicament.

The "pastoral backdrop" of The Enchanted Hunters provides the
setting for the "awakening" of Humbert Humbert's "romance" and is sustained throughout his year-long cross-country travels with Lolita. The
moment they settle back in suburban Beardsley the enchantment is lost,
the locations of Ramsdale and Beardsley serving to frame the novel's central idyllic episode and enhance its escapist appeal.

The screwball male also has a "pronounced tendency toward regression to childhood,"[42] and while he tends to be an innocent, the screwball heroine is not. The parallels between this scenario and that presented
by Humbert Humbert are plainly apparent. Humbert Humbert is trapped
in his childhood past and would have remained so if Lolita had not
seduced him, and thus their relationship adheres to screwball comedy's
inversion of conventionally accepted patterns of social behavior. The
world of the novel is confined to a chaotic space — the internalized set-
tings of the car, the motel room and suburban detached house — in which
the protagonists define the rules of conduct.

At the same time they are at the mercy of inexplicable, incongruous coincidence, which in screwball comedy would be presented as ludicrous but is strongly reminiscent of the intrusive, destructive forces of
fate in film noir. In contrast, fate manifests itself in absurd plot twists
which demand from the audience a suspension of disbelief. The extraordinary coincidences in Humbert Humbert's tale, while definable in
terms of noir, can also be interpreted as a black form of screwball comedy. Also, the celebration of comic humiliation and the typical dénouement of screwball comedy, the comic confrontation between the antihero
and the conventional heroic male, can also be applied to Humbert Humbert's final confrontation with Quilty, in which chaos triumphs over
banality.

Lolita's guise as screwball heroine exposes the novel's dark comedy,
its tragic absurdity. Lolita herself seems to be conscious of this, com-

menting that "this world was just one gag after another, if somebody
wrote up [my] life nobody would ever believe it" (p. 273). This element
of black humor is noted by Pauline Kael in her criticism of Kubrick's
Lolita, and it is interesting that it should be particularly evident as a cinematic mode. Kael describes the film as "the first *new* American comedy
since those great days in the forties when Preston Sturges recreated comedy with verbal slapstick [i.e., screwball comedy]. *Lolita* is black slapstick."[43] In terms of Humbert Humbert's relationship with Lolita,
however, the scenario provides yet another means of further divesting
him of any moral responsibility, underpinning his argument that he is a
mere victim of the nymphet's demonic power — he dubs her his "Frigid
Princess" (p. 166) — and absolving him of any crime against her.

Fate and the Noir "Double Bind"

Humbert Humbert's dilemma is primarily that of the noir protagonist. Having entrusted his destiny to fate, the "synchronizing phantom"
(p. 103), he places himself in a classic double bind from which there is
no escape. Like many noir heroes before him, he finds himself at the end
of his tale in the place where he began, behind bars, doomed. In realizing that no external force exists which will ultimately make sense of it
all, the noir hero's only salvation is in confession, yet Humbert Humbert's narrative is no true confession, but an elusive, shifting, confused
manipulation of events, which betrays the essential fallacy of his perceived control and its inherent flaws. Having told the reader his history
of psychosis and mental breakdowns, that he should begin to crack under
the pressure of Quilty's pursuit comes as no surprise.

> After all ... it was becoming abundantly clear that all those identical
> detectives in prismatically changing cars were figments of my persecu-
> tion mania, recurrent images based on coincidence and chance resem-
> blance [p. 238].

He even admits that his photographic memory is not so infallible, describing himself as "a murderer with a sensational but incomplete and unortho-
dox memory" (p. 217). At the same time, however, these slips into insanity
could also be a deliberate ploy to bolster his defense, these vacillations
being a means both of confusing the imaginary jury he addresses and of
introducing the notion of diminished responsibility, even innocence. This

The screwball hero, Nick Arden (Cary Grant, left), is persistently thwarted by his estranged wife, Ellen (Irene Dunn, right), and his adversary, Stephen Burkett (Randolph Scott, center). *My Favorite Wife* (RKO, 1940).

is implied in an earlier scene in which he presents himself as the victim of police brutality, forced to confess to crimes he did not commit:

> Humbert Humbert sweating in the fierce white light, and howled at, and trodden upon by sweating policemen, is now ready to make a further "statement" (*quel mot!*) as he turns his conscience inside out and rips off its innermost lining [p. 70].

Humbert Humbert's emotive complaint at the injustice of the proceedings signals that he is consciously parodying the interrogation scenes of countless gangster movies or, possibly more specifically, the extended sequence in Bruce Humberstone's film noir of 1942, *I Wake Up Screaming*, in which Frankie Christopher is bullied by plainclothes detectives under a "fierce white light" in a gloomy Manhattan police cell.

Fate is key to the noir protagonist's predicament and similarly plays a central role in the progress of Humbert Humbert's narrative. He falls victim to the vacillations of fate, which at first seem to work in his favor but then inexplicably turn against him. It is fate that brings him to the Haze house — the McCoos' house, where he was originally to stay, conveniently burning down. It is fate which prevents him from drowning Charlotte in Hourglass Lake when later it will do the job for him by having her run over by a car. "McFate" (p. 107) returns his coins in the telephone booth when he calls Lolita at Camp Q, as if signaling its approval of his plans, and similarly, when he loses his way in the park at Briceland, fate produces a couple from out of the darkness to direct him to The Enchanted Hunters. He is, however, conscious of fate's fickle loyalty and the dangers of trying to usurp its control over his destiny. It haunts him with "the awful feeling that if [he] meddled with fate in any way and tried to rationalize her fantastic gift, that gift would be snatched away" (p. 173). Nevertheless, he senses it working against him from the moment he collects Lolita from camp. He identifies this negative force as "secondary fate (McFate's inept secretary)," which "pettily [interferes] with the boss's generous and magnificent plan" (p. 116), and it is this force which he recognizes only once again, in Beardsley, when it contrives to make a telephone ring and enable Lolita's escape, an incident which he instantly associates with film, complaining that "with people in movies I seem to share the services of the machina telephonica and its sudden god" (p. 205). At the same time there is an implication that Lolita's betrayal is fated and that he can do nothing about it. As he begins to suspect her behavior in Beardsley, he describes the sensation of "being enmeshed" in some "[obscure] pattern of fate" (p. 215). This notion has intriguing ramifications for the scenario of revenge in the narrative, for if fate enables her escape, then neither she nor Quilty can be held responsible for conspiring against him, and thus his quest for vengeance is rendered utterly redundant.

Themes of noir and the Western dominate Humbert Humbert's depiction of his flight with Lolita and her flight with and his pursuit of Quilty. Alfred Appel comments on most of the predominant elements of noir in the novel, from guns to cars, lighting effects and theme songs.[44] The icon of the "vagabond" car as "home and haven, death chamber and prison cell"[45] is a notion reiterated by director Arthur Penn, in a discussion of the lives of Bonnie and Clyde:

> They lived in their automobile — it was not unusual for them to drive seven and eight hundred miles in a night, in one of those old automobiles. They literally spent their lives in the confines of the car. It was really

where they lived. Bonnie wrote her poetry in the car, they ate ginger snaps in the car, they played checkers in the car — that was their place of abode. In American Western mythology, the automobile replaced the horse in terms of the renegade figure. This was the transformation of the Western into the gangster.[46]

The central action of *Lolita* takes place in a car, Lolita and Humbert Humbert living in it just as Bonnie and Clyde, with Quilty in a kind of indistinct, ever-changing reflection as he trails after them. It is in a car that Humbert Humbert returns to pursue his rival, driving in a night the "eight hundred miles" (p. 267) from New York to Coalmont in an otherwise impossible journey made possible by these two infamous outlaws. Cars also function as plot catalysts — his first wife's adultery is revealed to him in the back of a taxi, with the double irony of her lover being the taxi driver, Charlotte is killed by an out-of-control Packard, and Humbert Humbert is finally apprehended in a car. As Alfred Appel comments, the "forward motion of the narrative"[47] is driven by these various automobiles, and it stops when Humbert Humbert's Melmoth rolls into a ditch. At the same time, however, the specifically American role of the car is used beyond the context of the United States, in the European setting of the novel's opening, thus establishing it as yet another feature of Humbert Humbert's cinematically inspired imagination and indicating the extent of his assimilation of an American identity to an extent where it infects his pre–American past.

Movie Violence and Movie Heroes

The violence of the novel is also reminiscent of noir and Western films. If *Lolita* is perceived as an initiation, then violence, in terms of American lore, is key.

> Violence is part of the American character. It began with the Western, the frontier. America is a country of people who act out their views in violent ways — there is not a strong tradition of persuasion, of ideation, and of law.[48]

Humbert Humbert's appropriation of a gun and the American myths attached to it is a gesture of acceptance and is fundamental to the process of his initiation. Ironically, his use of violence against Quilty,

At gunpoint, a bewildered Quilty (Peter Sellers) tries to make sense of Humbert Humbert's poem. Sellers and James Mason in *Lolita* (MGM/Seven Arts, 1962).

and particularly his adoption of the gun as his weapon, confirms that he is more American than his American adversary, relegating Quilty to the position of coward, who represents, in ironic inversion, the European tradition of "persuasion, ideation and law" which Humbert Humbert shuns. The murder scene itself dramatizes Humbert Humbert's transition, and the conflict of two opposing ideologies within him is illustrated by his possession of a poem in one hand and a gun in the other. The poem fails in its purpose; the gun does not. Even the very notion of murder serves to transform Humbert Humbert's image of himself and his predicament, such that he can declare, "Now that I have an altogether different mess on my conscience, I know that I am a courageous man" (p. 169). More fundamentally, however, it enables him to obliterate the "mess" of Lolita.

The murder of Quilty not only transforms Humbert Humbert into "a courageous man" but is necessary in order for his initiation to be complete. Quilty, as representative of America's worst failings, must be annihilated for Humbert Humbert, representative of America's true aspirations, to take his place.

Both Michael Wood and Alfred Appel note the quotation of slapstick comedy and Western films in the scene of Quilty's murder,[49] yet the most intriguing aspect of the sequence is where it fails cinematically. The murder scene itself is prefigured by an earlier description of Humbert Humbert's ideal Hollywood saloon fight:

> The pistol thrust through the shivered windowpane, the stupendous fist fight, the crashing mountain of dusty old-fashioned furniture, the table used as a weapon, the timely somersault, the pinned hand still groping for the dropped bowie knife, the grunt, the sweet crash of fist against chin, the kick in the belly, the flying tackle [p. 170].

If this is not a sufficient premonition of the violence to come, Humbert Humbert also cites two contemporary films, *Brute Force* and *Possessed* (p. 262), both 1944 releases, as particularly appropriate to his predicament,[50] along with two actual cases taken from newspapers. The first refers to G. Edward Grammar, who "bludgeoned" his wife to death, bundled her body into her "big blue Chrysler" and tipped it over a cliff (pp. 287–88),[51] and the second to "Frank Lasalle, a fifty-year-old mechanic" (p. 289) who murdered an eleven-year-old girl in 1948. On his way to Pavor Manor the atmosphere of impending doom is eloquently sustained by the evocation of film noir's moody and oppressive darkness, as inspired by the distinctive nighttime driving scenes in Chandler's fiction.

> Night had eliminated most of the landscape and as I followed the narrow winding highway, a series of short posts, ghostly white, with reflectors, borrowed my own lights to indicate this or that curve … in front of me, like derelict snowflakes, moths drifted out of the blackness into my probing aura [p. 292].

There is a further reference to the noir canon in the image of a gun which appears on a drive-in movie screen Humbert Humbert passes (p. 293), identified by Appel as a scene from *Double Indemnity*,[52] and there is an echo of another of Wilder's films, *Sunset Boulevard*, in the depiction of his arrival at Pavor Manor which seems to replicate almost exactly Joe Gillis's description of Norma Desmond's monstrous and dilapidated Hollywood mansion:

I had landed myself in the driveway of some big mansion that looked rundown and deserted. At the end of the drive was a lovely sight indeed — a great big empty garage just standing there going to waste. If ever there was a place to stash away a limping car with a hot license number. There was another occupant in the garage — an enormous foreign-built automobile. It must have burned up ten gallons to a mile. It had a 1932 license. I figured that's when the owners had moved out.... It was a great big white elephant of a place, the kind crazy movie people built in the crazy twenties. A neglected house gets an unhappy look. This one had it in spades.[53]

Humbert Humbert's description also has the casual, sardonic quality that Joe Gillis's narrative has, the phrases "burning like a man" and the image of the "loaded" garage echoing the tough-guy vernacular of the noir hero:

A thunderstorm accompanied me most of the way back to Grimm Road, but when I reached Pavor Manor, the sun was visible again, burning like a man, and the birds screamed in the drenched and steaming trees. The elaborate and decrepit house seemed to stand in a kind of daze.... A guardedly ironic silence answered my bell. The garage, however, was loaded with his car, a black convertible.... I tried the knocker.... I pushed the front door — and, how nice, it swung open as in a medieval fairy tale. Having softly closed it behind me, I made my way across a spacious and very ugly hall [pp. 293–94].

Quilty's murder is the event which transforms Humbert Humbert from a coward into a hero, yet it is a dismal failure in terms of emulating the dénouement of a Western or film noir. It even fails as a consistent piece of slapstick. The only aspect of it that goes according to plan is that Quilty dies, yet even this is a matter, practically, of accident. It is presented in a series of fits and starts, Quilty refusing to comply with Humbert Humbert's demands, resulting in a comic deflation of the narrative's climactic scene. First, in another echo of *Sunset Boulevard*, the encounter opens with a misunderstanding. Quilty mistakes Humbert Humbert for someone else — Jack Brewster, a telephone company representative — as Norma Desmond mistakes Joe Gillis for an animal undertaker, come to bury her pet chimpanzee. While Joe Gillis manages to rectify the misapprehension, Humbert Humbert does not, a detail which ultimately qualifies his mission as a failure. Having refused to acknowledge Humbert Humbert's real identity, Quilty then fails to respond in the expected way to having a gun pointed at him, and rather than cower with fear, he approaches Humbert Humbert as if this were an elaborate practical joke.

> "Say!" he drowled (now imitating the underworld numbskull of movies), "that's a swell little gun you've got there. What d'you want for her?" [p. 297].

Appel comments that Humbert Humbert's gun play is comical, and yet his ineptitude serves more as a self-conscious act of self-deprecation, an agonizing demonstration of inadequacy, made a greater torment by Quilty's cynical response. His first shot is hopelessly inaccurate, his incompetence magnified by the implication of sexual impotence in the imagined course of the bullet's trajectory through the floor, which confirms his total inability to command the scene; all the while Quilty's jibes serve to deepen his humiliation:

> I pointed Chum at his slippered foot and crushed the trigger. It clicked. He looked at his foot, at the pistol, again at his foot. I made another awful effort, and, with a ridiculously feeble and juvenile sound, it went off. The bullet entered the thick pink rug, and I had the paralyzing impression that it had merely trickled in and might come out again [p. 297].

When it comes to fighting, Humbert Humbert and Quilty tussle like schoolboys, falling over each other, rolling around on the floor ineffectively, the spectacle reminiscent of Smurov's fight with his lover's husband in *The Eye*, but far removed from the expert maneuvers of Dashiell Hammett's fight scenes.

> With a tremendous lurch he fell all over me, sending the pistol hurtling under a chest of drawers. Fortunately he was more impetuous than vigorous, and I had little difficulty in shoving him back in his chair.... Fussily, busybodily, cunningly, he had risen again while he talked. I groped under the chest trying at the same time to keep an eye on him.... We fell to wrestling again. We rolled all over the floor, in each other's arms, like two huge helpless children.... Our tussle, however, lacked the ox-stunning fisticuffs, the flying furniture.... It was a silent, soft, formless tussle on the part of two literati, one of whom was utterly disorganized by a drug while the other was handicapped by a heart condition and too much gin [pp. 298–99].

At the same time, Quilty also seems to be aware that he is participating in an absurd parody of a Western movie. Quilty's hysterical piano playing emulates the conventional role of the Western's saloon pianist in the midst of a barroom brawl, who spontaneously launches into, say, a "frenzied rendition of 'Buffalo Girls,'"[54] in bizarre accompaniment to the mayhem around him, as a means of ensuring that the farcical aspect of the scene is sustained. The distinction here, however, is that whereas the pianist, like the bartender who ducks behind the bar, never participates in the fighting, Quilty is the only contender in this brawl and his playing is therefore inappropriate and futile, for it fails to diffuse the sense of palpable threat Humbert Humbert generates.

In terms of the cinematic presentation of Quilty's murder, it is significant that tension is generated in the final moments before Humbert Humbert's fatal shots by the same visual emphasis used earlier to dramatize his emotional collapse before a bemused Dolly Schiller. In this instance, however, it is Quilty who seems to be on the verge of collapse. Trying, hopelessly, to talk his way out of the situation, Quilty stands before a silent Humbert Humbert. Throughout Quilty's speech the visual focus remains fixed on him, and, as in the scene with Lolita, the reader/audience gets only an indication of Humbert Humbert's responses via Quilty. Whereas in the earlier scene, Lolita's interjections imploring Humbert Humbert to stop crying communicate his pathetic state, Quilty's requests to him to "stop pointing ... that gun" (p. 301) present him in a completely different guise — the determined, steadfast, cold-blooded killer. Quilty's desperate prattle generates a sense of urgency, and the two interjections of "drop that gun" (p. 302) communicates his fear that Humbert Humbert is losing patience with him and that there is no way he is going to persuade him not to shoot. The first shot "*Feu*" (p. 302) interrupts Quilty in midsentence, confirming that his fear was not unfounded, and as the suspense is broken so the visual perspective shifts back to Humbert Humbert, and the action recommences.

This particular sequence could be interpreted as a calculated attempt by Humbert Humbert to salvage the dignity which he lost in the earlier scene with Dolly Schiller. This would certainly uphold his newly adopted guise as a man of courage, a true American hero. Yet the process of the murder scene as a whole is slow and messy, quite unlike the lethal and efficient rapid-fire sharpshooting of a Wild West hero like Wyatt Earp, who in John Ford's seminal Western of 1946, *My Darling Clementine*, takes on the criminal Clanton family in a "final, ritualistic showdown

[of] somnambulistic violence."[55] He cannot even emulate the glory of cinema's psychopathic gangsters, for example Cody Jarrett in Raoul Walsh's *White Heat* (1949), one of film noir's "most crippled and maladjusted protagonists,"[56] who murders indiscriminately yet still dies a hero. Humbert Humbert's only achievement lies in his persistence. Although his resolve to kill Quilty remains undiminished, his crowning moment is inglorious, shoddy and bathetic, and Quilty dies with no understanding of his murderer's motives, dealing his revenge fantasy a final, crushing blow.

Pauline Kael, however, comment that "if there is such a thing as an American tragedy, it must be funny.... Our heroes pick up the wrong fork and the basic figure of fun in the American theater and American movies is the man who puts on airs.... [W]e are used to failure."[57] If so, the farcical quality of Quilty's murder designates it as belonging to this particular tradition of American heroics, and thus Humbert Humbert's failure is transformed into his success. Not only this, but he also succeeds in presenting a dénouement which fulfils all the expectations of the cinematic revenge scenario that he initiated with his "Carmen" song, and yet there is a sense that he has succeeded too well, that the scene is excessive in its declaration of cinematic influence, that the protagonists fit too comfortably into recognizable Hollywood roles. This is, essentially, a synthetic attempt to reassert his authority, to reclaim creative autonomy over his narrative and the events they portray. He is determined to conclude his scenario in the style in which it was begun, to an extent where he is prepared to fabricate its final scenes in order to achieve it.

Humbert Humbert's meeting with Lolita in Coalmont is critical in terms of locating the narrative's true dénouement. It is a scene in which he claims to have experienced an acute and profound form of emotional and spiritual death, and yet it is an anticlimax. It is provoked, instantly, at the first sight of Lolita standing before him on her marital doorstep.

> Couple of inches taller. Pink-rimmed glasses. New, heaped-up hairdo, new ears. How simple! The moment, the death I had kept conjuring up for three years was as simple as a bit of dry wood [p. 269].

From this moment on, Humbert Humbert relinquishes his authority and allows Lolita complete command of the scene. This is the first time that she is permitted to speak more than a few words and the only point in the narrative where the reader/audience is allowed an insight into her experience, unadulterated and uncorrupted by Humbert Humbert. The cinematic guises, the highly styled filmic references, the calculated use of perspective and visual effect are abandoned in all but one moment, when Humbert Humbert deploys the camera eye in an attempt to minimize his state of utter collapse. The scene is key because it not only initiates a sincere reevaluation of Humbert Humbert's relationship with Lolita and its consequences but also reduces him to a state of weary incapacity which he has to struggle to overcome. This he does by reasserting the cinematic mode gradually in the subsequent scenes leading up to Quilty's murder, to produce a finale which explodes onto the narrative in an extravagant display of cinematic pyrotechnics. Yet how far does this successfully obliterate the impact of Coalmont when it seems still to be reverberating even as Humbert Humbert arrives in a drunken haze at Pavor Manor? If this is a false dénouement, designed by a psychotic egomaniac desperate to salvage any remaining vestige of dignity and pride before an imaginary audience by whatever creative means available to him, then where is the narrative's true dénouement, if such a thing exists, and what form does it take?

Light and Dark, Colors and Shadows: The Filmic Image as Revelation

On his way to Ramsdale to confront Quilty's Uncle Ivor, Humbert Humbert stops in an "anonymous town" (p. 281) for the night. He sits in his car in the dark and the rain, quietly drinking and watching the blinking neon signs and lighted store windows. There is a sense of mystery evoked by the lights—generating a familiarly noir mood—against which Humbert Humbert reminds the reader of his black purpose, cool and self-assured—"let me dally a little," he says, "he [Quilty] is as good as destroyed" (p. 282). The narrative focus returns to the street, to the glistening darkness and the crude, flashing neon signs which "[flicker] twice slower than [his] heart":

> The outline of a restaurant sign, a large coffee-pot, kept bursting, every full second or so, into emerald life, and every time it went out, pink letters saying Fine Foods relayed it, but the pot could still be made out as a latent shadow teasing the eye before its next emerald resurrection. We made shadowgraphs [p. 282].

He senses himself melting into the lights and shadows and is held mesmerized by the synchronized rhythms of his heart and the "teasing shadow" of the flashing "emerald" restaurant sign. The shadow reflects the imprint of the past; its illumination is memory brought to life and represents the elusive, amorphous quality of his narrative. Yet, more importantly, it functions as a revelation or, as Maxim Shrayer would call it, a "textual opening,"[58] which offers a sudden insight into Humbert Humbert's very being. As Shrayer notes of Ivanov, the hero of "Perfection," Humbert Humbert seems to be experiencing a similar "[state] of unique fusion" in which "the past and the present [combine] through memory"[59] in a process of "cosmic synchronization."[60] The "latent shadow teasing the eye" is, as it were, the shadow of Lolita, cast indelibly in his consciousness for eternity. This notion is confirmed by the phrase, "We made shadowgraphs," which recalls a trivial remark made by Lolita about her activities at Camp Q (p. 114), transformed here into a complex conceit, layered with meaning and implication. A shadowgraph is a primitive form of X ray, a picture made by a shadow cast on a lighted surface or an image refracted by light through different densities of fluid. In essence, it embodies the visual quality of Humbert Humbert's narrative, its gray obscurity, its distortion and refraction of characters and events, its fugitive atmosphere of transient illusion and ambiguity, but also the very visual nature of his memory. Images of the past appear in his mind's eye like stills projected on a screen, and likewise, the shadowgraph functions as a kind of slide, an apparently blank strip of celluloid brought vividly albeit briefly to life by a beam of light. The shadowgraph haunts his consciousness in the same way that the shadows haunt the flashing neon signs. The conceit is also significant in that it communicates Humbert Humbert's state of eclipse, his dissolution, his sense of having been reduced to a shadow by grief and loss.[61] Combined with the visual potency of the image of the shadowgraph are the connotations generated by the specific colors of the neon signs, which serve to reveal his tainted conscience. Green is a color associated with the Devil, and pink with seduction and debauchery,[62] suggesting that he is at last acknowledging the evil he has perpetrated. The conceit of the shadowgraph is elegiac, but its contamination by the colors of the neon lights transforms it from a vision of wistful, nostalgic indulgence into a potent expression of guilt, following as it does the episode in Coalmont in which Humbert Humbert perceives himself to have died, spiritually and emotionally. It is in this state of surrender and shame that he goes to take his revenge on Quilty, an act rendered meaningless by this realization of defeat.

The scene is also reminiscent, visually and conceptually, of the opening of "The Vane Sisters," a story written in 1951 while Nabokov was working on *Lolita*. It features a series of apparent coincidences which lead the story's narrator to an accidental meeting with D., a former teaching colleague and lover of a former student, Sybil Vane, who committed suicide as a result of their affair. D. informs the narrator that Sybil's sister, Cynthia, an amateur psychic, has also recently died, and this provokes a return to the past in an attempt to understand the circumstances of this chance meeting. The narrator's "trivial investigations"[63] are initiated by the visual spectacle of thawing ice, which, like the neon signs in Humbert Humbert's anonymous town, seem to be conspiring to distract him, to communicate a specific, yet elaborately elusive, design:

> In the midst of my usual afternoon stroll through the small hilly town attached to the girls' college where I taught French literature, I had stopped to watch a family of brilliant icicles drip-dripping from the eaves of a frame house. So clear-cut were their pointed shadows on the white boards behind them that I was sure the shadows of the falling drops would be visible too.... There was a rhythm, an alternation in the dripping that I found as teasing as a coin trick. It led me to inspect the corners of several house blocks, and this brought me to Kelly Road, and right to the house where D. used to live [p. 619].

The effect on the story's narrator of the rhythmic dripping of the ice is almost identical to that of the flashing neon signs on Humbert Humbert. Like the vision of the neon signs the icicles "tease" the spectator's eye, alluring and provocative. Gradually they "[sharpen his] appetite for other tidbits of light and shade" (p. 619), overwhelming his consciousness and obliterating all his other senses:

> I walked on in a state of raw awareness that seemed to transform the whole of my being into one big eyeball rolling in the world's socket [p. 619].[64]

The visual effect of the dripping icicles serves to reduce the spectator to this state of "raw awareness," enabling the lights and shadows to dictate his every move and guide him, imperceptibly and irrevocably, to D., in a way which emulates the cinematic process, the eye, as it were, transformed into a camera lens.

I walked up, and I walked down, and I walked straight into a delicately
dying sky, and finally the sequence of observed and observant things
brought me ... to a street so distant from my usual eating place that I
decided to try the restaurant which stood on the fringe of the town.
Night had fallen without sound or ceremony when I came out again.
The lean ghost, the elongated umbra cast by a parking meter upon some
damp snow, had a strange ruddy tinge; this I made out to be due to the
tawny red light of the restaurant sign above the sidewalk; and it was
then — as I loitered there ... that a car crunched to a standstill near me
and D. got out of it [p. 620].

The same combination of color, light and reflection captures the narrator's attention and holds him, as it does Humbert Humbert, for just a
fleeting moment, but long enough for the critical detail to register. The
acrostic at the end of the story — "Icicles by Cynthia, meter from me,
Sybil" (p. 631) — reveals that "the bright icicles and the tinted shadow,
and the consequent chain of events, were all arranged by [the dead sis-
ters]."[65] Ironically, the story's narrator remains oblivious to this super-
natural conspiracy, in spite of having experienced, through his associations
with Cynthia and her psychic activities, the spirit world's palpable presence. His skepticism renders him blind to the sisters' subtle interference,
and he is left with a feeling of frustration and impotence — "everything
seemed yellowly blurred, illusive, lost" (p. 631). Color also has a specific
function in this episode, as it has in the shadowgraph scene, but could
be further elaborated here to suggest an authorial presence, the colors
blue, purple and red serving as codes to denote, in Nabokov's chromes-
thetic perception, the letters *V* and *S* — the initials of his Christian name,
Vladimir, and pen name, Sirin, respectively.[66]

In terms of Humbert Humbert's experience, "The Vane Sisters" is
key in that, as Boyd argues, it "sums up a great deal of Nabokov's art."
The principle of its "meticulous attention to the outer world of shine and
sludge, [its] exact eye for the inner world of desire, despair, detachment,
and [its] urgent compulsion to discover something that might lie
beyond"[67] is significant in that it demonstrates the extent to which an
apparently incidental episode can possess extensive dramatic ramifications.
If, therefore, the details of such scenes are regarded as "a chance for us
to experience the surprise of a discovery that utterly transforms the story
and its world"[68] then the function of the shadowgraph conceit in *Lolita*
and all that it implies is instantly confirmed and, once realized, cannot
be ignored.

The conceit is also critical as a far more sophisticated demonstration of Humbert Humbert's cinematically inspired imagination than the parody of slapstick comedy, film noir and Western movies which he deploys to transform the banality of Quilty's murder into a sublime piece of cinema. It could be argued, therefore, that the murder scene functions merely as Humbert Humbert's "MacGuffin," a term Alfred Hitchcock used to describe a detail or a piece of action which serves as a plot catalyst, and apparently a very important one, but which proves, ultimately, to be of no consequence.[69] If this is the case, then it is the shadowgraph scene, with its depth of revelation and insight, which provides the narrative's pivotal cathartic moment. Quilty's murder is thus reduced to a hollow act serving merely to conclude the charade that is Humbert Humbert's revenge scenario.

Humbert Humbert and the American Cinematic Tradition

Humbert Humbert's initiation as an American hero is, nevertheless, determined by his successful engagement in a medium which is both a major "part of the American collective unconsciousness" and its "primary shared experience."[70] Film provides him with a crucial frame of reference enabling him to gain access to a nation and a culture which would otherwise have remained alien to him, and offers a means of both interpreting and delineating his environment in the dimensions of the actual and the imaginary. Humbert Humbert's Americanness is designated not only by his emulation of the heroes of film — the gangster, the noir victim, the Western outlaw, the screwball loser — but also the degree to which he continues in a tradition of compromised characters in American literature from Dos Passos's Jimmy Herf and Fitzgerald's Nick Carraway to Chandler's Philip Marlowe, while reflecting their cinematically-inspired consciousness. At the same time, he also anticipates the movie-obsessed hero of Walker Percy's *Moviegoer* (1961), Binx Bolling.

Bolling, like Humbert Humbert, uses film to create an alternative dimension of actuality, but for a very different purpose. He is suffering from an intense sense of alienation and isolation, a malaise generated by what he identifies as the "pain of loss"[71]:

> The world is lost to you, the world and the people in it, and there remains
> only you and the world and you no more able to be in the world than
> Banquo's ghost [p. 120].

"Moviegoing" offers him temporary relief from this malaise, and, like
Humbert Humbert's cinematic imaginings, every aspect of the filmic
experience plays a particular role in enabling this release, from the process
of movie-going itself, to the emulation of particular film roles, even reference to movie actors in their real-life guises. In the same way that Humbert Humbert emulates "movieland manhood," Bolling acquires a sense
of vaunted masculinity by referring to the heroes of contemporary Hollywood — William Holden, Gregory Peck, Dana Andrews, Clark Gable,
or Paul Newman, for example. His emulation of these stars serves as an
expedient device for handling problematic situations, and this grants him
a sense of control and self-assurance which, in an echo of Humbert Humbert's contrivances, is also particularly useful when trying to seduce
women. He "keeps a Gregory Peckish sort of distance" around his secretary, Sharon Kincaid, for example (p. 68), and when he crashes his
sports car on a date he even believes that he has surpassed the on-screen
heroics of Tony Curtis or Rory Calhoun, delighted that he has been
injured since it has given him an opportunity to demonstrate his courage. Most importantly, though, these transient flights of fancy release
him, albeit momentarily, from the grip of malaise.

The significance of these figures in Bolling's imagination also extends
beyond their screen manifestations to penetrate their real-life existence
so that they are made somehow more dynamic by their having been incar-
nated on the big screen:

> [William] Holden has turned down Toulouse shedding light as he goes.
> An aura of heightened reality moves with him and all who fall within it
> feel it [pp. 16–17].

The reverence Bolling expresses here, however, is not that of a fan. He
has no interest in following these actors' lives or in collecting autographs
or memorabilia. It is Holden's "peculiar reality which astounds" him (p.
17). The "aura of heightened reality" that the star leaves in his wake
infects the entire scene. The street is transformed into a "tremendous"
spectacle, but the effect quickly fades:

> Am I mistaken, or has a fog of uneasiness, a thin gas of malaise, settled
> on the street? ... Ah, William Holden, we already need you again. Already
> the fabric is wearing thin without you [p. 18].

Bolling's moviegoing is a quest, a search for a cure to the malaise he suffers, but it remains undefined and forever out of reach. Bolling is a veteran of the Korean War, and, paradoxically, the only time in his life when he felt that "the grip of everydayness was broken" was during that war, when he was wounded and "lay bleeding in a ditch" (p. 145). He cannot, and does not want to, replicate the same circumstances in peacetime simply in order to free himself of this malaise, but he has discovered in moviegoing a means of accessing another realm which allows him both a brief respite and an intensity of being that he longs to rediscover. Moviegoing offers more than simply an escape; it also offers a sense of belonging, of certification. This incorporates not only an identification with movie stars but also the notion of the power of film to capture and project the world in an alternative dimension that is more real than reality itself _ a form of hyperreality. The intensity and vitality of the cinematic experience is transferred also to everyday things, serving to certify ordinary people and the unremarkable places where they live:

> Nowadays when a person lives somewhere in a neighborhood, the place is not certified for him. More than likely he will live there sadly and the emptiness which is inside him will expand until it evacuates the entire neighborhood. But if he sees a movie which shows his very neighborhood, it becomes possible for him to live, for a time at least, as a person who is Somewhere and not Anywhere [p. 63].

The places which generate the most intense certification, however, are cinemas themselves. Bolling's literal moviegoing is part of this ritual of certification, whereby he will go to a movie theater in order to visit the place, to get a sense of its character, its atmosphere, its history and even to meet the people who work there. If he does not do this, then he would be "lost, cut loose," and there would be no point in seeing the film showing there because there would be no way of identifying that movie with that place and time. "There is a danger of slipping clean out of space and time," he explains. "It is possible to become a ghost and not know whether one is in downtown Leews or Denver or suburban Bijou in Jacksonville" (p. 75). The purpose of moviegoing, therefore, is to anchor himself in the world. In one theater he marks his seat with his thumbnail as if to confirm his presence in eternity — "Where, I wondered, will this particular piece of wood be twenty years from now, 543 years from now?" (p. 216) — but what he is really hoping to achieve is something he calls a "rotation." This he defines as "the experiencing of the new beyond the expectation of the experiencing of the new" (p. 144). By marking his presence he can return to this same place at any future time and have an instant means of comparing past and present experience and thus be able to define the new moment as something that has gone beyond his expectation of it. Better still, however, is the rare occurrence of what he calls a "repetition within a rotation." This is when the moviegoer returns to the same theater to see the same film to find that the content of the film being shown reflects the present situation, the place, the people in the audience and the time of year (see, for example, Bolling's *Dark Waters* experience on p. 144), combining in a single, synchronous moment that which would have been impossible to predict or contrive. And yet these moments do not last, they have no power to endure, and if they are sought out too often they also begin to fragment, and so the possibilities for relief diminish. As Bolling explains:

> But good as it is, my old place is used up (places get used up by rotary and repetitive use) and when I awake, I awake in the grip of everydayness [p. 145].

Bolling's life is reduced, therefore, to a matter of "deflat[ing] the pressure" of "everydayness" through his moviegoing. His emulation of film is neither cynical nor manipulative, but he echoes Humbert Humbert in his cinematic aspirations, although he is less successful than Humbert Humbert in establishing film as a permanent, alternative realm of existence. As Tony Tanner argues, Binx Bolling belongs to a long line of literary American heroes who pursue some form of quest (Jay Gatsby being one of them), and yet for Bolling "the search is finally for a true wonder, a maintained curiosity, an inviolable sense of reality."[72] While Bolling's search is "into the 'here and now,' [and] not away from it,"[73] Humbert Humbert rejects the "here and now" and replaces it with a cinematically inspired fantasy. Thus, although he establishes himself as an American hero, Humbert Humbert breaks away from the central idea of "wonder" in the American tradition, from the aspiration for a "true way of seeing" enabled by a "generous, open, even naive, undulled and reverent eye."[74] Humbert Humbert's rebellion continues that of his predecessors — Smurov, Albinus, Hermann Karlovich — and yet it is significant in that it prefigures a subversion of "true ways of seeing" in later American fiction, particularly evident in the film and television-informed manipulations of Brett Easton Ellis's psychotic anti-hero, Patrick Bateman.

Distinctive parallels can also be drawn with Faulkner's *Sanctuary*. Humbert Humbert's manipulation of the cinematic mode echoes Faulkner's, particularly with respect to Popeye. The camera eye in Faulkner's narrative functions voyeuristically, demonstrating the same sophistication and level of control and intent as Humbert Humbert's. In terms of characterization, Humbert Humbert can also be regarded as sharing Popeye's depthlessness. His command of the visual aspect of the narrative and its mode of presentation renders him, essentially, opaque. Humbert Humbert's depthless quality is generated not by enigmatic silence but, conversely, by his saturation of the narrative with a highly subjective and emotive perspective which is further complicated by ambiguity, contradiction and vacillation, serving, ultimately, to prevent any objective insight into his character. At the same time, the dynamics of Temple Drake and Popeye's relationship bear overt similarities to that of Humbert Humbert and Lolita. Humbert Humbert, like Popeye, is a voyeur, and in spite of the physical nature of his relationship with Lolita, the narrative's erotic drive is generated by an emphasis on spectacle, on ways of seeing, inspired, principally, by film. Lolita, too, shares Temple's qualities of precocious innocence, an innocence which is corrupted and destroyed by one man's depravity. Her presentation in the narrative also denies her an independent point of view, apart from the scene in Coalmont, where she is allowed to take command of the visual perspective, an episode which corresponds with the scenes in *Sanctuary* shortly after Temple's arrival at Miss Reba's brothel. In *Sanctuary*, Faulkner deploys the camera eye to generate a sense of estrangement and distilled horror. In *Lolita*, Humbert Humbert manipulates the modes, styles and techniques of film to communicate the overwhelming force of his desire, in a deeply cynical and highly complex act of deception, designed to transform the horror that he perpetrates into an evocative and compelling scenario of tragic romance.

Nabokov's deployment of cinematics in *Lolita* indicates a prevailing preoccupation with modes of presentation which extends into other contemporary works, particularly "The Assistant Producer" and *Bend Sinister*. In *Ada*, published eight years after his departure from America in 1961, Nabokov's affinity with the American cinematic experience is still evident as it was in his early Russian work, and his fascination with the medium extends even into his penultimate novel, *Transparent Things*, which reflects the concerns generated by the changing dynamics in film and television during the late 1960s and early 1970s. *Lolita*, however, was critical in Nabokov's oeuvre in its consolidation of his cinematic ideas. Not only did it demonstrate that film could be successfully and legitimately integrated into a work of fiction, but it also established a creative principle which offered new imaginative and conceptual realms and a means of further exploring the questions central to his art.

Six

Dream Distortions: Film and Visual Deceit in "The Assistant Producer," *Bend Sinister* and *Ada*

Every creator is a plotter; and all the pieces impersonating his ideas on the board were here as conspirators and sorcerers. Only in the final instant was their secret spectacularly exposed.[1]

In *Lolita*, film provides Humbert Humbert with the means to achieve the status of a true American hero, but it is also the medium which ultimately betrays him. In his "game of intricate enchantment and deception,"[2] Humbert Humbert deploys the cinematic mode to create a palpable and credible alternative reality. This reality is, essentially, a synthetic dimension constructed from a synthetic medium, and its inherent qualities of actuality and fantasy are exploited in a formidable celebration of artifice and "splendid insincerity."[3] Film is integral to *Lolita*'s "fine fabric of deceit"[4] but it is also fundamental in the portrayal of events in two other works that precede it, "The Assistant Producer" and *Bend Sinister*, as well as the 1969 novel, *Ada*, in which film is openly declared as both a narrative mode and a mnemonic tool, utilized in a complex process of deceit and unsustainable illusion.

Realms of Cinematic Existence in "The Assistant Producer" *and* Bend Sinister

"The Assistant Producer," published in America in 1943, is distinctive for two reasons. First, as Brian Boyd points out, it is because "for once [Nabokov] tells a story that really happened,"[5] and second, because of the way in which the story is told — as a film. In no other work to date does Nabokov utilize and deploy cinematics so explicitly. "Tonight we shall go to the movies,"[6] he announces at the story's opening, and indeed the entire piece is presented exactly as it would appear on screen, the scenes having a familiar quality of silent film melodramas, presented in a crude and amateurish style. On the surface, the very apparent mechanics of the assistant producer's film render it a failure, and yet the overt display of its technical artifice can also be interpreted as a smokescreen deployed to conceal the story's central premise. The layers of artifice in the story, therefore, do more than merely parody the synthetic, two-dimensional aspect of film. Rather, the story demonstrates the very essence of Nabokov's creative method in its calculated manipulation of illusion and its central evasive dynamic.[7]

"The Assistant Producer" demonstrates Nabokov's intimate knowledge of the techniques and styles of filmmaking but is also significant for its narrative manipulations, and particularly, its exploitation of authorial/directorial control. This is made evident in the series of weary and sardonic interjections made by the narrator/assistant producer throughout the story — "we are now going to witness a most weirdly monotonous series of events" (p. 549) — which deny the reader/audience the ability to formulate a subjective opinion on what it is being "shown." This betrays more than a simple lack of faith in the audience's interpretational abilities, however. Rather it smacks of veiled pride, undercut by an anxiety on the part of the assistant producer that his audience should not miss any crucial detail and thus be oblivious to his achievement. "By presenting everything as if on a movie screen, [Nabokov] makes the facts appear an impossibly trite romantic fiction," Boyd argues.[8] This is essentially the position taken by many critics with regard to this story: that Nabokov is using a second-rate art form to satirize the mediocrity and appalling banality of the real-life scenario.[9] Yet there is an innate paradox evident in the narrative in terms of authorial intent which demands closer examination, while on a more mundane level, the story is interesting for what it reveals about Nabokov's relationship to film, his experience of it and his knowledge of its workings, apart from the wider significance of producing a story written as a piece of American cinema.

The story recounts the scandal of a renowned Russian folk singer, Nadezhda Plevitskaia,[10] who was tried in Europe in 1938 "on charges of complicity, with her husband General Skoblin, in the kidnapping and murder, on the orders of the Soviet secret police, of several leaders of the Russian white movement."[11] True events are transformed into tawdry, absurd slapstick, with the characters' real identities only thinly disguised by the pseudonyms La Slavska and General Golubkov respectively. The story is an indictment of the revolution and its perpetrators, in particular its hypocritical leaders on both sides, for Golubkov, although a white, turns out to be a "triple agent" (p. 549). Poetic justice is offered in the form of its heroes' ultimate fall by the very same conspiracies and deceptions they use against their enemies.

Nabokov's choice of silent screen melodrama to present this scenario provides him with a perfect vehicle for parody. The style of the film seems ludicrously outmoded if set against the sophistication of contemporary talking pictures. The format of the film itself enables the events of several years to be condensed into a matter of minutes, deflating the principal protagonists' capacity for evil and reducing them to caricatures (the villain and the vamp). The story's fundamental impact, however, lies in its declaration of the essential artifice of the film itself. Every technical detail is brought starkly to the reader's attention in order to demystify the cinematic experience, to strip it of its magic.

> We get a gloomy glimpse of ravens, or crows, or whatever birds proved available, wheeling in the dusk and slowly descending upon a plain littered with bodies somewhere in Ventura County [p. 547].

The cinematic process, which involves laborious and elaborate contrivance, is repeatedly exposed. In this instance it is of no consequence that the actual landscape is American, and the birds nondescript. The scene would have convinced if its trickery had not been announced. As authenticity is sacrificed for effect in film, so it is in the lives of La Slavska and Golubkin. Every aspect of their existence is phony, every action calculated for maximum impact and maximum return. Even at moments of critical danger they continue their act, sacrificing their integrity and the possibility of salvation to the automatic response of a tired routine which culminates in La Slavska's fainting fit at the news of her husband's disappearance — "The Slavska said, 'Akh!' and crashed in a dead swoon, almost wrecking the parlor in the process" (p. 556).

The assistant producer, adopting, in addition, the role of projectionist, fights to control the film's unwieldy and cumbersome mechanics — "but my reel is going too fast" (p. 549) — yet at the same time he does not seem overly concerned by his clumsiness and technical incompetence. Paradoxically, his interjections also serve to defend the film — "these dreams may well strike the film pruners as an excrescence upon the main theme" (p. 550) — in a defiant assertion of authority which flies in the face of conventional processes of shooting and editing. His tyrannical aspirations are conveyed even in his comments on incidental character roles, for example the "Parisian *clochard*," which he qualifies as "an easy part" (p. 558), and gradually the parodic distance between narrator and subject begins to diminish.

The narrator's precise declaration of the details of the cinematic process has a celebratory quality, and at points, the film displays a technical virtuosity which far outstrips the capabilities of silent film. At the same time certain scenes have a visual quality reminiscent of Eisenstein's montage style. A scene of revelry at General Golubkov's camp, for example, is depicted in a series of obvious yet expert cuts, alternating from medium shots to choker close-ups and interspersed with "cutaways,"[12] in order that not only every sordid detail is captured but also the means by which it is rendered unequivocally acknowledged:

> A lithe Georgian dancing with a dagger, the self-conscious samovar reflecting distorted faces, the Slavska throwing her head back with a throaty laugh, and the fat man of the corps, horribly drunk, braided collar undone, greasy lips pursed for a bestial kiss, leaning across the table (close-up of an overturned glass) to hug — nothingness, for wiry and perfectly sober General Golubkov has deftly removed her [p. 548].

This is, in fact, a demonstration of highly skilled directing, rendered in a series of close-ups switching from the dancer to the samovar to La Slavska and the fat man, the scene closing with a "jump" cut to a medium shot which reveals Golubkov standing in the empty space where La Slavska had been. The sequence juxtaposes movement, stillness, sound and silence, its deliberate manipulation of visual effects signaled by the "self-conscious samovar," the level of artifice being such that even inanimate objects — the dagger, the samovar — participate in the scene. Another inanimate object, a bullet, serves to enable the scene's eloquent conclusion — the final shot resting on a shattered window accompanied by the clamor of an unseen crowd.

> And now as they both stand facing the gang [Golubkov] says in a cold, clear voice: "Gentlemen, I want to present to you my bride" — and in

the stunned silence that follows, a stray bullet from outside chances to shatter the dawn-blue window pane, after which a roar of applause greets the glamorous couple [p. 548].

The narrator/projectionist/assistant producer also draws overtly on silent comedy. The slapstick quality of these scenes is reiterated in Golubkov's abduction, which is reminiscent of a sequence from a Marx Brothers movie:

> General Golubkov cursed the wind at the top of his voice, and as this was the all-clear signal the green door opened and three pairs of hands with incredible speed and skill whisked the old man out of sight. The door slammed [p. 555].

As the two generals exit La Slavska's apartment having told her of her husband's disappearance, the visual comedy is sustained in an emulation of the absurd procrastinations of Laurel and Hardy or Abbott and Costello:

> They delicately touched each other's elbows in the doorway. Finally the slightly older man accepted the privilege and made a jaunty exit. Then they both paused on the landing, for the staircase struck them as being very still. "General!" cried the General L. in a downward direction. Then they looked at each other. Then hurriedly, clumsily, they stomped down the ugly steps, and emerged, and stopped under a black drizzle, and looked this way and that, and then at each other again [p. 557].

Also contributing to the scene's cinematic quality is the gradual and deliberate depiction of the action, amplified by the repeated use of the simple conjunctions "then" and "and," which indicate shifts in visual focus, marking, as it were, a series of "invisible cuts."[13]

The parodic stance of the assistant producer is further dissolved by the gentle humor of these episodes, and once again the notion that this film signifies more to him than a cynical manipulation of cinematic clichés is reasserted. Key to the revelation of the assistant producer's motives is the puzzle of his identity, which lies at the heart of the story. Gennady Barabtarlo points out that the elusive narrator, whose name is seen fading against the film's opening sequence, identifies himself as "a former White army priest,"[14] the priest whom Golubkov inexplicably mentions just before he disappears. Charles Nicol, however, argues that the assistant producer is Golubkov himself and that he is identified as such in the story's final paragraph,[15] serving to extend the theme of mirroring in the story which Nicol considers to be central. He also suggests, in support of this argument, the contemporary relevance of a real-life Hollywood episode and its fictional portrayal — Josef von Sternberg's use of Russian émigrés in his 1928 release, *The Last Command*, and an episode in F. Scott Fitzgerald's *Last Tycoon*, in which Hollywood producer Monroe Stahr considers casting a Russian prince in his film about the 1917 revolution.[16] Apart from providing a context of actuality, the notion of Nabokov's ready appropriation of Hollywood incidents indicates the extent of his regard for the medium, which generates a deeper resonance over and above the demonstration of a simple "[integration of] form and content"[17] for the purposes of parody.

Although "The Assistant Producer" is an attack on the absurdity of all politics, red or white, left wing or right, it is, more intrinsically, and more acutely, about loss. If the assistant producer's identity is taken to be that of the priest in the story, then in showing this film, he is recalling a past that was his also, for he accompanied La Slavska on her travels in Russia and Europe, and his memories are therefore inextricably linked with the events he depicts in his film. What is striking about his memory of the theaters of Berlin and Paris is the extent to which their all-pervasive artifice has permeated his own existence:

> I feel as if I were Technicoloring and sonorizing some very ancient motion picture where life had been a gray vibration ... and where only the sea had been tinted (a sickly blue), while some hand machine imitated off stage the hiss of synchronous surf [p. 551].[18]

It is his "gray" past[19] which he is bringing back to life in this film, and somehow the process of remembering is as overtly mechanical and ludicrously artificial as a staged scene. Yet what is critical about this passage is the notion that the past has not become gray with the passage of time but was already reduced to a colorless "vibration" and that no amount of technical wizardry can reanimate something that was always, essentially, dead. The skill, or lack of, on the part of the filmmaker therefore, is not, ultimately, significant.

The puzzle of the assistant producer's identity is further complicated in this respect by the close affinity between the predicaments of the priest and the "dove-gray" (p. 553) General Golubkov. The phony Russia of the film represents the loss of a country and a past which can never be reversed, and thus both the assistant producer and the general have become ghosts, desaturated like ageing celluloid. That Golubkov is associated with the story's other possible narrator — the white army priest — is also significant in that it somehow absolves him of his crimes. To extend this idea further still, the possibility of Golubkov himself being the film's anonymous director would account for the assistant producer's vehement defense of the film, at the same time elucidating the master/servant dynamic that typifies the director/assistant producer relationship, thus confirming the story's redemptive purpose. Thus Golubkov's appearance at the end of the story is sanctioned, as he is seen "emerging," appropriately, "from [an American] movie palace,"[20] discreetly anonymous, recognizable only by the production of his "old leathern cigarette case" (p. 559), a gesture he makes only once previously, moments before his abduction (see p. 555). If Golubkov is the film's absent director, then this final appearance could be considered an echo of Alfred Hitchcock's famous on-screen appearances, being a calculated gesture to assert his overriding directorial presence.

Like Delmore Schwartz's "In Dreams Begin Responsibilities," "The Assistant Producer" examines the experience of a recollected past. Both stories present this as film, fictionalizing the memories and reducing them to a depthless medium, while further depersonalizing them by delegating control to an anonymous, absent director. This is achieved in Schwartz's story by postponing the revelation that the scenario is dreamed, and in "The Assistant Producer" by sustaining the illusion of an unidentifiable narrator, compounded by the implication that his is a subordinate role and that ultimate control belongs elsewhere. This serves to dramatize the distance each narrator feels regarding his own past life. For Schwartz's protagonist, the alienation he feels is positive, for it enables him to divorce himself from circumstances which were and remain beyond his control and to experience the emotions he has denied himself by failing to confront the facts of the past. The film, therefore, acts as a catalyst, providing a metaphysical watershed between childhood and adulthood, the night of the dream marking the transition between his twentieth and twenty-first year. For Nabokov's assistant producer, the personal past is trivialized by the banality of the film's scenario, leading characters and shoddy production. Yet this is a ruse to deflect attention away from the narrator and the story's central idea of loss. The distinctive difference between the two stories, however, lies in the perceived reliability of each film. Schwartz's protagonist recognizes the images before him as real, whereas, although the scenario of "The Assistant Producer" is based on fact, its cinematic representation declares its essential artifice. Nabokov's assistant producer uses his film to dramatize — as he perceives them — the surreal quality of actuality and his own existence, and yet in terms of Nabokov's principle of "splendid insincerity," the assistant producer's purpose is to provoke his audience into solving the puzzle of his true motivations. Unlike Schwartz's protagonist, the assistant producer expresses neither anger nor frustration at his predicament but rather a quiet resignation to it, and the film seems to offer a means of achieving this state, in that it allows the individual the power to recombine and reconstitute reality according to his own personal vision.

This notion is echoed in *Bend Sinister*, Nabokov's second novel in English and the first to be published in America, in which he makes "a distinctive use of the devices and the symbolic implications of cinema."[21] As in "The Assistant Producer," film is presented both as a medium of terrifying banality and of "intricate enchantment and deception." The mass appeal of cinema is exploited as a propaganda tool by the novel's central tyrannical figure, Paduk, who capitalizes on its hypnotic impact, the druglike euphoria which it generates (as expressed by the hero of Delmore Schwartz's story). At the same time, film can be used more subtly and for more positive ends. Like the assistant producer, Nabokov openly declares the mechanics of film production in his narrative,[22] and this has a similar effect of disengaging the reader from the scenario, undercutting the emotive response to the horrors of Paduk's regime, and thus allows for a greater sensitivity to the intricacies of his presentation. Nabokov's "film" is, however, more discreetly manipulative than Paduk's. Here the process of transforming reality is not to realize it, as the assistant producer does, but to negate it. Apart from propaganda purposes, Paduk uses film to terrorize his people by subjecting them to brief glimpses of the senseless horror he perpetrates, exemplified by his "home movie" of Krug's son being tortured by a lunatic. Nabokov's response to this is to emphasize the dream quality of film, which also serves as a means of "halting the onward rush of time,"[23] and is in essence an attempt to defy mortality and thus the pain of human existence.

Most significant in this process is the role of memory, which is presented as shifting, malleable, fluid, and subject to the manipulations of both the conscious and unconscious mind:

> The script of daytime memory is far more subtle in regard to factual details, since a good deal of cutting and trimming and conventional recombination has to be done by the dream producers.[24]

Here, the "dream producers" function as the processes of remembering, which are somehow inherently flawed and inadequate. Krug's "dream producers" are "illiterate and middle-class" (p. 60), and yet, ironically, Nabokov too is a "dream producer."[25] The notion of the dreamquality of reality is also emphasized here—"the recurrent dream we all know ... was in Krug's case a fair rendering of the atmosphere of the original version" (p. 60). It is significant that the evocation of an "atmosphere" is sufficient to reconstitute the past, suggesting that the present also is nothing more than a sensation, intangible, illusory. This echoes the assistant producer's desire to withdraw, to become amorphous, a "gray vibration" even. The ultimate truth of the novel, therefore, is denial through art. Krug's reality exists only as long as Nabokov imagines it. Thus, the moment his creative trance is broken by the sound of the moth at the window, and just at the point where Krug is about to take the second and "better bullet," the scenario suddenly and conveniently dissolves, "like a rapidly withdrawn slide" (p. 200). Paduk is reduced to a mere "play upon words," and death to "a question of style" (p. 200), at once both diminishing the horrors of Krug's world and offering him a means of escape.

This final sequence is also an explicit revelation of the dimensions of narrative perspective covertly manipulated throughout the novel by Nabokov in his role as author/director. The events of the past have been reconstituted in the novel's film/narrative, bringing them into the immediate plane of experience, while a parallel actuality is exposed in the present scenario of Nabokov sitting in his study absorbed in the activities of his fictional protagonist. Nabokov, therefore, has used a synthetic medium not only to explore and express Krug's reality, but also, ultimately, to negate it, yet this is not an act of denial, but simply a transformation. The film/narrative enables a shift in perspective, and it is this that grants Krug a form of release from the tyranny of memory and mortality.

The manipulation of filmic perspective in *Bend Sinister* demonstrates what can be achieved by the deployment of "splendid insincerity," but it also echoes Nabokov's comment on Schwartz's story, the notion of the creative possibilities that arise from "a miraculous blend of an old cinema film with a personal past."[26] A key image fundamental to this concept is contained in Schwartz's story—"the long arm of light" which carries the delicate, translucent images of the film "[across] the darkness," "spinning" from projector to screen (p. 1). In Nabokov's fiction of the 1940s and later on, this "long arm of light" becomes synonymous with the act of remembering. In *Bend Sinister*, however, Nabokov, in his guise as "an anthropomorphic deity" (p. 11) "[slides] along an inclined beam of pale light" (p. 193) to reach his fictional protagonist incarcerated in a prison-house of torturous dreams and fears. The "inclined beam of pale light" is reminiscent of the projector's beam but is here also explicitly symbolic of the link between imagination and reality, serving as an amorphous bridge between two worlds, a notion which originates in *The Gift* (1938), when Fyodor realizes the power of light to reveal a parallel, otherwise invisible realm:

> Through the glass the ashen light from the street fell on both of them and the shadow of the iron design on the door undulated over her and continued obliquely over him ... while a prismatic rainbow lay on the wall. And as often happened to him ... Fyodor suddenly felt — in this

Norma Desmond (Gloria Swanson) relives her past for Joe Gillis (William Holden) courtesy of the film projector's beam. *Sunset Boulevard* (Paramount, 1950).

glassy darkness — the strangeness of life, the strangeness of its magic, as if a corner of it had been turned for an instant and he had glimpsed its unusual lining.[27]

A similar image appears again in *Speak, Memory* as Nabokov recalls "distant times whose long light finds so many ways to reach [him]."[28] Modified and presented in converse, as if in a gesture of triumph over time, the source of light is now not in the present but in the past, the light projected forward rather than back, powerful and persistent. Light, too, becomes a metaphor for life, the life of the past remaining undiminished by the passage of time. Combined with this is the notion that "our existence is but a brief crack of light between two eternities of darkness,"[29] an image again reminiscent of the vision of the film projector's beam cutting through the dark interior of a movie theater in both *Bend Sinister* and Schwartz's story.

In *Speak, Memory* the dilemma posed by the regressive progress of time is resolved by the conceit of the spiral, or helix, which, as it revolves, encompasses past, present and future in eternal, tireless succession: "The spiral is a spiritualized circle. In the spiral form, the circle, uncoiled, unwound, has ceased to be vicious; it has been set free."[30] This notion is also compounded by Nabokov's very visual system of memory, which has the power to defy time in its ability to regenerate the past. The "robust reality" of memory has the power to make a "ghost of the present," and thus time is subverted and mortality negated so that "everything is as it should be, nothing will ever change, nobody will ever die."[31]

As demonstrated in "The Assistant Producer" and *Bend Sinister*, film is Nabokov's primary synthetic visual means of projecting the past into the present and of reconstituting and recombining remembered images according to an individual's subjective requirements. This process is continued by Humbert Humbert, whose sole ambition is to transform the past into a perpetually repeating, infinite present reality, a reality in which Lolita remains forever a child and forever his. Film and photography are also central in the evocation of an idyllic past in *Ada*, in which Van Veen, its ninety-seven-year-old master "plotter" constructs an elaborate narrative illusion, a "fine fabric of deceit" marked by "false trails"[32] and dead ends, to produce a memoir that is devoid of meaning or moral and emotional integrity but is, nevertheless, a triumph of narcissistic self-indulgence.

Film and the Dilemma of Mortality in Ada

Ada was published over twenty years after *Bend Sinister* and "The Assistant Producer" and is widely considered to be a major postmodern work, demonstrating close affinities particularly with the fiction of American writers of the late 1950s and 1960s, including William Burroughs, Thomas Pynchon and John Barth.[33] John Stark defines the four key characteristics of the postmodernist text as "war with the audience (compare the false clues that Nabokov sprinkles throughout *Lolita*), self-consciousness, the dream of an ahistorical literature, and disinterest in communicating meanings."[34] *Ada* fulfills every one of these characteristics, and yet the deployment of film in the novel combines both modernist and postmodernist dynamics in ways that echo the role of film in works from "The Assistant Producer" on. Brian McHale, in discussing William Burroughs's use of the cinematic mode, also provides a particularly apposite description of the nature of Nabokov's deployment of the medium:

> William Burroughs not only uses movie discourse to capture various cinematic strategies in his texts ("Fadeout," "Cut"), but even goes so far as to compose entire episodes in the format of a screenplay or shooting script (e.g. in *The Wild Boys*, 1971, and *Exterminator!* 1973). In effect, the cinematic techniques here are laid bare: background structure, thrust into the foreground by self-reflective cinematic notations, becomes a distinct ontological level.[35]

In the postmodernist text, film functions as a common trope and, as McHale argues, often as "a master trope for control."[36] Considering the nature of the manipulation of the cinematic medium by Nabokov's protagonists, however, it is evident that the filmic trope extends back to the modernist era of *The Eye* and *Despair*, thus suggesting the instability of a perceived notion of a modernist/postmodernist divide. Van Veen's exploits serve as a continuation of a tradition of autocratic narrator/directors in Nabokov's fiction, his contribution being to challenge some of the most fundamental aspects of the visual experience and in doing so to dissolve, irrevocably, the distinguishing boundaries between modes of perception, from the mechanical to the metaphysical.

In *Ada*, as in Pynchon's *Gravity's Rainbow* (1973), "the distinction between literal reality and metaphorical vehicle becomes increasingly indeterminate, until we are left wondering whether the movie reality is only a trope after all, or belongs to the 'real' world of this fiction."[37] Perceptual ambiguity is fundamental to Van Veen's narrative, and its success is dependent upon it. Compounding this notion is the implication of the deceptive nature of the filmic medium, which has already been suggested by the cinematic manipulations of Nabokov in *Bend Sinister* and "The Assistant Producer." Van Veen, however, takes this a step further. Film is present in *Ada* in almost every conceivable form, and Van Veen's engagement with the medium extends from considerations of the camera as a visual and narrative tool, to a direct experience of the very mundane business of the cinema factory through the film careers of both his mother and sister. Film, therefore, exists as a form of "literal reality," to an extent where even the familiar centers of the industry — Hollywood and Pinewood — are included in Van Veen's fiction as "Houssaie" [hollygrove] and "Ivydell" respectively.[38] Yet it also functions as a trope, an ontological level, existing as "a world-within-the-world ... in competition with the primary diegetic world of the text," one which provides more than simply the "repertoire of representational techniques"[39] that, say, Humbert Humbert so deftly exploits.

The filmic world within the world of *Ada* functions both as an independent realm existing beyond the scope of Van Veen's control, and as a dimension which is consciously deployed as a narrative device. Van's incorporation of cinematic techniques into the narrative serves a dual function, to assert his overriding authority and omniscient stance, and to establish his superior mastery of the medium. He often refers to the visual perspectives of film in passages of casual description, for example:

> As he looks, the palm of a gipsy asking for alms fades into that of the almsgiver asking for a long life. (When will film-makers reach the stage *we* have reached?) (p. 85)

Van, however — in an echo of Hermann Karlovich — is here both emulating and undermining the cinematic medium by suggesting that it is the filmmakers who should be following his example. At the same time, it is ironic that Van should deploy the cinematic mode in order to demean the work of real filmmakers when he is indebted to them for giving him the tools with which to achieve his omniscient perspective, but this typifies his arrogant stance and the fundamentally paradoxical nature of his narrative. Casual references to the "bannister pause" (p. 101), dollying, close-ups and medium shots are mere gestures with which Van flaunts his knowledge of the medium, whereas in certain key scenes he deploys his cinematic skills to far greater dramatic effect. Abrupt declarations of cinematic technique also serve to disrupt narrative flow, calling attention to specific details or particular moments in a sequence, registering a discreet emotive shift or the shock of a fugitive recollection. A mnemonic flash can be initiated by the most obtuse image. For example, the repeated vision of "pink mushrooms" (pp. 160 and 161) in the key poolside sequence at Ardis Hall is dramatized by an explicit declaration of cinematic technique — "double take, double exposure"[40] (p. 161) — which serves, in this instance, as an ironic allusion to Van's sudden and conspicuous arousal, provoked by a fit of jealousy.

Although Van considers himself to be an artist with cinematic aspirations, his experience of film is, essentially, that of an onlooker, a member of the audience. Ada's vantage point is, conversely, from the inside out, since she is actively engaged in the business of making movies. It is this which throws Van's position into relief. Van has no firsthand experience of the industry, and while he is seduced by the fantasy of film, Ada's attitude is characterized by clinical pragmatism, informed by an acutely objective perspective which enables her to see the medium in all its absurdity and banality. Thus there is a tone of mockery in her comments quite distinct from Van's irony. For example, she finds the notion that "Marina's new director of artistic conscience defines Infinity as the furthest point from the camera which is still in fair focus" (p. 262) highly amusing, even though "infinity" is a legitimate cinematic term which she knows is being used here in its proper context,[41] and is thus devoid of any philosophical connotations.

At the same time, her descriptions of Hollywood suggest a degree of affection for its unique and bizarre incongruity, a quality which is, essentially, more satisfying than the "fourth-rate Westerns" it produces:

> As for me, I'm only an incidental waitress in a fourth-rate Western, hip-swinging between table-slapping drunks, but I rather enjoy the Houssaie atmosphere, the dutiful art, the winding hill roads, the reconstructions of streets, and the obligatory square, and a mauve shop sign on an ornate wooden façade, and around noon all the extras in period togs queuing before a glass booth [p. 262].

It is significant, however, that Ada should nevertheless support Van's choice of film as a narrative mode and that her reasons should coincide with his:

Van agreed with Ada that the talking screen was certainly preferable to the live theater for the simple reason that with the former a director could attain, and maintain, his own standards of perfection throughout an unlimited number of performances [p. 334].

Both literature and film offer a means of achieving immortality, and this is essentially the purpose of Van's narrative. Ada has already achieved this by being captured on celluloid, and this confirms her as an aspirational figure in Van's eyes. She is depicted throughout the narrative in terms of film — as a black-and-white photographic image — which is established from her very first appearance:

She wore a white frock with a black jacket and there was a white bow in her long hair. He never saw that dress again and when he mentioned it in retrospective evocation she invariably retorted that he must have dreamt it, she never could have put on a dark blazer on such a hot day, but he stuck to his initial image of her to the last [pp. 35–36].

It is significant that Van should persist in guarding a vision of Ada that she refutes, indicating the degree to which he is prepared to distort or ignore details in order to satisfy the demands of his imagination and his desire. Nevertheless, Ada maintains this filmic quality, and thus, on his second visit to Ardis, the black-and-white motif is reiterated. Here, "Ada's long figure [is] profiled in black" (p. 148), and later, at the "family" dinner with Demon and Marina, she wears a "sleeveless black sheath" (p. 193), while Demon's recent recollection of her is in "a raincoat with a white and black scarf" (p. 193). When they are finally reunited in Mont Roux, Ada is wearing black again (her reference to a change in color refers not to her dress, but to her hair, which has been dyed "bronze"):

Ada had warned him in a recent letter that she had "changed considerably, in contour as well as in color." She wore a corset which stressed the unfamiliar stateliness of her body enveloped in a black-velvet gown [p. 437].[42]

Ada's filmic qualities exist in spite of her unsuccessful career as a screen actress and the literal disintegration of the only film — *Don Juan's Last Fling* — in which something more of her than just the "perfectly distinct shadow" of her elbow appears.[43] Van witnesses the last remaining reel dissolve before his very eyes — "the film black-winked and shriveled" (p. 393) — but even from the outset it seems to be inexplicably doomed:

> A jinx has been cast on our poor girl's career. Howard Hool argued after the release that he had been made to play an impossible cross between two Dons…. Hool managed to buy up and destroy a number of copies while others have been locked up by the lawyer of the writer Osberg, who claims the gitanilla sequence was stolen from one of his own concoctions. In result it is impossible to purchase a reel of the picture which will vanish like the proverbial smoke once it has fizzled out on provincial screens [p. 392].

Ada exists in two cinematic dimensions, the real-life Hollywood product and Van's fictional emulation of it. Here, Van is seen to be directing both the course of the narrative and Ada's part in it:

> There is one exchange that it would be nice to enact against the green moving backdrop of one of our Ardis sets. The talk about "double guarantee" in eternity. Start just before that [p. 456].

The narrative, or rather, action, is staged with calculated deliberation taking into consideration every aspect of its visual impact, particularly scenery and lighting, critical scenes being precisely placed in the exact point of a sequence to generate maximum dramatic effect. In this instance, Van is openly declaring the manipulative artifice of the narrative process and asserting his omniscient directorial authority, but he is also engaged in the performance with Ada. Van's film-informed narrative not only offers him an opportunity to demonstrate his superior representational skills, but also, and equally significantly, provides him with a means of self-dramatization. Van's directorial stance is, essentially, a performance, and in turn this reflects upon the acute self-consciousness he displays throughout the narrative. "Kitchen Kim with his camera" (p. 126) for example, while violating his privacy, also flatters his ego, and there is even an implication that he *likes* the idea that he is being watched and enjoys the notion that Kim is not the only spy at Ardis, but that there may be many others, anonymous and invisible, hovering around him imperceptibly in "inquisitive skimmers or picture taking balloons" (p. 42). Preserving the secrecy of his relations with Ada becomes a game, and there are even occasions when he regrets the absence of a camera to capture their antics:

> *These* children … might also have been filmed rather entertainingly had snoopy Kim, the kitchen photo-fiend, possessed the necessary apparatus [p. 162].

The notion of performance is also extended to other, less pivotal characters. While Van imagines that he is starring in and directing his own film, and Ada and Marina make their careers as movie actresses, Van attributes Hollywood character traits to both his father, Demon Veen and the family maid, Blanche. Demon Veen's demonic qualities are amplified by allusions to film noir, most dramatically evident as he makes his final exit from Ardis Hall.

> Van and Ada saw him off. The night was very warm and dripping with what Ladore farmers called green rain. Demon's black sedan glinted elegantly among the varnished laurels in the moth-flaked porchlight.... Nobody paid any attention to Marina, who waved from a tengelo-colored oriel window a spangled shawl although all she could see was the sheen of the car's bonnet and the rain slanting in the light of its lamps.
>
> Demon pulled on his gloves and sped away with a great growl of damp gravel [pp. 207–08].

There can be no question that Van is deliberately emulating the noir mood — the "slanting" rain in the car's headlights,[44] the way the light is reflected in the darkness, and the jump cut from the close-up shot of Demon's gloves to the image of the churned-up gravel on the drive — to enhance not simply the atmosphere of enigmatic and seductive evil, glamour, and power he generates, but also the scene's dramatic impact. This is the first and only time that parents and children come together, and still at a point when Demon is ignorant of Van and Ada's incestuous affair. Perhaps more significant, however, is the stark contrast between Demon's depiction in this scene and the devastated figure he presents in Manhattan on discovering Van and Ada together, a revelation which destroys Demon absolutely, for he is killed soon after in a flying accident.

Van's attribution of a cinematic persona to Blanche serves, on the other hand, quite a different purpose. She is also making her exit from Ardis Hall, presumably in disgrace, pregnant with an illegitimate child:

> Blanche, standing by in a long gray skirt and straw hat, with her cheap valise painted mahogany red and secured with a criss-crossing cord, looked exactly like a young lady setting out to teach school in a Wild West movie [p. 236].

Although Van's allusion to Wild West movies appears, at this juncture, to be simply gratuitous, there is an underlying significance. As Brian

Boyd has elucidated, Blanche is inextricably bound up with Van and
Ada's affair, providing both a "comic counterpart"[45] to their lovemaking,
and an ironic subversion of notions of innocence and purity which characterize the "ardor of Ardis."[46] Blanche's appearance, therefore, in the
guise of a minor character from a Western, reflects not only her sub-
servient status in the narrative, but also — in its echo of the roles Ada
plays in Hollywood — the secondary role she has played as an object of
Van's desire and as a crude mirror to Ada's promiscuity. At the same time,
Blanche is key in exposing Ada's indiscretions to Van, and thus, although
she is predominantly a target for his abuse, and in spite of her subordinate position, she introduces an element of trust and honesty unique to
Van's experience. In a sense, therefore, Van's depiction of her here is an
expression of sympathetic regard, and not an attempt to denigrate her.

This scene, however, offers a rare moment of lucidity, for Van's
"chronicle" is dominated by ambivalence, illusion and obscurity. Through
elaborate distortion and visual deceit, Van asserts absolute control over
both the narrative and the version of his life that it presents, to attain
"the kind of subjectivity which, through the faculty of vision, considers
itself the origin of all meaning."[47] The success of Van Veen's exploit
depends upon the inability of his reader to perceive or accept the fraud
that he constructs because it is presented as film, a scheme based upon
the notion of the screen image's "immutable aura of validity," a notion
which has, in actuality, been proven to be sacred, as the mistake once
made by Alfred Hitchcock illustrates:

> In *Stage Fright* (1950), Alfred Hitchcock discovered, to his chagrin, that
> the first-person point of view in film is fraught with problems even when
> it is used perfunctorily. In that film, Hitchcock had one of his charac-
> ters narrate a flashback — and lie. Audiences saw the lie on screen and
> when they later found out that it was false they reacted angrily. They
> weren't able to accept the possibility that the *image* would lie, although
> they would have been quite willing to believe that the *character* had lied.
> The image on the screen is simply invested with an immutable aura of
> validity.[48]

That the reader/audience is never allowed to apprehend the visual
lie is key to Van Veen's success, and ironically, the very mode that he
abuses and subverts plays an integral part in the deception. Whereas in
"The Assistant Producer" and *Bend Sinister* neither protagonist is able to
sustain the fictions they construct through the medium of film, in *Ada*

film is deployed in such a way as to create an impregnable fiction and to generate the illusion of an underlying reality where there is, ultimately, none — a fiction which nevertheless provokes the reader/audience into pursuing a futile quest for an elusive and undisclosed meaning.[49]

Nabokov perceived "reality"[50] as "an infinite succession of steps, levels of perception, false bottoms," as something "unquenchable, unattainable."[51] The elusive quality of "reality" epitomizes the problematic nature of Van's narrative and is a central dilemma compounded by the inevitable distortion that takes place in the process of perception. The "objective existence of *all* events," Nabokov argues, is "a form of impure imagination," visual recognition and understanding being subject to "creative fancy, that drop of water on a glass slide which gives distinctness and relief to the observed organism."[52] In *Ada*, the distortion of places, characters and events is such that it is impossible to determine what, if anything in Van's narrative, is not an illusion — everything, that is, other than his lifelong love affair with Ada. Ada is the pivotal focal interest of Van's "chronicle"; his relationship with her is "the drop of water on a glass slide" and it alone receives the "distinctness and relief" that is the result of the process of imaginative refraction Nabokov describes, establishing it as the only tangible, stable aspect of the narrative, and reducing everything else to shadowy obscurity.

Themes of distortion are, therefore, central to the narrative. Distortion is both a given aspect of Van's environment — Antiterra being the "distorted glebe" reflected in the "distortive glass" (p. 21) of its mystical twin planet, Terra — and an element which is consciously manipulated and exploited to confuse, confound and distract the reader, so that ultimately the only feasible position available is one of profound skepticism. At the same time, however, it is impossible to ascertain whether or not Van deliberately engineers this response. The most overt example of the problem of narrative intent is the crass and incredible summary Van offers at the very end of his "chronicle":

> In spite of the many intricacies of plot and psychology, the story proceeds at a spanking pace. Before we can pause to take breath and quietly survey the new surroundings into which the writer's magic carpet has, as it were, spilled us, another attractive girl, Lucette Veen, Marina's younger daughter, has also been swept off her feet by Van, the irresistible rake. Her tragic destiny constitutes one of the highlights of this delightful book [pp. 460–61].

The total lack of any true perspective considering, particularly, the manner of Lucette's death is astonishing, and yet to claim that it is intentionally ironic would be to oversimplify the dynamics of Van's narrative, and to set an entirely inappropriate and untenable precedent by which to judge it. More obtuse still is the novel's final paragraph, which asks the reader to focus upon the visual aspect of the "chronicle," to relish its idyllic beauty, its "delicacy of pictorial detail" (p. 461). Once again, in the context of the multiple tragedies of Aqua, Lucette, Ivan Durmanov, Spencer Muldoon, Philip Rack, Percy De Prey, and even Demon Veen, the attention to such facile and essentially superficial elements is incongruous, and yet it offers a crucial clue to the central dynamic of Van's narrative — optical illusion.

It is significant that Van should give the reader this vital indication as to how best to approach his novel in the form, almost, of an afterword. It has a flippant quality, hurried and last-minute, as if inserted to oblige an imaginary publisher's requirement for an upbeat, "happy" ending, but on closer examination it contains a very specific and carefully chosen piece of "pictorial detail" — the "pretty plaything stranded among the forget-me-nots of a brook" (p. 461). This image epitomizes the dual nature of Van's narrative, for it refers to two things, equally. Firstly, this is a direct allusion to Lucette, and the image functions as a trigger, recalling an earlier episode on the grounds of Ardis Hall which, in retrospect, ironically encapsulates all the aspects of Lucette's tragic fate. Lucette is playing "on the brink of [a] brook" with her doll, while Ada sits reading and Van searches for his wristwatch, which he thinks he has "dropped among the forget-me-nots" (p. 115). Lucette accidentally lets go of the doll, it falls into the water and is swept away. Van pointedly refers the reader to this episode, which itself alludes to the later episode of Lucette's drowning. While Van is able to "[retrieve] the fugitive" doll (p. 115) from the brook, he is unable to save the real-life mannequin from the Atlantic Ocean — "the dark head of Van ... having been propelled out of the boat ... kept bobbing and bawling the drowned girl's name in the black, foam-veined, complicated waters" (p. 390) — and thus his remorse is communicated by the recurrence of the image of the forget-me-nots, and the explicit message contained in their name. At the same time, however, as Nabokov has pointed out, "the pretty plaything also refers to something else, the 'tubular thing' on p. 175"[53] (i.e., a condom), an allusion which instantly sours the apparently genuine declaration of remorse expressed in the initial image:

Van washed his hands in a lower shelf-pool of the brook and recognized, with amused embarrassment, the transparent, tubular thing, not unlike a sea-squirt, that had got caught up in its downstream course in a fringe of forget-me-nots, good name, too [p. 218].

Although it has been argued that Van's primary motive in writing his autobiography is to atone for past misdemeanors, and most critically, his responsibility for Lucette's suicide,[54] the suggestion of conscience is tempered by an innate paradox in the manner in which Van presents his world. In the novel's final paragraph, Van guides the reader's attention toward the visual aspect of the novel, and although this is key in revealing certain critical details concerning Van's admission of culpability in the demise not only of Lucette, but also Philip Rack, along with the suffering of countless others, the details themselves are obscured in a mass of complex allusions which serve to redirect and deflect attention away from them the instant they are registered.

It is significant also that Van considers his "chronicle" to be an artistic endeavor. As William Gass has commented, "art is a challenge *to* and denial *of* [the artist's] own manner of existence, an accusation concerning their own lack of reality."[55] This notion of artistry is fundamental to the representation of Van's past, and to his narrative manipulations, and is an enactment of Ada's contention that "in 'real' life we are creatures of chance in an absolute world — unless we are artists ourselves" (p. 335). Van asserts a governing authority over his narrative which obliterates interference from all external forces, be they "chance" or extraneous personalities. Unlike his predecessors — Smurov, Hermann Karlovich, Humbert Humbert or Charles Kinbote — Van's tyranny is absolute, and his deployment of the cinematic medium is distinctive for its skill and ingenuity. However, he is not alone in the narrative in his desire to create an idealized version of the past, not simply for posterity, but for his own personal gratification. In an echo of the "dream producers" in *Bend Sinister*, Marina is determined that "someday [her] past must be put in order" (p. 200), and that she should imagine the process in terms of film is not only appropriate as a reflection of her own immersion in the medium as a movie actress, but is also significant in that she inadvertently describes the exact process of Van's "chronicle":

Someday, she mused, one's past must be put in order. Retouched, retaken. Certain "wipes" and "inserts" will have to be made in the picture; certain telltale abrasions in the emulsion will have to be corrected; "dissolves"

in the sequence discreetly combined with the trimming out of the
unwanted, embarrassing "footage" and definite guarantees obtained; yes,
someday — before death with its clapstick closes the scene [p. 200].[56]

Van is plagued by "embarrassing footage," most overtly in the form
of illicit photographs taken by Kim, the kitchen boy at Ardis Hall, during the first years of Van's affair with Ada. These pictures violate his privacy, threaten the secrecy of his relations with Ada, and undermine both
his depiction of their romance and most fundamentally, his narrative
autonomy. Ironically, he has no suspicion of Kim's camerawork in spite
of the apparent knowledge of many of the other characters around him,
until Ada is presented with an album of his photographs, many years later,
with which he attempts to blackmail her. Van's blindness is further
magnified by the fact that even Marina, who is referred to, spitefully, as
the "dummy in human disguise" (p. 199), had always been aware of Kim's
activities:

> "I can't tell Kim, the kitchen boy, not to take photographs on the sly —
> he's a regular snap-shooting fiend, that Kim, though otherwise an
> adorable, gentle, honest boy" [p. 201].

Much of the narrative concerning Kim, therefore, focuses on notions of
voyeurism, spying and other forms of visual intrusion, as well as the
notion of blindness, which develops into a major thematic dynamic.

Kim is first mentioned in connection with the photographs and film
secreted away by Dan, Marina's husband, in the loft at Ardis Hall:

> A reel box containing what turned out to be (according to Kim, the
> kitchen boy, as will be understood later) a tremendous stretch of
> microfilm taken by the globetrotter, with many of its quaint bazaars,
> painted cherubs and pissing urchins reappearing three times at different
> points, in different shades of heliocolor.... Most of the film ... was run
> by Dan many times for his bride during their instructive honeymoon in
> Manhattan [p. 12].

Not only does this passage establish Kim's predilection for spying from
the novel's outset — associations which Van refers to consistently throughout the first part of his "chronicle" in order to demonstrate a knowledge
of Kim's activities where he had, in fact, none — but it is also revealing
in terms of the perceived function of film and the purpose it serves. In
this instance, the implication is that it is pornography, and the necessity

for discretion is suggested by the fact that the reel box does not contain standard film but microfilm, which reduces images to a size beyond the capabilities of the human eye and requires special projection apparatus to view. Also interesting is the fact that this film has evidently been tampered with by Dan. Many of its images appear "three times at different points, in different shades of heliocolor,"[57] implying some not inconsiderable amateur filmmaking skills and proving an ability to put into practice what Marina can only dream of and Van is only able to realize in the domain of fiction.

Apart from attempting to overcome the humiliation of Kim's activities and his blindness to them, Van has a far more exacting task to perform as a consequence of the impact of Kim's photographs on the depiction of his affair with Ada:

> "That ape has vulgarized our own mind-pictures. I will either horsewhip his eyes out or redeem our childhood by making a book of it: *Ardis*, a family chronicle" [p. 320].

The notion that Kim has "vulgarized" their "mind-pictures," that he has "spoofed and condemned" their "entire past" (p. 321) is critical, and yet the paradox here is that Van's response directly contradicts the mimetic quality of the photographic image. What Van objects to is the reality that Kim's photographs depict, that in their crude capturing of fleeting moments, they undermine the carefully constructed images that have replaced them in Van's imagination and subsequently in his narrative. At the same time, however, Van and Ada find the photographs sexually arousing, and the pornographic associations are played out in an ironic emulation of the experience of moviegoing, signaled by Ada's cry for an "intermission" and the notion of their partaking in a "peep show":

> "But look, girl, here I'm glutting your tongue, and there I'm glued to your epiglottis, and — "
> "Intermission," begged Ada, "quick-quick."
> "I'm ready to oblige till I'm ninety," said Van (the vulgarity of the peep show was catchy) [p. 317].

The relationship between imagination and film in Van's narrative is highly complex and often overtly contradictory. While the photograph is considered as a vulgarizing weapon, it is also recognized as an invaluable mnemonic tool. Van describes memory as "a photo-studio de luxe on an infinite Fifth Power Avenue" (p. 84), and yet the images stored there would not be the product of a camera lens, but the distorting glass of his subjective recollection. At the same time, Van, like Humbert Humbert, is inspired by the vitality of the photographic image, its ability to capture the essence of a moment and record it for eternity, and his assimilation of the techniques of photography in the mnemonic process is openly declared.

> In full, deliberate consciousness, at the moment of the hooded click, he bunched the recent past with the imminent future and thought to himself that this would remain an objective perception of the real present and that he must remember the flavor, the flash, the flesh of the present (as he, indeed, remembered it half a dozen years later — and now, in the second half of the next century) [p. 316].

Nevertheless, there is evidence elsewhere in the narrative which indicates that the photographic infallibility of memory is a delusion, that Van is unable to sustain the filmic process. The past as presented by Van Veen is a product of careful selection and omission, informed by imaginative and emotional bias, combined with the greater purpose of the narrative as a whole, to project the "mind-pictures" of an arrogant, egocentric, cruel and self-serving individual. While it becomes apparent that Van is unable to sustain this emulation of the processes of photography as a means of capturing his past, cinematic techniques serve him more favorably, and the nature of his recollections possess, very specifically, a quality reminiscent of montage.

> The Past ... is a constant accumulation of images. It can be easily contemplated and listened to, tested and tasted at random, so that it ceases to mean the orderly alternation of linked events that it does in the large theoretical sense [p. 428].

This recalls Marina's dream of being able to recut and recombine the past, and yet the distinctive element here is randomness, which evokes the process of montage. Not only this, but the technique of montage is ideally suited to Van's creative purpose, having a versatility and flexibility which offers supreme control over the fictional medium. In an earlier episode, Van combines the process of montage with specific camera techniques to demonstrate the particularly cinematic quality of memory in capturing a final vision of Ada:

He could not swear he did not look back, could not — by any optical chance, or in any prism — have seen her physically as he walked away; and yet, with dreadful distinction, he retained forever a composite picture of her standing where he left her. The picture — which penetrated him, through an eye in the back of his head, through his vitreous spinal canal, and could never be lived down, never — consisted of a selection and blend of such random images and expressions of hers that had affected him with a pang of intolerable remorse at various moments in the past. Tiffs between them had been very rare, very brief, but there had been enough of them to make up the enduring mosaic [pp. 234–35].

This "enduring mosaic" of "random images and expressions" is enabled by a reverse-angle shot which offers an otherwise physically impossible visual aspect on the scene. Although the vision is imaginary, it has the vivid and potent quality of film, "a definite picture that he knew he had never seen in reality" which "[remains] within him more real than any actual memory" (pp. 235–36). That the "actual memory" has been subordinated by a synthetic image is fundamental in revealing Van's concession not only to the devices of cinematic representation and the extent to which his imagination is informed by film, but also, and ultimately, his true creative priorities — the subjugation of actuality for the sake of artistic control.

Van's omniscient control is also, nevertheless, an illusion. Gavriel Moses argues that "when Nabokov's characters ... assume the actual role of a film director ... this happens at moments when they actually *lose* control altogether."[58] There are two key scenes in Van's narrative in which his adoption of the cinematic perspective is overt, and they are also episodes in which he is seen, paradoxically, to lose command of the action.

The first occurs at Ardis. Marina is entertaining friends by the pool and discussing her latest film project with her director, G. A. Vronsky:

> The shooting script was now ready. Marina, in dorean robe and coolie hat, reclined reading in a long-chair on the patio. Her director, G. A. Vronsky, elderly, baldheaded, with a spread of grizzled fur on his fat chest, was alternately sipping his vodka-and-tonic and feeding Marina typewritten pages from a folder. On her other side, crosslegged on a mat, sat Pedro ... a repulsively handsome, practically naked young actor ... whom she had brought from Mexico and was keeping at a hotel in Ladore.
>
> Ada, lying on the edge of the swimming pool, was doing her best to make the shy dackel face the camera in a reasonably upright and decent

position, while Philip Rack ... was trying to take a picture of the recalcitrant chop-licking animal and of the girl's parted breasts which her half-prone position helped to disclose in the opening of her bathing suit.

If one dollied now to another group standing a few paces away under the purple garlands of the patio porch, one might take a medium shot of the young maestro's pregnant wife in a polka-dotted dress replenishing goblets with salted almonds, and of our distinguished lady novelist resplendent with mauve flounces ... pressing a zebra vest on Lucette [p. 156].

This sequence takes the form of a series of distinct cuts which are contained in the structure of the text itself. The three paragraphs mark three overt switches in perspective, from a series of anatomized close-ups moving from Marina, to Vronsky, to Pedro, then switching to Ada and the dog and Philip Rack by the pool, and finally to a "medium shot" of the group in the background, providing as it were, a context shot for the scene.

The disruption of Van's casual gaze over the scene is marked, at the beginning of the final paragraph, by his overt reference to a cinematic device, the "dolly,"[59] and the subsequent switch in focus and camera angle to the medium shot of Philip Rack's pregnant wife. The very precise manipulation of cinematic techniques reveals Van's intimate familiarity with the processes of filmmaking, and would initially suggest a mastery of the medium which confirms his omniscient narrative authority. In the light of Moses's comment, however, the abrupt directorial intrusion suggests that the sudden change in perspective has been provoked by some other, undeclared aspect of the scene. That Van should announce the shift in visual focus away from the poolside implies that he is anxious to distract the reader's attention, and indeed his own, away from the vision of Rack leering at Ada, and that his impatience is an unconscious expression of a spontaneous and overwhelming pang of jealousy, compounded by combined feelings of revulsion and rejection. The overt declaration of cinematic technique and directorial intent that opens the final paragraph, therefore, indicates a loss of control on Van's part, and not an assertion of control which these details initially suggest. The sequence is concluded in a similar fashion, marking the point at which Van has had enough of the distasteful spectacle of Ada flirting with Rack and Pedro:

She had been casting sidelong glances, during that dreadful talk, and now saw pure, fierce Van under the tulip tree, quite a way off, one hand on his hip, head thrown back, drinking beer from a bottle. She left the pool edge ... and moved toward the tulip tree making a strategic detour between the authoress ... and the leading lady, now puzzling over a love scene where the young chatelaine's "radiant beauty" was mentioned.

"But," said Marina, "how can one act out 'radiant,' what does radiant beauty mean?"

"Pale beauty," said Pedro helpfully, glancing up at Ada as she passed by, "the beauty for which many men would cut off their members."

"Okay," said Vronsky. "Let us get on with this damned script. He leaves the pool-side patio, and since we contemplate doing it in color —"

Van left the pool-side patio and strode away [pp. 160–61].

The direct association Van establishes between himself and Vronsky's script epitomizes the self-reflexive nature of the narrative as a whole, here incorporating a real piece of movie action. The gesture that he makes in echoing the script by leaving the "pool-side patio" is, however, erroneous, considering that earlier on in the passage he is described as standing "quite a way off" under a tulip tree, a position which communicated his objection to and alienation from the scene, and was established at the very outset:

> As he approached from a side lawn, he saw a scene out of some new life being rehearsed for an unknown picture, without him, not for him [p. 148].

This sense of exclusion is compounded by the notion that he has been displaced as the central figure in the narrative, and this in turn undermines the cinematic trope that he has so carefully constructed. Van's sense of utter negation is expressed in terms of two alternatives: death, or demotion to a new, anonymous role in someone else's movie, as "an extra in a house rented for a motion picture" (p. 149). That Van should consider these two prospects as equally horrifying is both ludicrous and starkly revealing of the significance of his directorial aspirations. At the conclusion of the sequence his position has shifted, conveniently, for the purposes of making a dramatic exit, to a completely different location, indicating that this is, in fact, an imaginary point of exit, one which serves not only to dramatize his departure, but also to restore his rightful place (as he perceives it) at the center of narrative and visual attention. At the same time, Van's deliberate, parodic reflection of the movie script suggests that here too he has lost control, that this elaborate gesture is, in essence, merely an expression of irrepressible emotional pique.

Van's overt reference to cinematic device, therefore, functions as a smokescreen which serves to obscure emotional and mental distress and is evident again in the episode in Manhattan in which he and Ada seduce Lucette. The scene has the immediate visual quality of a highly romanticized, extravagant nineteenth-century oil painting, and yet it is presented as an anatomized, filmic sequence:

> Thus seen from above ... we have the large island of the bed illumined from our left (Lucette's right) by a lamp burning with a murmuring incandescence on the west-side bedtable. The top sheet and the newly landed eye starts on its northern trip, up the younger Miss Veen's pried-open legs. A dewdrop on russet moss eventually finds a stylistic response in the aquamarine tear on her flaming cheekbone. Another trip from the port to the interior reveals the central girl's long white left thigh ... Ada's red-lacquered talons, which lead a man's reasonably recalcitrant, pardonably yielding wrist out of the dim east to the bright russet west, and the sparkle of her diamond necklace.... The scarred male nude on the island's east coast is half-shaded.... The recently repapered wall immediately west of the now louder-murmuring ... dorocene lamp is ornamented in the central girl's honor with Peruvian "honeysuckle" ... while the bedtable on that side bears a lowly box of matches, a *karavanchik* of cigarettes, a Monaco ashtray, a copy of Voltemand's poor thriller, and a Lurid Oncidium Orchid in an amethystine vaselet. The companion piece on Van's side supports a similar superstrong but unlit lamp, a dorophone, a box of Wipex, a reading loupe, the returned Ardis album, and a separatum "Soft music as cause of brain tumors," by Dr Anbury.... Ten eager, evil, loving, long fingers belonging to two different young demons caress their helpless bed pet ... Unsigned and unframed [pp. 330–31].

The sequence opens with a high-angle shot of the bed, devoid of detail, but focusing specifically, and initially, on the principal source of light, the lamp on the "west-side bedtable." This attention to lighting is highly reminiscent of the distinctive cinematic quality of Chandler's fiction, in which the illumination of a scene is of primary importance and is delineated with an almost absurd degree of precision, exemplified by the following scene from *The High Window* (1943):

> I felt on the wall inside the door for the light switch, found one and tilted it up. Pale flame bulbs in pairs in wall brackets went on all around the room, showing me the big lamp Merle had spoken of, as well as other things. I went over to switch the lamp on, then back to switch the wall light off. The lamp had a big bulb inverted in a porcelain glass bowl.

You could get three different intensities of light. I clicked the button
switch around until I had all there was.[60]

Although here, light has a revelatory function, it can also serve to deepen
the obscurity of a scene, as in *The Big Sleep*, and it is this aspect which
Van seems to be emulating. In the meantime, visual perspective, in the
form of the "newly landed eye," functions exactly as a camera lens, trav-
eling, in acute close-up, gradually up Lucette's legs. It then switches to
Ada and follows the exact same sequence, on its conclusion switching
again to a choker close-up of Ada's fingers — the "red-lacquered talons" —
on Van's wrist and their passage toward Lucette, indicated by the close-
up shot of her "diamond necklace." Apart from the initial hazy vision of
the bed, which serves as a rather inadequate "establishing" shot,[61] there
is no visual context for these isolated, disembodied images, and the
reader/audience is compelled to piece together these various details in
order to achieve a composite picture. The sequence then abruptly cuts
to Van, presented as an anonymous nude on the other side of the bed,
lying in relative obscurity, "half-shaded," due to the absence of any light
source on that side of the room — "the companion piece on Van's side supports a similar superstrong but unlit lamp." In a sudden "jump" cut the
visual focus switches again away from the bed to a series of inconsequential details, in a sequence which moves from the wallpaper to the
clutter on the two bedside tables. This instantly suggests that the narrative attention is deliberately being shifted away from Van, who has already
been depicted in a way that suggests that he would rather not be part of
the scene, further implying that this is an episode that he does not, in
fact, relish. This is eventually followed by another jump cut back to the
bed, to yet another close-up of Van's and Ada's hands "caressing" Lucette.
Their disembodiment displaces any notion of responsibility, which, combined with the earlier anonymous vision of Van — the "scarred male nude"
lying in the shadows on the right-hand side of the bed — establishes the
sequence's proximity to pornography. Although the sequence concludes
with the comment, "unsigned and unframed," which directly indicates
Van's intention that the scene be regarded as a painting, its cinematic quality is unquestionable. The dichotomy between the two visual forms is
interesting, however, for by implying that this is a painting, by transforming the scene into a static work of art of transcendent beauty and
tantalizing detail, Van is attempting to divest himself of any feelings of
conscience. Ironically, in going to such lengths to obscure the reality of

the situation by generating such a carefully contrived optical illusion, Van's technical manipulations only serve to expose his feelings of guilt, his disgust at this episode in which Lucette is humiliated, tormented and defiled by his and Ada's combined depravity.

The scene, however, also serves the purpose of self-delusion and is a method which occurs again in Van's presentation of the circumstances and impact of Lucette's suicide, an episode which revolves, ironically, around a film. *Don Juan's Last Fling*, a movie in which Ada has only a minor part, is screened on the cruise ship, the *Admiral Tobakoff*, and seen, unintentionally, by Van and Lucette, who wander into the ship's movie theater seeking temporary diversion. Its effect is to provoke Lucette's suicide and to plunge Van into an Ada-obsessed reverie so overwhelming that it obliterates all other concerns for anyone or anything, and most crucially, Lucette. In retrospect, Van attempts to inject some element of remorse into his recollection of events, but the futility of this gesture is designated by the intensity of his experience and the resonances it generates:

> How sad, how significant that the picture projected upon the screen of his paroxysm ... was not the recent and pertinent image of Lucette, but the indelible vision of a bent bare neck and a divided flow of black hair and a purple-tinted paint brush [p. 386].

This vision of Ada recalls the one image of her that has the most enduring and potent effect upon Van, an image originating from their first tryst in the music room at Ardis Hall, which also, incidentally, has the quality of a hazily-lit, slow-motion sequence, filmed through a diffusion-filtered[62] lens, to evoke a dreamlike atmosphere:

> On those relentlessly hot July afternoons, Ada liked to sit on a cool piano stool of ivoried wood at a white-oilcloth'd table in the sunny music room, her favorite botanical atlas open before her, and copy out in color on creamy paper some singular flower.... The long beam slanting in from the french window glowed in the faceted tumbler, in the tinted water, and on the tin of the paintbox ... and as the sun looked on, the fantastic, black-blue-brown-haired child seemed in her turn to mimic the mirror-of-Venus blossom. Her flimsy, loose frock happened to be so deeply cut out behind that whenever she concaved her back while moving her prominent scapulae to and fro and tilting her head — as with air-poised brush she surveyed her damp achievement, or with the outside of her left wrist wiped a strand of hair off her temple — Van, who had drawn

up to her seat as close as he dared, could see down her sleek *ensellure* as far as her coccyx and inhale the warmth of her entire body [p. 81].

This scene, along with the initial black-and-white vision of Ada has the durability, in Van's memory, of a photographic image, or a movie sequence that endures "unlimited" repetitions:

> "One of these days," he said, "I will ask you for a repeat performance. You will sit as you did four years ago, at the same table, in the same light, drawing the same flower, and I shall go through the same scene with such joy, such pride, such — I don't know — gratitude!" [p. 209].

Indeed, Van has already transformed the scene in his memory into a piece of cinema, indicating the degree to which his consciousness is informed and inspired by film, and the notion of the immortality it affords that is central to his artistic purpose.

Although in retrospect, Van is surely aware of the consequences of his response to Ada's screen image, its impact upon his erotic consciousness remains an overriding preoccupation:

> Van, however, did not understand until much later (when he saw —*had* to see; and then see again and again — the entire film with its melancholy and grotesque ending...) that what seemed an incidental embrace constituted the Stone Cuckold's revenge [pp. 385–86].

It is astonishing that Van should be able to recollect this film without associating it in any way with Lucette's death. During the years of their separation, his only concern is the pursuit of Ada's image "from flick-house to flick-house" (p. 378), a concern which is here transformed into a matter of establishing her infidelity. As in the scene at Ardis by the pool and in many other instances throughout the narrative, Van is consumed by jealousy, and here to an extent that he even believes that the evidence contained in a piece of cinematic fiction is sufficient to cause him personal insult.

Self-delusion is also closely linked with themes of blindness in the novel, related, most overtly, to Van's blindness to Lucette's predicament and his attempts to delude himself and the reader into believing that he played no direct part in her suicide. Lucette's attempts to communicate her despair to Van on the *Admiral Tobakoff* fail, although, once again, in retrospect, Van attempts to imply some degree of sensitivity to her pain when in fact he demonstrates none. This conversation, for example, illustrates Van's narrative tamperings:

> "I enjoy — oh, loads of things," she continued in a melancholy, musing tone of voice, as she poked with a fork at her blue trout which, to judge by its contorted shape and bulging eyes, had boiled alive, convulsed by awful agonies. "I love Flemish and Dutch oils, flowers, food, Flaubert, Shakespeare, shopping, sheeing, swimming, the kisses of beauties and beasts — but somehow all of it, this sauce and all the riches of Holland, form only a kind of … (thin little) layer, under which there is absolutely nothing, except, of course, your image, and that only adds depth and a trout's agonies to the emptiness" [p. 365].

Ironically, as Van is tormented by Ada's elusive image, so Lucette is by Van's. Central in this dialogue, however, is the image of the trout. It is Van who imagines it to have been "boiled alive, convulsed by awful agonies," and yet Lucette reiterates the creature's pain by her reference to the "trout's agonies" at the end of her speech. Considering that Lucette's comment is rather incongruous and an essentially bizarre analogy, and that it echoes a little too conveniently the original image, it can be assumed that Van has inserted it deliberately to suggest empathy for her suffering. The violence communicated by the image of the trout's "bulging eyes" also introduces notions of extreme pain associated with blindness, or more specifically, blinding, in the narrative, recalling the particularly brutal punishment Van metes out to Kim for his "snap-shooting":

> Kim … would have bothered Ada again had he not been carried out of his cottage with one eye hanging on a red thread and the other drowned in its blood [p. 347].

Van devises the perfect means to ensure that Kim never spies on them again, but it is also a punishment he intends to inflict upon Philip Rack for his affair with Ada. Van takes the same cane to Kalugano that he is later to use on Kim, "a rude, stout article with a convenient grip and an alpenstockish point capable of gouging out translucent bulging eyes" (p. 241). Yet the sadistic brutality of Kim's blinding is not sufficient to satisfy Van's thirst for vengeance, and he continues to indulge in elaborate sadistic fantasies in which Kim's torture is cruelly perpetuated. "There are other possible forkings and continuations that occur to the dream-mind," he muses, "but these will do" (p. 351):

"Amends have been made," replied fat Van with a fat man's chuckle. "I'm keeping Kim safe and snug in a nice Home for Disabled Professional People, where he gets from me loads of nicely brailled books on new processes in chromophotography" [p. 351].

There are two other blind characters in the novel, Spencer Muldoon, Van's psychiatric patient, and Blanche's baby. Toward both Van exhibits uncharacteristic compassion. He demonstrates an unusual degree of concern for Blanche's blind baby, as if he feels in some way responsible for its handicap, although there is no conclusive evidence that the child is his (note that, ironically, he cites Kim's pictures as a means of demonstrating proof, as if, for once, Kim had done him a favor by not taking that particular shot):

> "They have a blind child," said Ada.
>   "Love is blind," said Van.
>   "She tells me you made a pass at her on the first morning of your first arrival."
>   "Not documented by Kim," said Van. "Will their child *remain* blind? I mean, did you get them a really first-rate physician?"
>   "Oh yes, hopelessly blind." [pp. 321–22]

There is no doubt that Van considers this to be the worst form of handicap, that the idea of blindness is somehow too awful for him to contemplate, and yet his comment, "love is blind" also has a self-reflexive quality, as if he is admitting to his own incapacity, implying that his love for Ada is essentially an infirmity which he is powerless to overcome.

Spencer Muldoon's tormented existence is also depicted with sensitivity, but it is tempered by detached curiosity:

> One Spencer Muldoon, born eyeless, aged forty, single, friendless ... had been known to hallucinate during fits of violent paranoia ... alternating with stupor, followed invariably by a return to his normal self, when for a week or two he would finger his blind books or listen, in red-lidded bliss, to records of music, bird songs, and Irish poetry [p. 368].

Although Van's interest in Spencer is principally as a clinical case, there is a sense that he is almost envious of Muldoon's ability to achieve a state of transcendent "bliss," that paradoxically, his incapacity enables him to access realms which remain remote and impenetrable to the sane and the seeing. Indeed, it is the likes of Muldoon, along with Aqua and many other psychiatric cases, who inspire Van's *Letters from Terra*, his first novel about the mythical planet with which lunatics seem exclusively able to establish metaphysical connections. Their visions tantalize Van's imagination and there is a sense that he envies their ability to experience Terra's elusive dimensions. Nevertheless, he overcomes any feelings of inadequacy by reassuring himself with the notion, evinced by his "chronicle," that although he may not be "quite a savant," he is "completely an artist" (p. 370). Although the ultimate success of a filmed version of *Letters from Terra* grants Van, at the end of his life, a few years of much-desired fame, it is ironic that he should object to the director's manipulations of his novel when he has indulged in so many in the presentation of his own autobiography.

> Van and Ada saw the film nine times, in seven different languages, and eventually acquired a copy for home use. They found the historical background absurdly farfetched and considered starting legal proceedings against Vitry — not for having stolen the L.F.T. idea, but for having distorted Terrestrial politics as obtained by Van with such diligence and skill from extra-sensorial sources and manic dreams [pp. 454–55].

That Victor Vitry, the film's director, is only guilty of distorting a fantasy, Terra being a mythical world, serves to compound the irony, for Van displays no compunction or conscience in his flagrant manipulations of Antiterran reality.

There is also, however, a suggestion of blindness being responsible for the film's success. Its controversial details provoke "nasty questions" from "philosophers," but this has no impact on cinema audiences, who Van describes as "wishing-to-be-gulled moviegoers" (p. 453). It is this exact same dynamic which Van attempts to exploit in his audience. The assumption that the reader also is "wishing-to-be-gulled" drives the narrative, the idea being that the reader/audience *wants* to suspend disbelief, it *wants* to be duped, that this is an acknowledged and accepted part of the reading/watching experience. At the same time, however, the illusion must be engineered so discreetly as to make the reader/audience believe that it is oblivious to the trickery, while their submission to the lie must never be exposed (as it was, disastrously, at the first screenings of Hitchcock's *Stage Fright*). This calculated blinding of the audience is precisely what Van endeavors to achieve in his "chronicle." Its narrative "forkings" are so convoluted and complex that the reader is rendered utterly at his mercy and denied any possibility of tangible revelation. Van likens the process of his autobiography to being sucked down into "the quicksand of the dream-like, dream-rephrased, legend-distorted past" (p. 221), and in this respect his reality is also the reader's experience.

Van's "chronicle" is, ultimately, as insubstantial and ephemeral as a "picture painted on air" (p. 365), a celluloid image. In rejecting the mimetic power of film and replacing it with his own form of filmic representation, Van relinquishes the possibility of achieving the superlative perceptive and mnemonic capabilities that he craves. Indeed, the closest he comes to emulating the vitality of film in his narrative is during his Mascodagama stage act when he walks on his hands, and yet this is merely a transient, futile gesture, serving not only to undermine his directorial but also, ultimately, his authorial feats:

> It was the standing of the metaphor on its head not for the sake of the trick's difficulty, but in order to perceive an ascending waterfall or a sunrise in reverse: a triumph, in a sense, over the ardis of time.... Van on the stage was performing organically what his figures of speech were to perform later in life — acrobatic wonders that had never been expected from him and which frightened little children [pp. 146–47].

Van believes himself to be not only defying time with his handstands, but by literally inverting his body he transforms himself into the image produced by a camera lens, a position which offers him a perspective as if from inside the camera. Yet this vantage point proves to be as short lived as the act itself, and like the assertion of photographic memory, Van cannot sustain such privileged perspectives. The extent of his self-delusion, however, is indicated by the notion that he is performing "acrobatic wonders," both visually and semantically — wonders which inspire awe and amazement — and yet the implication is that fundamentally, they are nothing more than meaningless, puerile tricks. This notion is extended into Van's treatise on the *Texture of Time*, which is logically, intellectually, and imaginatively barren.

> The "passage of time" is merely a figment of the mind with no objective counterpart, but with easy spatial analogies. It is seen only in rear view, shapes and shades, arollas and larches silently tumbling away [p. 427].

Van's treatise is formulated during and shaped by his very ordinary and uneventful drive to Mont Roux, and thus his theories are correspondingly banal, fundamentally flawed and curiously facile. The notion of "rear view" is a literal analogy to the car's rearview mirror, and the image of time "tumbling away" is a rather clumsy evocation of the vision of receding scenery that the rearview mirror affords.[63] Nevertheless, the treatise contains elements of particular significance to the themes of time and memory in the narrative. Van states that "Time is but memory in the making" (p. 440), which echoes the notion of "the Past [as] a constant accumulation of images" (p. 428), but this is a past that is "changeless, intangible, and 'never-to-be-revisited'" (p. 427). Thus, distinct from Nabokov's notion of the past as something to be perpetually drawn upon, never losing its vitality and vibrancy, the implication here is that while the past remains "changeless," the regressive force of time renders it perpetually out of reach, elusive, remote. Also absent is the concept of memory as, in Schwartz's terms, a "long arm of light" projecting from past to present, or the "inclined beam of pale light," which connects all dimensions of existence — past, present and future. It can be argued, therefore, that the distortions and manipulations that characterize Van's narrative are representative of his best recollection in the face of the "quicksand" of the past, and that the narrative as a whole is not merely his version of events, but inevitably, a fiction, a montage of disparate scenes and images, synthetically linked. Nor does film provide him with a mechanism to access his past, or a means by which to halt its inevitable disintegration, but rather offers him the potential for greater creative contortions. Eventually these amorphous mnemonic images and sensations replace past reality, as that last imagined vision of Ada "remains within him more real than any actual memory" (p. 236), thus confirming the notion that the only reality for Van *is* Ada.

During the years of her absence, Van's existence is reduced to a void, a void dominated by her image, and appropriately, yet ironically, a screen image:

> In the magic rays of the camera, in the controlled delirium of ballerina grace, ten years of her life had glanced off and she was again that slip of a girl.... She was absolutely perfect, and strange, and poignantly familiar [p. 385].

Ada's transformation into this immortalized cinematic vision is a magical process, inexplicable, mysterious, unfathomable, but nevertheless palpable, vital. Only in this mutated state does she achieve the victory over time that Van so desperately craves. Significantly, her triumph does not provoke envy in Van, but rather fuels his desire and admiration for her, and this is compounded by her innate cinematic quality, a quality that sets her apart and maintains her peerless, unrivalled dominance in Van's world. Ada's associations with film are reiterated by Van throughout the narrative by his depiction of her, consistently, in black and white, in an echo of her screen image, and this also serves to emphasize the contrast between her and her sister, who only ever appears in color.

In the poolside scene at Ardis Hall, Ada is depicted in black and white, in open contrast to the color around her. In her "faded, bluish-gray" (p. 158) swimsuit, Van watches her, in a reverse-angle shot, as she follows him away from the patio:

> Lifting one elbow, revealing the black star of her armpit, she tore off her bathing cap and with a shake of her head liberated a torrent of hair. Lucette, in color, trotted behind her [p. 161].

It is this exact same vision that Van recalls on the *Admiral Tobakoff*, when confronted by Lucette. The scene, once again, poolside, generates echoes of Hollywood — the "platinum sun" having an "aura of film-color" (p. 379) — and while Lucette is depicted, appropriately and consistently, in color, it is still against the black-and-white image of Ada that she is set and seen to clash:

> That mulatto skin, that silver-blond hair, those fat purple lips, reinacted in coarse negative *her* ivory, *her* raven, *her* pale pout [p. 379].

The contempt Van expresses here epitomizes his and Ada's response to Lucette throughout the narrative,[64] and yet this is irreconcilable with the remorse he seems to imply by his frequent, albeit discreet references to her demise. Ultimately this fundamental contradiction remains unresolved, eclipsed by Van's overwhelming compulsion to celebrate and glorify his lifelong romance with Ada. His memorial to Lucette — "his famous Lucinda Villa" (p. 264) — could be considered an eloquent demonstration of conscience, and yet there seems to be something more profound implied by the function Van attributes to it:

> A miniature museum just two stories high, with a still growing collection of microphotographed paintings from all public and private galleries in the world ... on one floor and a honeycomb of projection cells on the other: a most appetizing little memorial of Parian marble, administered by a considerable staff, guarded by three heavily armed stalwarts,

and open to the public only on Mondays for a token fee of one gold dollar regardless of age or condition [pp. 254–65].

Apart from the obvious irony that the building and its collection are lavished with more care and attention than Lucette ever was, it is intriguing that its collection should be of "microphotographed" images. This recalls the microfilm secreted by Dan in the loft at Ardis Hall, and while there is a sense of highly protected privacy about the Manhattan collection, there is no suggestion that it is at all illicit or obscene. In another, unrelated episode, however, Van describes the last moments of Percy de Prey's life in terms of microfilm images which seem to parallel, intriguingly, the role of the microphotographs at Lucinda Villa:

> One wonders, one always wonders, what had been the executed individual's brief, rapid series of impressions, as preserved somewhere, somehow, in some vast library of microfilmed last thoughts, between two moments: between, in the present case, our friend's becoming aware of those nice, quasi-Red Indian wrinkles beaming at him out of a serene sky not much different from Ladore's, and then feeling the mouth of steel violently push through tender skin and exploding bone [pp. 253–54].

In an extraordinary demonstration of sensitivity and empathy, Van seems to be suggesting that only such miniaturized images can adequately capture the essence of consciousness, its diverse and rapidly changing elements, and render its precious intensity with necessary discretion and subtlety. Yet this rare moment of insight is promptly obliterated by the violent images of the sequence's conclusion, depicted in a series of choker close-ups from which Van seems to derive particular relish (de Prey is after all, another of Van's intended targets for vengeance). That Van should feel any compassion for his rival is inexplicable, and on this basis, the only conclusion to be drawn is that this episode provokes yet another brief but resonant allusion to Lucette, the "vast library of microfilmed last thoughts" being an oblique reference to Lucinda Villa and Van's attempts to pay tribute to her, in essence, to express his "last thoughts" of her in the shape of hundreds of "microphotographed paintings." The nature of the collection is also significant in that its exclusivity, involving a level of intimacy and reverence absent in the other, more public mediums of photography and film, renders the larger cinematic distractions of the narrative meaningless and superfluous, reducing them to mere "half-hearted" flashbacks,[65] and yet, at the same time, the collection is compromised by its proximity in form to Dan's pornographic microfilms. Thus Lucinda Villa represents a physical manifestation of the fundamental and unresolved ambivalence of Van's chronicle, as demonstrated in the novel's final paragraph.

Although Van accuses Marina of having a "screen-corrupted mind" (p. 199), ironically it is Van's "screen-corrupted mind" that infects the entirety of his narrative and his representation of its principal characters. *Ada* offers neither spectacular revelations nor redemptive conceits, and Van's manipulation of the cinematic mode seems to be devoid of any purpose beyond the immediate game of "intricate enchantment and deception" that he plays. *Ada* is "a mirror or an image in a mirror," a text in which "depth is space upon a surface where every visual relationship is retained, though subtly inverted."[66] In other words, it is the epitome of a depthless text, narrated by a depthless protagonist and rendered by means of the depthless quality of film. Film extends and develops the central dynamic of mirroring in the narrative, providing Van with a format for endless self-reflection. While the films that are made and screened in the novel — Marina's *Torrid Affair*, Vronsky's *Les Enfants Maudits*, Ada's *Young and the Doomed* and *Don Juan's Last Fling*, and Vitry's *Letters from Terra* — reflect varying aspects and stages of Van and Ada's history, preoccupying themes of self-consciousness and performance are dramatized by the camera lens itself, to an extent where even inanimate objects seem to adopt the mechanisms of film:

> They crouched on the brink of one of the brook's crystal shelves, where, before falling, it stopped to have its picture taken and take pictures of itself [pp. 210–11].

Van's subversion of the mimetic qualities of film serves a very specific purpose, however, for it enables him to engineer the opacity which is integral to the narrative's central fraudulent dynamic. The "acrobatic wonders" Van achieves in his demonstrations of cinematic skill, even his expressions of conscience over Lucette's demise, are all mere distractions, serving to create the illusion of intellectual depth, imaginative complexity and emotional integrity where there is, essentially, none. Van's chronicle is a clandestine celebration of eroticism and sexual obsession, and it is this "spectacular secret" which is so carefully guarded through a calculated combination of illusion, deflection, distortion and controlled ambiguity. Thus it could be argued that Nabokov's Van Veen is, in his moral degeneracy and spiritual vacuity, nothing more than a supremely articulate and sophisticated descendant of William Faulkner's Popeye, and his chronicle a questionable attempt to achieve immortality which remains, ultimately, inconclusive. The narrative's overriding ambivalence, therefore, ultimately serves to confirm Richard Poirier's contention that "when it comes to dying or to the passage of time, ... all fictions are equally good and equally useless."[67]

In *Ada*, *Bend Sinister*, and "The Assistant Producer," Nabokov explores both the potential for illusion and transformation that the cinematic medium affords and its ability to generate alternative realms of experience. These ideas are developed further in Nabokov's penultimate novel, *Transparent Things* (1972), in which human and mechanical modes of perception merge in a conspiratorial association that irrevocably confirms his notion of reality as perpetually receding, amorphous, fragile and, ultimately, illusory.

Seven

Altered Perspectives and Visual Disruption in *Transparent Things* and American Film of the Early 1970s

The cinematic image has become the key to modern perception. It has created a new relationship between visual perception and emotion.[1]

When Nabokov began work on *Transparent Things* in 1969 he had been away from America for nearly a decade. As Brian Boyd points out, Nabokov's "natural audience was an American one, [but] he had lost touch with American slang and the rapid social changes of the 1960s."[2] Nevertheless, he wanted both the hero and narrator of this new novel to be American, and because he "always limited himself to milieus he could observe as well as or better than any of his readers,"[3] he placed them both in a literary environment as an editor and proofreader, and author respectively. The world of letters is, however, not the only milieu of *Transparent Things*. The novel demonstrates an acute filmic consciousness, manifested most overtly as a mode of narrative presentation, but which is also crucial to the exposition of its primary thematic concerns. At the same time, Nabokov's treatment of film, photography, and television is paralleled in the work of contemporary American writers, particularly Don DeLillo and Jerzy Kosinski, while the sophistication of his cinematic sensibility is echoed in the films of three leading directors, Roman Polanski, Francis Ford Coppola, and Robert Altman.

213

That Nabokov could produce a work of fiction that so closely reflected the preoccupations of contemporary America in spite of his long absence at first seems extraordinary. On examining the means by which he invokes those concerns, however, it quickly becomes apparent that he is merely proceeding along a course, inspired initially by America's dominant cultural medium which has led him, inexorably, to a point that happens to coincide with the state of the art at that time. *Transparent Things* responds to the primacy of film in the American psyche, but more fundamentally, challenges the perceived conventions of filmic fiction, as elucidated, for example, by Scott Simmon.

In discussing another contemporary novel, Thomas Pynchon's *Gravity's Rainbow*, Simmon comments on the extent to which the American reader's "whole way of approaching narrative itself has been altered by film."[4] Simmon argues that the "history of film is not so much a development of technique ... as it is a continuing education of an audience in the comprehension of film language" and thus the "seemingly unconscious knowledge of specific film conventions" that American audiences have accumulated over the decades "is now a resource for novelists as well as filmmakers."[5] *Transparent Things*, however, is distinctive not only for its integration of visual and filmic modes, but also for the ways it establishes a new dynamic of exchange between these two narrative forms, such that the novel becomes a "resource" for film, realigning itself to assume an engaged and interactive role, rather than the passive, merely receptive stance that Simmon emphasizes.

Transparent Things *and* the Mechanics of Perspective

Transparent Things contains Nabokov's most explicit exposition of "some of his oldest themes: the nature of time; the mystery and privacy of the human soul, and its simultaneous need to breach its solitude; the scope of consciousness beyond death; the possibility of design in the universe."[6] The novel is exceptional in Nabokov's oeuvre in that it comes closest to offering, not so much a finite solution, but a tangible resolution of these themes in the form of a reconciliation of conflicting modes of consciousness and shifting dimensions of perception.

Central to *Transparent Things* is the question of perspective. Whereas *Ada* is dominated by the solitary, narcissistic perspective of a megalomaniacal narrator/protagonist, *Transparent Things* presents the reader with two dominant parallel perspectives, that of the novel's inept hero, Hugh Person, the "sentimental simpleton,"[7] and its narrator, the spirit of the dead writer, R. The purpose of the primary narrative perspective offered by R. is to demonstrate a very particular visual process, one which consciously manipulates modes of perception, not as a means of distortion and deception, but of exposition and revelation.

Nabokov commented in a 1962 interview that "we live surrounded by more or less ghostly objects."[8] In an extension of the opposing "real" and "imaginary" worlds of Terra and Anti-Terra in *Ada*, *Transparent Things* dramatizes its ghostly world in a process of inversion, whereby the tangible proves to be illusory, and the intangible emphatically real. R.'s "ghostly" perspective enacts Nabokov's notion of reality as "an infinite succession of steps, levels of perception, false bottoms," a reality that is ultimately and inevitably "unquenchable, unattainable."[9] R. also represents an amalgam of two temporal forms of perspective, that of the scientist and the poet. The scientist "sees everything that happens in one point of space" whereas the poet "feels everything that happens in one point of time"[10]:

> Lost in thought, [the poet] taps his knee with his wandlike pencil, and at the same instant a car (New York license plate) passes along the road, a child bangs the screen door of a neighboring porch, an old man yawns in a misty Turkestan orchard, a granule of cinder-gray sand is rolled by the wind on Venus, a Docteur Jacques Hirsch in Grenoble puts on his reading glasses, and trillions of other such trifles occur — all forming an instantaneous and transparent organism of events, of which the poet (sitting in a lawn chair, at Ithaca, N.Y.) is the nucleus.[11]

R. is both a poet and a scientist. He shares the poet's privileged omniscient perspective but also possesses the ability to focus with scientific precision on a solitary, specific object. Indeed, this aspect of his perception is essential in safeguarding him from the primary hazard in the world of the dead, a process of "infinite regression in which the very identity and persistence of objects are hopelessly lost."[12] The dead can not only see all things at all times in all places, but they can see *through* things; they see their substance and their history in a series of endlessly unfolding layers.

> When *we* concentrate on a material object, whatever its situation, the very act of attention may lead to our involuntarily sinking into the history of that object [p. 1].

The process of "sinking" into an object is both figurative and literal. The dead can pass through any physical boundary and therefore risk falling headlong into an infinite chasm of receding time. Thus, in order both to remain in the present and prevent the "very identity and persistence of objects" from becoming "hopelessly lost," they must develop a means of perceptual control.

> A thin veneer of immediate reality is spread over natural and artificial matter, and whoever wishes to remain in the now, with the now, on the now, should please not break its tension film. Otherwise the inexperienced miracle-worker will find himself no longer walking on water but descending upright among staring fish [p. 2].

This, however, is not an easy task. As R. points out, "man-made objects, or natural ones, inert in themselves but much used by careless life ... are particularly difficult to keep in surface focus" (pp. 1–2). Preserving an object's fragile "tension film" requires a deliberate and highly conscious control of visual perspective; it is a skill which demands considerable effort, even for R., who is evidently a veteran "focus puller."[13] The role of film and photography in this process is crucial. R. adopts the camera perspective as a means of asserting perceptual authority. Rather than being a tool for sophisticated visual manipulation, however, it is deployed for its capability to render accurately the immediacy, fluidity and range of his vision, while providing a contained and defined medium in which to present it, one that is also instantly familiar to the reader.

The processes of R.'s visualization could be described, in cinematic terms, as a constantly repeating movement from "shallow" to "deep" focus.[14] This is first demonstrated in chapter three, when R.'s attention is distracted by a pencil Hugh finds in a drawer in his hotel room.[15] While Hugh continues to arrange his things, R. proceeds to trace the pencil's history in a sequence which describes every stage of its life, right back to the very tree that provided the wood for its shaft, "unfold[ing] in a twinkle" the "entire little drama, from crystallized carbon and felled pine to this humble implement, to this transparent thing" (p. 8). In order to retain the image of the pencil as a solid, opaque object, R. would have to hold it in shallow focus. As soon as his eye "sinks" through the pencil's surface "tension film" the visual focus rapidly adjusts to deep focus, revealing every layer and every detail of every layer of the pencil's history. Not only is the initial experience of sinking overtly cinematic, but the manner in which each episode of this history is presented also demonstrates a conscious manipulation of filmic techniques. In describing the pencil's manufacture, for example, R. deploys a series of "compilation cuts" which shift visual attention from one detail of the scene to another in a rapid sequence, serving to generate both pace and urgency and a sense of panorama:

> [The pencil] is now being cut into lengths required for these particular pencils [CUT] (we glimpse the cutter, old Elias Borrowdale, [CUT] and are about to mouse up his forearm on a side trip of inspection but we stop, stop and recoil, in our haste to identify the individual segment). [CUT] See it baked, [CUT] see it boiled in fat [CUT] (here a shot of the fleecy fat-giver being butchered, [CUT] a shot of the butcher, [CUT] a shot of the shepherd, [CUT] a shot of the shepherd's father, a Mexican) [CUT] and fitted into the wood [p. 7].

In a subsequent episode, the speed at which R. descends into and pulls back from this cosmic freefall is rendered with the abrupt impact of a jump cut. The bed in the boardinghouse in Geneva where Hugh is taken by a prostitute, Giulia Romeo, initiates another sudden shift in perspective, a flashback to a scene in the same room ninety-three years before:

> The bed — a different one, with brass knobs — was made, unmade, covered with a frock coat, made again; upon it stood a half-open green-checkered grip, and the frock coat was thrown over the shoulders of the night-shirted, bare-necked, dark-tousled traveler[16] whom we catch in the act of deciding what to take out of the valise [pp. 17–18].

Again, the direction and movement of visual perspective is overtly cinematic and eloquently dramatizes R.'s efforts to halt his fall into the past. R. manages to stop the rush of time portrayed by the bed being continually made and unmade by fixing his attention on the frock coat. He "pulls focus" as it were, and then allows his perspective to adjust sufficiently from a close-up to a medium shot so as to disclose the entirety of the scene. The scene is concluded with an equally abrupt shift in perspective which has the effect of a jump cut, serving to dramatize R.'s experience of being jolted back into the present.

> Instead of sorting his papers, [the traveler] uncorks his portable ink and moves nearer to the table, pen in hand. But at that minute there comes a joyful banging on the door. The door flies open and closes again. [CUT]
> Hugh Person followed his chance girl down the long steep stairs [p. 18].

This switch in visual focus is also combined with a parallel shift in tense, here from present to past, which emphasizes the movement of R.'s perspective through time. At the end of chapter eleven, for example, which considers the nature of Hugh's past relationship with Julia Moore, R. abruptly introduces the image, in close-up, of a detail of Hugh's hotel room — "We now see a torn piece of *La Stampa* and an empty wine bottle. A lot of construction work was going on" (p. 36) — thus bringing the narrative back to its primary chronology. By this process of perceptual fall, therefore, the past becomes a form of present, existing on an immediate, dynamic plane, and thus the notion of the past as something lost and remote is negated. The only limitation of R.'s perspective is that, having brought the past into a realm of greater proximity, he can still only replay events; he has neither the power to change them, nor any influence over the course of a future scenario.

R.'s primary concern, however, is to "remain in the now." A freefall into the past is not always useful, although it can offer a pleasant distraction and even sometimes impart such moments of "cosmic synchronization," but his immediate responsibility is to Hugh, and it is evident that keeping him at the center of his attention requires considerable effort.

> Now we have to bring into focus the main street of Witt as it was on Thursday, the day after [Armande's] telephone call. It teems with transparent people and processes, into which and through which we might sink with an angel's or author's delight, but we have to single out for this report only one Person [p. 44].

Although R. considers Hugh to be "somehow not a very *good* Person [but] merely a rather dear one" (p. 48), that he is deserving of his attention is never questioned. R. represents Nabokov's most overt manifestation of a "transcendent, non-material, timeless, and beneficent ordering and ordered realm of being that seems to provide for personal immortality, and that affects everything that exists in the mundane world."[17] He is "a tender ghost humoring a lucky mortal."[18] Not only does R.'s perspective evoke a mood of sympathy and tolerance, but unlike the didactic, autocratic narratives of Humbert Humbert or Van Veen, R.'s is distinctly democratic. Although his perspective is omniscient, it is not definitive, and whereas Humbert Humbert and Van Veen assert an unchallenged perceptual authority, R. prefers to emphasize the possibilities for alternative perspectives, the depiction of any character or situation being dependent upon the "angle of light and the position of the observer" (p. 16).

Nevertheless it is evident that R.'s perspective is, ultimately, the most reliable, as the discrepancies between his and Hugh's points of view become increasingly apparent. As the instances of Hugh's misapprehension accumulate, a sense of acute irony develops. The series of miscalculations, misconceptions and misinterpretations that leads to Hugh's ultimate demise occurs wholly independently and without any interference from R. His role is simply to "report" (p. 44) on the circumstances of Hugh's entrance into his world. His perspective is, however, supported and thus validated by several others. The first is Hugh's "umbral companion":

> All his life, we are glad to note, our Person had experienced the curious sensation (known to three famous theologians and two minor poets) of there existing behind him — at his shoulder, as it were — a larger, incredibly wiser, calmer and stronger stranger, morally better than he.... [H]ad he been without that transparent shadow, we would not have bothered to speak about our dear Person [p. 98].

Of the various perceptual tiers in operation in the novel, this discreet, anonymous perspective emerges only once, briefly, but at a critical point, sufficiently apparent for the reader to register its existence and to become conscious of its autonomous presence within and beyond the narrative:

> During the short stretch between his chair in the lounge and the girl's adorable neck, plump lips, long eyelashes, veiled charms, Person was conscious of something or somebody warning him that he should leave Witt there and then for Verona, Florence, Roma, Taormina, if Stresa was out. He did not heed his shadow, and fundamentally he may have been right. We thought that he had in him a few years of animal pleasure; we were ready to waft that girl into his bed, but after all it was for him to decide, for him to die, if he wished [pp. 98–99].

Other, less distinct perspectives, all of them spectral, appear at the novel's beginning and end. The novel opens with R. and another anonymous ghost beckoning to Hugh — "Hullo person! What's the matter, don't pull me. I'm *not* bothering him" (p. 1)[19] — while the novices described "humming" on their backs (p. 2) reappear in the form of the flames "mounting the stairs" of the Stresa hotel, "in pairs, in trios, in redskin file, hand in hand, tongue after tongue, conversing and humming happily" (p. 103). William Rowe argues that "unusual rising perspectives" in the narrative indicate the presence of ghosts, citing the scene at the Ascot Hotel in chapter two, when Hugh learns that the former manager, Kronig, is dead. The reiteration of the names of both of Kronig's hotels — the "Majestic" and the "Fantastic" (p. 4) — in the description of Hugh as he rides up in the lift indicates, according to Rowe, Kronig's "observing presence."[20]

There is also a suggestion that the spirit of Armande is present as yet another narrative perspective, indicated by the repeated use of the term "You" at the beginning of chapter thirteen, as R. relates Hugh's encounter with her and Julia at a pavement café in Witt:

> He decided it was time for some more refreshments — and saw her sitting at a sidewalk café. You swerved toward her, thinking she was alone; then noticed, too late, a second handbag on the opposite chair [pp. 44–45].

That this is Armande's voice is signaled by the mode of direct address which echoes her repeated mispronunciation of his name — "You" instead of Hugh — at the end of the previous chapter (pp. 42–43), and by the way it interrupts the novel's predominant, impersonal third-person narrative voice. The shift in perspective is also compounded by a switch in visual focus which follows the course of Hugh's attention as he registers the details of the scene before him. If this is Armande's interjection, then it communicates a level of sympathy and intimacy which she was incapable of either feeling or demonstrating in life, thus implying that in death, with the privileged insight it affords, Armande has perhaps found the means of engaging and empathizing with other souls.

Signs and Symbols and the Problems of Perception

The novel's ironic dynamic, however, is driven by Hugh's faulty vision. He believes that his destiny is governed by an esoteric patterning of "thematic designs,"[21] and that his life is "harrowed by coincident symbols" (p. 13). As R.'s narrative proves, Hugh is correct in his assumption, except that he responds to the wrong set of signs and motifs and is unable to recognize that not only are they vacuous and absurd, but that his pursuit of their perceived design is potentially disastrous.[22]

Hugh's world, according to Brian Boyd, is "arid and anguished,"[23] "everything frustrates [him], even inert matter," and thus he is driven to seek "refuge from the inimical outer world in the inner one of his emotions."[24] Hugh, however, is not a man of great passions. His hopes and desires are, in fact, very modest, yet his withdrawal into a private world of emotional fantasy reduces him to a state of perpetual disappointment, for nothing in his life can possibly live up to his imagined expectations. Hugh's refusal to revoke his misguided dreams, therefore, combines fatally with his inability to see the true pattern of his destiny.

Critics have noted the ways in which Hugh's predicament parallels that of Chorb in "The Return of Chorb" (1926), and the chess grandmaster, Luzhin, of *The Defense* (1930).[25] Hugh, like Chorb, endeavors to reincarnate his dead wife by embarking on a pilgrimage to the place where they spent their honeymoon. Whereas Chorb is intent on literally bringing his wife back from the dead by means of some bizarre form of inspired ritual, Hugh simply wishes to experience "a moment of contact with [Armande's] essential image" (p. 95). The folly of Hugh's aspirations is greater than Chorb's, however, because the form of Hugh's desired epiphany lacks all substance. He requires no bodily manifestation but merely an image, a two-dimensional, flat, depthless picture, the epitome of a transparent thing, which is, inevitably, unattainable. Chorb also possesses a greater awareness of the subliminal, yet sinister patterning of motifs and coincidences which seem to guide him in his quest. Luzhin, on the other hand, neither recognizes the presence nor discerns the significance of recurring motifs, except to sense a series of vague and muffled resonances, while the gradually encircling pattern of the chess motif which serves primarily as a means of communicating to the reader Luzhin's increasing sense of entrapment is only disclosed to him, finally, as "the image of the true eternity that awaits him."[26]

Hugh's demise could also be interpreted as an ironic inversion of Luzhin's suicide. Luzhin escapes the suffocating oppression of his world by falling to his death from a window. Hugh attempts to evade the fire in his hotel by escaping through, what he thinks, is a window but what is, in fact, a door, and thus he dies of smoke asphyxiation, suggesting that even at such a critical moment he fails to respond to the prospect he believes the window offers, perceiving it, wrongly, to be the "tension film" dividing the worlds of the living and the dead. It is also significant that he is stopped from jumping by the "graceful gesture" of a "long lavender-tipped flame" (p. 104), which, like the "humming" flames on the stairs, is another phantom presence that conspires to make him to stay inside the room. The apparent purpose of these spectral flames suggests that the window is not, as Hugh believes, an aperture that opens onto a terrifying void, and is, therefore, essentially redundant in the present scenario. Death, as R. discloses, occurs elsewhere and involves neither the tangible process of an exit through a window or a door, nor the "crude anguish" (p. 104) of a horrifying collapse, but manifests itself merely as a subtle and "mysterious mental maneuver" (p. 104).

The patterning of motifs in *Transparent Things* reaches its climax in this final scene,[27] but of the "three complexes of lethal motifs that sketch Hugh's life and death: fire, falling, and asphyxiation,"[28] "falling" is central to the exposition of the theme of perspective in the novel. R.'s perceptual "walking on water" (p. 2) prevents him from "falling," irrevocably, into the past. Hugh demonstrates a preoccupation with falling, or rather, a fear of falling, and this fear proves to be a fundamental motivation in governing almost every aspect of his existence and in influencing his perceptual capacities.

While falling means death to Hugh, to R. it is merely a matter of comic humiliation. The "after-fall pause of a bulky novice asprawl on his back in hopeless, good-humored repose" (pp. 52–53) is distinctly reminiscent of the suicidal antics of the indestructible heroes of American film comedy and cartoons. Although in this instance the "novice asprawl on his back" is the picture of himself that Hugh imagines having just fallen off his skis, it also alludes to R.'s "novice" ghosts, who, unlike Hugh, have no fear of injury and, in "learn[ing] to skim over matter" (p. 1), delight in the thrill of a perceptual plunge, "reveling with childish abandon" (p. 2) as they fall through layers of time.[29]

In spite of the extremity of Hugh's acrophobia, he not only repeatedly finds himself in situations that would provoke an attack of vertigo, but also seems to actively court them. His love for Armande causes him to follow her anywhere, whether it be up a mountain, onto a cable car, or out of a fourth-story hotel window. His acrophobia even extends from a fear of falling to a fear of things falling upon him from great heights and is manifested in recurring nightmares in which he is crushed to death beneath "collapsing colossuses" of rubbish (p. 60).

Hugh finds himself constantly confronted by precipices, in varying forms. Apart from the genuine terror they induce in him, the vision of Hugh staring into the abyss, gripped by vertigo, is distinctly comic in its combination of abject terror and farce, recalling the balancing acts of

Buster Keaton, Harold Lloyd or Charlie Chaplin.[30] Don Barton Johnson describes the narrative's comic tone as "uncharacteristically laconic,"[31] but at times it is far blacker than that. For example, the first incident that establishes the character of the novel's humor is that of Hugh's father's death. Person Senior dies of a heart attack while trying on a pair of trousers in a store:

> He died before reaching the floor, as if falling from some great height, and now lay on his back, one arm outstretched, umbrella and hat out of reach in the tall looking glass [p. 15].

The banality of the situation comically detracts from the genuinely unfortunate, undignified and distressing nature of Person Senior's demise. The idea of death as some form of rapid descent is clearly established, but its specific relation to Hugh and his father as a "coincident symbol" is anticipated by a sequence of images, beginning with Person Senior struggling with the Venetian blind in their hotel room which suddenly descends "in a rattling avalanche" (p. 10). This motif emerges again as they leave their room and pass through the hotel lobby, where a "local miracle of nature, the Tara cataract" (p. 11) is duplicated as a "huge photograph" on the wall and, ironically, as a painting on the watercloset door, in an attempt at an aesthetic indication of the prospect of a flushing cistern within.[32]

Hugh witnesses the aftermath of a fatal fall in the image of his father lying sprawled in the changing booth, and this serves to magnify his acrophobia, such that simply looking out of a window is sufficient to bring about an attack of vertigo:

> He opened wide both casements; they gave on a parking place four floors below; the thin meniscus overhead was too wan to illumine the roofs of the houses descending towards the invisible lake; the light of the garage picked out the steps of desolate stairs leading into a chaos of shadows [p. 19].

The vertiginous effect of this spectacle is rendered by sudden shifts in visual focus which descend rapidly in three stages: from the window down to the parking lot; from the sky down to the lake; and from the garage down into an infinite void. As the levels of R.'s perception are rendered cinematically, so the very specific visual character of this prospect has a cinematic quality, combining "crash" zooms and a distortion of perspective particularly reminiscent of the visual effects of Alfred Hitchcock's *Vertigo* (1958). In the following passage, James Monaco describes how Hitchcock developed a specific cinematic technique to evoke, visually, the sensation of vertigo which is experienced by the film's hero, John Ferguson:

> [Hitchcock used] a carefully controlled zoom combined with a track and models. Hitchcock laid the model stairwell on its side. The camera with zoom lens was mounted on a track looking "down" the stairwell. The shot began with the camera at the far end of the track and the zoom lens set at a moderate telephoto focal length. As the camera tracked in toward the stairwell, the zoom was adjusted backwards, eventually winding up at a wide-angle setting. The track and zoom were carefully coordinated so that the size of the image appeared not to change.... The effect relayed on the screen was that the shot began with normal depth perception which then became quickly exaggerated, mimicking the psychological feeling of vertigo.[33]

The combination of the rapid zooms and the movement from a moderate to a wide-angle shot deployed by Hitchcock exactly matches the course of Hugh's focal attention as he looks out of the window, and is compounded by the impact of the garage light, which draws Hugh's attention further into the abyss. This same visual experience is translated into his dreams and plays a crucial role in the dream he has on the night he strangles Armande.

Hugh dreams that their apartment block is on fire, and Armande, who has turned into "Julie," a composite of his former lovers, Julia Moore and Giulia Romeo, is about to leap from the window, in ironic echo of her honeymoon fire drill (see pp. 64–65). Hugh is forced to approach the window where Julie stands "prostrated" on the sill (p. 80), and as he looks out his eye is drawn down into the "chasm of the yard" (p. 80) by the red glow of the flames, which holds him mesmerized. Hugh grabs Julie by the neck to prevent her from falling, but "in her suicidal struggle" (p. 81) she slips and they both fall together "into the void" (p. 81). Hugh is incapacitated by the visual aspect of the scene, the vertiginous effect of the flames and the strange "luminous" quality of Julie's body in the window, which is magnified by the visual associations generated by the "Doppler shift" she is wearing. Although, as the electric sign flashing outside their sitting room window suggests, "Doppler" refers in this instance to a brand name for women's lingerie (see p. 77), the connotations of the scientific term "Doppler shift"[34] also suggest a vertiginous distortion of light, which compounds the surreal visual quality of the scene. As Hugh moves toward Julie, therefore, so the intensity of the light she seems to be emitting grows, having the same mesmeric effect as the fire.

Hitchcock's tower. *Vertigo* (Paramount, 1958).

Hugh's worst nightmare: Ferguson (James Stewart) clings to broken guttering, not daring to look down. *Vertigo* (Paramount, 1958).

The reflection of the scene in the image of the "writhing windpipe" which appears, appropriately, "on a screen of science cinema across the yard" (p. 81) offers an alternative close-up perspective on the reality of what is happening in the apartment, functioning as a "flash frame"[35] to reveal the scenario's actual horrific dimension. It is also significant that this is a perspective unavailable to Hugh. R.'s privileged ability to see through physical barriers, in this instance, beyond the apartment building and into the cinema's auditorium serves, therefore, to amplify the irony of Hugh's oblivious belief that he is, in fact, rescuing the girl.

The presence of the cinema is also significant in that it inspires the dream's conclusion. As they tumble from the window sill, Hugh is transformed into the gravity-defying American comic-book superhero, Superman, and thus their fall is reversed — "How they flew! Superman carrying a young soul in his embrace!" (p. 81).

At the same time, the naivety of this vision is undercut by the tragic nature of the episode's true consequences, which are also revealed cinematically. Hugh "gropes for the lamp" that has "collapsed" (appositely) along with the bedside table, as Hugh and Armande fall together to the ground. Hugh rights the lamp, switches it on and is abruptly confronted by a brutal, yet unequivocal reality. Light, therefore, functions as a revelationary force (it is significant that the episode had occurred in the dark), and the presentation of the scene's closing sequence — the silent depiction of the aftermath of violence and the final close-up image of Hugh's hands — his "bashful claws" — are distinctly reminiscent of the lighting devices deployed by Raymond Chandler and the visual quality of American film noir.

If the consequence of falling is death, then the ability to fly promises immortality. Armande in death seems, significantly, to adopt the pose of flight — "he wondered what his wife was doing there, prone on the floor, her fair hair spread as if she were flying" (p. 81). It is appropriate, there-fore, that Hugh, in his attempt to reincarnate Armande, should find him-self dreaming once again of flight, not as Superman, but this time as a passenger on an airplane. Here, the experience of flying is a matter of a shift in perspective, reminiscent of the "dizzying view of the world"[36] granted by Ivanov's flight into the earth's upper hemisphere at the end of "Perfection":

> At this moment of her now indelible dawning through the limpid door of his room he felt the elation a tourist feels, when taking off and ... the earth slants and then regains its horizontal position, and practically in no spacetime we are thousands of feet above land, and the clouds ... seem to lie on a flat sheet of glass in a celestial laboratory and, through this glass, far below it, bits of gingerbread earth show, a scarred hillside, a round indigo lake, the dark green of pine woods, the incrustations of villages [pp. 102–3].

The metaphor of flight which dramatizes Hugh's "elation" is transformed into an episode of "dream cinema,"[37] in which Hugh finds himself sit-ting in the plane, being served by Armande, now a flight attendant.[38] The folly of Hugh's "dream cinema," however, is confirmed, as it was in the previous Superman episode, by the abrupt and unwelcome intrusion of reality in the form of another fire.

Nevertheless, the sequence is significant in that Hugh is granted, if only briefly and incompletely, R.'s privileged perspective, at the same time corresponding with Rowe's notion of rising perspectives as indica-tive of the presence of spirits. Looking down from such a height, the clouds form a kind of transparent tension film, and unlike the opaque "meniscus" of sky (p. 19) that seems to constrain Hugh and magnify the pull of gravity as he looks up at it from his hotel room, this newfound vantage offers a panoramic spectacle and a deep focus visualization through layers of space. Most significantly, however, it is a perspective free of fear.[39]

Film and Television Dreams in
Transparent Things, Americana
and Being There

Hugh's "dream cinema" is a synthetic and transitory attempt to enter another realm of being, somewhere between life and death. That this realm should take the form of film is indicative of the medium's universal escapist appeal and the extent to which audiences concede their own reality to the fantasy projected on the screen before them. Even in waking hours, Hugh indulges in cinematically inspired fantasies, although they are more unconscious than conscious. For example, when Armande first invites Hugh to go skiing with her, he imagines a highly romanticized vision of the mountainside, with himself "stroll[ing] beside her, along a footpath not only provided for him by fancy but also swept clean with a snowman's broom" (p. 43). This "instant unverified vision" (p. 43) has the artificial, improbably tidy quality of a movie set, and yet such scenarios would be Hugh's only frame of reference, since this is, for him, an entirely new scenario.

His chance meeting with Armande and Julia Moore at the pavement café in Witt also provokes an absurd and highly clichéd scenario reminiscent of banal Hollywood romances, a scenario which he hopes, somehow, by the power of his imagination, will infect his present reality:

> [Hugh] was sorry that no music accompanied the scene, no Rumanian fiddler dipped heartward for two monogram-entangled sakes. There was not even a mechanical rendition of "Fascination" (a waltz) by the café's loudplayer. Still there did exist a kind of supporting rhythm formed by the voices of foot passengers, the clink of crockery, the mountain wind in the venerable mass of the corner chestnut [p. 48].

Hugh's "dream cinema" demonstrates the extent to which his consciousness has been informed by aspects of Hollywood culture, in the tradition of, say, Nick Carraway or Binx Bolling, and a more contemporary protagonist, the advertising executive David Bell of Don DeLillo's *Americana* (1971). Hugh's reference to American film is far less dynamic and evocative, but it nevertheless reflects the pivotal, inspirational role of cinema in the American psyche. Bell, for example, idolizes Burt Lancaster and Kirk Douglas, two Hollywood stars of the 1950s who made a profound impact on his consciousness as a young boy:

My own instincts led me to Kirk Douglas and Burt Lancaster. These were the American pyramids and they needed no underground to spread their fame. They were monumental. Their faces slashed across the screen.... They were men of action, running, leaping, loving with abandon.[40]

Apart from being aspirational figures, these actors represent a superior mode of being, distinct from mundane reality. For Binx Bolling, movie stars serve, in both their cinematic and real-life manifestations, to certify his existence. For David Bell, however, the vitality of both actor and image is such that they begin to replace his everyday reality, to a point where the very processes of conventional visual engagement and response are fundamentally disrupted and altered by the cinematic experience.

For the first time in my life I felt the true power of the image.... Within the conflux of shadow and time, there was room for all of us and I knew I must extend myself until the molecules parted and I was spread into the image [pp. 12–13].

In *Americana*, the world of film is set against the world of television, which is presented as an inferior medium, one which merely reflects mundane reality, serving not as a means of escape but rather providing a temporary distraction which has the power to neutralize, even obliterate, objective consciousness.

I looked at the TV screen for a moment and then found myself in a chair about a foot away from the set, watching intently. I could not tell what was happening on the screen and it didn't seem to matter. Sitting that close all I could perceive was that meshed effect, those stormy motes, but it drew me and held me as if I were an integral part of the set, my molecules mating with those millions of dots. I sat that way for half an hour or so [p. 43].

In *Transparent Things*, the same mesmeric state is echoed by the expression on the face of the elevator boy in the Ascot Hotel, who seems to be held rapt in a television-induced trance:

A handsome young fellow in black, with pustules on chin and throat, took Person up to a fourth-floor room and all the way kept staring with a telly viewer's absorption at the black bluish wall gliding down [p. 4].

A more extreme example of television's neutralizing force is embodied by Chance, the hero of Jerzy Kosinski's *Being There* (1970). As Cecelia

Tichi argues, "Kosinski acknowledges that television and its viewer form an interpenetrant unit,"[41] a relationship which causes the television audience to revoke any ability to discern or disseminate the sequence of arbitrary images that appears before it.

> The set created its own light, its own color, its own time. It did not follow the law of gravity.... Everything on TV was tangled and mixed and yet smoothed out: night and day, big and small, tough and brittle, soft and rough, hot and cold, far and near.[42]

Television's penetration of Chance's consciousness is total because he has no other available source with which to refer to or compare his world, and thus, unlike David Bell, he experiences no sense of disruption or alteration, but rather enjoys a fluid, interactive perceptual relationship with the images on the screen:

> By changing the channel he could change himself.... In some cases he could spread out onto the screen without stopping, just as on TV people spread out into the screen. By turning the dial, Chance could bring others inside his eyelids. Thus he came to believe that it was he, Chance, and no one else, who made himself be.[43]

For David Bell, however, the notion that television has the potential ability to control consciousness, to a point where it not only infects independent perception but can also govern existence itself, is deeply unsettling.

> There were times when I thought all of us at the network existed only on videotape. Our words and actions seemed to have a disturbingly elapsed quality. We had said and done all these things before and they had been frozen for a time, rolled up in little laboratory trays to await broadcast and rebroadcast when the proper time-slots became available. And there was the feeling that somebody's deadly pinky might nudge a button and we would all be erased forever [p. 23].

Bell's conflicting responses to the images produced by film and television indicate a generally perceived discrepancy between the two mediums. Bell is, throughout his life, continually "stirred by the power of the image," but it is essentially a cinematic image, one that certifies existence and inspires the imagination, not the television image which is perceived as a threat to the autonomous individual, possessing the capability to reduce all men to nothing "more than electronic signals [moving] through time and space with the stutter and shadowed insanity of a TV commercial" (p. 24).

Nabokov also clearly distinguishes Hugh's film-inspired dreamworld from the television world with which Armande regularly engages. The ludicrous fire drill Armande insists they embark upon on their honeymoon is initiated by a fire she sees on the television:

> For some reason or other, television producers consider that there is nothing more photogenic and universally fascinating than a good fire. Armande, viewing the Italian telenews, had been upset or feigned to be upset ... by one such calamity on the local screen [p. 64].

Thus yet another "plane of reality"[44] — TV reality — is established to complement the perspectives provided by R. and his phantom colleagues and the "dream cinema" of Hugh's waking and sleeping states. The television image magnifies both the reality and the proximity of the fire such that Armande feels that she is actually experiencing it as she watches it on the screen, even though what she sees is in fact an exaggerated distortion of the truth, dramatized for maximum effect by a highly skilled television crew. On another occasion, however, the relationship between Armande and the television set is reversed. Rather than allowing it to dictate to her, she wields control with her "deadly pinky":

> She ... turned it on, let it live for a moment, changed channels — and killed the picture with a snort of disgust (her likes and dislikes in these matters lacked all logic, she might watch one or two programmes with passionate regularity or on the contrary not touch the set for a week as if punishing that marvelous invention for a misdemeanor known only to her, and Hugh preferred to ignore her obscure feuds with actors and commentators) [p. 72].

Armande's command of the set may appear casual and arbitrary, but her engagement with it is nevertheless as compelling, her relationship with it as personal and intimate as if it were another unique and tangible entity in possession of an independent consciousness. It is significant, however, that R. should describe the television as a "marvelous invention," in spite of Hugh's indifference to it and Armande's illogical relationship with it, as if in acknowledgement of its intrinsic value as a medium of alternative perspectives.

A Parallel Realm of Existence:
Photography in Transparent Things

Apart from television and film, photography also features in *Transparent Things* as a tangible perceptual medium. In *Lolita* and *Ada*, photography offers a means of capturing and freezing a moment in time and is therefore an invaluable mnemonic tool, but for Hugh, it also offers a means of reincarnating the past. On returning finally to Stresa, Hugh's desire is not to bring Armande back to life, but merely to experience "a moment of contact with her essential image" (p. 95). Chorb's ambition proves to be disastrous, Hugh's promises to be even more so, since the intention is to reincarnate not a tangible presence, but something which is essentially amorphous, ephemeral, insubstantial. At the same time, it is appropriate that what Hugh should ultimately desire essentially reflects the nature of his relationship with Armande, whom he loved "in spite of her unlovableness" (p. 63), "despite her worst moods, her silliest caprices, her harshest demands" (p. 55). Hugh is, therefore, attempting to reincarnate a dream, a dream that from the first moment he met Armande took the form, in his mind, of a photographic image so potent that it instantly replaced the reality that inspired it.

> It was indeed all sham and waxworks as compared to the reality of Armande, whose image was stamped on the eye of his mind and shone through the show at various levels, sometimes upside down, sometimes on the teasing margin of his field of vision, but always there, always, true and thrilling [p. 30].

That Armande's image should sometimes appear in inverse form — "upside down"— confirms the innately photographic quality of Hugh's memory. This, however, only serves to compound the ironic nature of his mission at Stresa, designating it, categorically, as misguided and futile. Hugh not only attempts the impossible, but in doing so undermines the key element of the remembered vision that initiated and sustained its potency in his mind.

Hugh's misapprehension of the mnemonic process extends into other aspects of his bid to reincarnate "exactly remembered surroundings" (p. 95). On his return to the Villa Nastia, Hugh seeks out familiar details. "He would glance at the porch," for example, "as one uses a glazed envelope to slip in an image of the past" (p. 87). Hugh uses his eyes as a camera to take mental snapshots of significant locations, yet it is not their present prospect which he hopes to capture and immortalize, but rather a revived image of the past, in a kind of faulty simulation of R.'s process of visual retrieval. Hugh's imaginary photographs prove, however, to be devoid of any substance or useful function. He reaches the Villa Nastia to find it closed up, no porch in sight, and while Hugh's dream pictures only serve, ultimately, to disappoint, actual photographs also fail to meet his expectations.

On his first visit to Villa Nastia, in a vain excursion to seek out Armande, Hugh is welcomed by her mother, Madame Chamar, who ushers him into the house and then promptly excuses herself, leaving him in the sitting room with a set of photograph albums before him. The albums contain a "candid" series of snapshots taken of Armande "through all the phases of the past" (p. 40), the last album still waiting to be filled with present and future images. The intimate nature of many of the shots — many of a pre-pubescent Armande in the nude — causes Hugh to become aroused, and his perspective is instantly transformed from curious innocent to guilty, furtive voyeur. Apart from the very disconcerting effect the photographs have on Hugh, the pictures remain depthless, superficial, opaque, and Armande is presented as a two-dimensional object, a mere mannequin sporting various different outfits in various different locations.

David Packman has argued that photographs are inherently devoid of meaning because, unlike film, they are "discontinuous" and "fragmentary," they "arrest a frozen moment of time that is not located in any narrative sequence" and thus are "without beginning, middle, and end."[45] Although, in this instance, Packman is discussing the function of photographs in *Lolita*, the consequences of cataloguing a life in this way are essentially the same for Hugh as they are for Humbert Humbert.

> Because it involves a strip of celluloid, a sequence of shots, a film is decidedly narrative in character.... Like any narrative line, it contrives to elicit expectation and desire for its continued unfolding. To fragment that continuity would perhaps be to fetishize the nymphet.[46]

Armande, therefore, is, in this photographic form, reduced to precisely this — a "fetishized nymphet" — and although, initially, the vision excites Hugh, he is left with the unsettling sensation of having indulged in an act of sordid voyeurism. Ironically, while his dignity has been violated, Armande, in his eyes, remains uncompromised.

"Tell her that my system is poisoned by her, by her twenty sisters, her twenty dwindlings in backcast, and that I shall perish if I cannot have her."

He was still rather simple as lovers go. One might have said to fat, vulgar Madame Chamar: how dare you exhibit your child to sensitive strangers? But our Person vaguely imagined this was a case of modern immodesty current in Madame Chamar's set [p. 42].

The "backcast" perspective the albums afford is essentially a reverse sequence of the regressive stages of R.'s perception. Whereas R.'s perspective begins in the present and gradually sinks through layers of time into an infinite past, the albums offer Hugh a visual spectacle that begins at a finite stage in the not-so-distant past and progresses in chronological sequence to stop at a designated point in the recent present. Like the photographs, the dimensions of Hugh's perspective are fixed, and time is not an endless, boundless space of infinite dimensions, offering a multitude of diverse perceptual possibilities, as it is to R., but proscribed, limited, closed: a place which echoes Nabokov's conception of time as a kind of "prison" that is "spherical and without exits."[47]

Imaginary Boundaries, Invisible Barriers and the Filmic Perspective

The notion of Hugh being trapped in a prison of consciousness is compounded by the tension film motif. Invisible or transparent barriers serve, in the novel, not merely as devices enabling R. to maintain his perceptual focus, but also as the tangible boundaries of Hugh's existence, setting the limitations of his consciousness and amplifying the intensity of his solitude. The barriers tend to be made of glass and thus either obstruct, reflect or refract vision. Although objects on the other side of a window, for example, can be seen, they take on a remote, surreal quality. Likewise, while mirrors present a reverse image of whatever stands before them, the images they present appear to belong to another impenetrable realm, removed and inaccessible. It is significant that when Hugh's father collapses and dies in the changing booth his "umbrella and hat" are seen lying "out of reach in the tall looking glass" (p. 15), suggesting his entry in death into the dimension that lies behind the mirror, much in the same way that Alice passes into the fantastic world of Wonderland in Lewis Carroll's *Through the Looking Glass* (1871).[48] Carroll "attempts to naturalize Alice's extraordinary adventures by suggesting that she has merely been dreaming,"[49] there is no such suggestion in *Transparent Things* that Hugh's dreams bear any relation to the metaphysical realm which R. inhabits. Indeed, the notion that mirrors, windows, essentially all transparent or reflective surfaces serve as "holes between two universes," as "*leaks*"[50] which afford glimpses of and even access to other realms, is exclusively Hugh's misconception. The presence of barriers in the narrative demonstrates the fundamental dichotomy between Hugh's and R.'s perspectives, for, while Hugh perceives such surfaces as impenetrable obstructions, which at the same time enclose and protect him from the yawning abysses that lie behind them, to R. they merely provide a means of halting an infinite perceptual fall and simply define layers of time and space. The fact is that there is nothing in the novel that divides the worlds of the living and dead, for the dead, like R., are everywhere.

Nevertheless, for Hugh the barriers imply the presence of another realm, even though he is unable to fully apprehend or identify it. For example, as he looks out of his hotel window into an adjacent restaurant he is presented with the prospect of "phantoms of pale tables and underwater waiters" (p. 9). This vision can be interpreted not only as a revelation of R.'s world, but also as indicative of the extremity of Hugh's isolation, which in turn is magnified by these transparent barriers and is reminiscent of Ivanov's predicament in "Perfection." Ivanov's consciousness is described as "flutter[ing] and walk[ing] up and down the glass pane which for as long as he lived would prevent him from having direct contact with the world" (p. 340). Hugh, however, is not particularly concerned with achieving "direct contact" with the world until he meets Armande, and yet his desire for her increases his awareness of the barriers that constrain him — from the sky's "meniscus" (p. 19) to the glass walls, both real and imaginary, that confront him at every angle — "the blazing windows of a villa by Plam" (p. 28), or the movie of R.'s book "*Golden Windows*" (p. 32), and even his own "dazzled and watery eyes" (p. 53).

Armande's indifference to Hugh and his consequent frustration cause him to seek out objects upon which to transmit his affection. Thus the "green figurine of a female skier" (p. 13)[51] which he buys in a souvenir shop takes on a particular significance as a reminder not only of Armande, but of Armande in the guise in which he first kissed her, and also "the minor miracle" (p. 55) — a moment of blissful transparency — that the kiss initiated:

A shiver of tenderness rippled her features, as a breeze does a reflection. Her eyelashes were wet, her shoulders shook in his clasp. That moment of soft agony was never to be repeated — or rather would never be granted the time to come back again after completing the cycle innate in its rhythm; yet that brief vibration in which she dissolved with the sun, the cherry trees, the forgiven landscape, set the tone for his new existence with its sense of "all-is-well".... That kiss, and not anything preceding it, was the real beginning of their courtship [p. 55].

It could also be argued that the figurine serves as another of Hugh's "harrowing coincidences," that it anticipates this scene both in the narrative and in Hugh's consciousness. It is no coincidence in Hugh's mind, therefore, that Armande is clad in a green skiing outfit on this fateful day, and this serves to confirm the significance of the figurine in the store window as a signal of his destiny, a destiny which Hugh feels he must pursue, no matter how flawed the circumstances. The figurine, like the image imprinted on his memory, however, proves to be as remote as Armande herself. This quality is instantly designated by the fact that the figurine lies behind "show glass" (p. 13) and is therefore out of reach. Not only this, but the glass prevents Hugh from being able to discern what the figurine is made of; its very substance remains unidentifiable, mysterious, alien, even. It is deeply ironic, therefore, that Hugh should bring this figurine with him on his pilgrimage to Stresa as his most precious reminder of Armande and that it is rendered even more inaccessible by its new wrapping, this time a box. Nevertheless, Hugh's attachment to it is such that he can still sense it shining through the "double kix" (p. 101).[52]

The implication is, therefore, that the illusion of the object has become more real than the object itself, as the photographic illusion of Armande has the potential for greater substance and intimate proximity than any manifestation of her physical being. This notion even extends to Hugh, who throughout the narrative gradually assumes an incorporeal quality. The difficulty he experiences in distinguishing between actual and dreamed reality is transmitted to the reader, and so aspects of the two worlds seem to intertwine. This is particularly evident in the depiction of the three fires in the novel. In each instance the flames possess a similar synthetic quality, despite the fact that in the third instance, the flames are real. The first fire appears as a series of images on a television screen, and although it is an actual event, it poses no direct threat to Hugh or Armande and proves to be a danger only because of Armande's reaction to it. In the second fire, which Hugh dreams, the flames are likened to "scarlet strips of vitreous plastic" (p. 80) and are thus essentially harmless. That the flames of the Stresa fire also pose no threat but are, in a fantastic, magical way, friendly is expressed in their "humming" (p. 103) chatter and the elegant "long lavender-tipped flame" (p. 104) which stops Hugh from jumping from the window, saving him from the one thing that he most fears — falling. The illusory quality of the fires reflects, therefore, the dreamlike course of Hugh's existence, the inscrutability of his world, governed as it is by enigmatic forces manifested in baffling and often cruel coincidences, forces which Hugh senses but cannot apprehend. Indeed, Hugh's experience epitomizes the fundamental dilemma of human existence as outlined by R.:

> Another thing we are not supposed to do is explain the inexplicable. Men have learned to live with a black burden, a huge aching hump: the supposition that "reality" may only be a "dream" [p. 93].

Reality is equally illusory for Hugh and R. Hugh is plagued by faulty vision, an unreliable, emotionally driven, shifting perspective lacking in any objectivity or cognitive authority. R.'s perspective also emphasizes the illusory nature of things, their transparency, their infinite recession into the past, their constantly changing form and yet, unlike Hugh's, R.'s perspective is unequivocally positive. That Hugh is, throughout the narrative, standing on a brink between two worlds is demonstrated by his ability to sense the boundaries of his own world and the points at which he believes it to be infiltrated by R.'s. Hugh's inability to gain command over his world, either materially or perceptually, compounds the sense of his existing in a limbo, in a state of compromise, trapped between the physical and metaphysical, between waking and sleeping, between reality and dream. It is not, however, presented as a condition of antagonism or conflict, but merely as an inexplicable sensation, nagging yet elusive, as discreet and transitory as Hugh's physical presence in the narrative, which is indicated to the reader only twice, and ironically, as fleeting images in a mirror:

> The no less rapt mirror in the lift reflected, for a few lucid instants, the gentleman from Massachusetts, who had a long, lean, doleful face with a slightly undershot jaw and a pair of symmetrical folds framing his mouth in what would have been a rugged, horsey, mountain-climbing arrangement had not his melancholy stoop belied every inch of his fantastic majesty [p. 4].

The mirror here functions as a camera, it registers Hugh's reflection in the same brief flash of a lens shutter opening and closing, capturing in a "few lucid instants" not merely a faithful replica of Hugh as he stands waiting, unsuspecting, unaware that his presence is being recorded by this inconspicuous eye, but more significantly, the very essence of his nature. In a later scene, the only vision the mirror affords is of a "black hair" being "plucked ... out of a red nostril" (p. 49). The entirety of Hugh's reflected image is obliterated by this grotesque, Expressionistic, choker close-up of his nose, rendering him, utterly and conclusively, anonymous and inconsequential.

Brian Boyd comments that in *Transparent Things*, Nabokov "ruptures the relationship of reader, character, and author more radically than he has ever done."[53] The shifting narrative perspectives in the novel reflect Hugh's subjective confusion and his inability to engage with actuality, at the same time dramatizing the kaleidoscopic diversity of R.'s perceptual range and his ability to adopt the perspective of any passing individual in any place at any time. The rupture which this constant displacement of narrative focus generates is further compounded by the destabilizing effect of R.'s ready abandonment of his perceptual authority to any anonymous or invisible being, alive or dead. The reader, in turn, is thus forced to adopt a wide-angled, deep focus perspective which encompasses every detail of the narrative and to regard it, as it were, as a depthless plane upon which all things take on equal significance.

Transparent Things *and the New Hollywood*

In the context of American cinema of the early 1970s, *Transparent Things* demonstrates a remarkable affinity with the work of New Hollywood directors, in spite of Nabokov's declared ignorance of recent developments in film and television.[54] Nevertheless, consideration of the very specific origins, circumstances and character of these films makes it possible to account for this apparent coincidence and reveals a level of engagement with the medium unique in Nabokov's career.

By the mid–1960s, Hollywood had reached an impasse. Dominated by the outmoded production values of the 1940s and 1950s it resisted change at every level, but this rendered it vulnerable to a new generation of filmmakers who were determined to revolutionize the industry. Arthur Penn's *Bonnie and Clyde*, released in 1967, marked the beginning of a period, albeit brief, in American cinema which combined the very aspects of the classic Hollywood tradition that informed Nabokov's fiction and remained as the key source of inspiration for his cinematic explorations — the genre movie and the "stylistic innovations of European art cinema."[55] The dynamics that initiated the New Hollywood were essentially the same as those that produced its Golden Age thirty years before, except this time it was the work, predominantly, of French and Italian directors Godard, Truffaut, Fellini and Antonioni which introduced a new aesthetic of "ambiguity and allusionistic interplay"[56] and a revisionist approach to established film genres such as the Western, the gangster movie and film noir.

The success of *Bonnie and Clyde* enabled the emergence of an *auteurist* cinema in America led by producer-directors Warren Beatty, William Friedkin, Francis Ford Coppola, Robert Altman and Martin Scorsese, but it also established the tone and style of the New Holly-wood — its "disregard for time-honored pieties of plot, chronology, and motivation," its "promiscuous jumbling together of comedy and tragedy," its "sexual boldness," and its "new, ironic distance that [withheld] obvious moral judgments."[57] Not only were these elements to characterize Nabokov's penultimate novel, but they had also been key in *Ada* and *Lolita*, and even, to a certain extent, his pre-American work.

The preoccupying themes of perceptual instability and visual obstruction in *Transparent Things* are echoed in three contemporary films — Robert Altman's *The Long Goodbye* (1973), Francis Ford Coppola's *The Conversation* (1974) and Roman Polanski's *Chinatown* (1974). Each film disrupts the conventions of cinematic presentation and subverts the notion of the camera as a reliable, mimetic tool. In *Chinatown*, for example, as in *Transparent Things*, "an eloquent imagery of eyes and seeing and lenses and photography accumulates. Concepts involving the ways of seeing, the obstacles to seeing, the limitations of sight are embedded in the visual techniques which Polanski chooses for the presentation of his images."[58] In *The Conversation*, Coppola deploys a "consistent use of explicit framing, whereby subjects are turned into objects ... and the notions of subjectivity and objectivity are made problematic,"[59] while in *The Long Goodbye*, Altman uses "persistent camera movement, including short pans, zooms, and numerous cuts"[60] as a destabilizing force which consistently denies the audience any sense of resolution or perceptual authority.

The thematic links between these films and *Transparent Things* indicate a prevalent concern with visual dysfunction and its consequences, on both a narrative and structural level, reflective of the "ideology of defeat and powerlessness"[61] which, Robert Kolker argues, characterized 1970s' America. As in *Transparent Things*, the visual plane is depthless and the emphasis placed not on the action in the center or forefront of a scene, but in the background and on its peripheries. Polanski, for example, deploys "deep focus composition" reminiscent of the distinctive quality of R.'s perspective, as a "major visual means of revealing theme."[62] As in *Transparent Things*, this has a leveling effect which forces the audience's attention away from the planes occupied by the film's protagonists and their immediate concerns and toward a consideration of the "commentary"[63] provided by the objects or action occurring beside and behind them.

Polanski's visual method also has an ironic function, serving to alert the audience to the significant details which the central protagonist either misapprehends or misses altogether. In *Chinatown*, incidental objects such as Hollis Mulwray's spectacles, which lie at the bottom of the tide pool in his back garden, or the photograph of Mulwray arguing with his father-in-law, Noah Cross, prove to be "determinent"[64] in Jake Gittes's investigation.

The theme of flawed sight in *Chinatown*[65] parallels Hugh's dilemma in *Transparent Things* but extends also to the films of Coppola and Altman. A fundamental aspect of each protagonist's defective vision is his submission to some form of emotional ideal. In Hugh Person's case this takes the shape of Armande Chamar; for Jake Gittes, Evelyn Mulwray inspires his misguided heroic instincts. Harry Caul in *The Conversation* also tries to play the hero by becoming involved in a complex conspiracy of murder and betrayal, fueled by guilt over his responsibility for the brutal killings of a former client and his family, and in *The Long Goodbye* Philip Marlowe's vision is clouded by loyalty, by a naive belief in the "integrity of [the] bond"[66] between him and his best friend, Terry Lennox.

Marlowe, like Hugh, is depicted as "a character without physical or emotional anchorage in the world ... a man whose every connection with the world is faulty and non-comprehending."[67] Marlowe seems to be "operating in a void,"[68] and Altman's camerawork has the effect of magnifying this sense of meaninglessness and futility. Rather than being deployed in its conventional mode to "locate" and "illustrate," the camera moves in "helpless circles,"[69] offering no prospect of resolution, and, as Michael Tarantino points out, "camera movements frequently occur without any beginning or end," often "appear[ing] on the screen past their starting points" only to be "blocked from reaching their goals."[70] Altman's purpose, however, is not merely to dramatize Marlowe's subjective state. This disjointed, indeterminate mode of presentation has significant ramifications for the audience's expectations and understanding of film language. The rupture Brian Boyd identifies as being fundamental to the reader's experience of *Transparent Things* is achieved here by a deliberate subversion of familiar cinematic conventions. Apart from the destabilizing effect of Altman's constantly moving camera, the zoom and the tracking shot[71] are deployed not as routine devices, used to evoke a relationship of intimacy and collusion between the audience and the screen narrative, but as a means of communicating the filmmaker's perspective of detachment from and even indifference to the on-screen action, calling attention to the illusory nature of the cinematic process, which consequently generates a sense of dissociation in the audience.

Altman repeatedly uses the zoom and tracking shot together in sequences to establish a false set of visual priorities. For example, the film's protagonist, Marlowe, would conventionally command the principal focal attention of any scene in which he might appear. These shots, however, work in conjunction to dissipate Marlowe's central position in the narrative, most notably during his interrogation at the police station, and subsequently in the scenes at Roger Wade's house. Tracking shots are never completed; they follow Marlowe's course only part of the way before the focal attention cuts to another aspect of the scene. Likewise, zooms, rather than focusing in on Marlowe as he speaks, pull away, thus denying the audience the sense of intimacy and contact with a character that the zoom usually promises. In the scenes at Wade's beach house, for example, the camera moves through and across reflective surfaces, further amplifying Marlowe's dislocated position in the narrative and distancing the audience. The windows of the house serve as physical barriers, containing the action within the house but also preventing clear visual access to it. At the same time they reflect the action that occurs in front of them, which is equally abstract, the audience being granted only an indistinct image of Marlowe as he wanders about on the shore. As Tarantino comments, "by shooting a scene through a window, Altman ... plays off a dual presence — for not only do we have two frames for the action (window and screen frame), we have two actions (the one behind the window and the reflected image in front of it)."[72] The two-dimensional plane of this scene (repeated later in the film to depict Wade's suicide) is dis-

Layers of visual obstruction. The viewer's access to Marlowe (Elliott Gould) is blocked first by the enlarged foreground figure, then by the one-way glass partition, next by the handprint on the glass, and finally by the police interrogators. *The Long Goodbye* **(United Artists, 1973).**

tinctly reminiscent of R.'s layered vision and parallels the deliberate adjustments in focus required to disclose and fix its significant details.

Altman's shifts in focus are just as cumbersome as R.'s, yet they are calculated devices which not only call attention to the film's representational processes, but also indicate the presence of a perspective independent of both the audience and Marlowe, establishing a "complex spatial and perceptual interaction [that] serves as a metaphor for the film as a whole"[73]:

> The viewer is suspended between two points of view, seemingly unconnected with either.... The constant movement of the camera emphasizes this removal, this inability to confront the action as the viewer expects he or she has a right to.[74]

This sense of disconnectedness, which reflects Marlowe's situation within the narrative, is thus transmitted to the audience, and Marlowe's frustrated position on the peripheries of the action becomes the audience's predicament also. More fundamental, however, is the emphasis upon the voyeuristic aspect of the cinematic experience which this calculated visual disruption generates.

The "dislocation of space that makes up the visual world of [Altman's] films"[75] is also evident in the work of Polanski and Coppola. While Polanski emphasizes the significance of the peripheral area of a frame, he also generates a sense of dislocation by the use of reflective surfaces in the form of windows, picture frames, mirrors, camera and spectacle lenses, even eyes. In Coppola's work the camera itself serves as a "barrier between us and the events and the central character, refusing to reveal what we want to see or think we ought to see, revealing instead only the phenomenon and problem of observing."[76]

The notion of barriers — invisible, visible, physical, metaphysical — is a pivotal theme in Coppola's *The Conversation* and is embedded in the central protagonist's name, Harry Caul.[77] The motif of the caul extends from the ramifications of Harry's name to the transparent plastic raincoat that he wears whenever he is outside either his apartment or his workshop, a coat that, significantly, he does not remove even when he visits his lover. The coat communicates Harry's suspicious and distrustful nature, and his need for some form of barrier to protect him from a world that he perceives to be hostile. As James Palmer comments, "the caul ... is the most frequently recurring image in the film. Harry is seen dimly through screens, translucent glass, plastic curtains, or less frequently through bars and grillwork."[78] As in *Transparent Things*, these barriers suggest the possibility for some privileged form of existence, a promise of refuge, a notion which is compounded by the incorporeal quality Harry acquires whenever he is pictured standing, blurred and vague, behind them.

Initially, these transparent barriers contain and protect Harry, but as they serve to magnify Hugh's insecurity in *Transparent Things*, so in *The Conversation* they prove ultimately to offer no sanctuary, but rather a form of living hell, something which Hugh briefly experiences on his first visit to the "transparent" (p. 41) Villa Nastia:

> In full view of the public [Madame Chamar] ascended with ponderous
> energy the completely visible and audible stairs leading to a similarly

overt second floor, where one could see a bed through an open door and
a bidet through another. Armande used to say that this product of her
late father's art was a regular showpiece attracting tourists from distant
countries such as Rhodesia and Japan [p. 40].

Every aspect of the house reflects the flagrant immodesty displayed by
both Madame Chamar and her daughter, the barren, vacuous transparency of their lives serving as a bleak parody of R.'s transparent world.
In *The Conversation*, however, Harry's transparent barriers generate opacity, rendering him inaccessible, closed, remote, ultimately condemning
him to total abstraction and isolation.

Harry is a highly skilled professional surveillance operative. Having spent years spying on people and listening in to their conversations,
he has become reclusive and guarded. He lives alone, shunning all forms
of intimacy for fear that his privacy could be violated should he allow
anyone to get too close to him. The motif of the caul is also, therefore,
an eloquent image which communicates Harry's vulnerability and the pre-
cariousness of his solitary existence, an existence that depends upon his
ability to maintain a safe distance from those who threaten to invade his
world. In the film, Harry makes the fatal mistake of allowing himself to
become involved with the apparent predicament of two subjects under
surveillance, and in doing so compromises the objectivity essential not
only to his work, but also to the preservation of his autonomy. As Harry
becomes increasingly emotionally involved, his subjective perspective
begins to take over, and thus the sense of watching and being watched
develops in potency. Coppola focuses upon "a whole galaxy of monitor-
ing devices in such a way that the entire film seems like closed-circuit
television,"[79] which in turn serves to visually dramatize the discreet invasion of Harry's exclusive and secluded world and thus magnify his isolation. The overt use of the closed-circuit perspective is deployed in
conjunction with the device of "explicit framing,"[80] which consistently
presents Harry as enclosed within the perimeters of a defined space. His
workshop, for example, is contained in a corner of a vast and empty
warehouse floor, surrounded by a security cage; the bleak, modest space
of his one-bedroom apartment is magnified by a shot which tracks back
and forth from a corner of the ceiling; and at his client's office building,
Harry is seen walking along bare, uniform corridors, windows and walls
providing additional frames within the frame of the screen image serving to further communicate, in ironic correlation, the expanding dimensions of Harry's confinement.

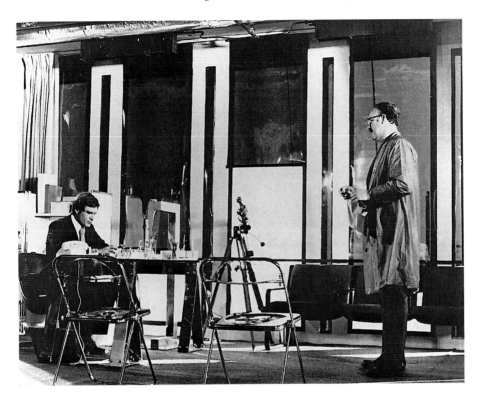

Confined but excluded. Harry (Gene Hackman)—wearing his plastic rain-coat—is framed by the stark vertical and horizontal lines of the windows and blinds, even the desk and chairs in his client's outer office. Harrison Ford (at desk) and Gene Hackman in *The Conversation* (Paramount, 1974).

Coppola develops a perceptual dichotomy between Harry's increasingly subjective perspective, which the audience is drawn into, and the conflicting objectivity generated by a detached camera perspective and the device of explicit framing. The audience, therefore, becomes subject to both a visual and narrative rupture and is thus denied any sense of independent cognition but forced to become "the buggers of film fiction, which is made for [the audience's] gaze, but pretends ignorance of it."[81] Thus the film has the effect of being "twice-viewed," the audience experiencing "simultaneously ... the life of a fictional surveillance man" and its own "surveillance of the fiction."[82]

As Harry's voyeuristic perspective turns in on him, so the motif of the caul turns against him. Rather than providing a protective barrier which prevents invasion by the outside world, the motif is reversed to prevent Harry from gaining any access to the outside world, and thus his isolation is no longer self-determined, but enforced and absolute.

This reversal takes place at the hotel where Harry's client, a company director, is murdered by the two subjects of his surveillance, who up until this point Harry has believed, mistakenly, to be his client's intended victims. The transparent plastic raincoat which represents the caul and has thus far been directly associated with Harry becomes displaced and is instead worn by the murderer to prevent the director's blood from staining his clothes. As he stabs the director to death, Harry stands listening in the adjacent room. He is denied any visual perspective on the murder scene; the adjoining balcony is divided by a frosted glass wall, yet another semi-transparent barrier which here serves to protect the murderers. The frosted glass is also significant in that it provides the context for the definitive moment at which the subversion of the caul motif is completed. Hearing the commotion in the next room, Harry goes out onto the balcony to try to see what is happening, thinking that perhaps he might be able to intervene, only to be confronted by the horrifying vision of a bloody hand pressed against the glass divide. Harry "retreats back into his room where he draws the curtains, turns on the TV set, and, in an action that visually parodies his surname, pulls the bedclothes over his head like a caul."[83] The irony of Harry's surrender to his fear is underlined by the way in which his actions mirror the fate of the director, whom he subsequently discovers lying dead on the bed in the next room, wrapped in a transparent plastic sheet. Thus the motif of the caul is not only displaced, but established irrevocably as a symbol of death.

Visual barriers are also a feature of Polanski's *Chinatown*. They accumulate during the course of the film in a pattern reminiscent of the layered quality of R.'s perception in *Transparent Things*. The barriers take the form of almost every conceivable transparent and reflective surface, creating increasing levels of obscurity and opacity in a series of impenetrable, cryptic surfaces which serve to magnify Jake's increasing sense of displacement and intensify his frustration. As William Palmer comments:

> Something, a camera lens, a windshield, drawn curtains, a pulled bamboo blind, always stands between Jake and reality. He spends the whole movie looking through things, attempting to penetrate the barrier between him and the world. The audience spends the whole movie looking over his shoulder through the barriers and having no more success than he.[84]

The conventional protagonist-oriented narrative perspective is further disrupted by the occasional use of this over-the-shoulder point of view, which, in conjunction with the deployment of reflected images serves to deepen the effect of visual dislocation in the film. The film's central preoccupation with ways of seeing is extended into the processes of photography itself. Jake is dependent on photographs and the privileged perspectives they afford in his investigations, relying upon them as the sole objective means of disclosing the truth. Polanski, however, confounds both the conventional role of the camera and the reliability of the images it captures by emphasizing the self-reflexive aspect of the photographic process. For example, early on in the film Jake is seen crouched on the roof of a Los Angeles apartment block taking pictures of Hollis Mulwray and an, as yet, unidentified young woman. The scene is presented to the audience through the sights of the camera Jake has trained on the couple, but almost exactly as the scene is registered, Polanski switches the perspective to disclose the reflected image of Mulwray and the girl on the camera's lens. As Palmer argues, "that reverse angle offers a photograph of the photographer caught in the midst of his photography," thus rendering the process redundant, for Jake's "photos, taken from the spy's distance, can only capture the surface of reality."[85] This highly potent visual device establishes the irony of Jake's dependence upon mechanical means of vision and the limitations of his own faculties, a notion which is developed during the course of the film as a commentary on Jake's visual incapacity.

Every optically related medium becomes a motif for Jake's defective vision, from the reflection in his camera lens, to the flaw in Evelyn Mulwray's iris. Even the revelation of the crucial pair of spectacles that lies at the bottom of the Mulwrays' tide pool is refracted by Jake's own reflection as he peers quizzically into the water. Jake is confronted at every turn by opaque and inscrutable images which seem to become increasingly impenetrable, to the extent that whenever he looks he is greeted by visions of himself caught in the act of looking reflected back at him, even in such mundane planes as the glass of the framed photographs hanging in Mulwray's office, or the rear and sideview mirrors of his car. In this respect, the film strongly echoes the central concerns of Coppola's *Conversation*, not merely in its preoccupation with the ways and means of apprehension, but also in the problems inherent in achieving a reliable objective perspective, or indeed, any perspective at all.

While the motif of the caul is central to Coppola's film, here the

Roman Polanski evokes a noir mood using high contrast lighting, obliquity and reflective surfaces, as well as the bandaged nose of Gittes (Jack Nicholson), which signals the ever-present threat of arbitrary violence. *Chinatown* (Paramount, 1974).

revelation of the flaw in Evelyn's iris initiates a sophisticated pattern of eye imagery, which, as Palmer elaborates, incorporates all manner of natural and synthetic objects — a broken taillight on the back of Mulwray's Packard, the black eye of a former client's unfaithful wife, the eye of a fish on the Albacore Club flag, the dead eye of a fish on Noah Cross's plate, the magnifying glass on Mulwray's desk, and the sunglasses minus one lens which sit on the end of Jake's broken nose[86] — all serving to amplify the futility of Jake's mission. The film's "metaphorical cycle of transpositions of images and cracked instruments of seeing"[87] culminates in the film's concluding scene with the spectacle of Evelyn Mulwray lying dead, slumped headlong out of a car door, her eye shot out by a bullet. Not only does this provide an eloquent comment on the violence that characterized 1930s' America, when the film is set, but it also reflects the "defeat and powerlessness" that Kolker identifies as the primary dynamic of America in the early 1970s.

In spite of Hugh's earthbound perspective of "defeat and power-lessness," *Transparent Things* ultimately presents a far more positive prospect than the films of Polanski, Altman and Coppola. Critics, inex-plicably, have described the novel's world as "squalid," its protagonists "heartless"[88] and "dehumanized,"[89] and Nabokov's authorial stance as cold and "arbitrary,"[90] yet the extended and overt elucidation of themes and processes of vision serve to reveal an alternative aspect which is benev-olent, compassionate and overwhelmingly affirmatory.

In their treatment of modes of perception and the fundamental chal-lenge they pose to conventions of narrative and visual presentation, *Chinatown*, *The Long Goodbye* and *The Conversation* demonstrate striking parallels with *Transparent Things*. The novel also marks the culmination of a preoccupation with ways of seeing — physical, mechanical and meta-physical — which dominated the entirety of Nabokov's oeuvre and served as a form of distraction, to varying degrees, for many of his protagonists, from Smurov and Hermann Karlovich, to Humbert Humbert and Van Veen. The novel also exists, in a sense, as a response to *Ada* in its explicit treatment of some of the key questions concerning the relationship between perception, perspective and mortality posed by Van Veen. Indeed, the notion of transparency is first introduced in *Ada*, during Van's Mascodagama stage act:

> Neither was the sheer physical pleasure of maniambulation a negligible factor, and the peacock blotches with which the carpet stained the palms of his hands during his gloveless dance routine seemed to be the reflections of a richly colored nether world that he had been the first to discover [p. 147].

Van is granted a privileged perspective on this "richly colored nether world" which leaves its imprint on his palms, in the same way that Hugh, in his dream airplane sees, for the first time, the world spread out beneath him through layers of clouds that "seem to lie on a flat sheet of glass" (p. 103). The distinction, however, is that Van looks down into a world that exists beneath the tangible surface of the earth; it is an impermanent, distorted vision, dependent upon a condition of transitory inversion, whereas Hugh's prospect is akin to R.'s, which, considering the dimen-sions of R.'s perspective, promises to be eternal and infinitely expansive.

Eight

Shimmers on a Screen: Cinematic Hyperreality in Recent American Fiction and Film

The power of the cinema, the awful power of it, the way from moron to genius it captivates us, it hypnotizes us.... What I don't know is how relevant attempts to initiate this instantaneity, this shuffle of images, are to the novelist's art.[1]

The relevance of film to the "novelist's art" remains a preoccupying question in recent American fiction. John Updike's concern is provoked by the increasing potency of the cinematic and televisual experience in late-twentieth-century American culture, such that writers are presented with two fundamental problems: first, whether to acknowledge the medium that is a defining element of America's collective unconscious and if so, how to deploy it successfully in a work of fiction. According to Dos Passos, however, the question of cinema's relevance to the literary process is no longer pertinent. In 1968, he commented that "there is probably less interest by writers in cinema because we have become so accustomed to this medium that it is less exciting than when it was very new."[2] Although this statement may initially appear to resolve Updike's dilemma, it also, albeit inadvertently, identifies the dynamic responsible for the altered relationship between viewer and screen. While Dos Passos considers acute familiarity with the cinematic mode a reductive force, it is precisely this familiarity — accelerated by television — that has created an even more profound and complex response to its persistent

250

"shuffle of images." In this respect, therefore, cinema is probably more relevant to the fictional exploration and dissemination of contemporary experience than it has ever been.

Particularly significant in America's development of a sophisticated viewing culture is the "interpenetrant"[3] aspect of television and its ability to ratify and certify experience, a notion developed by Don DeLillo in *White Noise* (1985) and *Libra* (1988). In the former, a mass evacuation provoked by a local toxic gas leak fails to attract the attention of television journalists. The outrage expressed by DeLillo's protagonist, Jack Gladney, is directed not at the negligence of the chemical plant, but at the absence of television, which causes the event to be negated, thus "depriving the participants of the certification of their own shared experience."[4] In *Libra*, Lee Harvey Oswald's death is certified by imagined television images, to an extent where he "becomes the on-screen simulacrum. Losing consciousness, dematerialized into a focus of pure pain, he understands his state in reference to TV watching."[5]

Oswald's experience reflects the "extraordinary cognitive change" which, Tichi argues, occurred in the early 1970s, whereby television audiences began to operate on two parallel planes of reality, the "ordinary" and the "televised"[6] (as discussed in the previous chapter). The television state is, essentially, a form of synthetic reality more potent than reality itself, a state which Umberto Eco identifies as "hyperreal."[7] As demonstrated by Humbert Humbert or Binx Bolling the hyperreal is not, however, exclusive to the domain of television, having its origins, rather, in the cinematic experience.

In *Americana*, the hyperreal is contained in David Bell's handheld movie camera. Passing strangers respond to the prospect of transformation, authentication and immortality that it offers with ease and grace. The warmth and spontaneity of their interaction is far removed from the affected, self-conscious, narcissistic displays of Hermann Karlovich or Van Veen and is a stance that DeLillo's cameraman is also attempting to dispel:

> I took the camera from my lap, raised it to my eye, leaned out of the window a bit, and trained it on the ladies as if I were shooting. One of them saw me and immediately nudged her companion but without taking her eyes off the camera. They waved. One by one the others reacted. They all smiled and waved. They seemed supremely happy. Maybe they sensed that they were waving at themselves, waving in the hope that someday if evidence is demanded of their passage through time,

demanded by their own doubts, a moment might be recalled when they
stood in a dazzling plaza in the sun and were registered on the transparent plastic ribbon; and thirty years away, on that day when proof is
needed, it could be hoped that their film is being projected on a screen
somewhere, and there they stand, verified, in chemical reincarnation,
waving at their own old age, smiling their reassurance to the decades....
I pretended to keep shooting, gathering their wasted light, letting their
smiles enter the lens and wander the camera-body seeking the magic
spool, the gelatin which captures the image, the film which threads
through the waiting gate [pp. 254–55].

The notion of the televisual or filmic experience as hyperreal is further extended in other recent American fiction. Robert Coover's *Night
at the Movies* (1987), for example, combines an overtly synthetic literary
emulation of the styles, devices and techniques of film with three
definitive aspects of the cinematic experience, that of the projectionist,
the moviegoer, and the movie actor. The volume's nine "fictions" present
the reader with revised versions of classic film genres: slapstick comedy,
the Western, the horror movie, an Astaire-Rogers musical, a romantic
thriller in the form of an irreverent reinterpretation of Michael Curtiz's
Casablanca, a cartoon and even an "intermission" which continues the
action within the movie theater while the "Operator Changes Reels."[8]

A constant "shuffle of images" is also a feature of Quentin Tarantino's *Pulp Fiction* (1994). This effect is rendered primarily by the film's
achronological structure and its interweaving of multiple plot lines which
demand from the audience a heightened level of engagement and deny
access to the complacent viewer. Every detail of every frame is significant
in the film's complex patterning, offering discreet clues not merely to the
exposition of its actual chronology but also to the revelation of story and
character. Critics have argued, however, that Tarantino exploits a prevailing fetish for "trivial pursuits" in contemporary American youth culture,[9] an interactive enterprise that is apparently void of meaning or
purpose beyond the process itself, and yet with each viewing new details
are registered and the interrelationships and overlapping of story and
character gradually revealed. Dana Polan argues that the film "offers a
shifting universe based on disjunction, substitution and fragmentation."[10]
Compounding this sense of visual and narrative instability is the range
of the film's allusiveness and the pace and proliferation of detail contained
in each frame. The film has a "breathless" quality[11] and, like Coover's
Night at the Movies, refers to, reworks and revises an array of familiar film

and television scenarios, generating its own hyperreality within the hyper-real experience of film viewing. The priority of *Pulp Fiction* is to maxi-mize the scope of the screen's depthless, two-dimensional visual plane. Tarantino presents the audience with a rich and bewildering visual expe-rience, amplified by his highly referential, hip and fast-paced dialogue. In many ways, the film echoes the preoccupation with the signs and sym-bols of contemporary America that dominates Bret Easton Ellis's *Amer-ican Psycho* (1991), an awareness of which grants the individual instant credibility and the audience a sense of collusion with the on-screen pro-tagonists, even though these elements are fleeting and insubstantial. Unlike the saturated narrative of Nabokov's *Ada* or the deceptive, eva-sive planes of *Chinatown* or *The Long Goodbye*, *Pulp Fiction* does not attempt to hide a significant subtext behind the film's foregrounded ref-erentiality. Its allusiveness and its play on movie cliché serve no greater purpose than to either confirm or confound the audience's expectations. Paradoxically, the fundamental meaninglessness of *Pulp Fiction*—dra-matized most provocatively by the cyclic nature of its framing story, in which Vincent Vega's death is negated and his cinematic immortality guaranteed—renders it valuable in a society that has become dependent upon the realms of film and television fiction as a means of escape from the malaise of mundane reality. In this sense, therefore, *Pulp Fiction* offers the ultimate, and sustained, hyperreal experience.

American Psycho: *New Dimensions in Cinematic Hyperreality*

Bret Easton Ellis's psychotic anti-hero, Patrick Bateman, represents the moviegoing sensibility in its most extreme manifestation. He has transformed Binx Bolling's fleeting experiences of the hyperreal into a continuous state of existence such that his only reality is movie reality. At the same time, Bateman is reminiscent of Humbert Humbert in his manipulation of filmic modes and techniques, but his highly self-con-scious need to assert his identity, to perform to and be acknowledged by an audience also echoes Van Veen's cinematic ambitions. The perspec-tive of his narrative is distinctly cinematic, characterized by the overt deployment of filmic device. Scenes are described as movie sequences, a process which is openly declared by Bateman's continual reference to specific shots—POV, close-ups, jump cuts, smash cuts, pans and dissolves. He also manipulates the pace of his narrative with a calculated use of representational effects — slow motion, freeze and flash frames. The opening section of the novel functions as an extended sequence, a slow, panoramic, establishing shot, with Bateman looking out at the New York City streets from inside a taxi cab. The shot moves in a cyclic pattern beginning and ending with the entrance and exit of a police car:

> Outside the cab, on the sidewalks, black and bloated pigeons fight over scraps of hot dogs ... while transvestites idly look on and a police car cruises silently the wrong way down a one-way street and the sky is low and gray.... Panning down to the sidewalk there's an ugly old homeless bag lady holding a whip and she cracks it at the pigeons who ignore it ... and the police car disappears into an underground parking lot.[12]

Bateman's "camera eye" visualization is distinctive in that, while he exploits the mechanical capabilities of film and photography, more significantly, he also allows his perceptual scope to be restricted equally by the medium's limitations. Here, Bateman's eye, like a camera lens, is facilitated by light. As the sun sets over the city and the light recedes, so his vision shuts down and takes on the quality of time-lapse photography — a technique that enables extended sequences to be condensed by running together at high speed a series of multiple still frames.[13] It is interesting that Bateman is very specific about his use of this device, deploying it not in its conventional mode, but in slow motion. Consequently, the visual scope of the scene is reduced such that his eyes are able to focus on only one large, brightly colored shape — the red Lamborghini — while sound becomes suddenly amplified:

> In what seems like time-lapse photography — but in slow motion, like a movie — the sun goes down, the city gets darker and all I can see is the red Lamborghini and all I can hear is my own, steady panting [p. 114].

The purpose of Bateman's cinematic manipulations is, specifically, to express his solipsistic perspective. Often this generates a wholly inappropriate exploitation of explicit filmic reference. Bateman's responses to certain characters, for example, takes on a more ludicrous aspect because of the way he chooses to depict them. In one particular scene, Bateman spots Luis Carruthers, who he is convinced is trying to seduce him (Carruthers's looming presence in the novel maintains an unresolved ambiguity as to Bateman's sexuality), looking as if he is about to approach him:

> Like a smash cut from a horror movie — a jump zoom — Luis Carruthers appears, suddenly, without warning, from behind his column [p. 292].

Bateman's response is highly reminiscent of Smurov's paranoid delusions concerning Roman Bogdanovich. Like Bogdanovich, however, Carruthers poses no real threat to Bateman (other than a rather vague one of sexual compromise).[14] Bateman's cowardice is incongruous, not simply because the situation is banal and Bateman's anxiety petty, but also because of what the reader knows he is actually capable of (or what he would like the reader to think he is capable of). The violence of the visual jolt deployed to depict the level of fear Bateman experiences is, therefore, absurd.

Bateman's filmic narrative is indicative of his complete immersion in movie lore, such that, like many of Nabokov's protagonists, he perceives himself to be directing and starring in his own production. He also extends Humbert Humbert's manipulation of contemporary cinematic genre to incorporate a range of familiar film and, significantly, television clichés — from Hollywood romance and horror movies to TV soap operas and chat shows.

Bateman's days are governed by the ritual watching of popular problem-solving and entertainment chat shows, hosted by the real-life presenters Patty Winters and David Letterman. These everyday forms of diversion become pivotal in affirming and communicating his manic existence, the topics on *The Patty Winters Show*, particularly, serving to objectify his deviant obsessions. They also establish a sense of routine, of consistency, of stability, simply by their daily presentation, morning and night, which remains constant throughout the narrative, even when Bateman's already precarious grasp of reality begins to collapse. Gradually, the real-life banality of these shows is metamorphosed in Bateman's imagination into a grotesque parody, whereby toward the end of the novel he claims to have been watching a "Cheerio [sitting] in a very small chair [being] interviewed for close to an hour" (p. 386). Bateman's other regular viewing activity is rented pornographic films. Anxiety over which films to choose, how many to rent and how soon they need to be returned is a persistent preoccupation. Like television, these films serve to certify Bateman's existence merely by the act of watching them, but they also are important in terms of the imaginary world he inhabits. Bateman's particular preference is for "snuff" movies — hard-core pornographic films featuring extreme violence and torture in which the female participants

are killed during sex. These films not only parallel his homicidal activities but, more importantly, provide him with ready-made scenarios to
reenact. At the same time, the daily press reports of bizarre deaths and
horrific accidents evidently feed his imagination, and there is even a suggestion that Bateman not only takes a vicarious pleasure in the mayhem
that surrounds him, but may also be responsible for some of these incidents. It is significant that Bateman should include the list of atrocities
read out from a magazine by his friend Tim in the narrative's opening
sequence. This serves to set the tone of the novel's world and legitimizes
Bateman's warped and depthless perspective. Bateman's New York is a
place where everything exists on an equal plane, where society's lurid fascination with indiscriminate acts of brutality is considered as normal as
being concerned about missing a favorite TV show:

> "In one issue — in *one* issue — let's see here ... strangled models, babies
> thrown from tenement rooftops, kids killed in the subway, a Commu-
> nist rally, Mafia boss wiped out, Nazis ... baseball players with AIDS ...
> faggots dropping like flies in the streets, surrogate mothers, the cancel-
> lation of a soap opera, kids who broke into a zoo and tortured and burned
> various animals alive, more Nazis..." [p. 4].

The central problem of *American Psycho*, however, is how to distinguish between actuality and Bateman's cinematic hyperreality. There
is much in the narrative to suggest that every violent episode is imagined, following the formulas of familiar horror and action movies. An
elaborate chase through the streets of Manhattan, for example, in which
Bateman escapes a police ambush and pursuit by a helicopter, is presented
as a sequence from a "blockbuster" movie[15] (see "Chase, Manhattan," pp.
347–52). Bateman survives the carnage, improbably but appropriately
unscathed. In terms of the contemporary horror genre, Bateman could
be perceived as a combined reincarnation of Abel Ferrara's *Driller Killer*
(1979), the original Hannibal Lecter of Michael Mann's *Manhunter*
(1986), Henry, of John McNaughton's seminal serial-killer movie (1986),
or even Charlie Reece of William Friedkin's *Rampage* (1988).[16]
       Bateman's existence is tormented by the conflict between his need
to remain anonymous in order to escape apprehension and his desperate
desire to be noticed. Obsession with image, with spectacle and the act
of watching dominates his world, and yet as his dependency upon this
filmic hyperreality for a sense of tangible certification develops, the more
elusive and insubstantial that world becomes. This, in turn, serves to

raise doubts concerning the reliability of the narrative as a whole. The question as to whether Bateman actually carries out any of his sadistic deeds or merely imagines them is also compounded by his instinct for performance. The "snuff" movies which he reenacts (either in the realms of the real or the hyperreal) demonstrate a shift in motivation from passive spectator to active participant. Participation, however, does not evidently provide Bateman with a sufficient sense of certification, and he is compelled to voyeuristically record his homicidal escapades on camera (although the tapes and photographs are never seen). The distance this affords him from the action taking place also echoes Hermann Karlovich's "dissociative splits," in which he withdraws further and further away from the scene in which he participates, allowing him a privileged vantage point and a total detachment from his corporeal being. Thus a conflicting and unresolved dynamic is generated by Bateman's compulsion to initiate and enact and his desire to passively observe. Bateman's private performances are, nevertheless, consistently undermined by his anonymous and inconsequential public demeanor, his unremarkable "boy next door" looks (p. 20) which, while enabling him to escape suspicion, also frequently cause his identity to be confused.[17] This confusion of identity is also pivotal to the depthlessness of *American Psycho*. Governed by a preoccupation with surfaces, the world of the novel has neither substance nor foundation. It is two-dimensional, deceptive, shifting, unstable, evasive, its tenuous credibility maintained by a barrage of inconsequential information — the endless cataloguing of brand names, for example — and a preoccupation with superficial appearances. The central manic and distorting dynamic of the novel extends from Bateman's highly solipsistic perspective to what could be deemed its tangible elements — distinctive characters, personalities, mundane objects — which merge and dissolve inexplicably. Paul Owen, for example, whom Bateman brutally murders and whose mutilated remains are left to decompose in a downtown apartment, vanishes, only to turn up again in London some weeks later, reportedly very much alive. Bateman's pristine apartment, decorated entirely in white and furnished throughout with reflective, transparent, shining objects, remains pristine, in spite of the amount of gore that he spreads all over it over a protracted period of time. No alarms are ever raised. Nobody makes any comment when Bateman starts an argument in the dry cleaners over the blood stains they fail to remove from his sheets. Messy killings on the streets of Manhattan never seem to disturb his immaculate looks — "I leave, almost slipping in the puddle of blood that has formed by the side of his head, and I'm down the street and out of darkness and like in a movie I appear in front of D'Agostino's, sales clerks beckoning for me to enter" (p. 166). None of his activities are ever reported, there is no mention of a serial killer at large in the city, either in the press or on television, and even Bateman's frequent, unprovoked pronouncements that he is an "evil psychopath" (p. 20) are completely ignored. It is possible that the dynamic of confusion in the novel, compounded by Bateman's filmic visualization, is deliberately generated by Bateman not only to deflect suspicion, but also to afford him an enigmatic ambiguity consistent with his excessive self-regard. Most crucially, however, it enables him to maintain, in the wake of Humbert Humbert and Van Veen, an unchallenged authority over the narrative. In terms of the very specific manner in which he achieves this, it could be argued that *American Psycho* revises *The Great Gatsby*'s central theme of "ocular confusion"[18] and extends it into the reader's experience of the novel.

That Bateman is unable to enter into any kind of genuinely intimate relationship is also significant in terms of his depthlessness. Like his predecessors in Nabokov's fiction (from Smurov to Humbert Humbert and Hugh Person), Bateman's romantic ideals are informed by highly sentimentalized Hollywood scenarios, and yet the distinction here is that Bateman is acutely aware of the movie world which inspires these dreams:

> I am so used to imagining everything happening the way it occurs in movies, visualizing things falling somehow into the shape of events on a screen, that I almost hear the swelling of the orchestra, can almost hallucinate the camera panning low around us, fireworks bursting in slow motion overhead, the seventy-millimeter image of her lips parting and the subsequent murmur of "I *want* you" in Dolby sound [p. 265].

It is also deeply ironic that a man capable of such extreme depravity (whether real or imagined) should be indulging in ridiculous fantasies, and yet it is particularly revealing of his fundamentally adolescent and naive mentality. In this sense, therefore, Bateman is the epitome of a late-twentieth-century "moviegoer," a 1980s' version of Walker Percy's disillusioned, disappointed, alienated romantic, victim to an all-pervasive cultural cynicism that has turned his life into "a blank canvas, a cliché, a soap opera" (p. 279). If, however, Bateman's condition is considered in terms of Dos Passos's Jimmy Herf, then he also stands squarely in the tradition of perceptually compromised American heroes, prone to the "variations of voyeuristic emptiness and who find that the 'center,' which they hope to approach through seeing images of it, does not exist."[19]

At the same time, Bateman's depthlessness enables his depravity. Existing in a state of eclipse, in a transient realm between reality and fantasy, dominated by worn-out movie scenarios played over and over in his imagination like the rented videos he watches interminably, there is no place for accountability or morality. He often refers to himself as something ghostly, ephemeral, but more as a fleeting celluloid shadow than the spirit of a dead man:

> I walk back to my place and say good night to a doorman I don't recognize (he could be anybody) and then dissolve into my living room high above the city [p. 24].

The notion, here, that "anybody" could be "anybody" applies equally to Bateman. As the narrative progresses, he seems to recede further into anonymity, and yet the filmic hyperreality he inhabits and which has offered him an alternative dimension of actuality ultimately fails him — he is unable to sustain it. Like the real world, his imaginary movies disintegrate, becoming remote and alien, muddled and anarchic, replaced, inevitably, by killing and death. "This is my reality," he claims, "Everything outside of this is like some movie I once saw" (p. 345).

In essence, *American Psycho* represents the culmination in the 1980s of Dos Passos's anti-image polemic of the 1920s. His conception of America as "image nation"[20] is now, in the postmodern era, so acutely developed that "the new primacy of spectacle" has become "a constitutive force of both state and economic power."[21] Patrick Bateman asserts both his narrative authority and his Americanness through his manipulation of the cinematic mode. Humbert Humbert deploys film as a means of achieving a level of engagement with contemporary America, but also and more significantly, as a means of acquiring the status of an American hero (whereas Bateman's ambition, conversely, is to achieve the status of "the bad guy"). The filmic consciousness of Nabokov's protagonists, from Smurov to Van Veen and even R., defines them as key contributors to America's ongoing cinematic dialogue.

While the hyperreal serves, in Bateman's case, to bring about an "eclipse of innate character,"[22] it can also, according to Vertov, function as a positive force and in this respect is closely aligned to Nabokov's filmic aesthetic. In Nabokov's fiction, the cinematic mode is deployed to corrupt and distort, being itself expressive of the "ocular confusions" and deluded apprehension of his dysfunctional protagonists, but it is depicted equally as a revelationary, liberating force. For Nabokov, the ideal apparatus with which to perceive "reality" is the "video" camera,[23] and the mechanisms of film enable the extension of both perception and perspective. That the dead and the dying — Ivanov, Mark Standfuss, R. and his ghostly companions, the Vane sisters — possess a superior visual capacity that parallels the vitality, dynamism and flexibility of Vertov's kino-eye is key in Nabokov's exposition of a metaphysical hyperreality. For Adam Krug and the assistant producer, the filmic mode offers a release from the tyranny of memory and the constantly repeating cycle of the past. At the same time, the image of the movie projector's beam is central to Nabokov's depiction of the processes of memory and the relationship between past, present and future, while the photographic "system of repeated exposure" is critical to the development of his artistic identity.

Ultimately, the proximity between Nabokov's cinematic manipulations and those of his film-informed protagonists reasserts the ambivalence that characterizes his early responses to the medium. It is a dynamic that remains unresolved, and yet it is also expressive of the nature of America's preoccupying and highly contentious fascination with image which, at the beginning of the twenty-first century, continues to endure.

Notes

Preface

1. F. R. Karl, *American Fictions 1940–1980: A Comprehensive History and Critical Evaluation*, New York: Harper & Row, 1983, p. 316.

2. David Cronenberg on Nabokov in Chris Rodley (ed.), *Cronenberg on Cronenberg*, London: Faber & Faber, 1997, pp. 52–53.

Chapter One

1. Walter Benjamin quoting Georges Duhamel's *Scènes de la vie future*, Paris, 1930, in his essay "The Work of Art in the Age of Mechanical Reproduction" (1936), collected in H. Arendt (ed.), *Illuminations*, New York: Schocken Books, 1968, p. 239.

2. Alfred Appel, Jr., *Nabokov's Dark Cinema*, New York and Oxford: Oxford University Press, 1974, p. 31. Hereafter, Appel.

3. Ibid., p. 58.

4. Letter dated 8 November 1974 in D. Nabokov and M. J. Bruccoli (eds.), *Vladimir Nabokov: Selected Letters 1940–77*, London: Vintage, 1991, p. 537. Hereafter, *Selected Letters*.

5. Ibid., pp. 537–38.

6. See V. Nabokov, "Philistines and Philistinism," in *Lectures on Russian Literature*, London: Picador, 1983, pp. 309–14; and *Strong Opinions*, New York: McGraw-Hill, 1973, pp. 100–01 (hereafter, *Strong Opinions*).

7. B. Boyd, *Vladimir Nabokov: The Russian Years*, London: Vintage, 1993, p. 363. Hereafter, *The Russian Years*.

8. D. Stuart, "*Laughter in the Dark*: The Novel as Film," in *Nabokov: The Dimensions of Parody*, Baton Rouge, LA: Louisiana State University Press, 1978, p. 89. Hereafter, Stuart.

9. See, particularly, Beverley Gray Bienstock, "Focus Pocus: Film Imagery in *Bend Sinister*" (hereafter, Bienstock), in C. Nicol and J. E. Rivers (eds.); *Nabokov's Fifth Arc: Nabokov and Others on His Life's Work*, Austin, TX: University of Texas Press, 1982 (hereafter, *Nabokov's Fifth Arc*), pp. 125–38; Gavriel Moses, *The Nickel Was for the Movies. Film in the Novel from Pirandello to Puig*, Berkeley and Los Angeles, CA: California University Press, 1995 (hereafter, Moses); and C. Nicol, "Finding the Assistant Producer," in C. Nicol, G. Barabtarlo (eds.), *A Small Alpine Form: Studies in Nabokov's Short Fiction*, New York: Garland, 1993, pp. 155–65 (hereafter, Nicol); and Stuart, pp. 87–113.

10. V. Nabokov, *Glory*, London: Penguin, 1974, p. 83. All Russian works are referred to in their translated versions, unless otherwise specified.

11. See *The Russian Years*, p. 205 and pp. 232–33.

12. See *Strong Opinions*, p. 161.

13. *The Russian Years*, p. 205.

14. Ibid., p. 376.

15. See *Selected Letters*, pp. 361–66 and 304, 311, 313–22, respectively.

16. Nabokov to Edmund Wilson, 22 October 1956, in S. Karlinsky (ed.), *Dear Bunny, Dear Volodya: The Nabokov-Wilson Letters, 1940–1971*, Berkeley and Los Angeles, CA, and London, University of California Press, 2001, p. 337. Hereafter, *The Nabokov-Wilson Letters*.

17. Appel, p. 208.
18. *Strong Opinions*, p. 161.
19. V. Nabokov, *Mary*, London: Penguin, 1973, p. 19. All references are to this edition.
20. Moses, p. 113.
21. *Strong Opinions*, p. 14.
22. D. Nabokov, "On Revisiting Father's Room," in P. Quennell (ed.), *Vladimir Nabokov: A Tribute*, London: Weidenfeld & Nicolson, 1979, p. 129. Hereafter, Quennell.
23. V. Nabokov, "My English Education," p. 9, in "*Conclusive Evidence*, excerpts in typescript (incomplete) of memoir, comprising 7 chapters, undated, 93 pp." Emphasis is mine. Nabokov's Papers at the Henry W. and Albert A. Berg Collection of English and American Literature, New York Public Library (hereafter, VN Berg).
24. See *Conclusive Evidence: A Memoir*, New York: Harper & Row, 1951, p. 54; and *Speak, Memory: An Autobiography Revisited*, London: Penguin, 1969, p. 70 (hereafter, *Speak, Memory*).
25. *Strong Opinions*, p. 154.

Chapter Two

1. J. D. Barlow, *German Expressionist Film*, Boston, MA: Twayne, 1982, p. 36 (hereafter, Barlow).
2. See entry in I. Konigsberg, *The Complete Film Dictionary*, second edition, London: Bloomsbury, 1997, p. 62 (hereafter, Konigsberg).
3. "An angle of view opposite to that in a preceding shot. A series of reverse angles is frequently used to alternate between the points of view of two characters in a conversation (called shot/reverse shot technique)" [ibid., p. 333].
4. Barlow, p. 115.
5. The "point of view shot" is "a subjective shot that shows a scene exactly the way a character would see it" [Konigsberg, pp. 298–99]. These shots tend to be combined with normal objective shots, since an extended use of point-of-view shots can disorientate the viewer, as it does in this instance.
6. Barlow, p. 96.
7. Ibid., p. 98.

8. See, for example, André Bazin's discussion of cinematic illusion in his essay "An Aesthetic of Reality: Neorealism" in *What Is Cinema? Volume 2*, trans. H. Gray, Berkeley/Los Angeles, CA: California University Press, 1971, pp. 26–27.
9. Reinhardt also worked in film, making three silent features between 1913 and 1919. He is perhaps best known, however, for his 1935 Hollywood production of *A Midsummer Night's Dream*.
10. For commentary, see Barlow, pp. 147–51.
11. V. Nabokov, "Details of a Sunset," in *Vladimir Nabokov: The Collected Stories*, London: Penguin, 1997 (hereafter, *Collected Stories*), pp. 79–80. All references are to this edition.
12. Nabokov commented on "the wonderful stylized chiaroscuro" of Murnau's film and Josef von Sternberg's *Shanghai Express* (1932). See Appel, p. 224.
13. Ibid., p. 137.
14. V. Nabokov, *The Eye*, London: Penguin, 1981, p. 9. All references are to this edition.
15. A scene which anticipates the confrontation between Humbert Humbert and Quilty in *Lolita*.
16. Murnau's film *Nosferatu* (1922), the first silent film feature based on Bram Stoker's novel *Dracula* (1897), which Nabokov described as "heavy-handed trash," is cited in Appel, p. 136.
17. Note the echoes of a similar furtive nighttime scene in Nabokov's story of 1924, "The Seaport": "She turned into a dark glistening alley. A streetlamp stretched her shadow. The shadows flashed along a wall and skewed.... An instant later he heard rapid footfalls behind him, and breathing, and the rustle of a dress. He looked back. There was no one. The square was deserted and dark. The night wind propelled a newspaper sheet across flagstones" (*Collected Stories*, p. 65).
18. See Appel; also Charles Nicol, "Did Luzhin Have Chess Fever?" *The Nabokovian*, 27, 1991, pp. 40–42.
19. D. Vertov, "Kinoks: A Revolution" (1923), in A. Michelson (ed.), *Kino-Eye: The Writings of Dziga Vertov*, London/Sydney: Pluto Press, 1984, p. 19 (hereafter, Michelson).

20. Ibid., p. 14.

21. As a process of editing individual shots into a sequence, the method was also deployed by Pudovkin to create fluid narratives, in a process of "linkage," as opposed to the conflict or "collision" premise of Eisenstein's method. See Konigsberg, pp. 245–46. Also S. M. Eisenstein, "Béla Forgets the Scissors" (1926), in R. Taylor (ed., trans.), *S. M. Eisenstein, Selected Works, Vol. 1: Writings, 1922–34*, London: BFI, 1988, pp. 77–81.

22. S. M. Eisenstein, "The Montage of Attractions" (1923), in ibid., p. 35.

23. Ibid., pp. 40–41.

24. S. M. Eisenstein, "The Montage of Film Attractions" (1924), in ibid., p. 45.

25. "The Montage of Attractions," in ibid., p. 41.

26. S. M. Eisenstein, "Béla Forgets the Scissors" (1926), in ibid., p. 79.

27. See V. Petrić, *Constructivism in Film: The Man with the Movie Camera: A Cinematic Analysis*, Cambridge: Cambridge University Press, 1987. Petrić also points out the similarities between Vertov's approach and that of Buster Keaton's *The Cameraman* (1928), directed by Edward Sedgwick: "Several sequences ... can be related to Vertov's film on a conceptual level (e.g., shooting a newsreel on the streets of New York, or accelerated motion to produce comic effects)" (p. 80), indicating the influence of Soviet experimental cinema in the United States.

28. "Letter from Berlin" (1929), in Michelson, p. 102.

29. Ibid., p. xxxvii.

30. "We: Variant of a Manifesto" (1922), in ibid., p. 7.

31. Ibid., p. 17.

32. V. Nabokov, "The Leonardo," in *Collected Stories*, p. 358. All references are to this edition.

33. "A transition between two scenes whereby the first gradually fades out as the second gradually fades in with some overlap between the two" (Konigsberg, p. 101).

34. The infamous twins from Lewis Carroll's *Alice in Wonderland*, which Nabokov translated into Russian in 1922. See Brian Boyd, "Chronology of Nabokov's Life and Works," in V. E. Alexandrov (ed.), *The Garland Companion to Vladimir Nabokov*, New York: Garland, 1995 (hereafter, *The Garland Companion*), p. xxxvi.

35. See Nabokov's explanation of the term in *Collected Stories*, p. 653.

36. "My task which I am trying to achieve is, by the power of the written word, to make you hear, to make you feel — it is, before all, to make you *see*." J. Conrad, "Introduction" to "The Nigger of the *Narcissus*," in *The Nigger of the "Narcissus," Typhoon and Other Stories*, London: Penguin, 1963, p. 13.

37. V. Nabokov, *Despair*, London: Penguin, 1981, p. 23. All references are to this edition.

38. Moses, p. 151.

39. Although this passage does not appear in either the Russian or English editions of 1936, it did exist in Nabokov's original manuscript having been "stupidly omitted" by censorious publishers. When he came to revise the original translation in 1964, Nabokov merely reinstated it. See pp. 9–10 and B. Boyd, *Vladimir Nabokov: The American Years*, London: Vintage, 1991, p. 489 (hereafter, *The American Years*).

40. Moses, p. 151.

Chapter Three

1. Wallace Stevens, "Imagination as Value," in *The Necessary Angel: Essays on Reality and the Imagination*, New York: Alfred A. Knopf, 1951, p. 151.

2. L. W. Wagner, *Dos Passos: Artist as American*, Austin, TX: University of Texas Press, 1979, p. xix.

3. A term adopted from the artists of the School of Paris, c. 1920. See J. Dos Passos, "What Makes a Novelist," in D. Pizer (ed.), *John Dos Passos: The Major Nonfictional Prose*, Detroit, MI: Wayne State University Press, 1988, p. 272. Hereafter, Pizer.

4. "The artist must record the fleeting world the way the motion picture film recorded it. By contrast, juxtaposition, montage, he could build drama into his narrative." Ibid.

5. J. Dos Passos, *Manhattan Transfer*, London: Penguin, 1986, p. 108. All references are to this edition.

6. Diary entry dated 16 April 1934 in Michelson, p. 174.

7. B. F. Kawin, *Faulkner and Film*, New York: Frederick Ungar, 1977, p. 6 (hereafter, Kawin).

8. Ibid., pp. 10–11.

9. C. Shloss, *In Visible Light: Photography and the American Writer, 1840–1940*, New York and Oxford: Oxford University Press, 1987, p. 146 (hereafter, Shloss).

10. Ibid., pp. 147–48.

11. Ibid., p. 148.

12. A cutaway is a shot which "momentarily takes us away from the main scene." Konigsberg, p. 82.

13. A fade is "a gradual means of closing or starting a scene." Ibid., p. 128.

14. Shloss, p. 144.

15. Ibid., p. 147.

16. See M. J. Bruccoli, *Some Sort of Epic Grandeur: The Life of F. Scott Fitzgerald*, London: Cardinal, 1991, pp. 627–33.

17. Ibid., pp. 670–71.

18. F. Scott Fitzgerald, *The Great Gatsby: The Authorized Text*, New York: Charles Scribner's Sons, 1995, p. 101. All references are to this edition.

19. See editor's note in the London Penguin edition, 1990, p. 174, n. 16.

20. Shloss, p. 148.

21. Ibid.

22. See R. Berman, "Seeing the Scene," in *The Great Gatsby and Modern Times*, Urbana/Chicago, IL: University of Illinois Press, 1994, pp. 137–59. Hereafter Berman.

23. Letter to John Peale Bishop, 1935, in L. W. Phillips (ed.), *F. Scott Fitzgerald on Writing*, London: Equation, 1988, p. 49.

24. See entry in Konigsberg, pp. 468–69.

25. Berman, p. 151.

26. W. W. Dixon, *The Cinematic Vision of F. Scott Fitzgerald*, Ann Arbor, MI: UMI Research Press, 1986, p. 30. Hereafter Dixon.

27. V. Nabokov, "Perfection," in *Collected Stories*, p. 340. All references are to this edition.

28. James Mason to Vladimir Nabokov, 21 August 1967, Hotel Belles-Rives, Jaun-les-Pins, France (VN Berg). Mason's emphasis.

29. According to Boyd, a "$100,000 contract had been negotiated for the movie rights" before its publication in April 1968. See *The American Years*, p. 532.

30. Ibid., p. 534.

31. J. Grayson, "Major Reworkings: *King, Queen, Knave*," in *Nabokov Translated: A Comparison of Nabokov's Russian and*

English Prose, Oxford: Oxford University Press, 1977, pp. 90–114.

32. Ibid., p. 112.

33. Ibid., p. 91.

34. V. Nabokov, *King, Queen, Knave*, London: Penguin, 1993, p. 6. All references are to this edition.

35. Although the explicit filmic analogy was added in Nabokov's 1968 translation, the distorting image of Dreyer is highly cinematic and specifically reminiscent of the vision of Mabuse in Murnau's film.

36. See V. Nabokov, *Korol', Dama, Valet*, Ann Arbor, MI: Ardis, 1979, p. 112. All references are to this edition.

37. Appel, pp. 258–59.

38. See *The Russian Years*, p. 445.

39. Appel, p. 259.

40. Stuart, p. 94, n. 9.

41. Appel, p. 259.

42. "A shot in which the camera moves up or down along a vertical axis from a fixed position [which can follow] the movement of a subject for the audience, expand our awareness of the environment, or show us the relationship between two areas of action.... The tilt shot is the opposite of a pan, in which the camera moves from a fixed position along a horizontal axis" (Konigsberg, p. 422).

43. V. Nabokov, *Laughter in the Dark*, New York: New Directions/James Laughlin, 1978, p. 236. All references are to this edition.

44. J. Connolly, "*Laughter in the Dark*," in *The Garland Companion*, p. 216.

45. *The Russian Years*, p. 363.

46. In, for example, Clarence Brown's *Flesh and the Devil* (1926) or *A Woman of Affairs* (1929).

47. *Collected Stories*, p. 138.

48. The reverse of a "flashback"; see Konigsberg, pp. 148–49. They occur early on in the narrative, when Albinus encounters Margot at the Argus cinema. The first appears as the final scene of a film — "a girl was receding among tumbled furniture before a masked man with a gun" (p. 20) — whereas the second is provoked directly by Margot's presence — "a car was spinning down a smooth road with hairpin turns between cliff and abyss" (p. 20).

49. Moses, p. 72.

50. V. Nabokov, "Spring in Fialta," in *Collected Stories*, p. 426. All references are to this edition.

Chapter Four

1. The term was first used by French cineaste Nino Frank in his article "Un nouveau genre 'policier': l'aventure criminelle," in *L'Écran Français* 61 (1946), pp. 8–9; 14 (p. 14). The French derived the term from translations of American *Black Mask* crime fiction, which they referred to as *Série Noire*.

2. These include R. Barton Palmer, *Hollywood's Dark Cinema: The American Film Noir*, Boston: Twayne, 1994; Bruce Crowther, *Film Noir: Reflections in a Dark Mirror*, London: Virgin, 1990; Glenn Erickson, "Expressionist Doom in *Night and the City*," and R. G. Porfiro, "No Way Out: Existential Motifs in the *Film Noir*," in A. Silver and J. Ursini (eds.), *Film Noir Reader*, New York: Limelight Editions, 1996 (hereafter, *Film Noir Reader*); S. Selby, *Dark City: The Film Noir*, Jefferson, NC: McFarland, 1984; and J. Tuska, *Dark Cinema: American Film Noir in Cultural Perspective*, Westport, CT: Greenwood Press, 1984 (hereafter, Tuska).

3. A. Silver and E. Ward (eds.), *Film Noir: An Encyclopedic Reference to the American Style*, third edition, New York: Overlook Press, 1992, p. 3. Hereafter, Silver and Ward.

4. J. R. Taylor, *Strangers in Paradise: The Hollywood Émigrés 1933–50*, New York: Holt, Rinehart & Winston, 1983, p. 62.

5. Ibid., pp. 62–63.

6. John Grabree, *Gangsters: From Little Caesar to the Godfather*, New York: Galahad Books, 1973, quoted in Tuska, p. 233.

7. R. Borde and E. Chaumeton, "Towards a Definition of *Film Noir*" (1955), in *Film Noir Reader*, p. 25. Borde and Chaumeton's italics.

8. K. Hollinger, "*Film Noir*, Voice-Over and the Femme Fatale," in ibid., p. 244.

9. Ibid., p. 258.

10. P. Schrader, "Notes on *Film Noir*," in ibid., p. 58. Hereafter, Schrader.

11. Ibid., p. 59.

12. Ibid.

13. Silver and Ward, p. 3. The names in square brackets denote directors and directors of photography.

14. J. Place and L. Peterson, "Some Visual Motifs of *Film Noir*," in *Film Noir Reader*, pp. 66–67. Place and Peterson's italics.

15. See Konigsberg, p. 54.

16. Schrader, p. 57.

17. R. Chandler, "The Simple Art of Murder" (1944); introduction to *Pearls Are a Nuisance*, London: Penguin, 1964, p. 8. Hereafter "The Simple Art of Murder."

18. Notes for *The Last Tycoon*, London: Penguin, 1960, p. 196. Hereafter, *The Last Tycoon*.

19. "The Simple Art of Murder," p. 8.

20. D. Dooley, *Dashiell Hammett*, New York: Frederick Ungar, 1984, p. 103.

21. Ibid.

22. Ibid., p. 102.

23. D. Hammett, *The Maltese Falcon*, New York: Vintage International, 1992, p. 46. All references are to this edition.

24. A. Spiegel, *Fiction and the Camera Eye: Visual Consciousness in Film and the Modern Novel*, Charlottesville, VA: University Press of Virginia, 1976, p. 156. Hereafter, Spiegel.

25. See Kawin, p. 2 and pp. 165–81.

26. Spiegel, p. 156.

27. Ibid., pp. 133–34.

28. Ibid., p. 153.

29. Ibid., p. 154.

30. W. Faulkner, *Sanctuary*, London: Picador, 1989, p. 5. All references are to this edition.

31. Silver and Ward, p. 3.

32. Ibid., p. 6.

33. Ibid., p. 4.

34. Ibid., p. 5.

35. Ibid.

36. See *King, Queen, Knave*, p. 160, and *Korol', Dama, Valet*, p. 157.

37. In the Russian version, it is an old lady who slips on the ice. See *Korol', Dama, Valet*, p. 125.

38. See D. Madden, *James M. Cain*, New York/Boston: Twayne, 1970 (hereafter, Madden). This was a label which Cain was himself to refute; see "James M. Cain: Tough Guy," an interview with Peter Brunette and Gerald Peary in P. McGillian (ed.), *Backstory: Interviews with Screenwriters of Hollywood's Golden Age*, Berkeley/Los Angeles, CA: University of California Press, 1986, p. 114.

39. Madden, p. 42. For Edmund Wilson's comment, see "The Boys in the Back Room" (1940), in *Classics and Commercials:*

A Literary Chronicle of the Forties, New York: Farrar, Straus, 1950, footnote to p. 49.

40. Madden, p. 117, quoted from A. Van Nostrand's *Denatured Novel*, Indianapolis/New York: Bobbs-Merrill, 1956, p. 117.

41. James M. Cain, *The Postman Always Rings Twice*, in *The Five Great Novels of James M. Cain*, London: Picador, 1985, p. 6. All references are to this edition.

42. "A cut between two shots that seems abrupt and calls attention to itself because of some obvious jump in time or space" (Konigsberg, pp. 200–01).

43. See L. Mulvey, *Citizen Kane*, London: BFI, 1992, pp. 41–43.

44. See pages 4, 58, 82, 83, 101, 173, 187 and 205.

45. R. Chandler, *The Big Sleep*, London: Penguin, 1948, p. 44. All references are to this edition.

46. *Collected Stories*, p. 137.

47. Most notably chapters 3 and 5, "Tristram in Movielove" and "Dark Cinema" in Appel; see also R. Corliss, *Lolita*, London: BFI, 1994.

Chapter Five

1. For more details see B. Boyd, "Chronology of Nabokov's Life and Works," in *The Garland Companion*, pp. xl–xlvi.

2. *Strong Opinions*, p. 98.

3. Ibid., p. 131.

4. John M. Kopper, "Correspondence," in *The Garland Companion*, p. 56.

5. S. Karlinsky, "Introduction" to *The Nabokov-Wilson Letters*, p. 12.

6. He also cites stories by Cheever, Updike, Salinger, Gold and Barth. See "On Inspiration," in *Strong Opinions*, pp. 312–13.

7. Ibid., p. 313.

8. Delmore Schwartz, "In Dreams Begin Responsibilities," in James Atlas (ed.), *In Dreams Begin Responsibilities and Other Stories*, London: Secker & Warburg, 1978, p. 1. All references are to this edition.

9. Note the parallels with Nabokov's response to the "homemade movies" taken a few weeks before his birth, featuring his expectant parents and a brand-new pram in *Speak, Memory*, p. 17.

10. *Strong Opinions*, pp. 163–64.

11. Correspondence from Dmitri Nabokov to the author, dated 1 July 1996.

12. See Appel, p. 57. Nabokov's favorite part of the film was "the clutter of the final sequence," reminiscent of the chaotic interior of Pavor Manor.

13. Ibid., p. 89.

14. *Strong Opinions*, p. 105.

15. V. Nabokov, *The Annotated Lolita*, A. Appel, Jr. (ed.), London: Penguin, 1995, p. 170. All references are to this edition.

16. This recalls the "front of a cinema" which "ripples in diamonds" in the story "A Letter That Never Reached Russia" (1924). See *Collected Stories*, p. 138.

17. For commentary on the song's implications in Humbert Humbert's revenge scenario, see B. Wyllie, "Resonances of Popular Music in *Lolita*, *Pale Fire* and *Ada*," in L. Zunshine (ed.), *Nabokov at the Limits: Redrawing Critical Boundaries*, New York: Garland, 1999, pp. 50–56.

18. See Gavriel Shapiro, *Delicate Markers: Subtexts in Vladimir Nabokov's "Invitation to a Beheading,"* New York: Peter Lang, 1998, p. 59. Hereafter, Shapiro.

19. "The first positive prints ... that are made the same night as the shooting and sent unedited to the director for viewing the next day." Konigsberg, p. 339.

20. "A series of cuts or shots unrelated by a continuous action or narration, but instead used in total to create the impression of a place, period of time, or a character's reactions to an event or memory of past events." Ibid., p. 69.

21. Spiegel, p. 88.

22. R. Chandler, "The Curtain," in *Killer in the Rain*, London: Penguin, 1966, p. 109.

23. Note that this is a device recognized and condemned by Hermann Karlovich and that also recalls the final scene of *Laughter in the Dark*.

24. Note how this sequence echoes the depiction of Miss Reba as disembodied in Temple's eyes, with the focus on isolated aspects of her person — her heavy breast and fat fingers.

25. "A zoom shot that suddenly and rapidly zooms in on the subject ... used to jolt and shock." Konigsberg, p. 78.

26. Ironically, Quilty wanted to take Lolita to Hollywood to play a "bit-part" in

a tennis scene in a film called *Golden Guts*. See p. 276.

27. Arclights "were a standard source of lighting in studios and are still, in spite of their noise and relatively short duration, used when great luminosity is needed from a single source." Konigsberg, p. 18.

28. See Appel, pp. 224–28.

29. For example, the anguish of Humbert Humbert's violent reaction to the news that Lolita has left the hospital in Elphinstone (p. 246) and the intense regret he experiences when he chances to hear the voices of children at play in some "transparent town" on his way from Pavor Manor (pp. 307–8).

30. P. Kael, "Crime and Poetry," in S. Wake and N. Hayden (eds.), *Bonnie and Clyde*, London: Faber & Faber, 1998, p. 196. Hereafter, "Crime and Poetry."

31. J. Kitses, *Gun Crazy*, London: BFI, 1996, p. 14.

32. Ibid., p. 27.

33. Ibid., p. 43.

34. Ibid., p. 66.

35. Ibid., pp. 42–43.

36. W. D. Gehring, *Screwball Comedy: A Genre of Madcap Romance*, Westport, CT: Greenwood Press, 1986, p. 3. Hereafter Gehring.

37. Ibid., p. 10.

38. Ibid., p. 38.

39. Ibid., p. 45.

40. Ibid., p. 47.

41. P. French, *Westerns: Aspects of a Movie Genre*, New York: Viking Press, 1973, p. 107. Hereafter French.

42. Gehring, p. 45.

43. Pauline Kael, "Lolita," in *I Lost It at the Movies: Film Writings 1954–1965*, New York: Marion Boyars, 1994, p. 205.

44. See Appel, pp. 201–25.

45. Ibid., p. 216.

46. Arthur Penn, "*Bonnie and Clyde*: Private Morality and Public Violence," in R. Koszarski (ed.), *Hollywood Directors 1941–1976*, New York and Oxford: Oxford University Press, 1977, p. 360. Hereafter *Hollywood Directors*.

47. Appel, p. 222.

48. Arthur Penn in *Hollywood Directors*, p. 360.

49. See Michael Wood, *The Magician's Doubts: Nabokov and the Risks of Fiction*,

London: Chatto & Windus, 1994, pp. 130–33, and Appel's introduction to *The Annotated Lolita*, p. xliii, particularly the account of Nabokov "quaking with laughter over the furiously climactic fight scene" of a television Western. Nabokov was also familiar with the Western scenario before the advent of film. In *Speak, Memory* he recalls reading the Wild West fiction of Captain Mayne Reid (1818–1883) as a boy. See p. 152 and pp. 156–57.

50. See Appel, p. 210.

51. Note the similarity to Papadakis's murder in Cain's *The Postman Always Rings Twice* and Humbert Humbert's comparison of the incident with Charlotte's "accident": "Alas, the woman's battered body did not match up with only minor damage suffered by the car. I did better" (p. 288).

52. Appel, p. 136.

53. *Sunset Boulevard*, screenplay by Charles Brackett, Billy Wilder, D. M. Marshman, Jr., Paramount Pictures, 1950.

54. French, p. 115. The comic aspect of this typical Western scene is also emphasized.

55. Silver and Ward, p. 325.

56. Ibid., p. 312.

57. "Crime and Poetry," p. 203.

58. See M. D. Shrayer, *The World of Nabokov's Stories*, Austin, TX: University of Texas Press, 1999, pp. 68–69. Hereafter Shrayer.

59. Ibid., p. 84.

60. See ibid. and *Speak, Memory*, p. 169.

61. The simultaneous projection and reflection of an experience of intense emotional agony is also apparent in Nabokov's story of 1938, "Lik," in which the protagonist's "heart pain colors his vision of the space outside his room," causing him to be "suspended in anticipation of the otherworldly abyss" (Shrayer, p. 84), whilst echoing the dissociative sensations provoked by Ivanov's weak heart in "Perfection."

62. See Shapiro, pp. 56–58 and 63–64.

63. V. Nabokov, "The Vane Sisters," in *Collected Stories*, p. 619. All references are to this edition.

64. Note the echoes of eye imagery in *The Eye* and *The Man with the Movie Camera*.

65. G. Barabtarlo, "English Short Stories," in *The Garland Companion*, p. 113.

66. See commentary on the color-cod-

ing of Nabokov's name in Shapiro, pp. 28–29.

67. *The American Years*, p. 194.

68. Ibid., p. 195.

69. For definitions, see S. Gottlieb (ed.), *Hitchcock on Hitchcock*, London: Faber & Faber, 1995, pp. 122–24, and Konigsberg, p. 225.

70. F. R. Karl, *American Fictions 1940–1980: A Comprehensive History and Critical Evaluation*, New York: Harper & Row, 1983, p. 316.

71. W. Percy, *The Moviegoer*, New York: Fawcett Columbine, 1988, p. 120. All references are to this edition.

72. T. Tanner, "Wonder and Alienation — The Mystic and the Moviegoer," in *The Reign of Wonder: Naivety and Reality in American Literature*, Cambridge: Cambridge University Press, 1965, p. 352.

73. Ibid.

74. Ibid., p. 355.

Chapter Six

1. V. Nabokov, *The Gift*, London: Penguin, 1981, p. 159. Hereafter *The Gift*.

2. *Speak, Memory*, p. 98.

3. V. Nabokov, *Poems and Problems*, New York: McGraw-Hill, 1970, p. 15.

4. *The Gift*, p. 160.

5. *The American Years*, p. 59.

6. V. Nabokov, "The Assistant Producer," in *Collected Stories*, p. 546. This is the first edition which prints the story in full, the final two paragraphs having been omitted in previous publications. All references are to this edition.

7. "Reading 'The Assistant Producer' to a composition class at Wellesley in May 1943, Nabokov had explained that he liked to 'lure the reader this way and that and then tickle him behind the ear just to see him whirl around.'" *The American Years*, p. 71.

8. Ibid., p. 59.

9. See G. Barabtarlo, "English Short Stories," in *The Garland Companion*, pp. 101–17 (hereafter, Barabtarlo), and id., *Aerial View: Essays on Nabokov's Art and Metaphysics*, New York: Peter Lang, 1993, pp. 84–85; *The American Years*, p. 59; Nicol, pp. 155–65.

10. Nabokov described her as "an Elvis Presley in period dress." Appel, p. 288.

11. Barabtarlo, p. 105.

12. A "cutaway" is a "shot away from the main action but used to join two shots of the main action ... to generate suspense or relief, or to show specific details outside the frame of the main action." Konigsberg, p. 82.

13. "Cutting from one shot to another so unobtrusively that viewers are virtually unaware of the change in the camera's position as they watch the action." Ibid., p. 197.

14. Barabtarlo, p. 106.

15. See Nicol, p. 160.

16. See ibid., pp. 160–63.

17. Ibid., p. 157.

18. This recalls the films Nabokov saw as a boy on Nevskii Avenue: "The art was progressing. Sea waves were tinted a sickly blue and as they rode in and burst into foam against a black, remembered rock ... there was a special machine that imitated the sound of the surf, making a kind of washy swish that never quite managed to stop short with the scene but for three or four seconds accompanied the next feature." *Speak, Memory*, pp. 182–83.

19. Note the parallels with the overwhelming grayness of Humbert Humbert's cinematically informed narrative.

20. Barabtarlo, p. 105.

21. Bienstock, p. 126.

22. Bienstock provides a detailed commentary. See ibid., pp. 127–34.

23. Ibid., p. 131.

24. V. Nabokov, *Bend Sinister*, London: Penguin, 1974, p. 60. All references are to this edition.

25. The role recalls the archetypal movie mogul Monroe Stahr as he watches the day's rushes: "Another hour passed. Dreams hung in fragments at the far end of the room, suffered analysis, passed — to be dreamed in crowds, or else discarded" (*The Last Tycoon*, p. 70).

26. *Strong Opinions*, p. 313.

27. *The Gift*, p. 169.

28. *Speak, Memory*, p. 93.

29. Ibid., p. 17.

30. Ibid., p. 211.

31. Ibid., p. 62.

32. *The Gift*, p. 160.

33. For commentaries on *Ada* and postmodernism, see Brian Boyd, *Nabokov's "Ada": The Place of Consciousness*, second edi-

tion, Christchurch, New Zealand: Cybereditions, 2002 (hereafter, *Nabokov's "Ada"*) and *The American Years*, pp. 536–62; Maurice Couturier (ed.), "Nabokov at the Crossroads of Modernism and Postmodernism," in *Cycnos*, 12, 1995, 2; Brian McHale, *Postmodernist Fiction*, London: Routledge, 1987 (hereafter McHale); Charles Nicol, "Ada or Disorder," in *Nabokov's Fifth Arc*, pp. 230–41; and John Stark, *The Literature of Exhaustion: Borges, Nabokov and Barth*, Durham, NC: Duke University Press, 1974 (hereafter Stark).

34. Stark, pp. 3–4.

35. McHale, p. 129.

36. Ibid., p. 130.

37. Ibid., p. 129. See, also, the relationship between the parallel realities of actuality and the television movie, *Cashiered* in chapter three of Pynchon's *Crying of Lot 49* (1965).

38. V. Nabokov, *Ada or Ardor: A Family Chronicle*, London: Penguin, 1971, pp. 262 and 335. All references are to this edition.

39. McHale, p. 128.

40. A "double take" is a cinematic term which refers to the "repetition of the same part of an action when the action is shot from two different angles" (see Konigsberg, p. 107), whilst "double exposure" is a clever pun on the processes of photography which emphasizes Van's self-consciousness.

41. See entry in Konigsberg, p. 192.

42. Ada's depiction in black and white also establishes her connection to Demon — her biological father — who is consistently identified by his black attire in explicit emphasis of his demonic qualities. For example, "Demon had dyed his hair a blacker black. He wore a diamond ring blazing like a Caucasian ridge. His long, black blue-ocellated wings trailed and quivered in the ocean breeze" (p. 143).

43. All that remains of the scene cut from Vronsky's film, *The Young and the Doomed*. See pp. 333–34.

44. "The light [from the headlights] hit pencils of rain and made silver wires of them." *The Big Sleep*, p. 182.

45. *Nabokov's "Ada,"* p. 153.

46. Ibid., p. 134.

47. Moses, p. 113.

48. James Monaco, *How to Read a Film: The Art, Technology, Language, History,* and *Theory of Film and Media*, revised edition, New York and Oxford: Oxford University Press, 1981, p. 173. Hereafter Monaco.

49. See also Boyd's commentary on the dynamic of "resistance" in *Nabokov's "Ada,"* pp. 50–63.

50. The quotations marks are Nabokov's. See *Strong Opinions*, p. 154.

51. Ibid., p. 11.

52. Ibid., p. 154. This statement was made in an interview given in the year of *Ada*'s publication.

53. Nabokov's correction to page 140 of the dissertation, *Nabokov's Garden*, by Bobbie Ann Mason (née Rawlings), undated, p. 6 of 8 pp. (VN Berg).

54. See, particularly, Brian Boyd's account in *Nabokov's "Ada,"* and *"Ada"* in *The Garland Companion*, pp. 3–18. Also Bobbie Ann Mason, *Nabokov's Garden: A Guide to "Ada,"* Ann Arbor, MI: Ardis, 1974; Robert Alter, "*Ada*, or the Perils of Paradise," in Quennell, pp. 103–18; and Ellen Pifer, "Dark Paradise: Shades of Heaven and Hell in *Ada*," in *Modern Fiction Studies*, 25, 1979, 481–97.

55. W. Gass, "The Artist and Society," in *Fiction and the Figures of Life*, Boston, MA: Nonpareil Books, 1971, p. 279. Hereafter Gass.

56. This also echoes Benjamin Franklin's comments on autobiography: "Were it offered to my Choice, I should have no Objection to a Repetition of the same Life from its Beginning, only asking the Advantages Authors have in a second Edition to correct some Faults of the first. So would I if I might, besides correcting the Faults, change some sinister Accidents & Events of it for others more favorable." *The Autobiography of Benjamin Franklin*, London: Penguin, 1986, pp. 3–4.

57. The color of the sun, or lit by the sun, i.e., by natural light.

58. Moses, p. 113. Moses cites Smurov's representation of others in *The Eye* and the concluding scene of *Despair*, but consider also the earlier dissociation episode and Felix's murder. This is, however, not true of Humbert Humbert, whose loss of self-control is signaled by his loss of directorial control.

59. "The movement of the camera during a shot by means of a wheeled support,

generally a dolly," the dolly being "a mobile platform on wheels that supports the camera, camera operator, and often the assistant cameraman, and allows the camera to make noiseless, moving shots in a relatively small area" (Konigsberg, pp. 105–6).

60. R. Chandler, *The High Window*, London: Penguin, 1951, p. 177.

61. "The opening shot of a sequence which establishes location but can also establish mood or give the viewer information concerning the time and general situation. Establishing shots generally are long shots or extreme long shots. Sometimes a series of establishing shots view the location from different angles and perspectives, or a panning or moving shot is employed for the same purpose" (Konigsberg, p. 122).

62. "Diffusion filters are employed to create soft focus." Ibid., p. 145.

63. Note the distinction between this notion of "rear view" and the depiction, in *Speak, Memory*, of Mademoiselle O's arrival in Vyra: "But what am I doing in this stereoscopic dreamland? ... All is still, spellbound, enthralled by the moon, fancy's rear-vision mirror" (p. 78). Compounding the role of the imagination in this scene is Nabokov's deployment of a cinematic "cross-fade" to establish a connection "across distances in time and in space." See Moses, p. 130.

64. Note also the reverse application, in photographic terms, of "negative" which designates Lucette as drab, in spite of her being presented in color, as opposed to Ada's 'positive' black-and-white brilliance.

65. Apart from being a feature of Vronsky's shooting script (p. 159), "flashback — or perhaps 'half-hearted flashback'" is also, as Neil Cornwell argues, "an overriding technique" of *Ada*. N. Cornwell, *Vladimir Nabokov*, Plymouth, UK: Northcote Publishers, 1999, p. 89.

66. "Mirror, Mirror" in Gass, p. 110.

67. R. Poirier, *The Performing Self: Compositions and Decompositions in the Languages of Contemporary Life*, New Brunswick, NJ: Rutgers University Press, 1992, p. 41.

Chapter Seven

1. J. Kosinski, *The Art of Self: Essays à propos "Steps,"* New York: Scienta-Factum, 1968, p. 15.

2. *The American Years*, p. 588.

3. Ibid.

4. S. Simmon, "Beyond the Theater of War: *Gravity's Rainbow* as Film," in R. Pearce (ed.), *Critical Essays on Thomas Pynchon*, Boston, MA: G. K. Hall, 1981, p. 127.

5. Ibid., p. 128. Whilst Simmon has Pynchon specifically in mind, his statement could also apply to the work of Don DeLillo, Kurt Vonnegut, Jr., Jerzy Kosinski and Gilbert Sorrentino.

6. *The American Years*, p. 601.

7. V. Nabokov, *Transparent Things*, New York: Vintage International, 1989, p. 48. All references are to this edition.

8. *Strong Opinions*, p. 11.

9. Ibid.

10. *Speak, Memory*, p. 169.

11. Ibid.

12. D. Barton Johnson, "*Transparent Things*," in *The Garland Companion*, p. 731 (hereafter Barton Johnson).

13. An assistant cameraperson who is responsible for maintaining focus during a take. See Konigsberg, p. 146, and Monaco, p. 433.

14. "Deep" focus has "great depth of field and brings all planes of the image — foreground, middle ground, and background — into sharp focus." "Shallow" focus enables "a narrow area of sharp definition in the film image, with the surrounding area out of focus or blurred." Konigsberg, pp. 86 and 356.

15. Nabokov describes this chapter as "not only an integral part of the [novel's] theme, but ... the clue to the whole story." Letter to Katherine Fox, 24 January 1973 in *Selected Letters*, p. 506.

16. "A Russian traveler, a minor Dostoevski, occupying that room, between a Swiss gambling house and Italy." *Strong Opinions*, pp. 194–95.

17. V. E. Alexandrov, *Nabokov's Otherworld*, Princeton, NJ: Princeton University Press, 1991, p. 5 (hereafter Alexandrov).

18. *Speak, Memory*, p. 110.

19. R. is identified by the repeated and distinctive unconventional spelling of "hello." He greets Hugh directly three times in the novel — "Hullo, person! Doesn't hear me"; "Hullo, person ... (last time in a very small voice)" (p. 1), and "Hullo, Person!" (p. 30) — which designates his Germanic origins.

"In conversation R. has an annoying habit of introducing here and there the automatic 'you know' of the German *émigré* and, more painfully yet, of misusing, garbling, or padding the commonest American cliché." *Strong Opinions,* p. 195.

20. See W. W. Rowe, *Nabokov's Spectral Dimension,* Ann Arbor, MI: Ardis, 1981, pp. 15–16.

21. *Speak, Memory,* p. 23.

22. Hugh's pursuit by inanimate objects echoes the predicament of the Expressionist hero, in that their perceived significance is merely the projection of subjective emotional and psychological fears and aspirations.

23. *The American Years,* p. 601.

24. Ibid., p. 589.

25. See Alexandrov, pp. 34–35 and the chapter on *The Defense,* pp. 58–83; *The American Years,* pp. 592–93; Barton Johnson, pp. 729–30; and M. T. Naumann, *Blue Evenings in Berlin: Nabokov's Short Stories of the 1920s,* New York: New York University Press, 1978, pp. 214–16 and p. 221.

26. Alexandrov, p. 82.

27. For detailed commentary see M. Rosenblum, "Finding What the Sailor Has Hidden: Narrative as Patternmaking in *Transparent Things,*" in *Contemporary Literature,* 19, 1978, pp. 219–32 (hereafter Rosenblum).

28. Barton Johnson, p. 727.

29. This also echoes Kern's idea of death as "a gliding dream, a fluffy fall" in "Wingstroke" (1924), in *Collected Stories,* p. 31.

30. See Appel, pp. 160–61. Very early in his career, Nabokov wrote "commercial sketches" which featured what he called "Locomotions" (p. 155). These, as Appel points out, anticipated the chaotic character of American film comedy, particularly the work of Keaton, Chaplin, Harold Lloyd and Laurel and Hardy. In an interview with Appel, Nabokov describes a scene from Charlie Chaplin's *The Great Dictator* (1940), in which a "parachute inventor ... jumps out of the window and ends in a messy fall which we only see in the expression on the dictator's face" (*Strong Opinions,* p. 163). These scenes reemerge not only as the various death plunges in *Transparent Things* but also as a highly orchestrated element of *Invitation to a Beheading* and *Pale Fire.* See Appel, pp. 153–67.

31. Barton Johnson, p. 729.

32. The image also recalls the "veritable Niagara" of the neighboring toilet at the Enchanted Hunters. See *The Annotated Lolita,* p. 130.

33. Monaco, p. 63. Although Monaco is referring to the pivotal tower scenes, the device was also deployed in the film's opening sequence in a dramatic chase across rooftops which culminates in a policeman plunging to his death whilst Ferguson watches in horror as he clings to a piece of broken guttering.

34. Meaning an increase or decrease in the frequency of sound, light, or other waves as the source and observer move toward (or away from) each other.

35. "A single frame ... of a different image inserted into a shot for effect." Konigsberg, p. 149.

36. Moses, p. 113.

37. Rosenblum, p. 226.

38. This image of Armande is prefigured in chapter seventeen — "her figure as trim as that of an air hostess, in that blue coat with flat buttons as bright as counters of gold" (p. 67).

39. This is also reminiscent of the ecstasy Hermann Karlovich experiences during his dissociative "splits" whilst Hugh's earthbound state echoes the image of the penguin who "flies only in its sleep" (*Despair,* pp. 32–33; 34).

40. D. DeLillo, *Americana,* London: Penguin, 1990, p. 12. All references are to this edition.

41. C. Tichi, *Electronic Hearth: Creating an American Television Culture,* New York and Oxford: Oxford University Press, 1991, p. 205 (hereafter Tichi).

42. J. Kosinski, *Being There,* London: Black Swan, 1970, p. 10.

43. Ibid., pp. 10–11.

44. Rosenblum, p. 226.

45. D. Packman, *Vladimir Nabokov: The Structure of Literary Desire,* Columbia, MO: University of Missouri Press, 1982, p. 49.

46. Ibid., pp. 49–50.

47. *Speak, Memory,* p. 18.

48. Nabokov considered Carroll to be "the greatest children's story writer of all time" (*Strong Opinions,* p. 119). His Russian translation of *Alice in Wonderland* was pub-

lished in 1923, and allusions to the Alice stories are evident throughout his fiction, particularly in the novels *Invitation to a
Beheading* and *The Real Life of Sebastian
Knight*. See Julian W. Connolly, *"Ania v
Strane Chudes,"* in *The Garland Companion*,
pp. 18–25, and J. B. Sisson, *"The Real Life
of Sebastian Knight,"* in ibid., pp. 637–39.

49. Beverly Lyon Clark, *Reflections of
Fantasy: The Mirror Worlds of Carroll,
Nabokov and Pynchon*, New York: Peter
Lang, 1986, p. 143.

50. A notion voiced by Kilgore Trout,
the hero of Kurt Vonnegut, Jr.'s 1973 novel,
Breakfast of Champions: "Trout did another
thing which some people might have considered eccentric: he called mirrors *leaks*. It
amused him to pretend that mirrors were
holes between two universes." K. Vonnegut,
Jr., *Breakfast of Champions*, London: Vintage, 1992, p. 19.

51. Note the associations of green as a
color of evil signaled by Armande's ski outfit.
See Shapiro, pp. 56–58.

52. In a typed transcript of the novel
dated 1 April 1972, the following annotation
appears in the margin of page 103 — "kix =
kex" (VN Berg). In Russian, "keks" means
"fruit-cake," the allusion serving to emphasize the box's dense opacity.

53. *The American Years*, p. 601.

54. In a letter to Alfred Appel dated 8
November 1974, Nabokov comments that
"my wife and I have virtually not been to the
cinema more than two or three times in
fifteen years, nor do we have a TV at home
(except when soccer competitions take
place)." *Selected Letters*, p. 537. This is, however, contradicted by another statement to
Appel concerning Welles's *Citizen Kane*,
which Nabokov saw for the first time on
Swiss television in 1972. See Appel, p. 57.

55. N. King, "Three New Versions of
Hollywood," in P. Cook and M. Bernink
(eds.), *The Cinema Book,* second edition,
London: BFI, 1999, p. 100 (hereafter King).

56. Ibid., p. 101.

57. P. Biskind, *Easy Riders, Raging Bulls:
How the Sex 'n' Drugs 'n' Rock 'n' Roll Generation Saved Hollywood*, London: Bloomsbury,
1999, p. 45 (hereafter Biskind).

58. W. J. Palmer, *The Films of the Seventies: A Social History*, Metuchen, NJ: Scarecrow Press, 1987, p. 129 (hereafter Palmer).

59. L. Shaffer, *"The Conversation,"* in
Film Quarterly, 28, 1974, 1, pp. 54–60 (59).
Hereafter Shaffer.

60. H. Keyssar, *Robert Altman's America*, New York: Oxford University Press,
1991, p. 100 (hereafter Keyssar).

61. R. P. Kolker, *A Cinema of Loneliness: Penn, Kubrick, Scorsese, Spielberg, Altman*, second edition, New York and Oxford:
Oxford University Press, 1988, p. 332 (hereafter Kolker).

62. Palmer, p. 143.

63. Ibid.

64. M. Eaton, *Chinatown*, London:
BFI, 1997, p. 29 (hereafter Eaton).

65. Although only one scene is set in
Los Angeles's Chinatown, the place has a
metaphorical significance in the film directly
related to its central themes. Chinatown is
"a synecdoche for the entire City of Los
Angeles," a place "where nothing is ever what
it seems, where everyone's vision is flawed,
where any attempt to understand is
doomed." Palmer, p. 120.

66. Keyssar, p. 100.

67. Kolker, p. 320.

68. M. Tarantino, "Movement as
Metaphor: *The Long Goodbye*," in *Sight and
Sound*, 44, 1975, pp. 98–102 (98). Hereafter
Tarantino.

69. Ibid.

70. Ibid., p. 99.

71. A shot which "allows the audience
to stay with a character" by moving with
them. Konigsberg cites, for example, the long
tracking shot that opens Murnau's *Der letzte
Mann*, in which "the camera rides down an
elevator and moves across the [hotel] lobby
to the revolving doors." See Konigsberg, pp.
45–46 and 426.

72. Tarantino, p. 102.

73. Kolker, p. 346.

74. Ibid., pp. 346–47.

75. Ibid., p. 320.

76. R. P. Kolker, *A Cinema of Loneliness: Penn, Kubrick, Scorsese, Coppola, Altman*, first edition, New York and Oxford:
Oxford University Press, 1980, p. 95. The
chapter on Coppola was omitted from the
volume's second edition (hereafter Kolker,
1st ed.).

77. A "caul" is the thin membrane that
envelops an unborn child in the womb.

78. J. W. Palmer, *"The Conversation*:

Coppola's Biography of an Unborn Man," in *Film Heritage*, 12, 1976, 1, pp. 26–32 (27). Hereafter "*The Conversation*."

79. Shaffer, p. 59.

80. Ibid.

81. Kolker, 1st ed., p. 95.

82. Ibid.

83. "*The Conversation*," p. 29.

84. Palmer, p. 138.

85. Ibid., p. 131.

86. Ibid., p. 133.

87. Eaton, p. 69.

88. *The American Years*, p. 601.

89. D. Rampton, *Vladimir Nabokov: A Critical Study of the Novels*, Cambridge: Cambridge University Press, 1984, p. 166.

90. Ibid., p. 168.

Chapter Eight

1. John Updike in G. Plimpton (ed.), *Writers at Work: The Paris Review Interviews*, fourth series, New York: Viking Press, 1976, p. 448.

2. Pizer, p. 288.

3. Tichi, p. 205.

4. Tichi, p. 145. See also D. DeLillo, *White Noise*, London: Picador, 1986, pp. 161–62.

5. Tichi, p. 149. See also D. DeLillo, *Libra*, London: Penguin, 1989, pp. 439–40.

6. Tichi, p. 129.

7. Being the "absolute fake" constructed out of a desire for "the real thing," a means of authentication through a synthetic process. See Tichi, p. 130, and Umberto Eco, "Travels in Hyperreality" (1975), in W. Weaver (trans.), *Faith in Fakes: Travels in Hyperreality*, London: Minerva, 1995, pp. 3–58.

8. R. Coover, *A Night at the Movies, Or, You Must Remember This*, Normal, IL: Dalkey Archive Press, 1992, p. 113.

9. See commentary in Dana Polan, *Pulp Fiction*, London: BFI, 2000.

10. Ibid., p. 35.

11. Ibid., p. 17.

12. Bret Easton Ellis, *American Psycho*, London: Picador, 1991, p. 5. All references are to this edition.

13. See Konigsberg, p. 424.

14. Bateman's narcissism, combined with Carruthers's misinterpretation of his "designs" upon him (Bateman tries to strangle him in a toilet), also echoes the ambiguous nature of Smurov's sexuality. For commentary, see Galina Rylkova, "Okrylyonnyy Soglyadatay— The Winged Eavesdropper: Nabokov and Kuzmin," in D. H. J. Larmour (ed.), *Discourse and Ideology in Nabokov's Prose*, London and New York: Routledge, 2002, pp. 43–58.

15. The dominant film genre of the 1980s and 1990s, initiated by Steven Spielberg's *Jaws* (1975) and George Lucas's *Star Wars* (1977). See King, pp. 102–3 and Biskind, pp. 343–45.

16. Coincidentally, this movie ran with the tagline, "In modern America, the boy next door isn't what he appears to be." See the IMDb website http://us.imdb.com/Title?0095958.

17. For discussion of the question of identity in the novel, see Elizabeth Young, "The Beast in the Jungle, the Figure in the Carpet: Bret Easton Ellis's *American Psycho*," in E. Young and G. Caveney, *Shopping in Space: Essays on American "Blank Generation" Fiction*, London: Serpent's Tail, 1992, pp. 85–122.

18. Dixon, p. 30.

19. Shloss, p. 146.

20. Ibid., p. 147.

21. J. Cohen, *Spectacular Allegories: Postmodern American Writing and the Politics of Seeing*, London: Pluto Press, p. 2.

22. Shloss, p. 148.

23. *Strong Opinions*, p. 154.

Filmography

German Expressionist and Early Soviet Film

Bronenosets Potiomkin (*Battleship Potemkin*), First Studio Goskino, 1925, dir. Sergei Eisenstein.

Das Kabinet des Dr. Caligari, Decle-Film-Ges. Holz and Co., 1919, dir. Robert Wiene.

Dr. Mabuse, der Spieler, Uco-Film, 1922, dir. Fritz Lang.

Der letzte Mann (*The Last Laugh*), Ufa, 1924, dir. F. W. Murnau.

M, Nero, 1931, dir. Fritz Lang.

Chelovek s kinoapparatum (*The Man with the Movie Camera*), VUFKU, 1929, dir. Dziga Vertov.

Metropolis, Ufa, 1926, dir. Fritz Lang.

Nosferatu, Ufa, 1922, dir. F. W. Murnau.

Oktiabr (*October*), First Studio Goskino, 1927, dir. Sergei Eisenstein.

Orlacs Hände (*The Hands of Orlac*), Pan Films, 1924, dir. Robert Wiene.

Shakhmatnaia goriachka (*Chess Fever*), Mezhrabpom-Rus', 1925, dir. Vsevelod Pudovkin.

Comedy

Abbott and Costello

Hold That Ghost, Universal, 1941, dir. Arthur Lubin.

Ride 'Em Cowboy, Universal, 1942, dir. Arthur Lubin.

Who Done It? Universal, 1942, dir. Erle C. Kenton.

Charlie Chaplin

The Circus, Charles Chaplin Productions, 1928.

The Gold Rush, Charles Chaplin Productions, 1925.

The Great Dictator, United Artists, 1940.

Buster Keaton

The Cameraman, Metro-Goldwyn-Mayer, 1928, dir. Edward Sedgwick.

The General, Buster Keaton Productions, 1926, dir. Buster Keaton and Clyde Bruckman.

Steamboat Bill, Jr., Buster Keaton Productions, 1928, dir. Buster Keaton and Charles Reisner.

Laurel and Hardy

A Chump at Oxford, Hal Roach Studios, 1940, dir. Afred J. Goulding.
County Hospital, Hal Roach Studios, 1932, dir. James Parrott.
Helpmates, Hal Roach Studios, 1932, dir. James Parrott.
Perfect Day, Hal Roach Studios, 1929, dir. James Parrott.
Sons of the Desert, Hal Roach Studios, 1933, dir. William A. Seiter.

Harold Lloyd

Feet First, The Harold Lloyd Corporation, 1930, dir. Clyde Bruckman.
The Freshman, The Harold Lloyd Corporation, 1925, dir. Fred C. Newmeyer and Sam Taylor.

The Marx Brothers

Duck Soup, Paramount, 1933, dir. Leo McCarey.

A Night at the Opera, Metro-Goldwyn-Mayer, 1935, dir. Sam Wood.
Ninotchka, Metro-Goldwyn-Mayer, 1935, dir. Ernst Lubitsch.

Melodrama

Marlene Dietrich

Blonde Venus, Paramount, 1932, dir. Josef von Sternberg.
Morocco, Paramount, 1930, dir. Josef von Sternberg.
Shanghai Express, Paramount, 1932, dir. Josef von Sternberg.

Greta Garbo

Flesh and the Devil, Metro-Goldwyn-Mayer, 1926, dir. Clarence Brown.
A Woman of Affairs, Metro-Goldwyn-Mayer, 1929, dir. Clarence Brown.

Casablanca, Warner Bros., 1942, dir. Michael Curtiz.
Gone with the Wind, Selznick, 1939, dir. Victor Fleming.
Intolerance, Triangle Productions, 1916, dir. D. W. Griffith.

Film Noir

Angel Face, RKO, 1953, dir. Otto Preminger.
The Asphalt Jungle, Metro-Goldwyn-Mayer, 1950, dir. John Huston.
The Big Heat, Columbia, 1953, dir. Fritz Lang.
The Big Sleep, Warner Bros., 1946, dir. Howard Hawks.
The Blue Dahlia, Paramount, 1946, dir. George Marshall.
Brute Force, Universal, 1947, dir. Jules Dassin.
Citizen Kane, RKO, 1941, dir. Orson Welles.
Criss Cross, Universal, 1949, dir. Robert Siodmak.
Crossfire, RKO, 1947, dir. Edward Dmytryk.
Cry of the City, 20th Century–Fox, 1948, dir. Robert Siodmak.
The Dark Mirror, Universal, 1946, dir. Robert Siodmak.
D.O.A., United Artists, 1949, dir. Rudolph Maté.
Double Indemnity, Paramount, 1944, dir. Billy Wilder.

The File on Thelma Jordan, 20th Century–Fox, 1949, dir. Robert Siodmak.
Fury, Metro-Goldwyn-Mayer, 1936, dir. Fritz Lang.
The Glass Key, Paramount, 1942, dir. Samuel Heisler.
Gun Crazy, United Artists, 1950, dir. J. M. Lewis.
I Wake Up Screaming, 20th Century–Fox, 1942, dir. Bruce Humberstone.
Key Largo, Warner Bros., 1948, dir. John Huston.
The Killers, Universal, 1946, dir. Robert Siodmak.
The Lady in the Lake, Metro-Goldwyn-Mayer, 1947, dir. Robert Montgomery.
The Lady from Shanghai, Columbia, 1948, dir. Orson Welles.
Laura, 20th Century–Fox, 1944, dir. Otto Preminger.
The Maltese Falcon, Warner Bros., 1941, dir. John Huston.
Mildred Pierce, Warner Bros., 1945, dir. Michael Curtiz.
Murder, My Sweet, RKO, 1944, dir. Edward Dmytryk.
Night and the City, 20th Century–Fox, 1950, dir. Jules Dassin.
Out of the Past, RKO, 1947, dir. Jacques Tourneur.
Phantom Lady, Universal, 1944, dir. Robert Siodmak.
Pickup on South Street, 20th Century–Fox, 1953, dir. Samuel Fuller.
Possessed, Warner Bros., 1947, dir. Charles Bernhardt.
The Postman Always Rings Twice, Metro-Goldwyn-Mayer, 1946, dir. Terence Garnett.
Pursued, United States, 1947, dir. Raoul Walsh.
The Racket, Paramount Famous Players Lasky, 1928, dir. Lewis Milestone; RKO, 1951, dir. John Cromwell.
Scarlet Street, Universal, 1945, dir. Fritz Lang.
Sorry, Wrong Number, Paramount, 1948, dir. Anatole Litvak.
The Strange Love of Martha Ivers, Paramount, 1946, dir. Lewis Milestone.
Strangers on a Train, Warner Bros., 1951, dir. Alfred Hitchcock.
Sunset Boulevard, Paramount, 1950, dir. Billy Wilder.
Suspicion, RKO, 1941, dir. Alfred Hitchcock.
They Live by Night, RKO, 1948, dir. Nicholas Ray.
This Gun for Hire, Paramount, 1942, dir. Frank Tuttle.
To Have and Have Not, Warner Bros., 1944, dir. Howard Hawks.
White Heat, Warner Bros., 1949, dir. Raoul Walsh.
The Woman in the Window, RKO, 1945, dir. Fritz Lang.
You Only Live Once, Walter Wanger Productions, 1937, dir. Fritz Lang.

Screwball Comedy

The Awful Truth, Columbia, 1937, dir. Leo McCarey.
Ball of Fire, RKO, 1941, dir. Howard Hawks.
Bluebeard's Eighth Wife, Universal, 1938, dir. Ernst Lubitsch.
Bringing Up Baby, RKO, 1938, dir. Howard Hawks.
His Girl Friday, Columbia, 1940, dir. Howard Hawks.
It Happened One Night, Columbia, 1934, dir. Frank Capra.
It's a Wonderful World, Loew's Inc. & Metro-Goldwyn-Mayer, 1939, dir. W. S. Van Dyke.
The Major and the Minor, Paramount, 1942, dir. Billy Wilder.
Mr. and Mrs. Smith, RKO, 1941, dir. Alfred Hitchcock.
My Favorite Wife, RKO, 1940, dir. Garson Kanin.
Nothing Sacred, United Artists, 1937, dir. William Wellman.
The Palm Beach Story, Paramount, 1942, dir. Preston Sturges.
Too Hot to Handle, Loew's Inc. & Metro-Goldwyn-Mayer, 1938, dir. Jack Conway.
Vivacious Lady, RKO, 1938, dir. George Stevens.

Westerns

Destry Rides Again, Universal, 1939, dir. George Marshall.
Dodge City, Warner Bros., 1939, dir. Michael Curtiz.
Duel in the Sun, Selznick, 1946, dir. King Vidor.
The Gunfighter, 20th Century–Fox, 1950, dir. Henry King.
My Darling Clementine, 20th Century–Fox, 1946, dir. John Ford.
The Plainsman, Paramount, 1936, dir. Cecil B. DeMille.
Stagecoach, United Artists, 1939, dir. John Ford.
They Died with Their Boots On, Warner Bros., 1941, dir. Raoul Walsh.
Winchester '73, Universal, 1950, dir. Anthony Mann.

Alfred Hitchcock

Blackmail, British International Pictures, 1929.
North by Northwest, Metro-Goldwyn-Mayer, 1959.
Notorious, RKO, 1946.
Psycho, Paramount, 1960.
Rear Window, Paramount, 1954.
Stage Fright, Warner Bros., 1949.
Vertigo, Paramount, 1958.

Stanley Kubrick

The Killing, United Artists, 1956.
Lolita, Metro-Goldwyn-Mayer/Seven Arts, 1962.
2001: A Space Odyssey, Hawk/Metro-Goldwyn-Mayer, 1968.

European "New Wave" Cinema

À bout de souffle (*Breathless*), Imperia/SNC, 1959, dir. Jean-Luc Godard.
Alphaville, Athos/Chaumian/Filmstudio, 1965, dir. Jean-Luc Godard.
Blow-Up, Bridge Films, 1966, dir. Michelangelo Antonioni.
Farenheit 451, Vineyard/Universal Pictures, 1966, dir. François Truffaut.
Jules et Jim, Carosse, 1962, dir. François Truffaut.
La Dolce Vita, Riama/Pathé/Gray, 1960, dir. Frederico Fellini.
Les quatre cent coups (*The 400 Blows*), Carosse/SEDIF, 1959, dir. François Truffaut.
La Strada (*The Road*) Ponti-De Laurentiis Cinematografica, 1954, dir. Frederico Fellini.

The New Hollywood

Bonnie and Clyde, Warner Bros., 1967, dir. Arthur Penn.
Chinatown, Paramount, 1974, dir. Roman Polanski.
The Conversation, Paramount, 1974, dir. Francis Ford Coppola.
Easy Rider, Pando/Raybert, 1969, dir. Dennis Hopper.
Five Easy Pieces, Columbia, 1970, dir. Bob Rafelson.
The French Connection, 20th Century–Fox, 1971, dir. William Friedkin.
The Godfather, Paramount, 1972, dir. Frances Ford Coppola.
The Long Goodbye, United Artists, 1973, dir. Robert Altman.
M*A*S*H, Aspen, 1970, dir. Robert Altman.

Mean Streets, TPS, 1973, dir. Martin Scorsese.
Taxi Driver, Columbia, 1976, dir. Martin Scorsese.

Blockbusters

Die Hard, Gordon/Silver, 1988, dir. John McTiernan.
Jaws, Universal, 1975, dir. Steven Spielberg.
Lethal Weapon, Warner Bros., 1987, dir. Richard Donner.
Star Wars, 20th Century–Fox, 1977, dir. George Lucas.

1980s and 1990s Independents

Crash, Alliance Communications Corp., 1996, dir. David Cronenberg.
Dead Ringers, Mantle Clinic II, 1988, dir. David Cronenberg.
The Driller Killer, Navaron Productions, 1979, dir. Abel Ferrara.
Henry: Portrait of a Serial Killer, Filmcat, 1986, dir. John McNaughton.
Manhunter, De Laurentiis Entertainment Group, 1986, dir. Michael Mann.
Pulp Fiction, Miramax, 1994, dir. Quentin Tarantino.
Rampage, De Laurentiis Entertainment Group, 1988, dir. William Friedkin.

Bibliography

Nabokov

Works

Ada or Ardor: A Family Chronicle, London: Penguin, 1971.
The Annotated Lolita, A. Appel, Jr. (ed.), London: Penguin, 1995.
Bend Sinister, London: Penguin, 1974.
Conclusive Evidence, New York: Harper & Row, 1951.
Dear Bunny, Dear Volodya: The Nabokov-Wilson Letters, 1940–1971, revised and expanded edition, edited by M. Karlinsky, Berkeley/Los Angeles, CA, and London: University of California Press, 2001.
Despair, London: Penguin, 1981.
Details of a Sunset and Other Stories, London: Penguin, 1994.
The Enchanter, D. Nabokov, trans. London: Picador, 1986.
The Eye, London: Penguin, 1992.
The Gift, London: Penguin, 1981.
Glory, London: Penguin, 1974.
Invitation to a Beheading, London: Penguin, 1963.
King, Queen, Knave, London: Penguin, 1993.
Korol', Dama, Valet, Ann Arbor, MI: Ardis, 1979.
Laughter in the Dark, New York: New Directions, 1978.
Lectures on Literature, London: Weidenfeld & Nicholson, 1981.
Lectures on Russian Literature, London: Weidenfeld & Nicholson, 1982.
Lolita: A Screenplay, New York: Vintage International, 1997.
Look at the Harlequins! London: Penguin, 1980.
The Luzhin Defense, M. Scammell, trans. London: Penguin, 1994.
Mary, London: Penguin, 1973.
Nabokov's Dozen: Thirteen Stories, London: Penguin, 1960.
Nikolai Gogol, London: Editions Poetry London, 1947.
Pale Fire, London: Penguin, 1973.
Pnin, London: Penguin, 1960.
Poems and Problems, New York: McGraw Hill, 1970.
The Real Life of Sebastian Knight, London: Penguin, 1964.
A Russian Beauty and Other Stories, London: Penguin, 1975.
Sogliadatei, Ann Arbor, MI: Ardis, 1978.
Speak, Memory: An Autobiography Revisited, London: Penguin, 1969.
Stikhi (Poems), Ann Arbor, MI: Ardis, 1979.
Strong Opinions, New York: McGraw Hill, 1973.
Transparent Things, New York: McGraw Hill, 1972.

Tyrants Destroyed and Other Stories, London: Penguin, 1981.

Vesna v Fial'te i drugie rasskazy, New York: Izdatel'stvo imeni Chekhova, 1956.

Vladimir Nabokov: The Collected Stories, London: Penguin, 1997.

Vladimir Nabokov: Selected Letters 1940–1977, edited by M. J. Bruccoli, and D. Nabokov, London: Weidenfeld & Nicholson, 1990.

Materials from the Archive of Nabokov's Papers Held at the Henry W. and Albert A. Berg Collection of English and American Literature, New York Public Library

Ada or Ardor: A Family Chronicle on 2,049 index cards. Palace Hotel, Montreux, 1967–16 October 1968.

Camera Obscura: A Novel by Vladimir Nabokoff-Sirin, Winifred Roy (trans.), London: John Long, 1935 (annotated).

Conclusive Evidence: A Memoir, New York: Harper & Row, 1951.

Conclusive Evidence, excerpts in typescript (incomplete) of memoir, comprising 7 chapters, undated, 93 pp.

"Conversations with Nabokov" by Alfred Appel (draft).

Corrections to *Nabokov's Garden*, dissertation by Bobbie Ann Mason (née Rawlings), undated, 8 pp.

Correspondence: Ira Gershwin, 1960; James Harris/Stanley Kubrick, 1958–1972; Alfred Hitchcock, 1964; James Mason, 1967.

Despair by Vladimir Nabokoff-Sirin, London: John Long, 1937 (annotated).

Favourite Hates, October 1964.

Interviews: Alfred Appel, 1966, 1970; George Feifer, 1976; Herbert Mitgang, 1967–1975; Carl Proffer, 1966–1968.

Lolita: A Screenplay, typescript, first version, undated.

Notes for Work in Progress on index cards. Includes "Notes for a second volume of *Speak, Memory*, twenty years in America."

Notes on Various Subjects on index cards. Contains undated first translation of "The Leonardo" by Véra Nabokov on 37 index cards.

Philistines and Philistinism, holograph and typescript draft of lecture notes, unsigned and undated, 21 pp. with illustrative newspaper clippings, 4 pieces.

Strong Opinions, typescript, undated, 399 pp.

Transparent Things on 348 index cards, and typescript, 1 April 1972.

Criticism

Alexandrov, V. E. (ed.), *The Garland Companion to Vladimir Nabokov*, New York: Garland, 1995.

_____, *Nabokov's Otherworld*, Princeton, NJ: Princeton University Press, 1991.

Alter, R., "Nabokov and the Art of Politics," "*Ada* or the Perils of Paradise" in *Motives for Fiction*, Cambridge, MA; London: Harvard University Press, 1984, pp. 61–75; 76–91.

Anastasiev, N., "The Tower and Around: A View of Vladimir Nabokov" in S. Chakovsky, M. Thomas Inge (eds.), *Russian Eyes on American Literature*, Jackson: University of Mississippi, 1992, pp. 173–201.

Appel, A., Jr. (ed.), *The Annotated* Lolita, London: Penguin, 1995.

_____, *Nabokov's Dark Cinema*, New York and Oxford: Oxford University Press, 1974.

_____, "Nabokov's Dark Cinema: A Diptych," in S. Karlinsky, A. Appel, Jr. (eds.), *The Bitter Air of Exile: Russian Writers in the West 1922–1972*, Berkeley/Los Angeles: University of California Press, 1973, pp. 196–273.

_____, "Tristram in Movielove: *Lolita* at the Movies," in C. R. Proffer (ed.), *A Book of Things About Vladimir Nabokov*, Ann Arbor, MI: Ardis, 1974, pp. 122–70.

Bader, Julia, *Crystal Land: Artifice in Nabokov's English Novels*, Berkeley and Los Angeles: University of California Press, 1972.

Barabtarlo, G., *Aerial View: Essays on Nabokov's Art and Metaphysics*, New York: Peter Lang, 1993.

Berdjis, N. W., *Imagery in Vladimir Nabokov's Last Russian Novel (Dar), Its English Translation (The Gift), and Other Prose Works of the 1930s*, Frankfurt am Main: Peter Lang, 1995.

Bloom, H. (ed.), *Vladimir Nabokov's* Lolita, New York: Chelsea House, 1987.

Boyd, B., *Nabokov's* Ada*: The Place of Consciousness*, second edition, Christchurch, NZ: Cybereditions, 2002.

_____, *Vladimir Nabokov: The Russian Years*, London: Vintage, 1993.

_____, *Vladimir Nabokov: The American Years*, London: Vintage, 1993.

Clancy, L., *The Novels of Vladimir Nabokov*, London: Macmillan, 1984.

Connolly, J. W. (ed.), *Nabokov and His Fiction: New Perspectives*, Cambridge: Cambridge University Press, 1999.

_____, *Nabokov's Early Fiction: Patterns of Self and Other*, Cambridge: Cambridge University Press, 1992.

_____, *Nabokov's "Invitation to a Beheading": A Critical Companion*, Evanston, IL: Northwestern University Press, 1997.

Cornwell, N., *Vladimir Nabokov*, Plymouth, UK: Northcote House, 1999.

Couturier, M. (ed.), "Nabokov at the Crossroads of Modernism and Postmodernism," *Cycnos*, 12:2, 1995.

Dembo, L. S. (ed.), *Nabokov: The Man and His Work*, Madison: University of Wisconsin Press, 1967.

Field, A., *VN: The Life and Art of Vladimir Nabokov*, London: Macdonald, 1987.

Foster, J. Burt, Jr., *Nabokov's Art of Memory and European Modernism*, Princeton, NJ: Princeton University Press, 1993.

Gibian G., and Jan, Parker S. (eds.), *The Achievements of Vladimir Nabokov*, Ithaca, NY: Cornell University Press, 1984.

Giles, P., "Virtual Eden: *Lolita*, Pornography, and the Perversions of American Studies," *Journal of American Studies*, 34, 2000, 1, pp. 41–66.

Grayson, J., *Nabokov Translated: A Comparison of Nabokov's Russian and English Prose*, Oxford: Oxford University Press, 1977.

Green, M., "Tolstoy and Nabokov: The Morality of *Lolita*," in H. Bloom (ed.), *Vladimir Nabokov's Lolita*, New York: Chelsea House, 1987, pp. 13–33.

Johnson, D. Barton, *Worlds in Regression: Some Novels of Vladimir Nabokov*, Ann Arbor, MI: Ardis, 1985.

Kellman, S. G., and Malin, I. (eds.), *Torpid Smoke: The Stories of Vladimir Nabokov*, Amsterdam and Atlanta, GA: Rodopi, 2000.

Larmour, D. H. J. (ed.), *Discourse and Ideology in Nabokov's Prose*. London and New York: Routledge, 2002.

Lee, L. L., *Vladimir Nabokov*, New York: Frederick Ungar, 1974.

Mason, B. A., *Nabokov's Garden: A Guide to* Ada, Ann Arbor, MI: Ardis, 1974.

Merivale, P., "The Flaunting of Artifice in Vladimir Nabokov and Jorge Luis Borges," in L. S. Dembo (ed.), *Nabokov: The Man and His Work*, Madison: University of Wisconsin Press, 1967, pp. 209–24.

Meyer, P., *Find What the Sailor Has Hidden: Vladimir Nabokov's* Pale Fire, Middletown, CT: Wesleyan University Press, 1988.

Moraru, C., "Vile Scripts: Games of Double-Crossing in Vladimir Nabokov's The Assistant Producer,'" in S. G. Kellman and I. Malin (eds.), *Torpid Smoke: The Stories of Vladimir Nabokov*, Amsterdam and Atlanta, GA: Rodopi, 2000, pp. 173–87.

Naumann, M. T., *Blue Evenings in Berlin: Nabokov's Short Stories of the 1920s*, New York: New York University Press, 1978.

Nicol, C., "Did Luzhin Have Chess Fever?" *The Nabokovian*, 27, 1991, pp. 40–42.

Nicol, C., and Barabtarlo, G. (eds.), *A Small Alpine Form: Studies in Nabokov's Short Fiction*, New York: Garland, 1993.

Olsen, L., *Lolita: A Janus Text*, New York: Twayne, 1995.

Packman, D., *Vladimir Nabokov: The Structure of Literary Desire*, Columbia: University of Missouri Press, 1982.

Pifer, E., "Dark Paradise: Shades of Heaven and Hell in *Ada*," *Modern Fiction Studies*, 25, 1979, pp. 481–97.

_____, *Nabokov and the Novel*, Cambridge, MA, and London: Harvard University Press, 1980

Proffer, C. R. (ed.), *A Book of Things About Vladimir Nabokov*, Ann Arbor, MI: Ardis, 1974.

_____, *Keys to* Lolita, Bloomington: Indiana University Press, 1968.

Quennell, P. (ed.), *Vladimir Nabokov: A Tribute*, London: Weidenfeld & Nicolson, 1979.

Rampton, D., *Vladimir Nabokov: A Critical Study of the Novels*, Cambridge: Cambridge University Press, 1984.

Rivers, J. E., and Nicol, C. (eds.), *Nabokov's Fifth Arc: Nabokov and Others on His Life's Work*, Austin: University of Texas Press, 1982.

Rosenblum, M., "Finding What the Sailor Has Hidden: Narrative as Patternmaking in *Transparent Things*," *Contemporary Literature*, 19, 1978, pp. 219–32.

Rowe, W. W., *Nabokov and Others*, Ann Arbor, MI: Ardis, 1979.

_____, *Nabokov's Deceptive World*, New York: New York University Press, 1971.

_____, *Nabokov's Spectral Dimension*, Ann Arbor, MI: Ardis, 1981.

Schiff, S., *Véra, Mrs. Vladimir Nabokov: Portrait of a Marriage*, New York: Random House, 1999.

Shapiro, G., *Delicate Markers: Subtexts in Vladimir Nabokov's "Invitation to a Beheading,"* New York: Peter Lang, 1998.

Shrayer, M. D., *The World of Nabokov's Stories*, Austin: University of Texas Press, 1999.

Stuart, D., *Vladimir Nabokov: The Dimensions of Parody*, Baton Rouge: Louisiana State University Press, 1978.

Tammi, P., *Problems of Nabokov's Poetics: A Narratological Analysis*, Helsinki: Suomalainen Tiedeakatemia, 1985.

_____, *Russian Subtexts in Vladimir Nabokov's Fiction: Four Essays*, Tampere, Finland: Tampere University Press, 1999.

Tekiner, C., "Time in *Lolita*," *Modern Fiction Studies*, 25, 1979, pp. 463–69.

Toker, L., *Nabokov: The Mystery of Literary Structures*, Ithaca, NY, and London: Cornell University Press, 1989.

_____, "Nabokov's *Torpid Smoke*," *Studies in Twentieth Century Literature*, 12, 1988, pp. 238–48.

Trilling, L., "The Last Lover: Vladimir Nabokov's *Lolita*', *Encounter*, 11, 1958, 4, pp. 9–19.

Updike, J., "Grandmaster Nabokov," in *Assorted Prose*, London: André Deutsch, 1965, pp. 318–27.

Williams, C. T., "Nabokov's Dialectical Structure," *Wisconsin Studies in Contemporary Literature*, 8, 1967, 2, pp. 250–67.

Wilson, E., "Vladimir Nabokov on Gogol" in *Classics and Commercials*, New York: Farrar, Strauss, 1950, pp. 215–18.

Wood, M., *The Magician's Doubts: Nabokov and the Risks of Fiction*, London: Chatto & Windus, 1994.

Zunshine, L. (ed.), *Nabokov at the Limits: Redrawing Critical Boundaries*, New York: Garland, 1999.

American Fiction

Works

Apple, M., *The Oranging of America and Other Stories*, New York: Grossman, 1976.
Auster, P., *In the Country of Last Things*, London: Faber & Faber, 1988.
_____, *The Invention of Solitude*, London: Faber & Faber, 1988.
_____, *Leviathan*, London: Faber & Faber, 1992.
_____, *The New York Trilogy: City of Words, Ghosts, The Locked Room,* London: Faber & Faber, 1987.
Barnes, D., *Nightwood*, London: Faber & Faber, 1963.
Barth, J., *The Floating Opera*, London: Penguin, 1970.
_____, *Lost in the Funhouse*, London: Penguin, 1972.
Barthelme, D., *City Life*, New York: Farrar, Straus & Giroux, 1970.
Brautigan, R., *In Watermelon Sugar*, New York: Dell, 1968.
_____, *Richard Brautigan's* Trout Fishing in America, New York: Delacourte, 1972.
Burnett, W. R., *Four Novels by W. R. Burnett: Little Caesar; The Asphalt Jungle; High Sierra; Vanity Row*, London: Zomba Books, 1984.
Burroughs, W. S., *The Burroughs File*, San Francisco, CA: City Lights Books, 1984.
_____, *Exterminator!*, New York: Viking Press, 1966–1973.
_____, *Nova Express*, London: Jonathan Cape, 1966.
_____, *The Wild Boys: A Book of the Dead*, New York: Grove Press, 1969–1971.
Cain, J. M., *The Baby in the Ice Box and Other Short Fiction*, R. Hoopes (ed.), New York and London: Penguin, 1984.
_____, "Camera Obscura," *The American Mercury*, 30, October 1933, 118, pp. 138–46.
_____, *The Five Great Novels of James M. Cain: The Postman Always Rings Twice; Double Indemnity; Serenade; Mildred Pierce; The Butterfly*, London: Picador, 1985.
_____, "Paradise," *The American Mercury*, 28, March 1933, 111, pp. 266–80.
Capote, T., *In Cold Blood: A True Account of a Multiple Murder and Its Consequences*, London: Penguin, 1966.
_____, *Music for Chameleons*, New York: Vintage International, 1994.
_____, *Other Voices, Other Rooms*, New York: Random House, 1948.
Carver, R., *The Stories of Raymond Carver*, London: Picador, 1985.
Chandler, R., *The Big Sleep*, London: Penguin, 1948.
_____, *Farewell, My Lovely*, London: Penguin, 1949.
_____, *The High Window*, London: Penguin, 1951.
_____, *Killer in the Rain*, London: Penguin, 1966.
_____, *The Lady in the Lake*, London: Penguin, 1952.
_____, *The Little Sister*, London: Penguin, 1955.
_____, *The Long Good-Bye*, London: Penguin, 1959.
_____, *Pearls Are a Nuisance*, London: Penguin, 1964.
_____, *Trouble Is My Business*, London: Penguin, 1950.
Cheever, J., *Collected Stories*, London: Vintage, 1990.
Coover, R., *Pricksongs and Descants*, New York: Plume, 1970.
_____, *A Night at the Movies Or, You Must Remember This*, Normal, IL: Dalkey Archive Press, 1992.
_____, *The Universal Baseball Association, Inc. J. Henry Waugh, PROP.*, London: Minerva, 1992.
DeLillo, D., *Americana*, London: Penguin, 1990.
_____, *Libra*, London: Penguin, 1989.
_____, *Players*, London: Vintage, 1991.
_____, *White Noise*, London: Picador, 1985.
Dick, P. K., *The Man in the High Castle*, London: Penguin, 1965.
Ellis, B. Easton, *American Psycho*, London: Picador, 1991.

_____, *Less Than Zero*, London: Picador, 1986.
Faulkner, W., *As I Lay Dying*, London: Penguin, 1963.
_____, *Intruder in the Dust*, London: Picador, 1989.
_____, *Light in August*, New York: Vintage International, 1985.
_____, *Sanctuary*, London: Picador, 1989.
_____, *The Sound and the Fury*, London: Penguin, 1964.
Fitzgerald, F. Scott, *The Beautiful and the Damned*, London: Penguin, 1966.
_____, *The Crack-Up and Other Stories*, London: Penguin, 1965.
_____, *The Great Gatsby*, New York: Scribner's, 1995; London: Penguin, 1950.
_____, *The Last Tycoon*, London: Penguin, 1965.
_____, *The Lost Decade*, London: Penguin, 1968.
_____, *The Pat Hobby Stories*, London: Penguin, 1967.
_____, *Tender Is the Night*, London: Penguin, 1955.
_____, *This Side of Paradise*, London: Penguin, 1963.
_____, *The Letters of F. Scott Fitzgerald*, A. Turnbull (ed.), London: Penguin, 1968.
Franklin, B., *The Autobiography of Benjamin Franklin*, London: Penguin, 1986.
French, P., and Wlaschin, K. (eds.), *The Faber Book of Movie Verse*, London: Faber & Faber, 1994.
Frost, R., *Selected Poems*, I. Hamilton (ed.), London: Penguin, 1973.
Goodis, D., *Four Novels by David Goodis: Nightfall; Down There; Dark Passage; The Moon in the Gutter*, London: Zomba Books, 1983.
Hammett, D., *The Big Knockover and Other Stories*, London: Penguin, 1969.
_____, *The Glass Key*, London: Pan, 1975.
_____, *The Maltese Falcon*, New York: Vintage International, 1992.
_____, *The Thin Man*, London: Penguin, 1935.
Hemingway, E., "The Killers" in *Men Without Women*, London: Arrow Books, 1994.
_____, *In Our Time*, New York: Scribner's, 1930.
Hollander, J., *Movie-Going and Other Poems*, New York: Atheneum, 1962.
Lowell, R., *Robert Lowell's Poems: A Selection*, J. Raban (ed.), London: Faber & Faber, 1974.
Jakubowski, M. (ed.), *The Mammoth Book of Pulp Fiction*, London: Robinson, 1996.
Kesey, K., *One Flew Over the Cuckoo's Nest*, London: Picador, 1973.
Kosinski, J., *The Art of Self: Essays à propos Steps*, New York: Scientia-Factum, 1968.
_____, *Being There*, London: Black Swan, 1970.
_____, *The Devil Tree*, New York: Harcourt Brace Javonovich, 1973.
_____, *Steps*, New York: Random House, 1968.
McCarthy, M., *A Charmed Life*, London: Penguin, 1964.
_____, *The Company She Keeps*, London: Penguin, 1965.
McCullers, C., *The Ballad of the Sad Café* and *The Member of the Wedding* in *Collected Stories of Carson McCullers,* Boston: Houghton Mifflin, 1987.
_____, *Clock Without Hands*, London: Penguin, 1965.
_____, *The Heart Is a Lonely Hunter*, London: Penguin, 1961.
_____, *Reflections in a Golden Eye*, London: Penguin, 1967.
McCoy, H., *Kiss Tomorrow Goodbye*, London and New York: Serpent's Tail, 1996.
Mailer, N., *An American Dream*, London: Flamingo, 1994.
_____, *The Naked and the Dead*, London: André Deutsch, 1949.
Miller, H., *The Air-Conditioned Nightmare*, London: Heinemann, 1962.
_____, *Tropic of Cancer*, London: Flamingo, 1993.
Passos, J. Dos, *Manhattan Transfer*, London: Penguin, 1986.
_____, *U.S.A.*, London: Penguin, 1966.
Percy, W., *Lost in the Cosmos: The Last Self-Help Book*, New York: Farrar, Straus & Giroux, 1983.
_____, *The Moviegoer*, New York: Fawcett Columbine, 1988.
Poe, E. A., *The Fall of the House of Usher and Other Writings*, London: Penguin, 1967.
Pronzini, B, and Adrian, J. (eds.), *Hard-Boiled: An Anthology of American Crime Stories*, New York: Oxford University Press, 1995.

Pynchon, T., *The Crying of Lot 49*, London: Picador, 1979.
_____, *Gravity's Rainbow*, London: Vintage, 1995.
_____, *The Secret Integration*, London: Aloes Books, 1964.
_____, *Slow Learner*, Boston: Little, Brown, 1985.
_____, *V.*, London: Picador, 1975.
_____, *Vineland*, London: Vintage, 1990.
Roth, P., *Reading Myself and Others*, London: Penguin, 1985.
Ruhm, H. (ed.), *The Hard-Boiled Detective: Stories from "Black Mask" Magazine 1920–1951*, Sevenoaks, Kent, UK: Coronet Books, 1979.
Salinger, J. D., *The Catcher in the Rye*, London: Penguin, 1994.
_____, *For Esmé, with Love and Squalor*, London: Penguin, 1986.
_____, *Franny and Zooey*, London: Penguin, 1994.
_____, *Raise High the Roof Beam, Carpenters; Seymour: An Introduction*, London: Penguin, 1994.
Schulberg, B., *What Makes Sammy Run?* London: Penguin, 1978.
Schwartz, D., *In Dreams Begin Responsibilities and Other Stories*, James Atlas (ed.), London: Secker & Warburg, 1978.
Sorrentino, G., *Imaginative Qualities of Actual Things*, Normal, IL: Dalkey Archive Press, 1991.
_____, "The Moon in Its Flight," *New American Review*, 13, 1971, pp. 153–63.
Southern, T., *Flash and Filigree*, London: Bloomsbury, 1997.
_____, *The Magic Christian*, London: Bloomsbury, 1997.
_____, *Red-Dirt Marijuana and Other Stories*, London: Bloomsbury, 1997.
Steinbeck, J., *The Grapes of Wrath*, London: Minerva, 1990.
_____, *The Short Novels: Tortilla Flat; Of Mice and Men; The Moon Is Down; Cannery Row; The Red Pony; The Pearl*, London: Minerva, 1992.
Stevens, W., *Collected Poems*, London: Faber & Faber, 1955.
_____, *The Necessary Angel: Essays on Reality and the Imagination*, New York: Alfred A. Knopf, 1951.
Styron, W., *Lie Down in Darkness*, New York: Random House, 1979.
Thompson, H. S., *Fear and Loathing in Las Vegas: A Savage Journey to the Heart of the American Dream*, London: Paladin, 1972.
Thompson, J., *Omnibus: The Getaway; The Grifters; The Killer Inside Me; Pop. 1280*, London: Picador, 1995.
_____, *Omnibus 2: After Dark, My Sweet; A Hell of a Woman; Savage Night; A Swell Looking Babe; Nothing More Than Murder*, London: Picador, 1997.
Updike, J., *Assorted Prose*, London: André Deutsch, 1965.
_____, *Forty Stories*, London: Penguin, 1987.
_____, *A Rabbit Omnibus: Rabbit, Run; Rabbit Redux; Rabbit Is Rich*, London: Penguin, 1991.
_____, *Roger's Version*, New York: Alfred A. Knopf, 1986.
Vonnegut, K., *Breakfast of Champions*, London: Vintage, 1992.
_____, *Cat's Cradle*, London: Penguin, 1965.
_____, *God Bless You, Mr. Rosewater*, London: Vintage, 1992.
_____, *The Sirens of Titan*, London: Coronet, 1967.
_____, *Slapstick*, London: Vintage, 1991.
_____, *Slaughterhouse Five*, London: Vintage, 1991.
West, N., *Selections: Novels and Other Writings (The Dream Life of Balso Snell; Miss Lonelyhearts; A Cool Million; Day of the Locust)*, New York: Library of America, 1997.
Williams, W. Carlos, *Kora in Hell: Improvisations; The Great American Novel* in W. Schott (ed.), *Imaginations*, London: MacGibbon & Kee, 1970, pp. 6–82; 158–227.
_____, *Selected Poems*, London: Penguin, 1976.
Woolrich, C., *Four by Cornell Woolrich: The Bride Wore Black; Phantom Lady; Rear Window; Waltz Into Darkness*, London: Zomba Books, 1983.

Criticism

Allen, W. R., *Conversations with Kurt Vonnegut*, Jackson, MS, and London: University of Mississippi, 1988.

Alter, R., *Motives for Fiction*, Cambridge, MA: Harvard University Press, 1984.

_____, *Partial Magic: The Novel as a Self-Conscious Genre*, Berkeley and Los Angeles: University of California Press, 1975.

Berman, R., *The Great Gatsby and Modern Times*, Urbana: University of Illinois Press, 1994.

Bradbury, M., *The Modern American Novel*, Oxford: Oxford University Press, 1984.

Brooks, C., and Warren R. Penn (eds.), *Understanding Fiction*, New York: Appleton-Century-Crofts, 1959.

Bruccoli, M. J. (ed.), *New Essays on the Great Gatsby*, Cambridge: Cambridge University Press, 1985.

_____, *Some Sort of Epic Grandeur: The Life of F. Scott Fitzgerald*, London: Cardinal, 1991.

Clark, B. L., *Reflections of Fantasy: The Mirror-Worlds of Carroll, Nabokov and Pynchon*, New York: Peter Lang, 1986.

Coale, S., "The Cinematic Self of Jerzy Kosinski," *Modern Fiction Studies*, 20, 1974, pp. 359–70.

Cohen, J., *Spectacular Allegories: Postmodern American Writing and the Politics of Seeing*, London: Pluto Press, 1998.

Cohen, S. Blacher, *Comic Relief: Humor in Contemporary American Literature*, Urbana: University of Illinois Press, 1978.

Didion, J., *The White Album* (1979), London: Flamingo, 1993.

Dike, D. A., and Zucker, D. H. (eds.) *Selected Essays of Delmore Schwartz*, Chicago, IL, and London: University of Chicago Press, 1970.

Dixon, W. W., *The Cinematic Vision of F. Scott Fitzgerald*, Ann Arbor, MI: UMI Research Press, 1986.

Dooley, D., *Dashiell Hammett*, New York: Frederick Ungar, 1984.

Eidsvik, C., "Demonstrating Film Influence," *Literature/Film Quarterly*, 1, 1973, pp. 113–21.

Eisinger, C. E., *Fiction of the Forties*, Chicago, IL, and London: University of Chicago Press, 1963.

Eliot, T. S., "American Literature and the American Language," in *To Criticize the Critic and Other Writings*, London: Faber & Faber, 1978, pp. 43–60.

_____, *Selected Essays*, New York: Harcourt, Brace & World, 1964.

French, B., "The Celluloid Lolita: A Not-So-Crazy Quilt," in G. Peary and R. Shatzkin (eds.), *The Modern American Novel and the Movies*, New York: Frederick Ungar, 1978, pp. 224–35.

Gardiner, D., Sorley, Walker K. (eds.), *Raymond Chandler Speaking*, Berkeley and Los Angeles: University of California Press, 1962.

Gass, W., *Fiction and the Figures of Life*, Boston, MA: Nonpareil Books, 1971.

Goldstein, L., *The American Poet at the Movies*, Ann Arbor: University of Michigan Press, 1994.

Hansen, A. J., "The Celebration of Solipsism: A New Trend in American Fiction," *Modern Fiction Studies*, 19, 1973, pp. 5–15.

Karl, F. R., *American Fictions 1940–1980: A Comprehensive History and Critical Evaluation*, New York: Harper & Row, 1983.

Kawin, B. F., *Faulkner and Film*, New York: Frederick Ungar, 1977.

Kellman, S. G., "The Cinematic Novel: Tracking a Concept," *Modern Fiction Studies*, 33, 1987, pp. 467–77.

Klinkowitz, J., *Literary Disruptions: The Making of Post-Contemporary American Fiction*, second edition, Urbana: University of Illinois Press, 1980.

Lavers, N., *Jerzy Kosinski*, Boston, MA: Twayne, 1982.

Lawrence, D. H., *Studies in Classic American Literature*, London: Penguin, 1971.

Lawson, L., "Moviegoing in *The Moviegoer*," in J. Tharpe (ed.), *Walker Percy: Art and Ethics*, Jackson: University Press of Mississippi, 1980.

MacShane, F. (ed.), *Selected Letters of Raymond Chandler*, London: Macmillan, 1981.

Madden, D., *James M. Cain*, New York: Twayne, 1970.

———, "James M. Cain and the Movies of the Thirties and Forties," *Film Heritage*, 2, 1967, 4, pp. 9–25.

——— (ed.), *Tough Guy Writers of the Thirties*, Carbondale and Edwardsville: Southern Illinois University Press, 1968.

Martin, J., *Nathanael West: The Art of His Life*, New York: Farrar, Strauss & Giroux, 1970.

Moore, T., *The Style of Connectedness: "Gravity's Rainbow" and Thomas Pynchon*, Columbia: University of Missouri Press, 1987.

Moses, G., *The Nickel Was for the Movies: Film in the Novel from Pirandello to Puig*, Berkeley and Los Angeles: University of California Press, 1995.

Nostrand, A. Van, *The Denatured Novel*, Indianapolis and New York: Bobbs-Merill, 1956.

Oates, J. Carol, "Man Under Sentence of Death: The Novels of James M. Cain," in D. Madden (ed.), *Tough Guy Writers of the Thirties*, Carbondale and Edwardsville: Southern Illinois University Press, 1968, pp. 110–28.

Orvell, M., *The Real Thing: Imitation and Authenticity in American Culture, 1880–1940*, Chapel Hill: University of North Carolina Press, 1989.

Pearce, R. (ed.), *Critical Essays on Thomas Pynchon*, Boston, MA: G. K. Hall, 1981.

Phillips, L. W. (ed.), *F. Scott Fitzgerald on Writing*, London: Equation, 1988.

Pizer, D., *John Dos Passos: The Major Nonfictional Prose*, Detroit, MI: Wayne State University Press, 1988.

Plimpton, G. (ed.), *Writers at Work: The Paris Review Interviews*, fourth series, New York: Viking Press, 1976.

Polito, R., *Savage Art: A Biography of Jim Thompson*, London: Serpent's Tail, 1997.

Richardson, R., *Literature and Film*, Bloomington, IN, and London: Indiana University Press, 1969.

Shattuck, R., "The Alibi of Art: What Baudelaire, Nabokov and Quentin Tarantino Have in Common," *LA Times*, 26 April 1998.

Shloss, C., *In Visible Light: Photography and the American Writer, 1840–1940*, New York: Oxford University Press, 1987.

Stark, J., *Pynchon's Fictions: Thomas Pynchon and the Literature of Information*, Athens: Ohio University Press, 1980.

Stevick, P., *Alternative Pleasures: Postrealist Fiction and the Tradition*, Urbana: University of Illinois Press, 1981.

Tanner, T., *City of Words: American Fiction 1950–1970*, London: Cape, 1971.

———, *The Reign of Wonder: Naivety and Reality in American Literature*, Cambridge: Cambridge University Press, 1965.

Trilling, L., *The Liberal Imagination: Essays on Literature and Society*, New York and London: Harcourt Brace Jovanovich, 1978.

Vidal, G., *Collected Essays, 1952–1972*, London: Heinemann, 1974.

Wagner, L. W., *Dos Passos: Artist as American*, Austin: University of Texas Press, 1979.

Wilson, E., *The Shores of Light: A Literary Chronicle of the Twenties and Thirties*, London: W. H. Allen, 1952.

———, *Classics and Commercials*, New York: Farrar, Straus, 1950.

———, *Letters on Literature and Politics: 1912–1972*, London: Routledge, 1977.

Young, E., and Caveney, G., *Shopping in Space: Essays on America's "Blank Generation" Fiction*, London: Serpent's Tail, 1992.

Literary Theory/Philosophy

Agheana, I. T., *The Meaning of Experience in the Prose of Jorge Luis Borges*, New York: Peter Lang, 1988.

Alazraki, J. (ed.), *Critical Essays on Jorge Luis Borges*, Boston, MA: G. K. Hall, 1987.

Barthes, R., *Elements of Semiology*, A. Lavers and C. Smith (trans.), London: Jonathan Cape, 1967.

_____, "From Work to Text," in J. V. Harari (ed.), *Textual Strategies: Perspectives in Post-Structuralist Criticism*, London: Methuen, 1980, pp. 73–81.

_____, *Image-Music-Text*, S. Heath (trans.), London: Fontana, 1977.

_____, *Mythologies*, A. Lavers (trans.), London: Cape, 1972.

_____, *The Pleasure of the Text*, R. Miller (trans.), New York: Hill & Wang, 1975.

_____, "Power and 'Cool'" in *The Eiffel Tower and Other Mythologies*, R. Howard (trans.), Berkeley and Los Angeles: University of California Press, 1997, pp. 43–45.

_____, *Writing Degree Zero*, A. Lavers and C. Smith (trans.), New York: Hill and Wang, 1968.

Baudrillard, J., *America*, Chris Turner (trans.), London and New York: Verso, 1998.

_____, *Selected Writings*, Mark Poster (ed.), second edition, London: Polity, 1988.

Benjamin, W., *Illuminations*, H. Arendt (ed.), New York: Schocken Books, 1968.

Bergson, H., *Creative Evolution* (1911), New York: Dover, 1998.

Bradbury, M., and McFarlane, J. (eds.), *Modernism 1890–1930*, London: Penguin, 1976.

Culler, J., *On Deconstruction*, London: Routledge, 1983.

_____, *The Pursuit of Signs: Semiotics, Literature, Deconstruction*, London: Routledge, 1981.

_____, *Structuralist Poetics*, London: Routledge, 1975.

Eco, U., *A Theory of Semiotics*, Bloomington: Indiana University Press, 1976.

_____, *Faith in Fakes: Travels in Hyperreality*, W. Weaver (trans.), London: Minerva, 1995.

_____, *The Limits of Interpretation*, Bloomington: Indiana University Press, 1990.

_____, *Misreadings*, London: Picador, 1994.

Erlich, V., *Russian Formalism: History-Doctrine*, New Haven, NJ, and London: Yale University Press, 1965.

Hassan, I., "The Question of Postmodernism," in H. R. Garvin (ed.), *Romanticism, Modernism, Postmodernism*, Lewisburg, PA: Bucknell University Press, 1980, pp. 117–26.

_____, *The Postmodern Turn: Essays in Postmodern Theory and Culture*, Columbus: Ohio State University Press, 1987.

Horkheimer, M., and Adorno, T. W., "The Culture Industry: Enlightenment as Mass Deception," in *Dialectic of Enlightenment*, J. Cumming (trans.), London: Allen Lane, 1973.

Irwin, J. T., *The Mystery to a Solution: Poe, Borges and the Analytic Detective Story*, Baltimore, MD, and London: John Hopkins University Press, 1994.

Jackson, R., *Fantasy: The Literature of Subversion*, London and New York: Methuen, 1981.

Jameson, F. *The Cultural Turn: Selected Writings on the Postmodern, 1983–1998*, London and New York: Verso, 1998.

_____, *The Prison-House of Language: A Critical Account of Structuralism and Russian Formalism*, Princeton, NJ: Princeton University Press, 1972.

Lodge, D. J., *The Modes of Modern Writing*, London: Edward Arnold, 1977.

McHale, B., *Postmodernist Fiction*, New York and London: Methuen, 1987.

Poirier, R., *The Performing Self: Compositions and Decompositions in the Languages of Contemporary Life*, New Brunswick, NJ: Rutgers University Press, 1992.

Pound, E., *ABC of Reading*, London: Faber & Faber, 1961.

Pyman, A., *A History of Russian Symbolism*, Cambridge: Cambridge University Press, 1994.

Robbe-Grillet, A., *For a New Novel: Essays on Fiction*, Richard Howard (trans.), New York: Grove Press, 1965.

Sontag, S., "The Aesthetics of Silence," in *Styles of Radical Will*, London: Secker & Warburg, 1969, pp. 3–34.

Stark, J. O., *The Literature of Exhaustion: Borges, Nabokov and Barth*, Durham, NC: Duke University Press, 1974.

Wellek, R., *Concepts of Criticism*, S. G. Nicols, Jr. (ed.), New Haven, CT, London: Yale University Press, 1963.

_____, and Warren, A., *Theory of Literature*, London: Penguin, 1963.

Social/Cultural History

Issel, W., *Social Change in the United States, 1945–1983*, London: Macmillan, 1985.

Jones, M. A., *The Limits of Liberty: American History 1607–1980*, Oxford: Oxford University Press, 1983.

Raeff, M., *Russia Abroad: A Cultural History of the Russian Emigration 1919–1939*, New York and Oxford: Oxford University Press, 1990.

Cinema

Balázs, B., *Theory of the Film: Character and Growth of a New Art*, E. Bone (trans.), New York: Dover, 1970.

Barlow, J. D., *German Expressionist Film*, Boston, MA: Twayne, 1982.

Barthes, R., "En sortant du cinéma," *Communications*, 23, 1975, pp. 104–7.

Bazin, A., "An Aesthetic of Reality: Neorealism," in *What Is Cinema? Volume 2*, H. Gray (trans.), Berkeley and Los Angeles: University of California Press, 1971, pp. 16–40.

_____, *What Is Cinema?* H. Gray (trans.), Berkeley and Los Angeles: University of California Press, 1967.

Belton, J. (ed.), *Alfred Hitchcock's "Rear Window,"* Cambridge: Cambridge University Press, 2000.

Biskind, P., *Easy Riders, Raging Bulls: How the Sex 'n' Drugs 'n' Rock 'n' Roll Generation Saved Hollywood*, London: Bloomsbury, 1999.

Branigan, E., *Point of View in the Cinema: A Theory of Narration and Subjectivity in Classical Film*, New York: Mouton, 1984.

Buss, R., *French Film Noir*, London and New York: Marion Boyars, 1994.

Cagin, S., and Dray P., *Hollywood Films of the Seventies: Sex, Drugs, Violence, Rock 'n' Roll and Politics*, New York: Harper & Row, 1984.

Chown, J., *Hollywood Auteur: Francis Coppola*, New York: Praeger, 1988.

Clark, A., *Raymond Chandler in Hollywood*, Los Angeles, CA: Silman-James Press, 1982.

Cook, C. (ed.), *The Dilys Powell Film Reader*, Manchester, UK: Carcanet Press, 1991.

Cook, D., "Auteur Cinema and the 'Film Generation' in 1970s Hollywood," in J. Lewis (ed.), *The New American Cinema*, Durham, NC: Duke University Press, 1998, pp. 11–37.

Cook, P., and Bernink, M. (eds.), *The Cinema Book*, second edition, London: BFI, 1999.

Corliss, R., *Lolita*, London: BFI, 1994.

Crowe, C., *Conversations with Wilder*, New York: Alfred A. Knopf, 1999.

Crowther, B., *Film Noir: Reflections in a Dark Mirror*, London: Virgin Books, 1990.

Denby, D., "Stolen Privacy: Coppola's *The Conversation*," *Sight and Sound*, 43, 1974, pp. 131–33.

Eaton, M., *Chinatown*, London: BFI, 1997.

Eisenstein, S. M., *The Film Form and the Film Sense: Two Complete and Unabridged Works*, J. Leyda (ed., trans.), New York: Meridian Books, 1957.

Fox, K., Grant, E., and Imeson, J. (eds.), *The Seventh Virgin Film Guide*, London: Virgin, 1998.

Frank, A., *Frank's 500: The Thriller Film Guide*, London: B.T. Batsford, 1997.

Frank, N., "Un nouveau genre 'policier': l'aventure criminelle," *L'Écran Français*, 61, 1946, pp. 8–9, 14.

French, P., *Westerns: Aspects of a Movie Genre*, New York: Viking Press, 1973.

Friedman, L. D., *Bonnie and Clyde*, London: BFI, 2000.

Gehring, W. D., *Screwball Comedy: A Genre of Madcap Romance*, Westport, CT: Greenwood Press, 1986.

Gottlieb, S. (ed.), *Hitchcock on Hitchcock*, London: Faber & Faber, 1995.

Grabree, J., *Gangsters: From Little Caesar to the Godfather*, New York: Galahad Books, 1973.

Gunning, T., *The Films of Fritz Lang: Allegories of Vision and Modernity*, London: BFI, 2000.

Hayward, S., *Key Concepts in Cinema Studies*, London: Routledge, 1996.

Johnson, W., "*The Long Goodbye* from *Chinatown*," *Film Quarterly*, 28, 1974–1975, 2, pp. 25–32.

Kael, P., *I Lost It at the Movies: Film Writings 1954–1965*, New York: Marion Boyars, 1994.

———, *Kiss Kiss Bang Bang*, Boston, MA: Little, Brown, 1968.

———, *Reeling*, New York: Marion Boyars, 1977.

Kaminsky, S. M., *American Film Genres*, second edition, Chicago, IL: Nelson Hall, 1985.

Kanfer, S., "The New Cinema: Violence ... Sex ... Art...," *Time*, 8 December 1967, pp. 52–56.

Keyssar, H., *Robert Altman's America*, New York: Oxford University Press, 1991.

Kitses, J., *Gun Crazy*, London: BFI, 1996.

Kolker, R. P., *A Cinema of Loneliness: Penn, Kubrick, Scorsese, Coppola, Altman*, New York and Oxford: Oxford University Press, 1980.

———, *A Cinema of Loneliness: Penn, Kubrick, Scorsese, Spielberg, Altman*, second edition, New York and Oxford: Oxford University Press, 1988.

Konigsberg, I., *The Complete Film Dictionary*, second edition, London: Bloomsbury, 1997.

Koszarski, R., *Hollywood Directors 1941–1976*, New York and Oxford: Oxford University Press, 1977.

Lewis, J. (ed.), *The End of Cinema as We Know It: American Film in the Nineties*, London: Pluto Press, 2001.

——— (ed.), *The New American Cinema*, Durham, NC: Duke University Press, 1998.

Leyda, J., *Kino: A History of the Russian and Soviet Film*, third edition, London: George Allen & Unwin, 1983.

McArthur, C., *The Big Heat*, London: BFI, 1992.

McBride, J. (ed.), *Hawks on Hawks*, London: Faber & Faber, 1996.

McGilligan, P. (ed.), *Backstory: Interviews with Screenwriters of Hollywood's Golden Age*, Berkeley and Los Angeles: University of California Press, 1986.

Mailer, N., "A Course in Film-Making," *New American Review*, 12, 1971, pp. 200–41.

Mason, J., *Before I Forget*, London: Hamish Hamilton, 1981.

Marshall, H., *Masters of the Soviet Cinema: Crippled Creative Biographies*, Boston, MA, and London: Routledge & Kegan Paul, 1983.

Mast, G., Cohen, M., and Braudy, L. (eds.), *Film Theory and Criticism: Introductory Readings*, fourth edition, New York and Oxford: Oxford University Press, 1992.

Michelson, A. (ed.), *Kino-Eye: The Writings of Dziga Vertov*, Berkeley and Los Angeles, CA: Pluto Press, 1984.

Monaco, J., *How to Read a Film: The Art, Technology, Language, History, and Theory of Film and Media*, revised edition, New York and Oxford: Oxford University Press, 1981.

Mordden, E., *Medium Cool: The Movies of the 1960s*, New York: Alfred A. Knopf, 1990.

Mulvey, L., *Citizen Kane*, London: BFI, 1992.

Neale, S., *Genre and Hollywood*, London and New York: Routledge, 2000.

Nelson, T. A., *Kubrick: Inside a Film Artist's Maze*, Bloomington: University of Indiana Press, 1982.

Orr, J., *Cinema and Modernity*, Cambridge: Polity Press, 1993.

Palmer, J. W., "*The Conversation*: Coppola's Biography of an Unborn Man," *Film Heritage*, 12, 1976, pp. 26–32.

Palmer, R. B., *Hollywood's Dark Cinema: The American Film Noir*, Boston, MA: Twayne, 1994.

Palmer, W. J., *The Films of the Seventies: A Social History*, Metuchen, NJ: Scarecrow, 1987.

Petrić, V., *Constructivism in Film: The Man with the Movie Camera: A Cinematic Analysis*, Cambridge: Cambridge University Press, 1987.

Place, J., "Women in Film Noir," in E. Ann Kaplan (ed.), *Women in Film Noir*, London: BFI, 1998, pp. 47–68.

Polan, D., *Pulp Fiction*, London: BFI, 2000.

Pudovkin, V. I., *Film Technique and Film Acting*, I. Montagu (trans.), London: Vision, 1954.
Pym, J., *The Palm Beach Story*, London: BFI, 1998.
Rander, H., and Preacher, A. (eds.), *Film Theory Goes to the Movies*, New York: Routledge, 1993.
Robinson, D., *Das Cabinet des Dr. Caligari*, London: BFI, 1997.
Rodley, C. (ed.), *Cronenberg on Cronenberg*, London: Faber & Faber, 1997.
Ross, H., *Film as Literature, Literature as Film: An Introduction to and Bibliography of Film's Relationship to Literature*, Westport, CT, and New York: Greenwood Press, 1987.
Rosso, D. de, *James Mason: A Personal Biography*, Oxford, UK: Lennard, 1989.
Sarris, A., "Toward a Theory of Film History," in *The American Cinema: Directors and Directions 1929–1968*, New York: Dutton, 1968, pp. 19–37.
Schickel, R., *Double Indemnity*, London: BFI, 1992.
Selby, S., *Dark City: The Film Noir*, Jefferson, NC: McFarland, 1984.
Shaffer, L., "*The Conversation*," *Film Quarterly*, 28, 1974, 1, pp. 54–60.
Shipman, D., *The Story of Cinema, Volume 1: From the Beginnings to "Gone with the Wind,"* London: Hodder & Stoughton, 1982.
Sikov, E., *On Sunset Boulevard: The Life and Times of Billy Wilder*, New York: Hyperion, 1998.
Silver, A., and Ursini, J. (eds.), *Film Noir Reader*, New York: Limelight Editions, 1996.
Silver, A., and Ward E. (eds.), *Film Noir: An Encyclopedic Reference to the American Style*, Woodstock, NY: Overlook Press, 1979.
Sinclair, I. *Crash*, London: BFI, 1999.
Spiegel, A., *Fiction and the Camera Eye: Visual Consciousness in Film and the Modern Novel*, Charlottesville: University Press of Virginia, 1976.
Sweeney, K., *James Mason: A Bio-Bibliography*, Westport, CT, and London: Greenwood Press, 1999.
Tarantino, M., "Movement as Metaphor: *The Long Goodbye*," *Sight and Sound*, 44, 1975, pp. 98–102.
Taylor, J. R., *Strangers in Paradise: The Hollywood Émigrés 1933–1950*, New York: Holt, Rinehart & Winston, 1983.
Taylor, R. (ed., trans.), *S. M. Eisenstein: Selected Works, Volume 1. Writings, 1922–1934*, London: BFI, 1988.
Tichi, C., *Electronic Hearth: Creating an American Television Culture*, New York and Oxford: Oxford University Press, 1991.
Tsivian, Y., *Early Cinema in Russia and Its Cultural Reception*, Alan Bodger (trans.), Richard Taylor (ed.), Chicago, IL, and London: University of Chicago Press, 1998.
Turner, D., "The Subject of *The Conversation*," *Cinema Journal*, 24, 1985, 4, pp. 4–22.
Tuska, J., *Dark Cinema: American Film Noir in Cultural Perspective*, Westport, CT: Greenwood Press, 1984.
Wake, S., and Hayden N. (eds.), *Bonnie and Clyde*, London: Faber & Faber, 1998.
Walker, A., *Garbo: A Portrait*, London: Sphere Books, 1982.
Wilbur, R., "A Poet at the Movies," in W. R. Robinson (ed.), *Man and the Movies*, Baton Rouge: Louisiana State University Press, 1967, pp. 223–26.
Williams, C. (ed.), *Realism and the Cinema: A Reader*, London: Routledge & Kegan Paul, 1980.
Woolf, V., "The Cinema," in *The Crowded Dance of Modern Life: Selected Essays*, Volume 2, R. Bowlby (ed.), London: Penguin, 1993, pp. 54–58.
Zolotow, M., *Billy Wilder in Hollywood*, New York: Putnam's, 1977.

Internet Sites

The Internet Movie Database: http://www.imdb.com.
{waxwing} — the Vladimir Nabokov appreciation site: http://www.fulmerford.com/waxwing/nabokov.html.
Zembla — the Nabokov website: http://www.libraries.psu.edu/tas/nabokov/zembla.htm.

Index

Numbers in **boldface** indicate photographs.